Other Books
by Stefan Aarnio

The Oracle, the Queen, the Princess, and the Whore,
Hard Times Vol IV

Letters to a Scorpion, Hard Times Vol III

Dead Man Walking, Hard Times Vol II

Hard Times Create Strong Men

Money People Deal:
The Fastest Way To Real Estate Wealth

Self Made

The Ten Commandments of Negotiation

The Close:
7 Level Selling

Visit <u>StefanAarnio.com</u> for 1on1
coaching or to order books

HARD TIMES CREATE
STRONG
MEN

*What does it mean to be a man in the modern world?
This book is the Man Bible on money, sex, religion, and
politics: what has worked in the past and what didn't work
based on proven history and results—not on feelings.*

STEFAN AARNIO

Clovercroft Publishing

Hard Times Create Strong Men

Published by Clovercroft Publishing, Franklin, Tennessee

Edited by Tammy Kling, Tiarra Tompkins, and Beth Brown

Cover Design by Marla Beth Thompson

Illustrations and Interior Design by Adept Content Solutions

Printed in Canada

ISBN: 978-1-949572-05-6

Bloody are the pages of history.

CONTENTS

"The path to paradise begins in hell."

DANTE

DEDICATION

"A creative man is motivated by the desire to achieve, not by the desire to beat others."

AYN RAND

I write this book without ego.

It's not about me; it was never about me.

What does it mean to be a man? Possibly one of the most important questions a man can ask, but it is one of the least answered. I asked myself this very question at several key junctures in my life, and, as most men do, I struggled to find the answer. This book cross-examines that vital question and sets forth my answers to that and other hard questions and brutal realities that men need to ask themselves to survive and be men.

I, like every man, have had problems in my life. I have solved some of these problems, but I still grapple with others. It is through the struggle to find solutions that I am able to examine myself and my life and finally answer the question, what does it mean to be a man?

This book started as a blog entitled *Weak Men Create Hard Times, Hard Times Create Strong Men*. It was a big hit as far as my blogs go, and it got people talking. Nearly one year later, in a moment of frustration while trying to deal with a group of young men who were acting like boys, I sat down to write out my thoughts on being a man. My goal was to teach those young men and to show them how to succeed in life. The problems these young men struggle with today are the same ones I faced when I was a very young man.

As I discovered, there is no instruction manual or bible on how to be a man, and there are a million ideas on what it takes to be a man. In his book *The Way of Men*, Jack Donovan offers one perspective on becoming a man:

> For decades, people have been talking about a "crisis" of masculinity. Our leaders have created a world in spite of men, a world that refuses to accept who men are and doesn't care what they want. Our world asks men to change "for the better," but offers men less of value to them than their fathers and grandfathers had. The voices who speak for the future say that men must abandon their old way and find a new way. But what is that way and where does it lead?

I write this book out of brotherly love for the young men out there who struggle because their fathers weren't willing, able, or present to help them answer the question, what does it mean to be a man?

Let this book serve as a guidepost and a sort of "man bible" or "father in a box" that will deliver a series of lessons that have helped me become a stronger man as I grew up and entered the cruel realities of the world of men. The lessons in this book cover four categories: money, sex, religion, and politics. These are the big four offensive topics that you aren't supposed to talk about at the dinner table. We will also weave in conversations about the zeitgeist of the present time and how modern attitudes and trends shape and mold the idea of what it means to be a man in today's world.

I write this book as it were a brutally honest conversation that a father would have with his son, away from the women and away from people who force political correctness for power and control.

This book is raw, real, and offensive, and it should threaten and challenge you. After all, being a man and facing the frontiers of survival—both literally and figuratively—is threatening. If something in this book threatens you, then work through my argument rationally. I have done my best to back up my arguments with examples from history that have worked, and I contrasted them with examples from history that have not worked.

At the end of the day, being a man is a functional task: things either work or they don't. Everything I give you in this book works in a practical sense, and I back it up with working examples from history. I offer only results here—no feelings—so buckle up and please don't cry if I hurt your feelings.

I dedicate this book to Tyler, Andrew, and my father D. Aarle Aarnio. May you find your path to becoming the strong men that the world needs. My heart is heavy with emotion to give you this manual on how to be a man. Unfortunately, the delivery systems of this information have been systematically destroyed over the years by cultural shifts, men of power, political correctness, women, and feminism. May this book serve as the father you never had to guide you to becoming a Strong Man.

I also dedicate this book to young males everywhere—boys, men, strong men, weak men—males of all types who wonder what a man is and who challenge modern ideas that purport to answer that question. This is an increasingly difficult question to answer in the modern world. Today, people can effectively switch genders in the morning by changing clothes, hair, and makeup or can even choose a different gender before kindergarten. This is confusing, and I feel your frustration and confusion. If you have a penis and testicles, you are probably a man or are at least a male; you are explicitly not a woman. As Chuck Palahniuk said in *Fight Club*, "Sticking feathers up your butt does not make you a chicken!"

> Why are we confused as men? Shouldn't being a man be simple and fundamental?

> If "how to be a man" seems confusing, it is because there are many groups with a vested interest in what it means to be a man. Men of wealth and power have always wanted men to believe that being a man was about obedience and duty or that manhood can be attained by wealth and power through

established channels. Religious men have always wanted to make manhood about spiritual or moral righteousness and that becoming a man could be achieved through mastery of the self, self-denial, self-sacrifice or evangelism. Merchants, and men with something to sell, have always wanted men to believe that masculinity could be bought or improved by buying what they have to sell.

In a united tribe with a well-defined identity, there is harmony between the interests of male groups, and answering the question "how to be a man" is simple. In a large, sprawling super tribe made up of cosmopolitan, individualistic, fragmented civilization with unlimited choices of unique identities, answering the question "how to be a man" is unclear. The ways of the rich and powerful men are mixed with the ways of gurus, ideologies, religions, and co-mingled with macho trinkets that "how to be a man" can mean anything, everything or nothing at all. Add to this concoction the suggestions and "improvements" by women and the question of "how to be a man" becomes an unreadable map to a junkyard of ideals.

The Way of Men is the way of that gang"

JACK DONOVAN, *THE WAY OF MEN*

I wrote this book for you, young man, to help you sort out all the problems that come with being a Strong Man in today's modern society and to guide you in how to be a leader whom the world craves.

"The truth is not for all men, but only for those who seek it."

AYN RAND

Just as this book is for men and about men, it is specifically not about women. If I mention women, it is only to define a man in relation to a woman so that we can flesh out what a man truly is. Men and women are two halves of a whole, so it makes sense to examine them together, but this is not a book about women.

I do not intend to exclude women as an audience from this book; women just simply are not the focus. Women have expressed interest in this book and will buy it for their men. Women want men, not other women, as partners. I empathize with female emotions from this perspective because I want a woman, not another man, as my partner. There is a polarity in the opposite gender; there is an attraction. Women want men, and men want women. They want the otherness, not the sameness. This is even true for homosexual couples where the masculine energy and feminine energy still exist between two men or two women. The otherness is endlessly attractive.

This book is written by me, a man, for other men struggling with the idea of masculinity and manhood. As a female you are certainly welcome to read this book, but I want you to know that it is not designed for you and may not contain the messages you want to read. So, I have warned you. Please don't send me hate mail. I mean you no harm. My goal, and the primary focus of this book, is to enhance men. Ladies, buy this book for your men. Give it to a man who you wish would be stronger and better defined in his life. Or read it for yourself. You don't need to learn how to be a man, but perhaps defining what a man is will give you a better idea of what you want. Men as a group are caught in a junkyard of ideals and need lots of help right now to sort out the mess. Please offer this book to the men in your life.

> "If someone is able to show me that what I think or do is not right, I will happily change, for I seek the truth, by which no one was ever truly harmed. It is the person who continues in his self-deception and ignorance who is harmed."
>
> MARCUS AURELIUS, *MEDITATIONS*

"We are much beholden to Machiavelli
and others, that write what men do,
and not what they ought to do."

FRANCIS BACON

GROUND ZERO

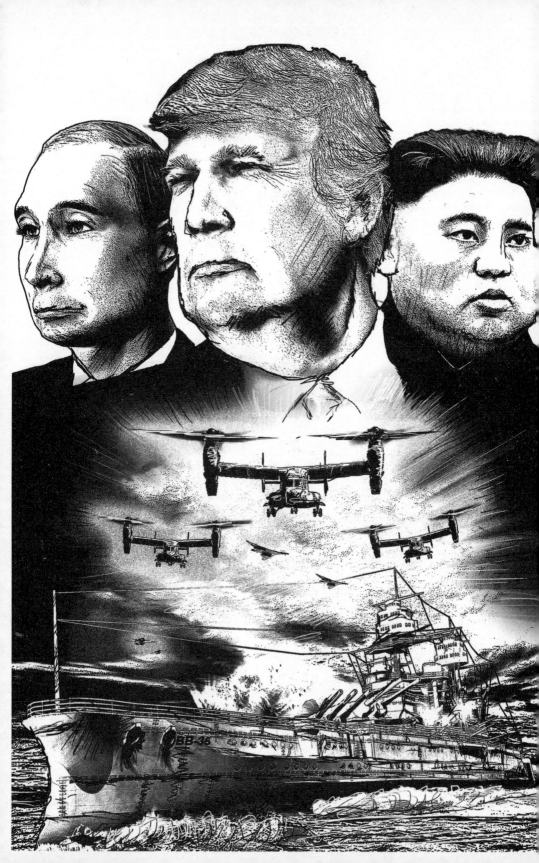

ZEITGEIST
A Spirit of the Times

zeit·geist
'tsīt ˌgīst,'zīt ˌgīst/
noun

    the defining spirit or mood of a particular period of history as shown by the ideas and beliefs of the time.

WARNING: Do not read this book if you are easily offended! Burn this book instead!

This Book is Rated R for Relevant

Political correctness tells us that nothing is more important than the way people feel. If something offends us, if it hurts our feelings, if it makes us feel that we have been treated unfairly, it is to be shunned and snuffed out from the public discourse. We believe this because we are trying to love one another. Because the road to hell is paved with good intentions, and we are afraid: afraid of not accomplishing our goals or seizing our dreams, afraid of death. We want to construct an artificial world around us ... that will shield us from these negative and unnecessary parts of life, but in doing so, we leave ourselves unprepared for the realities of the world. When the realities of life hit, they are that much more surprising, that much more brutal, and that much more devastating.

Gene Simmons, *On Power*

This book discusses **money, sex, religion,** and **politics**—major topics that are offensive to large groups of people because they challenge popular core belief systems fed to us by major sources like schools, parents, and churches. Many of us have belief systems that we never really chose but rather just inherited without thinking for ourselves.

My views may not be popular, but they are grounded in the reality of what works and what doesn't work. The ideas and arguments in this book are backed up by experts and reinforced by examples from the past. I use history to highlight times when humanity functioned well and also times when society fell apart and led to violence and extinction. This book will deliver the truth about how to create Strong Men.

"Devotion to the truth is the hallmark of morality; there is no greater, nobler, more heroic form of devotion than the act of a man who assumes the responsibility of thinking."

AYN RAND, *ATLAS SHRUGGED*

Too many people would rather be popular than discuss the truth. This book contains unpopular viewpoints that go against the narrative of current society. The Strong Men of the past created good times for us, but the current good times have created weak men. We now live in a time of weak men with weak bodies, weak minds, weak spirits, weak attitudes, weak emotions, weak activity, and most of all weak philosophy.

"The object of life is not to be on the side of the majority, but to escape finding oneself in the ranks of the insane."

MARCUS AURELIUS, *MEDITATIONS*

I developed this book from a philosophy of strength and from the independence of men throughout history who were strong and who faced oblivion on the frontiers of survival.

There is no more time left for weakness or weak men; it is time to bring back Strong Men and a Strong Man mentality. If we leave society in the hands of weak men, we in the Western world will cease to exist just as all great empires of the world have fallen when in the custody of weak men. When the empire falls, the tribe becomes extinct. Historically, good times created weak men, and weak men succumbed to hard times.

Today, hard times are coming. History repeats itself on an eighty-year social cycle from good times to hard times, and at the time of writing we are at the end of the cycle. This is explained later in this book. Men will be forced to become strong once more. Do not be offended by this book; rather, open your mind to the counter viewpoints inside and allow them to challenge society's popular narrative. What is popular certainly is not always right, and what is right is not always popular.

"Reject the basic assumptions of civilization."

CHUCK PALAHNIUK, *FIGHT CLUB*

If this book offends you, good.

Offense taken to the truth laid down in these pages means that something you believe is based on weakness.

This book is based on a philosophy of stoicism and strength from a time when men were strong, admired by women, feared by their enemies, and respected by their families.

Today we have the opposite—men are weak, disrespected by women, laughed at by their enemies, and paid little respect by their children. The weak men of today deserve little respect as they drift from job to job and never actually take responsibility for their lives and problems.

Some of us have neither book smarts nor street smarts and are simply not very bright. Period. It's harsh, but it's true. Some people out there are stupid—accept it. But regardless of where you are on Mother Nature's intelligence scale, you need to do what all animals in the wild do: adapt. Take your weaknesses as realities and acknowledge them, find your strengths, and find a way. Recognize that your situation is unfair and then get over it. Succeed anyway.

GENE SIMMONS, *ON POWER*

This book rather painfully rips off the politically correct Band-Aids that society has placed over fragile, bleeding wounds of weakness. When we expose bleeding wounds to the air, they clot, form scabs, and eventually heal into scar tissue. Through pain and exposure to the ways that things naturally are, we can heal those wounds in ways that the artificial bandages of society cannot.

To attempt to heal our wounds, the words on these pages will specifically focus on men. Men have been left out of important conversations in modern Western society in favor of women and women's rights. Several of the ideological patterns that are destroying today's men, and the strength of our society can be traced back as far as the 1960s, when the women's movement began in earnest. If you want a conversation on women, this is the wrong book for you. There are a glut of books on women stored in the dark basements of most libraries and universities that you can read instead. If you want to read about women or women's studies, just go to the universities of the world. They will welcome you with open arms, offer you a comprehensive degree on the subject, and expose you to a huge selection of work.

"You have power over your mind—not outside events. Realize this, and you will find strength."

MARCUS AURELIUS, *MEDITATIONS*

*"If I had asked people what they wanted,
they would have said faster horses."*

HENRY FORD, INVENTOR OF THE
AUTOMOBILE AND THE ASSEMBLY LINE AND
FATHER OF THE AMERICAN MIDDLE CLASS.

WHY I HAD TO WRITE
THIS BOOK

"Begin each day by telling yourself: Today I shall be meeting with interference, ingratitude, insolence, disloyalty, ill-will, and selfishness—all of them due to the offenders' ignorance of what is good or evil."

MARCUS AURELIUS, *MEDITATIONS*

"You're mean" was the message my staff gave me.

I am the founder, owner, and proprietor of a real estate company. During one weekly staff meeting, I gazed in disbelief at my eight full-time staff members sitting around my board room table rebelling against my leadership. I had been away from the office for an extended period of time and returned to discover that the inmates had taken over the prison!

"You're mean," one of them repeated.

The children were ganging up on Dad; I was Dad.

I had been out of the country for more than thirty days and had left the office alone. I fasted for 18 days in the jungle of Costa Rica, subsisting on pure water—no food, no supplements, no vitamins, no drugs—and came home to a small mutiny started by my employees.

"You're mean," they whined as I sat at the head of the table and listened.

That morning, two of my female staff showed up more than one hour and forty minutes late for their jobs in customer service. The office hours are Monday to Friday, 9 a.m. to 5 p.m. The young women in question took the liberty of showing up at the office at 10:40 and 10:45 respectively that morning and didn't even blink at the fact that they were late. In another office, they would have been fired. I had been away for so long that the culture of the office had begun to unravel.

One of my young salesmen, a 21-year-old man, made zero sales calls the day before. He told me he didn't like me, and he got emotional at the boardroom table, telling me that I made him feel like "a piece of shit" while he turned red and had a temper tantrum like a baby. He, in fact, was acting like a piece of shit and desperately needed a spanking.

My manager—my young COO—had not conducted the 11:00 a.m. team meeting where the team reviews the daily stats in over a month. We had an open discussion later that morning about why. During our meeting, he told me he didn't like me, that I was mean, and that he didn't like working there anymore.

My young staff consisted of mostly millennials—an entitled, weak, babied generation of kids who never want to grow up or do any real work. Fuck me. Ironically, I know this generation all too well. I am a millennial.

Over the next two days, I had to do six hours of one-on-one bomb defusal—listening, debugging, and cleaning out all the dog shit that these young men had in their brains.

"You're mean," they protested again.

I countered with, "You four young people should be fired for your bad behavior."

I didn't fire anyone; instead, I listened to the protests and the complaints.

In the world of work and business, you have to do your job. You may not like your job or your boss, or even the company you work for, but you have bills to pay, so you must do your work.

Work is the purpose of a man, and I had to have a "how to be a man" conversation with these young men to straighten them out and get them on the path to productivity.

Such is the challenge of a small company. You can't fire everyone when they act badly; it's too expensive. So instead I listened to them and their complaints, and something became very apparent to me.

None of these young men have real fathers to teach them how to be a man. Even my own father failed to teach me that most basic lesson because his father was a drunk who beat him. The lesson was missing from his own growing-up experience.

I sat at my boardroom table, one-on-one, having the "how to be a man and do your work conversation" with my young millennial men who were, in fact, still boys.

What the fuck? I thought to myself. This man-boy-never-growing-up weakness is an epidemic, a pandemic, a disease that is plaguing our young people today. During my meetings, I heard an entire laundry list of emotional, shitty excuses coming from their mouths:

1) I don't love it here.
2) I don't love selling this.
3) I don't believe in this.
4) I want to go traveling.
5) I want to be a business owner of my own one day.
6) This isn't my dream.
7) This doesn't make me happy.
8) You make me feel like shit.
9) I don't like you.
10) You're mean to me.
11) I don't want to do my job.
12) I would rather do another job in the company that I find to be more interesting.
13) The work you want me to do is not what I want to do.

The list goes on and on, but I will save your eyeballs from reading it; reading their emotional excuses is a waste of your time.

Where is this nonsense coming from? These young men I hired are good men. They are smart, good looking, well dressed, and speak well—the cream of the crop for their age. Yet they still think and say this bullshit when faced with the challenges of real work, their real purpose, and the discomforts of living life as a man.

> *"Contradictions do not exist. Whenever you think that*
> *you are facing a contradiction, check your premises.*
> *You will find that one of them is wrong."*

> Ayn Rand, *Atlas Shrugged*

I spent hours lecturing the young men, interviewing them, and trying to find the contradictions in their thinking. There were several. After having a lecture from me on how to be a man and do your work to gain the trust of your women and your tribe of other men, the message sank in. It was as though I had activated some of the original software in the male's brain. I spoke to them, and they listened and understood. The definition of how to be a man was clear for them, and they immediately made the right changes. No one had ever activated the software for them before.

In the days that followed, the young men showed up to work, the bitching and whining stopped, and they adjusted their attitudes. Best of all, they became productive! They thanked me for listening to them and said that I straightened them out and pointed them in the right direction; their own fathers had failed to teach them how to be men.

I realized in that moment that this is not a local problem, but rather a massive problem across the entire Western world. We have multiple generations of men raised by women who never learned how to be a man.

> *"The problem with this generation is there are not enough*
> *black eyes. Mommy or the teachers are always stepping in*
> *and fighting the battles for the boy. You need to let them*
> *fight it out in the school yard and learn for themselves."*

> J. Douglas Edwards

I normally write books on business, sales, negotiation, real estate, and making money because that is what I have learned by virtue of being a man. I entered the world with nothing and had to learn to survive on the modern frontier of survival in work, money, negotiations, and business. But I am going to step into the "how to be a man" niche briefly because I believe that the young men of today are rotten, not necessarily by choice, but rather because they are steeped in mental and philosophical poison that ruins their minds. This systematic poisoning of the minds of our young men originates from

1) the school system.
2) the universities.
3) the bullshit media telling them to chase their happiness and dreams—mostly a false idea that will stop them from really succeeding in life (I'll explain why later).
4) women and their mommies asking them to be more like women than like men. This often makes women unhappy in the long run because at some point they find out that they want real men, strong men, and not the badly behaved girls that they have created by inadvertently trying to make their men into another woman.
5) an absence of real men or dads in the lives of young men to mentor them and show them how being a man actually works.
6) the Care Bear society we live in where everyone is a racist, sexist, or homophobe if you speak out against any of the doublespeak, nonsense, or cultural subversion taking place in the Western world.
7) feminism, which has destroyed both men and women as a functioning and reciprocating complementary unit in the last 70 years. Now we have nonfunctioning relationships between men and women, and this is a result of the social subversion of feminism.
8) a plethora of other poisons that are systematically wiping real men, strong men, off the face of the earth in the Western world and making strong men into an endangered species.

This eradication of strong men is bad in so many ways. It makes our society weak, our workers weak, our philosophy weak, and heaven forbid if these little girlie-boy Starbucks barista type men with their beards and scarves and fake glasses ever had to fight a war to defend our freedom and our way of life ... we would be so screwed!

It's time to call out some of the problems that are destroying the stock of men in our Western world. Surprisingly, women have embraced the idea of this book more than men, because women after all *want* strong men, not some losers they have to support who live in their mother's basement playing video games and masturbating into oblivion.

> *"Mortal danger is an effective antidote for fixed ideas."*
>
> ERWIN ROMMEL

My messages in this book will be offensive to several groups of people, and they will be unpopular with the narrative of today's media and political agenda, but please stick with me.

I do not aim to hurt your feelings or harm you (the fact that I should have to type that fucking nonsense into my book is a testament to the weakness that we have become). I simply want to lay the issues out on the table, put together a framework for what a man is, and restore the idea of what it takes to be a real man and a strong man at that. Not a man forced into a female framework or anything artificial that our society has wrongfully placed upon men.

If your reaction to this book is "you're mean," then give your head a shake and look at the results in your life: do you have all the things you want? The freedom you want? The life you want? Or did you settle for less?

If the answer to any of those questions is no, then keep reading! If you feel like there is more to be had out of life, that you can be happier, that you can be stronger, and that you can get better results, then keep reading! This book is for you!

Every time you walk out your door and expect the world to cater to your fragile feelings and subtle, sensitive ideas about right and wrong, you rob yourself of power. It's a jungle out there. Being idealistic is fine, but being prepared is more useful and will allow you to navigate the world and use reality to your advantage, instead of being "oppressed" by it.

GENE SIMMONS, *ON POWER*

My employees emoting to me "you're mean" is fucking nonsense and bullshit.

If my company was bigger, the whiney babies who say "you're mean" would get the real-world rebuttal—"you're fired."

I'm not their friend; I'm their employer and their boss. Work isn't always fun, so suck it up—*snowflake!*

This is the reality of life and the reality of work as it stands, and we have to deal with it— as men, not as little boys or little girls or children. When the *Titanic* famously sank in the frigid waters of the North Atlantic in April 1912, the women and children—the little boys and little girls—got the lifeboats. The men were expected to stay behind and go down with the ship. There has been a clear division in history between men, who had to do the hard, brutal, and dangerous work of life, and women and children, who were in a sheltered, separate category. Over the decades, the line between these two divisions has grown blurred, and now men routinely inhabit the protected, more delicate category. It is time for men to leave that area to the women and the children and move back into the category of men—where they belong!

We are men, and we have to take charge as men and be the leaders who are missing from our society before our own proverbial boat sinks, just like the *Titanic*.

"You better work, bitch."

Britney Spears

THE MILLENNIAL PROBLEM

"If a man knows not what harbor he seeks, any wind is the right wind."

LUCIUS ANNAEUS SENECA

I am a millennial, born in 1986. By definition, the millennial generation starts in the early 1980s and ends around the 2000s. Millennials are also sometimes referred to as *echo boomers* because they are the "echo" of the baby boomers by representing a second surge in population.

Another name for the millennial generation is the *Peter Pan generation* or the *boomerang generation* because millennials have had a hard time growing up like Peter Pan and navigating the rites of passage of adulthood, so they return home to their parents like boomerangs.

We have reached a point in the history of the Western world where it is more challenging than ever to be a man. In fact, we live in an environment that is openly hostile to men. Men have fewer rights than ever. Men—specifically white, Christian men—used to be a majority in America and are now a minority. White Christian men are currently treated worse than minority groups, who have recently seized tremendous power in the media and government. Both the media and the government have made it their agenda to pander to minorities as the lowest bidder for votes and popularity in exchange for political power. Votes are always being sold for the lowest price possible, and politicians and the media will buy votes from whomever they can sell to. Such is the bottom-feeding nature of a democratic political system.

This book is not filled with popular opinion. You can turn on the sewer pipe of television and popular media and get that bottom-feeding message on tap 24/7—you don't need me for that. My goal with this book is to give you the counter argument to the sewer sludge oozing out of the mouths of the popular media that is prevalent in the political agendas of today. Most of the content in this book is counter to what they teach you in school or in the universities. They shovel pure horse-shit philosophy, communism, socialism, collectivism, and general garbage into the minds of today's youth—ideas riddled with feelings and emotional arguments that are not grounded in reality. As the old wisdom says, "garbage in, garbage out." I only wish that were true. In reality, it's "garbage in, garbage multiplies!" We are experiencing a multigenerational multiplication of garbage, and it is time for a major cleanup.

I am here to deliver nothing but pure reason, functional logic, and practical advice to young men to fix the "tire fire" issues that continue to burn our civilizations, societies, families, established religions, militaries, young men, and countries to the ground.

"The smallest minority on earth is the individual. Those who deny individual rights cannot claim to be defenders of minorities."

AYN RAND

The greatest generation, the World War II generation, was born in the 1920s. By the time they were 10 years old, they were living in the Great Depression, a hard time that created strong men. After the Depression, these strong men fought in Europe in the 1940s, storming the beaches of Normandy. Wounded or not, they returned home to build a house with their bare hands, have several children, raise a family, and work at a job they may or may not have loved for 40 years until retirement. They married early and stayed married; there was no option for divorce, and they dealt with their problems as they arose.

The men did their work, the hard times created strong men, and there was no question of happiness or backpacking around Europe after high school to "find yourself." There were no safe spaces in universities or gender neutralization of men and women. Men were men and women were women; there were only two options. The World War II generation lived through hard times, sacrificed, and gave everything they could, and America and other Western countries became strong out of the hard times.

> *"The U.S. Constitution doesn't guarantee*
> *happiness, only the pursuit of it."*
>
> BENJAMIN FRANKLIN

Of course, the poem reads: Strong men create good times, good times create weak men, weak men create hard times, hard times create strong men.

Today I am 31, I am a millennial, and I run a business. I hire young men who cannot find their footing in life. Young men—boys, really—walk into my office looking for work. Rather than taking up the required work, they tell me about their feelings and their dreams. This is weak. Good times have created weak men.

We have enjoyed so much comfort and surplus in the Western world after World War II. The postwar era gave way to the baby boomer generation—the richest and most prosperous generation in Western history—and weakness crept in like a cancerous tumor that must be painfully removed.

The great economic times of the past century fostered weakness in the baby boomers. This weakness was compounded by Generation X, and now it is really rearing its ugly head in my generation: the millennials. Thus, the millennial problem.

A man these days is no longer a man. He is confused, raised by women, and explicitly not raised by other men. Divorce rates hover around 50% for modern marriages, removing fathers from half of the families and leaving boys without a strong male influence. Mom usually gets the kids and Dad gets removed, but he gets to pay the child support.

Many millennial men do not have fathers at all, and learning "how to be a man" is an endeavor that is no longer taught anywhere. In fact, this important skill is swept under the rug in the schools of today. We have reached a boiling point where four-year-old boys can now choose to become girls. How can a four-year-old determine his identity? I would argue that he cannot. Why not wait to make a sex identity decision until you are an adult? How can you know your identity when you are four years old?

This is madness.

The politically correct dialogue and narrative of society has created such weakness in young men that they are now nothing like the strong men from successful previous generations.

I do not say that esoterically. Millennials are on track to have worse lives than their parents, with lower wages, lower home ownership, lower marriage rates, and lower birth rates. The American dream that the boomers enjoyed will not look anything like the scraps left for the millennial generation. This is not progress, but rather is a move backward—we are going backward right now.

Young men of today are somewhat avoidant of women. Many no longer desire to get married to a woman, leaving an entire generation of women family-less and childless and forced into the workforce to do tasks that are far less sacred and important than motherhood.

Instead, these women are "empowered" and are statistically devoid of family or children and meaningful relationships with a man. Women are more empowered than ever, but statistics prove that women are more unhappy than ever without a husband and a family. What is the most satisfying job for women in the modern world? Out of all professions, women still find being a housewife to be the most satisfying (http://

www.dailymail.co.uk/news/article-3634473/The-job-makes-happiest-Housewife-Survey-finds-stay-home-mothers-satisfied-profession. html). The traditional biological roles of men and women have been a source of happiness and meaning throughout history for both sexes.

In the last 70 years, we have started to improvise with the roles of men and women. The results are ugly.

Twelve ugly and uncomfortable side effects of our 70-year improvisation experiment:

1) Divorce in the Western world has climbed to rates of around 50% in most Western countries, including those in North America and Europe. The USA is hovering around 53% while other European countries have divorce rates of 60% or higher (http://www.businessinsider.com/ map-divorce-rates-around-the-world-2014-5).

2) Birth rates are down, under 2.1 or 2.2 children per family. In Canada, where I live, the birth rate is currently 1.2 children per family. We subsidize our deficit of children and population with people from non-Western countries. This will have its own side effects because these immigrants come from countries Westerners would not want to live in (Syria, Nigeria, Congo, Haiti, Afghanistan, Iraq, etc.). These immigrants come from incompatible cultures; they come here and have eight children and literally outbreed the declining Western population. Their cultures could overtake our culture at some point. This is not xenophobia; it's math. Eight children are more than 1.2. In fact, if those numbers persist, we will be extinct, and our Western culture will cease to exist. By merely having 1.2 children per family, Westerners do not even statistically replace the two parents who created the child.

3) Unlike centuries past, women now have careers and one or two jobs to make ends meet. They get paid less than men, and some employers argue that they pay women

less because they work less (due to raising children and managing families). As an employer, I can verify that this is somewhat true. Women typically get paid less because they have to take a little more time off for family, whereas men do not typically take any time off and will put in more overtime. Women also gravitate to support roles with less economic upside, whereas men end up with dangerous and riskier jobs with higher economic upside.

4) Women, when saddled with the masculine responsibilities of careers and money, must sacrifice becoming mothers and having families. This has been measured as a decrease in happiness in several studies (http://www.dailymail. co.uk/news/article-2381647/Stay-home-mothers-happiest-Women-dont-return-work-suffer-feelings-boredom-worthlessness.html). Biologically, women want families and children to be happy; this is a fundamental biological and sacred need.

5) Women who work in corporate jobs at companies like Google are encouraged to freeze their eggs to have children in their 40s instead of their 20s so they can advance their careers. This is now a new corporate perk of companies like Google, Apple and Facebook who encourage women to defer having families when they are young in favor of working like a man *for the Man*. Female pregnancy at 40 has now overtaken teen pregnancy in the UK, which is biologically strange when compared to human recorded history. Is this an upgrade? Is this better? I'm not convinced.

6) If a man's family dissolves through divorce (as over half do), he has virtually no power in the court systems over divorce, family, sex, and children. In fact, men and women are supposed to be "equal" today, but when it comes to legal power in the arenas above, men have nothing at all and virtually no rights.

7) We have reached a point in the Western world where, if a woman even suggests that she was sexually assaulted or

"raped" by a man, then the man has no recourse. I use the quotes around the word "rape" because there is real rape, where a woman is attacked and forced to have violent sex with a man—which is horrible and psychotic and the worst crime a man could ever commit towards a woman—and then there are unsubstantiated, damaging, and untrue claims of "rape." In war, men are killed, and women are raped. Those are certainly two of the darkest things that humans can do to one another. However, we are in a "me too" culture now where every single woman has a "me too" story. Some are true, and some are psychologically constructed in the mind and imagined. There is also the challenge of consent generally around sex and the danger of a woman changing her mind after the fact. This is called buyer's remorse—you bought an item, and after the fact you feel like you shouldn't have bought it. This is confusing to men because, if a woman experiences buyer's remorse, she can claim "rape," and the man has no power to defend himself and can have his life ruined with no recourse.

Another confusing case with "rape" is where a woman doesn't explicitly say no to sex, but maybe *never really* said yes. She can claim that she was "raped," and that poor man's life is over. He suffers a character assassination, even if he's not guilty, and he will likely go to jail. The power is so skewed that some men have just said "fuck it" and have unplugged from dating all together in favor of pornography and video games with no downside or risk of becoming accidental rapists.

8) Ultimately, the strange reversal or homogenization of gender roles has created a new set of problems. The biggest one is that men don't need women anymore. Young men are opting out of the woman/man love equation to become video game or porno addicts because they don't want to deal with the pain and wrath of a woman. This has crept into American society and is a major problem in Asia right now, where government policies of female infanticide have

created a surplus of men and a deficit of women. The other side of the equation is if a man is feeling a little bit gay or bisexual, he'll just say "fuck it" and become full-blown gay. Then he can play around in boy-land forever, having lots of sex with other men and never having to put the man–woman–family equation together. He gets to avoid the responsibilities of being a man. Also, being gay today is almost an upgrade over being a straight male. There is a lot of social power and special attention given to the homosexual group—it's "cool" in today's pop culture.

9) Some men opt out of Western women by flying to countries that are literally 70 years behind America culturally, specifically Asia and Eastern Europe, including Russia. You could call the women "mail order brides." Or you could call it men seeking relief from the fattest, most opinionated, most expensive, most man-hating, most offensive, most entitled women in the world—that is, those women found in the United States of America, Canada, and parts of Europe. Men get almost no respect from these "empowered" women, and I have noticed another subset of men who have said "fuck it" to that part of the man–woman equation and have looked to countries with traditional man–woman roles for wives so that they can have a traditional family and just get some basic respect. This is sad; these women in the Western world need and want men, strong men, to be with them, but the culture and strange reversal of power in the Western world are driving some men to import better options.

10) To further the point above, a growing trend in sophisticated civilized countries is for men to marry their sex dolls (joking aside, this is real). Some men in Japan have said "fuck it" to the man–woman equation. They claim that women are too cruel, and they would rather marry their sex dolls that they parade around in wheel chairs, dress up however they like, that stay skinny forever, and that don't talk back. You may think this sounds sick or weird. I think it's unmanly to

opt out of women all together, but at the same time I understand the lack of power men have today in marriage, sex, children, and divorce, and I think there is a certain rationality to "marrying a sex doll" that could never hurt you.

11)   In the future, these sex dolls will become more lifelike and will be seeded with artificial intelligence. I can imagine a time when there will be a reversal of the man–woman power structure in that a man can buy one of these sex dolls for $12,000. It would serve the emotional support a man would need, give him all the sex he wants, and be another way for men to say "fuck it" to the man–woman equation. This will be a major problem and could single-handedly destroy Western civilization as birthrates that are already negative would plummet close to zero. I don't think a sex doll is really the answer that these men crave, or what women want, but it's becoming a real functional option in today's world.

12)   In my own parents' marriage, my mother made significantly more money than my father and resented him for it. Our family had the gender reversal of power where my mother was responsible for masculine roles such as work and making money, and my father was in a feminine role almost like a "stay-at-home dad." This tragically ended because of the massive disrespect that my mother felt toward my father. The gender reversal was a breeding ground of resentment and did not fulfill my mother's biological needs. Since then, several of my friends and family members have divorced, and the divorces were sad and unnecessary in most cases. I believe that the primary cause for the rise in divorce rates is that men and women are no longer complementary reciprocals. They are no longer two opposite halves of a whole. Instead, they are both the same half, neither needing the other. There has been a huge push in the popular narrative of society to make men and women equal, and I think this is generally wrong and a ridiculous idea.

When men and women are "equal" and don't need each other, then there is no reason to be together. If you have two heads who always agree, you don't need one of them. The ancient, sacred ideals of familial roles that sprung from various religions and that worked historically have been cannibalized by feminism and equality over the last seventy years. The idea that men and women are equal is preposterous, and it clearly does not bring real value to the Western world. In fact, I would say it's somewhat responsible for the decline of families, which make up the basic social fabric of a society.

The functional and correct idea, as outlined in several ancient religions, is that men and women are complementary and reciprocal. Men—real men—have special talents they can bring to the table to enhance the lives of women. Likewise, women, with their own sacred energies and life-giving abilities, have an entirely exclusive set of special attributes that they bring to the table. For us as modern humans to try to reverse biology, equalize it artificially with drugs, and homogenize it is somewhat backward and perhaps evil. With divorce rates over 50%, I can say that whatever we are doing currently is not working well for families, happiness, raising children, and the general fabric of society, which I believe to be in decline right now.

There are not many "real" men left. What we have is a generation of weak men, raised by women, with no fathers.

These weak men are the beard-wearing, toque-wearing, scarf-sporting Starbucks barista men who cannot find meaningful work.

The women of today crave men to date and marry one day to live out their feminine and biological purposes of having children and raising a family, but when they go into the dating marketplace to find a man, they find weak, unmanly men who run away from their problems, cry, need safe spaces, do not have any economic power, do not have real careers, do not have father role models, avoid commitment, avoid responsibility, have no religion or spiritual guidance at all, are more educated than ever, and are more useless than ever. These men can't work with their hands or build anything, hunt or fish, they can't sell or do business, they can't lead, and they don't follow either.

Women want real men; they don't want men who resemble women. The men we have today, I would argue, classify more as women than as men. I will define "what it means to be a man" throughout this book and the problems with being a man today.

In the last week, I had to have the "how to be a man talk" with several young men in my office. In reality, their fathers should have had the talk with them, but their fathers are incompetent or gone, so I have to "be the dad."I have, out of necessity, had to teach the young men about work, their responsibilities in life, and that work is not always fun and will not always serve their esoteric "dreams" or "happiness."Is there hope? Can we reverse the trends that are slowly destroying our society?

Yes, we can absolutely return to times of strong men, but it will be a painful return filled with hardship and perhaps a struggle for the survival of Western civilization. The weak men of today will bring hard times, and the hard times will create strong men again.

All things move in cycles. Today we are in a cycle of weakness, but hardship will bring strength, courage, and manliness back.

The sad part is that only pain and suffering will bring back the strong men, and no one knows the kind of darkness that we will have to endure to have such men again.

I write this book for all men out there, weak or strong, to find their footing in the world and bring great value to themselves, their women, and their families. You have greatness inside of you, and by asking yourself, "what does it mean to be a man?" you can unlock the leadership that both men and women crave in today's world.

Don't talk about the change; be the change and be the leader of men. But first you must follow the rules ...

AT THE RISK OF BEING HATED FOR LAYING DOWN A DOSE OF COLD BRUTAL TRUTH

"Don't fight a battle if you don't gain anything by winning."

ERWIN ROMMEL

I write this book with great risk of peril and hatred towards the ideas in this book. Several of the ideas in this book are threatening to the reigning popular belief systems in the current Western world. However, what is popular is not always right, and what is right is not always popular.

"The hardest thing to explain is the glaringly evident which everybody has decided not to see."

AYN RAND, *THE FOUNTAINHEAD*

Right and wrong can be simplified to their basic tenets. If something is right and everyone did it, the world would be a better place. The converse is true as well—if something is wrong and everyone did it, the world would fall apart.

In this book I will discuss right and wrong as per those definitions above. We live in a world of extreme tolerance today, and extreme tolerance is weakness. Tolerant societies throughout history are violently murdered by intolerant societies that are strong in their moral beliefs, values, and code.

We live in a time when everyone has a voice through the internet and social media, and some of these voices scream so loudly that you cannot hear any reason coming through the constant noise. Arguments are made today on the basis of emotions and feelings instead of reason and sound logic. People are judged as good or bad based on how the masses feel about their ideas instead of on pure rational thought.

We live in a world today where it is blasphemous, racist, sexist, homophobic, or any other number of labels to identify real problems in our Western world. We cannot even say certain words or criticize certain groups of people without getting hit with a label as a racist, sexist, homophobic, or other hate label.

I assure you that there is no hate in this book, and I do not wish to be hated by others. What I will do is examine some of the problems in the Western world in a rational way, from a philosophical standpoint and removed from emotion.

There was a time in ancient Greece when the warriors were philosophers, so the warriors were smart. Likewise, the philosophers were also warriors, so your philosophers were tough. Today our warriors are dumb, and our philosophers are wimps. This book will study the nature of man and how he was meant to live, meant to be respected, and meant to fit into a functioning world.

Why We Need This Book and Strong Men More than Ever Before

We live in a world today where the weak men, women, boys, children, and everything but strong men have taken over the power in society.

In fact, to be a strong man these days is to walk on eggshells for fear of offending a group of minorities that has become an overwhelming majority. This strange shift in the balance of power has caused a gap in leadership and a hole that only a strong man can fill.

Missing today are the good fathers who once presided over stable families. Fathers are important for raising good girls into good women and good boys into strong men.

Missing today are the strong men who lead their communities, churches, sports teams, cub scouts, and other groups that need to be led by men to be examples for young men to follow.

Missing today are the strong men who become mentors, fathers, business leaders, coaches, philanthropists, educators, and role models, and who serve as guideposts for others to follow.

The world craves leadership from strong men in so many ways. But instead of filling the need with strong men, we settle for weak effeminate men, cowards, men who look and sound good but have no substance, posers, fakes, and other imposters who look like men but act like boys.

The Case for Donald Trump as a Zeitgeist and Strong Men Throughout History

In 2016 Americans elected Donald J. Trump to be president of the United States. Love him or hate him, Donald Trump is a zeitgeist—a sign of the times—and he fills the need for a strong man and a strong leader. But many people criticize him for his actions as a strong man and leader, and that criticism deafens the media to all the good things he does as a leader.

Trump is an embodiment of the clash between the unpopular work a strong man must do to protect his tribe, as he always has done throughout history, and the popular narrative of the media and the weakness in society that attacks the general idea of having a strong man in charge. For the first time in my life, there is a major clash between the leader who plays the role of father to a very sick and screwed-up country and the role of the popular media, which is playing the role of the teenager or badly behaved child.

In most strong man countries that respect their leaders, like China or Russia, the people are disciplined by their "father." In short, the badly behaved reporters and other media would be shot, disciplined, jailed, hanged, tortured, or "publicly spanked" like an errant child. There are no spankings in America anymore, and the children have overtaken the father in power.

Trump is a highly competent president. No American leader has been more effective based on actions, business success, and real tangible results. However, we do not value our leaders based on their actions and results; we now value leaders based on their words and how we were made to *feel* about their words.

Trump has succeeded in several major endeavors in life, whereas weak leaders like former president Obama speak pleasing words but have no tangible success to add weight to the soothing words he speaks. Actions versus words is part of the clash between weakness and strength with the popular narrative in society. The popular media violently attacks the character and idea of a strong man every day as being racist, homophobic, sexist, xenophobic, or Islamophobic. These attacking words are somewhat baseless claims but nonetheless are the fundamental slings and arrows used to destroy the idea that a strong man can govern and rule by getting the necessary work done and solving the real problems at hand.

This same "weak man–favored" media is the same media that tore down the president hopeful and strong man John Kerry. Kerry was a proven war hero, but the media transformed him into a baby killer. The media also took George W. Bush, a proven coward who stayed home partying during the Vietnam War, and made him into an acceptable weak man. In countries like China, Russia, and other non–Western powers, reporters and badly behaved media who would criticize their strong leaders would simply be assassinated, and the media channels would be nationalized. I'm surprised the same thing has not happened in America—yet. America is still the land of the free and home of the brave, but government agendas such as the Patriot Act, where the

government can label anyone as a terrorist and throw him in jail for any reason as "national security," can enforce a regime of tyranny in the blink of an eye; during hard times, it could happen sooner than you think through martial law.

Donald Trump is a modern strong man, and he is publicly attacked, criticized, and even hated because of his success and his strength. Objectively, I believe it is wrong to ever criticize success.

If you criticize success, what does that make you? How can you ever take control of your life and become a success yourself if you criticize and hate success?

The answer is that you will never be successful if you criticize those who succeed.

> *"The man who does not value himself,*
> *cannot value anything or anyone."*
>
> Ayn Rand, *The Virtue of Selfishness:*
> *A New Concept of Egoism*

You can never solve a problem you do not own. Trump is a proven success and a modern strong man who is hated by the popular narrative because he

- is a self-made billionaire.

- is explicitly not sexist. Trump Tower, his flagship building, was the first skyscraper to be project managed by a woman.

- is a father of 5 impressive, civilized, effective children. His daughter Ivanka is very impressive and runs his empire and her own.

- Prior to becoming president, the public billionaire and celebrity Donald Trump was not portrayed as a womanizer. When the media tried to dig dirt on him for being a womanizer and sexist, all they could find was some locker room talk from 2005 on a concealed audiotape on a tour bus. If he was as bad as they said he is, there would be an abundance of verifiable proof that he was sexually abusing and assaulting women. The claims that came forward after he became president were proven to be underwhelming for a man with so much fame, wealth, and power.

- Trump is not a racist. Champion African-American boxer Floyd Mayweather supported that idea in a radio interview. "Racism still exists. You never heard anything about Donald Trump being racist until he ran for president" (http://www.abc.net.au/news/2017-09-15/floyd-mayweather-defends-donald-trump-locker-room-talk/8948942). Mayweather, a strong man himself, stated that Trump was never a racist, homophobe, or sexist until he became president. He was a popular public television personality and self-made billionaire, but the negative claims never came out until the media engineered a plot to destroy him.

- is a decent husband for a man with so much power, wealth, fame, and status (yes, he cheated on his first wife, and divorced his second wife, but he still holds it together on his third marriage).

- owns approximately 500 companies. He is criticized for some corporate bankruptcies that he was able to maneuver through and a handful of failed business ventures, including Trump Education, Trump Steaks, Trump Airlines, and Trump Casinos, but this is a handful of failures when compared to his successes. Considering 99% of businesses fail in the first 10 years of operation, Trump has a very high success rate in business.

- employs more than 10,000 employees and is not racist or sexist in his hiring practices. Several positions of power in the Trump organization are filled by women and minorities.

- has a multibillion dollar net worth.

- owns some of the finest real estate in the world.

- speaks out against his enemies and real problems that are happening in the United States, even though his views may be unpopular with the social narrative.

- is not a homophobe. Somehow, the press has classified Trump as a homophobe or "gay hater," but I have never seen him actually do or say anything that would classify him as such.

- is a master of the media (able to command $2 billion of free media in the election).

- single-handedly cleaned out all other professional lifetime politicians in the Republican race of the election.

- has no prior history in politics, but dominated the 2016 election nonetheless.

- supposedly has a very high IQ of 155. I would say, based on results in his life, this claim may be true.

- seeks solutions that are common sense, such as eliminating sixteen regulations for every new one passed and simplifying the US tax code back to the size it was in 1960 and 1970, which makes practical sense.

- has not resorted to violence or assassination of members of the media who are against him or nationalized the media outlets who criticize him in unfair ways. Vladimir Putin in Russia assassinates all reporters who are against him and controls the media with an iron fist. It's violent, it's effective, and it's a little bit gangster, but Putin doesn't mess around. I find it amazing that Trump does not exercise his power for violence, and that is admirable, but his passivity towards getting violent with the media gains him no respect with the popular narrative in the media, which makes the popular idea that he is bad or doing a bad job. There are statistics and results to show that he is, in fact, doing good things, especially economically for the country, and this is important for a country that is in as much trouble as America is currently in.

I would argue that *any strong man* in Trump's position as the president of the United States in the modern world would face the exact same criticism, hatred, and accusations of being a racist, homophobe, and sexist from the popular media narrative simply because Trump is calling out and identifying real problems that are destroying the country. We live in such a world now where we cannot even identify problems with words for fear of being racist, sexist, and homophobic. I will likely be attacked and called racist, sexist, and homophobic for even suggesting some of the ideas in this book. This book is threatening and dangerous, especially to the popular media and the narrative of society.

History has always loved and remembered strong leaders: Marcus Aurelius, Julius Caesar, Alexander the Great, Vercingetorix, Charlemagne, General George S. Patton, Napoleon, Winston Churchill, Genghis Khan, Attila the Hun, Moses, Aristotle, and Socrates. Some of these men were cold-blooded mass killers, some were loved, and some were hated, but they all were incredibility strong and led their groups through both good and bad times.

You can love him or hate him, but Donald Trump is strong. When the weak world wants a soft message from "mommy" like Hillary Clinton or Barack Obama to sugarcoat the basic problems around finance, social issues, illegal immigration, and enemies of the country, Donald Trump is the voice of "dad." He doesn't tell you what you want to hear; instead, he tells you the truth. Dad says, "Stop partying and be home at 11 p.m." The teenager narrative of the American media and society says, "Fuck you, Dad. I'm coming home whenever I want." Thus, the problem with the message from "dad." The entire country has no dads and no spankings for bad behavior.

Here's the truth about the America that craved strong leadership in 2017 and needed a strong leader to take over:

1) The nation has more national debt than ever with no hope of paying it off.

2) America is involved in unofficial, illegal wars with more than 7 Muslim countries. The wars are dragging on and on forever and wasting the treasury.

3) The country lacks high quality, value-added manufacturing jobs and instead has an abundance of low quality service jobs that slowly destroy the middle class.

4) Trump banned people from 7 Muslim countries that the United States is involved in illegal wars with from entering the country. People said the ban was "racist," but look at history. America did not take anyone from Germany during WWII—not even Jewish refugees. America is acting as per normal. It is not out of America's normal historical behavior to disallow the entry of people from countries they are at war with.

5) The country has a massive trade deficit to several countries, primarily China.

6) Terror groups are rampant and expanding around the world.

7) America has a fake and weak currency that could collapse at any time if China and Russia make a deal to trade oil in non-US dollars—this is a major threat to America's power base.

8) Inflation in the United States is beginning to spiral out of control.

9) The American middle class is rapidly shrinking.

10) The US has a hollowed-out interior of the country with "no jobs" in the once mighty industrial Steel Belt, which is now called the Rust Belt. People in the Rust Belt have been getting screwed for the last 40 years by the government, and they are pissed off and broke.

11) America has rampant unemployment. The official number at the time of writing according to Google was 4.1% in the United States, but the statistics are manipulated to remove workers who have been out of work too long. The real official number is estimated much higher, somewhere at 30%

to 42%, but it's almost impossible to determine. A huge portion of the United States lives on food stamps.

12) The gold reserves are empty.
13) The nation has increasing violence and political dissent.
14) American society has increasingly polarized population and viewpoints, some of which are breaching upon Nazism, and others are full-blown Communist, which could lead to civil war.
15) Another American civil war is realistic and possible.
16) America garners little respect on the world stage.

The world is entering a hard time, and in hard times we crave strong leaders. This is shown throughout history time and time again. In World War II, there were Hitler, Stalin, Churchill, Eisenhower, Rommel, Zhukov, de Gaulle, and other legendary strong men who led their tribes to victory or defeat.

In our good times, we tend to elect weak leaders with no substance. America had George W. Bush, a weak leader, followed by Barack Obama, another weak leader with no substance, followed by a strong leader, Donald Trump. In Canada, we currently have Justin Trudeau, a girlie man weak leader with no substance whatsoever. In Canada we are usually 4 to 8 years behind the United States politically, so we will have a strong leader next to match Trump, Putin, and other strong leaders around the world as we enter hard times.

The cover of this book is a painting by Thomas Cole called "The Course of Empire—Destruction." The painting is the fourth painting of a series of five that illustrates the rise and fall of an empire. Violently across the cover of this book, you can see the brutality of the fall of Rome. Rome was once an intolerant nation of strong philosophers and strong warriors. It was a nation of strong men, born out of war. As I describe Rome, it sounds much like modern-day America. Born strong in war, intolerant, strong philosophy, strong warriors but with such prosperity, America is growing weak.

When Rome became tolerant and weak, the philosophy became weak, the men became weak, and the warriors became weak. In fact, many legendary Roman armies were replaced by foreign mercenaries, which is also happening in America today. The Roman Empire divided itself into an eastern section and a western section. Each side robbed the treasury to hire mercenaries like the Huns to terrorize the opposite side of the empire. The Huns were barbaric and so good at killing and extortion that they were awarded a piece of land that is known today as Hungary.

"Look back over the past, with its changing empires that rose and fell, and you can foresee the future too."

MARCUS AURELIUS, *MEDITATIONS*

Eventually, Rome fell to the Germanic tribes of barbarians who were strong men; they invaded and conquered the Roman men who had become weak, tolerant, and unprincipled. The Germanic tribes were pissed off about the horrible taxes that the Roman Empire imposed on them, similar to the way that the English imposed high taxes on the American colonies. High taxes lead to revolt. The cover of this book is a violent image as a reminder of a once great strong society like Rome—advanced in medicine, philosophy, the arts, and other faculties of higher thinking that eventually degraded into "bread and circuses" made of unprincipled people who were binge-eating gluttons and lived for Roman sex orgies. Obsessed with pleasure and feelings over reason, this group of sophisticated, civilized people—the greatest empire ever known at the time—was sacked by a group of Strong Men from the north. The invaders were barbarians, named after the sounds of their harsh language that sounded like "bar-bar-bar" on Roman ears. The fall of Rome plunged Europe into a nearly 1,000-year economic depression. Half the population of Europe died from famine, plague, violence, and darkness—the Dark Ages. This continued until nearly 1600, when the world was introduced to the printing press, Martin Luther, and the Renaissance. It was religion, after all, that united the broken tribes of a fallen Rome into the Roman Catholic Empire and facilitated a return to the fundamentals and principles that made that civilization great.

There is great danger in becoming weak like Rome. We could create the next dark age and go backwards in civilization if we allow weakness to take over. It has happened before in history, and it could happen again. The question is, will we choose to be weak or strong?

"Unfairness, hardship, asymmetry: these are sources of pressure, and pressure turns coal into diamonds. This is a concept that, sadly, we seem to be on the verge of forgetting in this country (USA). The more compassionate we become, the more we cater to one another's feelings, and the more we attempt to make life easier for the less fortunate—though these are all worthy endeavors— the more we forget that these utopian ideals are not the natural order of things. The further we manage to get from the feral reality of natural selection and competition, the less prepared we are to face the realities of our world. Nature may be cruel, but this is neither right nor wrong, Nature simply is, and we must be aware of and prepared for this fact in our quest to gain power."

GENE SIMMONS

Democracy usually only lasts 200 to 250 years until the people realize that they can vote themselves prizes from the treasury, and weakness takes over strength.

"A democracy cannot exist as a permanent form of government. It can only exist until the majority discovers it can vote itself largess out of the public treasury. After that, the majority always votes for the candidate promising the most benefits with the result the democracy collapses because of the loose fiscal policy ensuing, always to be followed by a dictatorship, then a monarchy."

ELMER T. PETERSON

Just as strong men create good times, good times create weak men, weak men create hard times, and hard times create strong men. Society has cycles and transitions from bondage to abundance and right back to bondage once more. We are heading back towards a time of bondage, and weakness in our society is creating a need for dependency and bondage. This is not a forward-moving part of the historical cycle; rather, we are moving backward.

"The historical cycle seems to be: From bondage to spiritual faith; from spiritual faith to courage; from courage to liberty; from liberty to abundance, from abundance to selfishness; from selfishness to apathy, from apathy to dependency; and from dependency back to bondage once more."

HENNING W. PRENTIS, JR.

I write this book for you today to slow or reverse the process back into bondage. I'm a strong believer in freedom, but unfortunately freedom is never free. We do need to examine the weak philosophy of our society and how it has created these weak men and what we can do to return to strength and freedom instead of succumbing to apathy, dependency, and bondage. Too many people have fought and died throughout history for freedom, and we simply cannot squander such a precious gift that has been bought and paid for with the blood of our forefathers.

"*A wise man ought always to follow the paths beaten by great men, and to imitate those who have been supreme, so that if his ability does not equal theirs, at least it will savor of it.*"

NICCOLO MACHIAVELLI

WHY THIS BOOK IS NOT ABOUT STRONG PEOPLE OR STRONG WOMEN

There are dump trucks of books filling our libraries and bookstores about female empowerment and empowerment of minorities. I had some criticism online when I unveiled the title and cover of this book as well as a short description of the main focus—Strong Men. The criticism came from certain women asking, "What about strong women?" or why not make the title "strong people"? Those comments are precisely why this book must be about only men, and Strong Men at that.

There is too much narrative in our social fabric right now about women, female empowerment, and a myriad of other social devices empowering minorities into majority power. Today, it seems that whoever screams the loudest gets the best service from the media and the government (who are generally weak men and women) begging, bartering, lying, cheating, and stealing for votes and popularity at the lowest wholesale price. The media and the government are weak and will drive the race to the lowest common denominator, which generally is not pretty, not intelligent, and not something that will move our civilization ahead into a better place.

Political correctness is not the aim of this book; in fact, political correctness is part of our dysfunction. Political correctness is degrading and dissolving society like a strong acid eating away at hard metal or bone. It's time to throw away the political correctness and to see things for what they truly are with rational eyes and not emotional hearts. Sure, compassion and sympathy are virtues, but to have too much of anything is poison, and weakness that is not needed right now.

Women are doing fine; in fact, they are getting more powerful every day, especially in the Western world. In some cases, women are too powerful, such as when it comes to divorce law, common law, and anything to do with children or sex. The people who have lost too much ground in the last 70 years are men, specifically strong men who were previously the leaders of families, militaries, churches, homes, businesses, and other groups of people. Those men are nearly extinct today in a philosophical sense because it is anathema and almost evil to be a proud strong man these days.

Strong men are not popular or favored right now, much like you might dislike your dad when he says, "Don't drink and drive." But if you do drink and drive, crash your car, and spend the night in jail, you love your dad when he comes to bail you out and take you home for a hot shower and hot breakfast.

When times get hard, you don't want Mom; you don't want some pussy man-child who can't even bail you out; you don't want a safe space, or a cry space, or a counselor. You want Dad to come rescue you. Strong men will be very much needed and very much wanted when our weakness unveils the hard situations we have created for ourselves in the near future. You will want Dad again, not Mom.

Remember that in the story of Little Red Riding Hood, it was the strong woodsman who saved the little girl from the big bad wolf hiding in Grandma's bed wearing Grandma's pajamas. The wolf was a killer, and he literally ate Grandma for breakfast with his sharp teeth, claws, and jaws. The strong man chopped that wolf up with an axe and saved the little girl. It was not a woman or Little Red Riding Hood's younger sister or Mom who rushed in to save the little girl. It was not a Starbucks barista boy wearing a scarf, a toque, a beard, and fake glasses to look smarter and older. It was a strong man, a woodsman with an axe, who saved the girl and chopped the wolf up into lunch meat. When things get tough, you want the strong woodsman to come save you because he's likely the only one who is ready and willing to do the dangerous and life-threatening work that ensures your survival.

PART I
MONEY AND WORK

"*Someone is sitting in the shade
today because someone planted
a tree a long time ago.*"

WARREN BUFFET

CHAPTER 1
HARD TIMES CREATE
STRONG MEN

On June 6, 1944, America led the largest land-sea invasion in history to storm the beaches of Normandy in France and take back Europe from Hitler and the unstoppable Nazi war machine.

Young men—15, 16, and 17—too young to fight, but lied about their ages to defend their country—crammed 36 at a time into rickety Higgins boats made of wood and metal to fight an uphill battle against seasoned Nazi war veterans who had blitzkrieged across Europe and had violently brought Europe to its knees.

The young men were scared, and some vomited before the front door of the Higgins boat would open and display the beach of death ahead. Their guns were wrapped in plastic to keep the gunpowder dry so they could still swim through the water and onto dry land and fire a bullet when the time came.

Some of the boats exploded on water mines before reaching the shore, killing the young men inside, some boats were riddled with machine gun fire before landing, tearing up the young men into a bloody box of death. Other boats would be strafed by Nazi planes while the bullets pierced through their bodies and sunk the boat, drowning them all inside. Some boats would reach the shore, where scores and scores of young men were mutilated by Nazi machine gun fire.

Still, the young Allied men had to press on, they had to move forward, they had to storm the beaches and kill their enemies, or they knew that eventually the Nazis would storm their Allied beaches and kill them. It was "us" or "them." Two hundred and nine thousand Allied men died that day taking the beach, and they didn't stop when their best friend was gunned down. They didn't stop when the rest of the platoon was lit on fire by a flamethrower. They didn't stop when their boat couldn't land and they had to swim to shore; they stopped at nothing less than victory.

I read a short poem online, and it read:

> Hard times create strong men,
> Strong men create good times,
> Good times create weak men,
> Weak men create hard times.

G. Michael Hopf

The poem struck me as I read it as though it were mana from the mouth of God or divine truth. Truth lasts throughout history; truth lasts the test of time. Lies and deceit fall away, but the truth always remains.

This poem represents the circle of life, the cycles of history—what goes up must come down. The rise and fall of empires, the rise and fall of men, the rise and fall of power, which eventually gives way to weakness. The words are visceral, you can feel them in your guts, and even just the phrase "Hard Times Create Strong Men" appeals to anyone and everyone who has ever faced a hard time and had to be strong.

Unfortunately, as I write these words, I believe that we are living in the "weak men create hard times" part of the cycle.

"A nation is born a stoic and dies an epicurean."

WILL DURANT

Strength and success are born out of stoic values.

The stoics elaborated a detailed taxonomy of virtue, dividing virtue into four main types: wisdom, justice, courage, and moderation.

To have wisdom, justice, courage, and moderation is to be strong enough where one will defer his or her own happiness and pleasure for virtue.

To the stoics, virtue was more important than happiness in life.

In contrast, Epicurean values stem from Epicurus. He believed that what he called "pleasure" was the greatest good, but that the way to attain such pleasure was to live modestly, to gain knowledge of the workings of the world, and to limit one's desires. This would lead one to attain a state of tranquility (*ataraxia*) and freedom from fear as well as an absence of bodily pain (*aponia*). The combination of these two states constitutes happiness in its highest form ... Epicureanism is a form of hedonism (Wikipedia).

When pleasure, personal happiness, limited desire, modest living, knowledge without action, tranquility, absence of bodily pain, and hedonism take over, a weak man is born.

As a millennial, I can say that my generation is certainly Epicurean in nature. We are indeed living in a time of weak men who create hard times.

Today's young man between 20 and 30 drowns in pleasure through video games and pornography. He will not have a serious or real relationship with a woman to make a family or bear children until late in life, or perhaps ever. Our birth rates are down, and costs of living are high, so traditional families are in decline. Today's young man puts his personal happiness first, above all else. He has limited desire and ambition and, in effect, must live modestly. He is the most educated that a young man has ever been in history, but he takes little action to use his education to reach his potential in life. He has an absence of bodily pain, and we now have "safe spaces" and "cry spaces" on campuses to validate our generation's weak emotional fortitude.

"He is free to evade reality, he is free to unfocus his mind and stumble blindly down any road he pleases, but not free to avoid the abyss he refuses to see."

AYN RAND

My grandmother's generation (born in 1920s) lived through the Great Depression, fought in World War II, built a house and a family, and went on to be one of the most successful, virtuous, happy, and wealthy generations in history.

Men of 18 years of age stormed the beaches of Normandy on D-Day in World War II with bullets flying past their faces. These men brutally killed Nazis in close-quarters combat with rifles, pistols, bayonets, shovels, helmets, and sometimes with their bare hands in the name of service and freedom to their families. In contrast, today's 18-year-old kids need "cry spaces" because their feelings are hurt.

Where did all the strong men go?

"We don't have a great war in our generation, or a great depression, but we do, we have a great war of the spirit. We have a great revolution against the culture. The great depression is our lives. We have a spiritual depression."

CHUCK PALAHNIUK, *FIGHT CLUB*

I'm not saying all millennials are weak. To be weak is to choose to be weak. There are strong millennials out there who go against the grain and work harder than ever to ignore the pleasures and distractions of modern life.

You determine your level of strength and your own level of greatness.

I am sad to say that we live in a time of weak men, and we will plunge into a very dark, very hard time ahead of us.

This dark time of hardship will galvanize men and women to become strong, like my grandmother, who became strong living through the Depression and World War II, while other weak men and women simply won't survive.

Strength and greatness are choices; do not be tempted by pleasure and the distractions of weak men and women.

If you want to be strong, it is time to rise up; this is your time to *seize everything you have ever wanted*. Such rampant weakness has created a huge gap in the market for you to fill, but it can only be filled by strength.

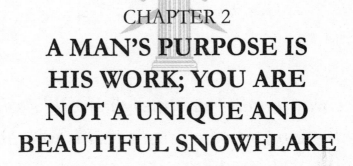

CHAPTER 2
A MAN'S PURPOSE IS HIS WORK; YOU ARE NOT A UNIQUE AND BEAUTIFUL SNOWFLAKE

When You Are Living Your Purpose

When you are living your purpose, you get up early in the morning without an alarm.

You stay up late, focused, without getting tired.

You never tire from your purpose or get bored with it.

Your purpose is an obsession.

You forget to eat, forget to drink water, forget everything else.

Fear doesn't stop you, weakness doesn't tempt you and you become relentless ...

People who are not living their purpose say "slow down," "take a break," "have a little fun," "take a vacation." They don't understand that your purpose makes you happy, and that to you, every day is Saturday.

Time is no matter and it never matters what day it is.

Screw the TGIF clock-punching mentality; you are seizing everything you ever wanted in life!

You only get one shot in this life; don't waste it living someone else's dream.

Live your purpose; there is no other way ...

Stefan Aarnio

"The way a man penetrates the world should be the same way he penetrates his woman: not merely for personal gain or pleasure, but to magnify love, openness, and depth."

DEIDA, WAY OF THE SUPERIOR MAN

In his bestselling book *Fight Club,* which became a hit movie in the '90s, Chuck Palahniuk is credited with being one of the first to use the word "snowflake" to describe the modern man: "You are not special. You're not a beautiful and unique snowflake. You're the same decaying organic matter as everything else. We're all part of the same compost heap. We're all singing, all dancing crap of the world." The modern man has been a generation of men, raised by women and by television.

Palahniuk goes on to say: "I see in the fight club the strongest and smartest men who've ever lived. I see all this potential, and I see squandering. God damn it, an entire generation pumping gas, waiting tables, slaves with white collars; advertising has us chasing cars and clothes, working jobs we hate so we can buy shit we don't need. We're the middle children of the history man, no purpose or place; we have no great war, no great depression, our great war is a spiritual war, our great depression is our lives, we've been all raised by television to believe that one day we'd all be millionaires and movie gods and rock stars, but we won't, and we're slowly learning that fact, and we're very, very pissed off."

Why the lies? Why did we buy the lies that TV and our overprotective mothers sold us? In the old days, in warrior culture, in the agrarian age, or in the tribes, there were groups of women and groups of men. In these cultures, men and women were honest with who they were and what they were. Typically, in these old cultures, the children were raised by women until they were 12 or so, and then the boys would be taken from their mothers to be raised by groups of men. If it was a warrior culture, the boys learned to fight. If it was a farming culture, they learned to farm. In a tribal culture, they learned to hunt and fish. In essence, they learned to be men from their fathers and the group of other men who made up the masculine side of the equation in such a society.

If a man had an incompetent father, then an uncle, a friend of the father, or another man would raise and mentor the boy. The word *mentor* has been nearly eradicated from society by virtue of the modern industrial school system that has a "one teacher to many students" structure. Teaching young kids is an assembly line, but the mass production model doesn't work as well for creating strong men as the old holistic mentorship style.

There are no mentors anymore with modern state-run education taking over. In ancient Greece, every boy had a mentor, and he would have to do whatever his mentor wanted. Severus was mentor to Marcus Aurelius, the greatest Roman emperor of all time, who learned the lessons passed down by Aristotle, one of the greatest philosophers of all time. In mentorship, sometimes the boy would have to sexually service his mentor to pay for his mentorship. Nothing in this life is free.

Mentorship was common in several warrior cultures, along with homosexuality. The Samurai had a culture of mentorship with young boys and men. The Spartans had it, and even the medieval knights and crusaders had squires. This has been common throughout history.

Modern schools have destroyed the master/apprentice relationship that survived throughout history. Mentors and mentees, masters and apprentices, the immersion of your work and your knowledge to transfer real knowledge and information from one generation to the next.

In the industrial age, we tried to violate the mentor-mentee relationship and tried to cram all the young boys and girls into factory assembly lines called schools. The young people no longer had mentors, and when the divorces hit and the families started dissolving, child-rearing became the responsibility of the state. This is ugly, because the state can impose its philosophy and will over the population, which creates a lack of counterbalance to the state. Strong homes, strong families are the basic unit of society, and the strength of the basic unit allows a family to make its own decisions, independent of the whims of the state.

The educational institutions have been serving Marxist, communist philosophy and communist propaganda. They have taken religion and families out of schools along with nearly everything that this successful society has been built on. As KGB defector Yuri Beznemov observed, "Marxist-Leninist ideology is being pumped into the soft heads of at least three generations of American students without being challenged, or counterbalanced by the basic values of Americanism."

Most of the old useful life lessons have been removed from the schools, and the school system and have been replaced with impractical subjects such as sexuality and gender studies.

They don't teach commerce, business, money, freedom, how to have a family, how to be married, or anything useful to an individual person. Instead, we get communist philosophy and harebrain ideas, where subjectivity overtakes objectivity, and the greater good is more important than the individual. This is all backwards from the philosophy upon which our great Western society, and especially American culture, was built.

America became successful by being a bastion of freedom and a beacon of hope around the world. The freedom, hope, and, most importantly, philosophical and religious freedom that made America great are now getting choked out by claims of "racist," "sexist," "homophobic," or whatever other labels the popular narrative is using.

In the old days, if your father was a blacksmith and you wanted to be a cobbler (a shoe maker), you lived with the cobbler and learned your trade. Your father, the blacksmith, took on another boy who wished to be a blacksmith. The men raised the boys and taught them how to be honorable strong men. There was no TV or MTV, iPads raising babies, or state-run schools. Men raised the boys into men, and women raised the girls into women who the men would want to marry and have families with. The men were desirable; the women were desirable and were not the type that men would want to "opt out of" for a lifestyle of video games and pornography or a foreign wife from a more traditional society, such as eastern Europe or Asia.

A boy learned to be a man from other men, and he learned what a man's purpose was—his work!

A man's main purpose in life is to work,
whatever that work may be.

To paraphrase the great Roman emperor, Marcus Aurelius, "Do the work of men" and "do the work that only you can do ... as bees make honey, so you must do your work!" Marcus Aurelius ruled Rome at the height of its power; he was a great emperor, a warrior, a philosopher, and a strong man. He understood that men had to do their work, and in his collection of memoirs—*Meditations*—his words ring throughout history as an example of exemplary leadership. His book is highly regarded in the military, in business, and by leadership around the world today where strength is still valued.

The bees are a great example. The bees do not stop; they do not think about "should I make honey or not?" The bees do not go to Europe to take a year off and find themselves; they don't need a guidance counselor at their high school to help them select a career they would be happy with. Bees don't follow the "follow-your-dreams" horseshit advice that we give to young people today. Instead, the bees just work—every day and every night. The bees work around the clock to make honey and serve their purpose, which is their work. The bees do the work that only they can do, and thus men must do the work that only they can do—the work in front of their face. The work that the group needs done. The work in front of them that validates their purpose, builds trust with the tribe, and makes them capable of serving their purpose—being a man.

Will a man always love his work? Hell no! Work is work; it is not play. Play is grounded in feminine energy and is reserved for women, children, girls, and little boys. Play is not reserved for men. In fact, when the ship is sinking, women and children get the lifeboats, not the men. Nobody promised that work was going to be fun. Work is not dreaming; it is not becoming a rock star, movie star, or pro athlete! Those are mostly vain fantasies that teenage boys have and are not based in reality. Sure, there are a few rock stars kicking around, a handful of movie stars who have grinded it out, and some pro athletes who have put in the work. But there is nothing but work and grinding in this life, and the day you stop filling your purpose with work as a man is the day you become useless, retired, and ready to be tossed from the ship of society into an early grave. Retirement has never really existed throughout history and cultures. You worked until you were no longer useful or you died, whichever came first.

"There is joy in work."

HENRY FORD

Rock stars are a fantasy. I used to want to be a rock star, and today in my industry, I am an influencer with public exposure, so I could be crudely labeled as a rock star. But a rock star is a fantasy and detached from reality.

As Slash from Guns N' Roses says on being a rock star, "A rock star is the intersection of who you are and who you wish to become." By virtue of this definition, a man can never become a rock star because who we wish to become is always attached to a fantasy. Fantasyland is attached to boy-land and is right beside Disneyland as the happiest place on earth. This is not a place for men; it's for children, women, little girls, and little boys. Men do not hang out at Disneyland alone; if you did, they would escort you out as a potential pedophile and sex offender. Men do not belong at Disneyland or fantasyland unless they are bringing their family along and paying the bill. Men live in reality, and reality can be mundane and "suck" a lot of the time.

Men, real men, do not live in fantasyland.

Real men, strong men, do not live virtually in their World of Warcraft accounts where they fantasize about being a wizard and shooting magical spells at one another. They are not drowning in video games and pornography. These are unmanly pursuits. Instead, real men wake up early in the morning, go to work, and do the work that is required! Even now, I'm writing this book straight out of bed, because it's my job, and I am doing my work! Real men may love their work, and they may love their purpose; they also may not love their work or purpose. At the end of the day, no one cares if you love your work or not, and it doesn't really matter to the tribe, to women, or to the other men you know. Your feelings do not matter, *snowflake*. Men must work to support themselves, their women, and their families. Your "feelings" about this don't matter, have never mattered, and never will matter! Welcome to your life as a man.

"All of this stupid bullshit that children have been so crippled by has grown out of something called the self-esteem movement ... and I'm happy to say it has been a complete failure, because studies have repeatedly shown that having high self-esteem does not improve grades, does not improve career achievement, it does not even lower the use of alcohol, it most certainly does not reduce the incidence of violence of any sort, because as it turns out, extremely aggressive, violent people think very highly of themselves. Imagine that, sociopaths have high self-esteem ...

I love when these politically correct ideas crash and burn ...
The self-esteem movement revolved around a single notion, the
idea ... that every child is special ... every child is clearly not
special... but let's say it's true. Let's grant this ... isn't every adult
special too? ... and if every adult is special, then that means we're
all special and the whole idea loses all its fucking meaning."

GEORGE CARLIN

My father struggled with the idea of work for years. As such, he never really had a job. With a small amount of seed money, my father and mother purchased a promotional products brokerage to sell printed T-shirts, printed mugs, and other promotional products when I was just a baby. My father was never truly successful in his business and ran it for 16 years sideways. He really wasn't in business for 16 years; instead, he did the same year 16 times. No one in my family or friends ever really addressed the fact that my dad was perpetually sideways with his work and his business for 16 years. He called himself an entrepreneur for 16 years, but he really wasn't. He never raised capital or started a business from scratch with a product, which is what most true entrepreneurs do. He was a broker, and to be clear, brokers of anything are not entre-preneurs; they are salespeople. My dad was a salesperson, a broker of printed materials, a middleman. He sold shit, as many men do in this life. Sadly, I believe that my father used his business to live in fantasy and to hide from the fact that he was unemployable, unable to lead or follow, and incapable of listening to directions and doing the work. Essentially all the things that real men must choose to do every day.

My parents divorced when I was 17. At that time, my dad's business, which was supported by my mother and her job as a teacher, lost its financing. My mother made $80,000 a year with the teacher's union at the time as a government worker—guaranteed income. My father made $30,000 a year at his business and didn't always bring home money to pay bills. Sometimes he brought home money, sometimes he didn't, as many undisciplined, amateur businessmen do. He had unpredictable results based on unpredictable actions and a lack of discipline.

My mother resented this fact; she hated his lack of manliness in his work. He did not embrace his work and instead used the fantasy of being a business owner to avoid the real work of building a business.

When my dad's company closed due to lack of credit (supported by my mother and lost in the divorce), my dad never got back up on his feet to become an entrepreneur again. He never was an entrepreneur, never worked on his skills of work, never read a book, and never took a class to improve his work and his purpose.

He drove a limo for 13 years, taking minimum responsibility for his life. He took pilot lessons because it was his dream, his fantasy, and it made him happy. He put himself into over $100,000 of credit card debt.

Last April my dad called me. I was in Houston, Texas, going on a real estate cruise for rich successful real estate investors and their hot, beautiful, Barbie doll–looking wives.

My dad says in the receiver, "I owe the bank a lot of money."

"How much?" I ask.

"Over $100,000 on credit cards, and I can't make the interest payments; it's over 20%," replies my dad.

I waited for him to say more, but he didn't. He was ashamed and rightfully so. He thought that taking pilot lessons for years on the side would somehow provide him with economic salvation from his money problems. After the divorce he followed the advice of "go to school and get a good job," but this advice had been outdated for years, plus no one wants a sixty-year-old rookie pilot. Getting a real job with an airline was out of the question for someone with his age and experience.

I later learned that my dad was driving out of town to fly for a shitty little sky dive company and got paid $100 to drive an hour out of town to show up to work and then $5 a flight. He could maybe do two flights an hour if he was lucky. This was less than minimum wage.

What the fuck, Dad? I said to myself when I heard what he was making. That's poor decision making! You are putting yourself on the poverty line?! Working at McDonald's pays better than that, and you don't have to drive, fly a fucking plane, or get $100,000 of training to make minimum wage! Fuck!

"You have to go bankrupt," I said flatly into the phone. "It's okay, though. We live in Canada. There's no debtor's prison, and this isn't Dubai, where they will throw you in jail for being a deadbeat. In fact, you're poor, and Canada loves poor people. This is an awesome country to be poor in! Give the bank the shitty swamp land you own, give them your shitty old car that's broken, and go bankrupt. This is the best financial move you will ever make in your life."

"But I don't want to do it," my dad protested, sounding immensely ashamed.

"Well I know, it sucks, but if you could sell that shitty land and car for $100,000 right now, would you do it?"

"Yes, of course."

"Good. Go bankrupt then."

That was effectively the end of the conversation. The bank never should have given my dad $100,000 of credit; he wasn't smart enough to use it.

> "A man's capacity to receive another man's direct criticism is
> a measure of his capacity to receive masculine energy. If he
> doesn't have a good relationship to masculine energy (e.g.,
> his father), then he will act like a woman and be hurt or
> defensive rather than make use of other men's criticism."
>
> DEIDA, WAY OF THE SUPERIOR MAN

My mother divorced my father over his unmanly relationship with work.

My mother's mother was a stay-at-home mom who was the stereotypical '50s housewife. My mother wanted to live like her mother and stay at home and raise the babies; she wanted to live her feminine purpose and be a mom. My dad seemed like he could pull off his entrepreneur dream, so she took a gamble on him and married him. She had kids with him, and I was one of the kids. When the gamble didn't pay off, my mother was very angry at being forced into the masculine energy of working and becoming the breadwinner. She wanted a man to handle the masculine duty of work, and she could live in the feminine duty of the family and the home.

After my mother announced she wanted a divorce, I moved in with grandma, my mother's mother, the seasoned '50s housewife to get away from all the bullshit of the divorce at home.

Grandma was amazing!

Grandma, the perfect '50s housewife, was a relic of a forgotten and better time.

She cooked traditional homemade dinners every day and set the table with fine silverware and china every day. She packed a cooler with a "sandwich du jour" every day (she didn't want me to get bored with the food as the working man of the house). I painted houses in the summer, and it was boring but manly work. Grandma stocked my lunch with pickles, homemade cookies of the week, sandwich of the day, drinks, baby carrots, and dip. I couldn't believe the level of service that working men had in the '50s and '60s.

Grandma had my clothes washed, folded, and starched (I had never experienced starch until living with Grandma). If I got home late from work, dinner was waiting in the oven, kept warm with a hand-written note for me and a table set with silverware and fine china.

Grandma was from the World War II generation. Men were men, and women were women. My mother wanted to be a stay-at-home mom and do what she was programmed to do as she saw her mother do. She wanted her purpose to be feminine and about the family. She needed a man who was masculine to do the work, make the money, shut the fuck up, and pay the bills, just as her dad did for her mom in the glorious days of the 1950s, 1960s, and 1970s.

She never got a man; she got a boy in a man's body—my father. He had an aversion to work and hid behind a shitty business that wasn't really a business. It was a T-shirt brokerage. He played games with money and never stepped up to be the man.

When I was 17 she said, "Fuck this."

I walked in on my parents in the kitchen one day at 17 after music school and saw my 5'4" mother towering over my 6'2" father , who was on his knees crying and begging her for a second chance. She had just told him that she wanted a divorce, and he got down on his knees and begged while she towered over him, hands on hips in a Darth Vader "don't come near me" power pose.

While my dad was begging on his knees like a dog for his life, my mother lost her composure and laughed at him. She didn't help him, she didn't give him another chance, and she betrayed him in his moment of weakness, as many women would. A woman who must support a man is forced into the masculine purpose of work. The man is forced into the feminine, and this is unmanly. Unmanly men are savagely attacked, discounted, and thrown out by women everywhere. If you can't fill your masculine role of work, your woman will divorce you and find a man who can fill the job description. Those are the rules.

An unmanly man who can't work and can't support a family is of no use to a feminine woman. A feminine woman's purpose is the family, and she needs a masculine man to do the work, make the money, and be the man.

My mother had enough, and as a feminine woman forced into the masculine role as the breadwinner, she metaphorically stabbed him in the back as a woman always eventually will to a man who fails to fill her needs to be feminine. She was forced into the masculine role in the relationship and hated him every day for it. She hated his weakness, and she hated who she had to become to make it work.

"Fuck him," she probably thought.

I sometimes feel guilty for my parents' divorce because one day I came home from working with my dad at a summer job, and I said to my mother, "Mom, I don't get it." We would secretly complain about my dad's business and bash him behind his back. This was a very unmanly thing to do on my part, but I was 16 and didn't know any better than to engage in womanly gossip with my mother. She gossiped about him, so I did too.

No one had laid down the rules for how to be a man.

"I don't get it, Mom. Dad goes to work at 10:00 and comes home at 2:00 with a one-hour lunch break. What does he do? How can he be making money?"

My mother has attributed her decision to leave my father to that information that I let out of the bag. Do I feel guilty for telling her that? Yes. My mother worked full time as a teacher, and, as teachers often do, she worked into the night with special clubs, assignments, and marking exams and papers.

My dad would make lunches for us like a housewife, bring home some discount groceries from the discount grocery store, and then fall asleep in front of the TV. He didn't always bring home a paycheck, and this pissed my mom off! It angered her to see such incompetence and work avoidance in a man. Avoiding his purpose and his work, making lunches like a mommy, and falling asleep in front of the TV like a baby instead of getting better at what he had to do. He didn't train, didn't read, didn't study, and he didn't take a course or hire a coach or mentor to make him great at his work and purpose. Instead, he avoided the reality that he was shitty at his work, and his inability to own his problems made him a boy and not a man.

She wanted a man, but she was forced to become the man, and manly she became. My mother often said, "I felt like I had three sons and no husband." I don't blame her for this feeling when I look back on how my father treated his work and purpose.

"If a man never discovers his deepest purpose, or if he permanently compromises it and uses his family as an excuse for doing so, then his core becomes weakened and he loses depth and presence. His woman loses trust and sexual polarity with him, even though he may be putting much energy into parenting their children

and doing the housework. A man should, of course, be a full
participant in caring for children and the household. But if he
gives up his deepest purpose to do so, ultimately, everyone suffers."

DEIDA, WAY OF THE SUPERIOR MAN

My mother, being forced into the masculine energy and masculine role of work and supporting the family, became more masculine to become the breadwinner and man of the house. The masculine energy made her skin tougher, she grew into a stocky build, she cut her hair short like a man, and she had to take on masculine qualities, such as assertiveness to do the work and make the money. She didn't get the choice to be feminine and look after the family as she wanted.

If she were free to live in the feminine essence, she could have kept her skin fair, stayed slim and feminine, kept her hair long, and allowed her man to be assertive and provide the money. She didn't get any of that, so she transformed into a man.

As a consequence, my father transformed into the woman. The roles reversed.

Perversely, my dad sacrificed his business to make lunches, drive my brother and me to school, and take on a stay-at-home dad role. This was unsexy, unmanly, and a gender reversal that ultimately pissed my mother off. This unmanly display made my mother lose respect for my dad and reversed the gender polarity and sexual attraction towards my father. After they divorced I learned they had not kissed in years and rarely had sex.

All of these problems stem from my father never learning how to live his masculine purpose and do the work.

"A man must he prepared to give 100% to his purpose, fulfill
his karma or dissolve it, and then let go of that specific form
of living. He must be capable of not knowing what to do with
his life, entering a period of unknowingness and waiting for

a vision or a new form of purpose to emerge. These cycles of strong specific action followed by periods of not knowing what the hell is going on are natural for a man who is shedding layers of karma in his relaxation into truth."

DEIDA, *WAY OF THE SUPERIOR MAN*

Years later, when my father phoned me about not being able to pay his bills, I was 30 years old and a successful entrepreneur. My father came to me in a sideways way looking for a job and looking for more help.

I was a real entrepreneur with two multimillion dollar companies at the time and nearly 10 employees in real estate and my consulting businesses.

My dad needed a job, so he had his girlfriend's daughter help make a résumé with his last job being from 1985 and a testimonial from 1985, his last boss from the last century. It was 2017, and he hadn't had a valuable job in 30 years. The top of his résumé read "proud father of two great boys."

I looked at this piece-of-shit résumé as an owner of a business and said, "Dad, no one cares that you have two great boys. That's irrelevant to work. No one cares about your last job in 1985. That's from the last century; it's irrelevant. Go get a job at McDonald's today and start flipping burgers to get some money, any money. It doesn't matter, just go, or go on welfare and forget it all."

My dad looked at the floor, defeated, terrified, and a little depressed. He had been running from the reality of work and manly work, mundane work, work that needed to be done for 30 years.

Miraculously, after my mother left my father, he found a woman exactly the same as my mother and started to date her. He didn't marry her, as would be a manly thing to do. Instead, he "dated her" and will likely date her forever, but never claim responsibility and marry her.

This woman was 100% the same as my mother. She was the same age, a teacher as well—in fact a resource teacher just like my mom. She had the same socioeconomic background, the same European background, lived in the south part of the city, the same part of town, and had the same idioms, taste in eclectic design of her home décor, loved the same shops and was essentially the closest thing my dad could get to my mother—his ex-wife whom he still secretly loved. This woman's name was Val. She was cool. I liked her, and I was happy for them. Everyone needs love.

Val liked that fact that my dad was fun loving and took her in his plane and on his sailboat. A real playboy—what a show the guy could put on! But when he moved into her house and had no money to pay for things, shit got real.

"Val is going to kick me out," my dad revealed to me in a moment of shame and weakness.

"What the fuck, Dad?!" I exclaimed. "This is the same bullshit you went through with Mom! If you don't change, you are going to be thrown out, and I'll have to move you into my basement! Fuck!"

They say that in life the same problems happen over and over again until you learn your lesson. My dad had not learned his lesson. He still hadn't learned to work, do manly work, work that is required, and make money to support his woman.

"Get a job at McDonald's," I said. "Just get some money, get going, there's a gas station by your house, just start pumping gas, get going! Go!"

"But I don't want to do those jobs. They don't help me get to my dreams!" my dad protested.

"Fuck your dreams!" I exclaimed to him, "Your dreams don't matter right now. What matters is that you bring some money in to show your girlfriend that you are a man and you get it done. Fuck your feelings, and fuck your dreams. That's not what work is about."

"But I'd rather start my own business."

Fuck, this guy was out to lunch so hard I started to lose it.

"Dad, you haven't earned the right to have your own business. You have to have a job first and save up some capital. Then you will have earned the right to be a business owner; you aren't there right now."

"Well, I was thinking of a cleaning or painting business. I could start those fairly easily."

"Dad, you suck at painting, and you suck at cleaning. Then you have to go sell that shit and handle the fulfillment, the employees, and the money. That's way harder than you think it is. Just get a job."

My dad looked at the floor. "Maybe I could work for you on one of your construction crews."

My dad was looking for a handout. He wanted me to hire him to paint or clean one of the several homes I was flipping at the time. I didn't take the bait. I was smarter than that.

"Go get a job at McDonald's or go on welfare. You have to get something, anything. You have to prove that you can do some work."

My dad was caught in the fantasy of being exempt from work by being an entrepreneur. What a mental disease that is. I've been an entrepreneur for a decade, and I work two working days on every working day to get ahead. The reality of entrepreneurship is ten times harder than having a job.

What was apparent in that moment was that my dad was a work-avoidant boy who did not understand the most basic purpose of being a man— doing the work even if you don't like it and support your family. This basic lesson was lost on him because his father was a drunk and his family dissolved when he was 12.

A boy is obsessed with fantasy and dreams, but a man understands the reality of the situation and does the work required from him in front of his face.

A man builds trust with other men by doing the work and by being good at his work. A man who is not good at his work is untrusted by both men and women alike.

In war, deserters are shot; these are unmanly men who run away from their work and their problems.

In the corporate world, men who don't work are fired.

Men who don't work have their women leave them and cheat on them behind their backs. These men are ultimately discarded by women in favor of a man who can be masculine, do his work, and allow women to be feminine.

There is no place in this world for men who do not work, and your place in the world must be earned every day if you are a man. It is your purpose to do the work that only you can do. Suck it up, snowflake; no one asked you what your dreams are. In fact, I didn't start to succeed in business until I gave up my dreams of being a rock star, gave up the fantasy, and focused on building the dreams of others.

As Warren Buffet, the world's richest investor, says, "What you love about you is your hobby; what other people love about you is your business."

Zig Ziglar says, "You can have anything you want in life as long as you help enough people get what they want."

A man understands that it isn't about him, it never was about him, and it never will be about him. It's about his group, his tribe, his family, his wife, and his kids—never about him. Leaders eat last. The world craves leadership from men who are willing to do the work and eat last.

Do the work that only you can do and be a man.

Your dreams can exist, but no one cares; they don't matter to anyone else but you.

Do the fucking work.

If you work first, maybe you can have a shot at your dreams.

CHAPTER 3
MAKING THE LEAP FROM GOOD TO GREAT

"I honestly believe that if you're focused and passionate and driven, you can achieve anything you want to achieve in life. I honestly believe that. Because you'll fucking figure it out ... I never took lessons to play... I just figured it out ... But I would listen and practice by myself in my bedroom obsessively. And so, throughout life I've always kind of figured that's just how you do stuff."

Dave Grohl, lead singer, front man, and songwriter of Foo Fighters and drummer of the legendary Nirvana.

There is a never-ending conflict in the popular advice for young men. One side says in regards to a man's work: do what you love. The other side says: do what's required of you. At the end of the day, both of these statements are true, but there is an order of operations required for a man to be effective in the world.

A man must have a job, he must have work, he must do something every day with some sort of purpose. Whatever purpose he puts on his work is up to him. Is he laying brick or building a cathedral? He decides in his own mind.

Two men are laying bricks. One man is miserable, and each brick he lays upon another brick hurts his muscles more and more. He whines and complains about the task of laying brick and can see nothing but endless bricks laid upon one another as his body atrophies and aches under the hot sun each day.

A second man working next to the first man is excited each day. He knows he is building a cathedral, and in his mind he can see the most beautiful structure known to man being built right in front of his face. He is proud and excited to a part of the project each day. Sure, the sun is hot on his skin. Sure, it's hard work laying brick. But the vision, the meaning, and the spirit of the work allow him to be great at his job each day.

What separates these two men? Simply said, it's the meaning they place on their work. Bricklaying may be the highest and greatest value you can bring to the world as a man, or maybe bricklaying is a stepping stone towards a greater and bigger vision in your life. But in the end, the only meaning we have on any experience or event in our life is the meaning we subjectively place upon it.

In his book *Man's Search for Meaning*, Viktor E. Frankl, who was thrown into a series of death camps in Nazi Germany, noticed that it was the optimists who died first. The death camps in Nazi Germany were miserable, horrific places for all prisoners living there, but there were two types of people: those who survived and those who didn't. The ones who died were the optimists. They would say "we will be free by Christmas." Of course, this little lie they told themselves turned out to be false. Christmas came, and the optimists died of severe heart-break or depression. They gave up when the lies they told themselves were found to be false.

The survivors, on the other hand, lived for any number of reasons. But the survivors all had a reason to make it through. Frankl wrote a book manuscript; the guards seized it from him and destroyed it. Part of what kept him alive was the thought that he had to complete his purpose and his mission of publishing his book.

If a man does not have a purpose or a mission, he will die on the inside. Worse, he could simply die. There are countless stories of men who

worked at a job every day of their lives and shortly after they retired—
which means "to take out of useful service"—they failed to find a new
purpose and died shortly thereafter.

First you must do the work that is in front of you. It is unmanly to be
without work and to be jobless. Welfare and the welfare system have
killed the desire and the need for work, as a large portion of men and
women in the United States now live on food stamps. The number
of food-stamp dependent Americans grew each year until President
Trump reversed the trend during his first year in office.

The welfare system is a beautiful idea. It is a safety net to catch those
who fall in society, but it's an ugly mentality to adopt. The welfare
system promotes a welfare mentality. At the zoo there is a sign that
says, "Do not feed the bears; they will get dependent and weak and will
not be able to forage for themselves." It's odd that we understand that
feeding the bears will ruin them, but we don't think about feeding the
welfare humans in perpetuity. This ruins them and kills the desire to
work and produce.

First, a man must have some work. Once he has his basics handled and
a steady income earned by service, then he can focus his energy in his
off time on that which he loves. Only then can he move into a profession of passion and a labor of love.

Nowadays we have a bullshit idea that it is the labor of love first, and
that is a wrong idea. That is like eating dessert but not your normal dinner. If you eat nothing but dessert, you will get sick. The same applies
to work. The labor of love is what you earn in your off time; turn off the
TV and work on your passion.

When I decided I wanted to go into real estate, and real estate would be
my calling in life, I had to take four jobs to support myself enough to
get into the industry. From 4:00 a.m. until noon I put chips on shelves
for Frito Lay as a merchandiser. I didn't really love the job, but it paid
my bills and gave me a chance for credit to get into the real estate game.
From noon until 5:00 p.m. I worked on my real estate deals. From 5:00
p.m. until 7:00 p.m. or so I taught guitar, and from 7:00 p.m. until 9:00
p.m. I worked on my debt-buying business. It was a grueling death

march for six months until I quit my day job, but that's what it takes to get into the labor of love—it takes everything and much more.

"Success always demands a greater effort."

WINSTON CHURCHILL

Gene Simmons is an American businessman and rock star known for his famous rock group KISS. The last time I heard Gene's annual income, it was $35,000,000 a year from royalty and business deals surrounding KISS; not bad for a school teacher from New York City:

"If KISS had not taken off, I might still be a teacher in New York City, and proud of it. Or I might be doing something different. My point is I would be doing something, and I would be doing it successfully. I would have found a way, because that's what I've always done. I've always had a plan B and a plan C because I know that life is not fair, and when reality takes everything away from you, you must be ready to start all over again."

GENE SIMMONS, *ON POWER*

Gene knew that his labor of love may or may not work out for him. That's why he became a school teacher and had plan B, plan C, and every other plan ready to go if his first choice of profession didn't work out. Gene swung for the fences and hit a home run. He understood the work ethic that it takes to get the labor of love off the ground and did not subscribe to the loser mentality that so many musicians have nowadays.

"So many of my fellow musicians are, pardon the expression, bums. They are merely lucky that their music took off, because without it, they would have no recourse in the real world

*and would likely still be living in their parents' basements.
I've seen people ascend to the status of international
icon, only to blow every last cent on trivialities and break
up their bands over relationships, drugs and ego."*

GENE SIMMONS, ON POWER

You can be good at your day job, but you can aspire to be great at your passion and labor of love:

*"Find something you never have to take a break from, and
you will find your path to power. And in the meantime,
there is no shame in taking a day job. But your time off
from your day job should not be spent sitting around and
watching TV. Your free time should be spent pursuing
your passion, the job you actually want to be doing."*

GENE SIMMONS, ON POWER

Turn off the TV, or better, throw away your TV or give it to the welfare people who stay at home all day and don't change out of their pajamas. I don't say that to insult people, but I frequently walk through welfare homes in my real estate career, and the same poverty picture is shown over and over again: 8 TVs in the house, one in every room, Mom and Dad are home on a Tuesday afternoon and are still in bed wearing pajamas, their 6 kids are all at home not going to school, they have Xbox and PlayStation, they have pornography lying around, Cheetos and other salty snacks like chips and candy strewn about the house. They likely have pets that they shouldn't own because they can't even take care of themselves. On the stove is a pot of Kraft macaroni and cheese and a pan of bacon frying in its own grease until it's crispy. There are 2-liter after 2-liter bottles of Coke, Pepsi, and other soft drinks and cases and cases of beer and liquor. It smells like marijuana because Mom and Dad woke up and "lit up a joint" in the morning to mellow out, and the curtains on the windows are either Budweiser promotional towels that came with a case of beer or marijuana flags, as the only political platform they subscribe to is "legalize pot."

I don't say my words above to be mean or threaten you in any way, but as a young man trying to find my way in the world, I kept seeing the same poverty picture in the same poverty homes over and over again. When you go home at the end of your work day, it's your job to not succumb to all of the weakness and temptation that I described above and work on your labor of love and passion instead. If you work hard enough on your passion, it can become your plan A, and you will earn the right to transition from being good at your work to being great.

I made the transition myself and do not even own a TV; instead, I have a large library.

Avoid the traps of comfort and the traps of poverty and instead choose to use your heart and mind for creation, for good, for passion, and for becoming great at your work. Start with what you are curious about because curiosity is the base ingredient for all passion. Curiosity, when followed, will lead to passion and adventure—just the thing that all men need. But when you numb your curiosity and kill your passion with TV, porn, videogames, sex with women you don't love, Cheetos, beer, marijuana, fatty bacon, and Kraft dinners, you can never find the things that will add the ultimate color and excitement to your life. You will be stuck in a land of mediocrity, average—or worse, less than average. Do not trade the greatness of tomorrow for the pleasures of today. Learn to delay gratification to earn the right to do things that only you love to do!

"You will only be great at things you love to do."

Dave Grohl

"This is key to power. When we look at people who have achieved excellence in a certain field, these are not people who chose their field haphazardly or due to peer pressure. Whatever industry

these people are in, they're doing it because they loved it. They also practiced and worked at what they do. All day long. They did not take breaks. They did not take vacations. They did not get tired of it. Because when you love what you do, you won't tire of it. You will get more done, and you will do it better and faster."

GENE SIMMONS, *ON POWER*

Yes, you read that correctly. Passionate, excited people who enjoy their work do not take vacations; they do not get tired of their work. I always get criticized by average people for working too hard. "Take a break," they say. "You are going too hard," they say.

These are the same people who were negative about my choice to pursue my passions in the first place.

I love the words of Grant Cardone, a $100-million-dollar man. He says to "be obsessed or be average"—BOBA for short. I subscribe to the idea of BOBA, and Grant understood at the young age of around 25 that his drug addictions, drinking addictions, women problems, and fighting were merely his obsessive attitude obsessing about the wrong things. If you take your obsessive attitude and turn it from your vices to your virtues and passions, you can not only shoot for the moon, but you will become a star in the process. I share that sentiment with Cardone. If I take my eyes off the ball and get comfortable, I eat the wrong foods, spend time with the wrong women, and get into all my vices. As the book of Proverbs says in the Bible, "Idle hands are the devil's workshop." When I focus on bigger goals, bigger ideas, and bigger passions that are 10 times larger than I even imagined, the vision is so big and so exciting that I forget about my vices and work much harder on my passions to hit the next level.

"Passionate work stimulates the mind like a car engine recharges its battery—by running, not resting."

GENE SIMMONS

As Tony Robbins says, when you are passionate about your work and your labor of love, you get more energy by spending more energy. Spending energy is the way to get more. In the words of famous actress Helen Hayes, "If you rest, you rust."

You have to take your work and merge it with your labor of love if you ever want to go from being a good man to a great man. Good is the enemy of great, and once your basics are taken care of in the field of work, you can start planning your escape plan into your passions and your dream job. I work today as an entrepreneur, and my passion is "making things." I love writing books, making courses, making marketing materials, etc. I realized early on that no one would pay me in a meaningful way to "make things," so instead I became an entrepreneur.

As an entrepreneur, you will have two years of making no money and being broke and maybe living on the poverty line. This is okay because you have to reinvest in your business to become successful. If you survive five years in business you might be affluent, and if you can make it to ten years and grow the whole time, chances are you will be rich. It takes 20 years to be an overnight success, and it takes 10 years and 10,000 hours to be a master according to Malcolm Gladwell in his book *Outliers*. I subscribe to the philosophy of 10 years and 10,000 hours, and that's why I say, "Respect the grind." The grinding never stops, the pushing on the world never stops, and you have to respect the process of those who have gone before you. There are no shortcuts, and you can't skip the process of paying your dues.

"I was in the same fucking position you are in twenty fucking years ago. That was it. I worked at a fucking furniture warehouse and I wanted people to like my music, so I played out as much as I could. If you are passionate and driven and focused on what you do, and if you're really fucking good at it, people are gonna take notice."

DAVE GROHL

Dave Grohl's current band, the Foo Fighters, does over $100 million a year in sales, and his work ethic is unparalleled and unmatched in the industry. Is Dave Grohl the best musician? No, far from it, but his work ethic is what keeps him winning year after year. It is also the main reason why the Foo Fighters surpassed his original legendary band, Nirvana. Nirvana burned twice as hot for a very short time with legendary musician Kurt Cobain as the front man. Grohl is no Cobain, not even close, but his work ethic and persistence have made the Foo Fighters surpass Nirvana in longevity and sales. This makes him great on grit, grind, and work ethic alone.

"Whether your industry is making shoes, data crunching, running a restaurant, or anything else, there is much to be gleaned from Grohl's work ethic and strategy. He even toured the world with his band with a broken leg, bound to a chair he had constructed out of recycled guitar necks, like some rock-opera Game of Thrones. The actual accident occurred during a concert in Gothenburg, Sweden in 2015 when Grohl fell off the stage. He announced over the mic that drummer Taylor Hawkins would lead the band and cover some of the songs while he was rushed to the hospital. But before he was carted off in an ambulance, he promised the audience that he would be back to finish the show. Hawkins carried on, and Grohl returned an hour later and proceeded to play a further two-hour set, perched on a chair with a fresh cast on his leg. This is yet another situation in which it would have been totally understandable to just take some time off, to rest, to rust, like any normal person would, like the doctor probably ordered. But not Grohl. This story is a microcosm for Grohl's life and work ethic. He is someone who seems incapable of sitting still, of stopping, of giving up. What kind of person doesn't take time off, even for injury and hospitalization? The kind who loves what he does. The kind whose vacation is his work. The kind who succeeds. The kind who seizes power and lives by his

own terms. This is what separates the powerful from the rest, in any field. Never take vacations. Never take breaks. Unless I am absolutely bedridden, I work every day. Life is work, and if your work is something you love, it will never feel like work."

GENE SIMMONS

In the movie *Fight Club*, Brad Pitt plays Tyler Durden. Durden embodies everything that the modern man is not. He is masculine, rough, an entrepreneur, a hustler, fearless, a fighter, dresses the way he wants, and represents everything that men have lost over the years. The narrator, played by Edward Norton, is the opposite of Durden; he is effeminate, soft, a corporate bitch, compliant, fearful, not a fighter, wears what his boss makes him wear to work, wastes his life on meaningless corporate work, succumbs to the status quo, and represents the devolved version of a man that we have today.

In the book version of *Fight Club*, there is a key scene in which Tyler Durden breaks into the back of a convenience store and drags the clerk behind the desk into the back ally. Durden forces the clerk to the ground and points a hand gun point blank at his head. The narrator watches in terror as Durden says:

> *"A vet, you said. You want to be a vet, a veterinarian.*
>
> *You could be in school working your ass off, Raymond Hessel, or you could be dead. You choose. I stuffed your wallet into the back of your jeans ...*
>
> *... Go back to school. If you wake up tomorrow morning, you find a way to get back into school.*
>
> *I have your license.*
>
> *I know who you are. I know where you live. I'm keeping your license, and I'm going to check on you, mister Raymond K. Hessel. In three months, and then six months, and then a year, and if you aren't back in school on your way to being a veterinarian, you will be dead ...*

Raymond K. K. Hessel, your dinner is going to taste better than any meal you've ever eaten, and tomorrow will be the most beautiful day of your life."

The soft person inside of us would say, *"Oh my god, what a horrible thing to do to someone."* But the flipside of the argument that the author, Palahniuk, is trying to show us is follow your dreams as if someone was pointing a gun to your head—your life will become beautiful, the colors will be brighter, and you will live the most beautiful life.

"The soul becomes dyed with the color of its thoughts."

Marcus Aurelius, *Meditations*

Stop the bullshit, stop the fear, stop living the life that everyone else says you should live. Yes, you must work and do your duty as a man. But if you fail to work on your passions in your spare time, if you go home and masturbate, play video games, get drunk, watch TV, get fat, and get covered in potato chips, what's the point of life? Play this game of life to win. Play as if someone is threatening you with a gun. You will think differently if you knew you would be dead at the end of this day.

"It is not death that a man should fear, but he should fear never beginning to live."

Marcus Aurelius, *Meditations*

The question you must ask yourself is how would you live differently if you knew you were going to die tonight? Would you sit in that corporate cubicle as a corporate bitch doing meaningless work? Or would you do something else?

I often challenge myself with this question. What if it ended all today? Would I be happy? Would I still go to work? Would I still sit here on my laptop and pound out 10,000 words in one sitting in one day? The answer is probably yes. I do what I love; if I don't love it, I get someone else to do it for me. My position of power today has come from working at my job and working on my passion relentlessly at night. As I type this it's 8:45 at night on a Sunday, and I started typing the second I woke up in the morning.

I finished one 63,000 word book this month, and I'm furiously finishing this book, a second book, 148,500 words one week later. I love to write, I live my passions, and I want to write three books this year. I will do it because I live as though Tyler Durden was going to come to my house and threaten to kill me each day.

There was an old story about a young man who came to a seminar and said to the old guru, "I want to be a success in business, just like you. Will you mentor me?"

The old guru said, "Sure. Show up at the beach tomorrow at 4:00 a.m."

The next day, the young man showed up at the beach at 4:00 a.m. in a full suit, white shirt, and solid color tie, and the guru showed up in swim trunks and a T-shirt. The young man suddenly felt out of place in a suit; he thought they were going to talk business.

"Come in the water with me," said the old man as he began to wade into the water, first up to his knees, then up to his waist, and then finally up to his shoulders. The young man in the suit reluctantly followed deeper and deeper into the water in his full two-piece suit.

When they were deep enough in the water, the old man ambushed the young man, forcing his head under the water and holding him in submission.

The young man struggled and flailed around, trying break from the old man's grip. The young man fought and fought until finally the old man sensed that the young man was going to pass out. So he pulled the young man's head above the water and said, "What did you want more than anything when your head was under the water and you felt as if you were going to drown?!"

"I WANTED TO BREATHE!" exclaimed the young man, fighting for air.

"Good," said the old man. "You will not succeed in business or in life until you want to succeed so badly that success becomes your oxygen and you want to breathe as though your life depends on it!

"It is honorable for a man to admit his fears, resistance, and edge of practice. It is simply true that each man has his limit, his capacity for growth, and his destiny. But it is dishonorable for him to lie to himself or others about his real place. He shouldn't pretend he is more enlightened than he is—nor should he stop short of his actual edge. The more a man is playing his real edge, the more valuable he is as good company for other men, the more he can be trusted to be authentic and fully present. Where a man's edge is located is less important than whether he is actually living his edge in truth, rather than being lazy or deluded ...

In any given moment, a man's growth is optimized if he leans just beyond his edge, his capacity, his fear. He should not be too lazy, happily stagnating in the zone of security and comfort. Nor should he push far beyond his edge, stressing himself unnecessarily, unable to metabolize his experience. He should lean just slightly beyond the edge of fear and discomfort. Constantly. In everything he does."

DEIDA, *WAY OF THE SUPERIOR MAN*

"Life is neither good or evil, but only a place for good and evil."

MARCUS AURELIUS, *MEDITATIONS*

CHAPTER 4

GOOD MEN ARE NOT NICE MEN

The Way of Men Is the Way of the Gang

Most traditions have viewed masculinity and femininity as complementary opposites. It makes sense to say that masculinity is that which is least feminine and femininity is that which is least masculine, but saying that doesn't tell us much about The Way of Men.

Women believe they can improve men by making masculinity about what women want from men. Men want women to want them, but female approval isn't the only thing men care about. When men compete against each other for status, they are competing for each other's approval. The women whom men find most desirable have historically been attracted to— or been claimed by—men who were feared or revered by other men. Female approval has regularly been a consequence of male approval.

Masculinity is about being a man within a group of men. Above all things, masculinity is about what men want from each other.

Jack Donovan, *The Way of Men*

> ## *"Waste no more time arguing about what a good man should be. Be one."*
>
> ## MARCUS AURELIUS, *MEDITATIONS*

There is a fallacy about men, nice men. Men must be nice; women lie and say they want "nice men," but the truth is that they do not want nice men.

> *"Among our structurally closest analogues—the primates—the male does not feed the female. Heavy with young, making her way laboriously along, she fends for herself. He may fight to protect her or to possess her, but he does not nurture her."*
>
> ## MARGARET MEAD, *MALE AND FEMALE*

Nice men are not men at all.

Let me be specific about this. There are good men—men who follow through, they do their jobs, and you can trust them to do their work. Their word is their bond, they lead or follow other men, and you could trust them to have your back in a war if you were to fight on the same side. They could pull the trigger and kill if called upon to do it; they could also pick up the kids from school if that was what was required for them and their job at hand.

However, good men can also be criminals in organized crime or soldiers from an enemy army doing their duty. They could be your enemies, and you can trust your enemies to be enemies if they are good men.

Being a man is about living to your word and your bond; that is what integrity is. When the words you speak become true, you are a man of integrity, whether your profession is for good or for evil; a good man gets the job done no matter what. Men can only trust men who get the job done, and women crave men who get the job done. Everyone likes a man who is good at his job or who can walk his walk. This is what being a good man is.

However, a good man is different from a nice man.

The word *nice* used to describe "lame" or "stupid" or "ignorant."

In middle English, the word *nice* means "stupid." From old French and Latin, *nice* is derived from *nescius*, or "ignorant," and *nescire*, which means "not to know."

No one wants a man who is nice. Nice is bad. Nice is a pushover.

Women are programmed biologically to select the alpha male out of their tribe and mate with him; this is how women have survived throughout written and unwritten history. Out of the 50 men that a woman knows, she usually selects the leader of the pack to be her mate. If her pool of 50 men changes, she will choose out of the new 50 men.

For example, we all know the prettiest girl in high school, the prom queen, the leader of the cheerleading squad. The most beautiful girl who has her choice of any man. In an almost cliché way, this young woman will choose the most alpha male man she can find out of her pool of high school boys. Most likely he will be the best athlete of the highest prestige sports team. This is the way of life in high school—it's medieval in every way.

Attraction is based on social stature and looks; it's primitive, much like medieval times.

When that young girl graduates from high school and enters a new pool of men in college or university, she will typically break up with her boyfriend, who is no longer the alpha male in the new tribe, and she will select whoever the new alpha is: the associate professor, the old man professor, the new sports team captain, a med student—whoever she believes the leader of her tribe to be. If she's a party girl and in her early 20s in bars and clubs, she might find the alpha male to be a DJ, a drug dealer, a bartender, or a club owner, as those are the alpha males of the nightclub scene.

When she graduates from university and enters the real world, she will give up on the losers in the club scene or the still-in-school boyfriend who has no money and go for a man who can handle responsibility—aka real money and economic support. Enter the doctor, lawyer, or businessman—whatever is the new alpha to her.

She will always choose the most alpha male of the tribe. If you are dating or married to a woman, you must be the alpha male of her tribe or you risk losing her.

It's not nice. It's not fair. It's just biology.

On the flip side, men are also looking for strong men to lead them.

That basketball captain or football captain in high school is respected by the men of the high school tribe.

In university, the professor, associate professor, drug dealer, DJ, and bartender are all respected by men in their own tribes. They are the leaders of their tribes.

In the real world, the doctor, lawyer, or successful businessman is the leader of his male tribe.

Both men and women want the leadership of an alpha male, a male who can lead the tribe to survival and success. He can bring economic gain to the men and protection and survival value to the women. This is hardwired into our biology; men and women both want a strong man to be their leader.

There is a case against patriarchy coming from the feminist camps inside of our society's think tanks (universities) that is seeping into our culture against Strong Men.

Patriarchy, or "to be ruled by the father," is different from a "matriarchy," where a mother or woman is in charge. Humans have been a patriarchal society throughout history because the environments we lived in were hostile, violent, and dangerous—we needed strong men for protection. Even female leaders—if they ever manage to take on a leadership role in the tribe—take on such masculine traits that I would consider them to be playing the game of leadership as men rather than women. Such is the nature of the pecking order and competition for dominance of the tribe. To lead the tribe is a masculine trait. Women can do it, but they become masculine in the process.

As the frontier of survival moves farther and farther from us every day, the need for patriarchs, warrior kings, and Strong Men to protect us has begun to evaporate. There are no raiding bandits, hostile neighboring tribes coming to kill the men, rape the women, and cast the children into slavery.

Instead, we have weak men because we have a lack of need for Strong Men today.

Women blame patriarchy for their problems and for power structures, but this just comes from having the frontiers of survival close to home. When there is physical danger, imminent danger, a strong man is needed to protect the tribe.

A nice man can never be a leader.

As Steve Jobs said, "If you want to make everyone happy, don't be a leader—go sell ice cream."

Nice men can sell ice cream and be nice.

Strong men are leaders. They might piss people off once in a while, get violent in words or actions, be mean, or make decisions that ensure the survival of the tribe.

A strong man might have dissenters in the tribe killed once in a while as tribal and country leaders do around the world. He might have to set an example or instigate a public hanging to scare the tribe and make everyone act accordingly.

Not everyone will like the leader. He is not nice, but he is strong, and he is a good man in that he serves the tribe and ensures the survival of the men, women, and children of his tribe.

The real world is not a nice place; in fact, it is generally a hostile place.

In the caveman days, a caveman from another tribe would bash your head in with a stick and take your woman as his prisoner, concubine, or slave.

This was not good for you or for her.

Today, we have much less physical violence in the civilized world, and as such, strong men have become less valuable in a physical sense.

However, we have raiders and bandits through the banks, financial systems, tax systems, educational systems, and health systems. At every level of humanity there is someone looking to take advantage of you. The strong always take advantage of the weak, and we still need strong men to protect us from the frontier of survival.

The men who must deal with the daily decisions that keep the modern tribe alive are not nice men. They are, however, good men in that they do their work, serve their purpose, and keep the tribe functioning and alive.

That is what a good man is. Do not succumb to the whining of mostly women and weak men to be "nice" and become weak yourself.

No one respects nice men. As the old adage says, "Nice guys finish last." It's true in real life as well.

> *On Being a Good Man*
>
> *Most men would agree that it is better to be a good man who stands up to bad men. They would rather be heroes than villains. Most men want to see themselves as good men fighting for something greater than survival or gain.*
>
> *When you ask men about what makes a real man, a lot of them will get up on their high horses and start talking about what it means to be a good man.*
>
> *"A real man would never hit a woman."*
>
> *"A man who doesn't spend time with his family can never be a real man."*
>
> *"A real man takes responsibility for his actions."*
>
> *"A real man pays his debts."*
>
> *"Real men love Jesus."*

However, if you ask the same men to list their favorite "guy movies," many of them will include films like The Godfather, Scarface, Goodfellas, *and* Fight Club.

Was Darth Vader a pussy?

Despite the moral posturing, men are attracted to these characters precisely because they are manly. Bad guys tend to operate in brutal, indelicate, and unmoderated boys' clubs, and they seem to be particularly concerned with the business of being a man. Gangsters are status conscious, aggressive, tactically-oriented, ballsy, brother-bonded men's men. The loner hitmen are portrayed as capable but careful smooth operators who are masters of their dangerous craft. They are not good men, but they are good at doing the kinds of things that have been demanded of men throughout human history. They are not good men, but they are good at being men.

We want our external enemies to be defective and unsympathetic. Many have written about our tendency to dehumanize our foes. Emasculating them is another aspect of that—it adds insult to injury. We also want to puff ourselves up and psych them out. It's good strategy. Insulting a man's honor— his masculine identity—is a good way to test him. It's a good way to get his blood up. It's a good way to pick a fight.

We want our villains within to be equally unsympathetic. Portraying bad men as unmanly men is a good way to dissuade young men from behaving badly. Making your own cultural heroes seem bigger than life men elevates group pride and morale. It makes sense to want your young men to emulate men who champion your people's values, and young men especially tend to choose the stronger horse.

Jack Donovan, *The Way of Men*

I don't want to get nice men mixed up with merciful, kind, or generous. Those are all virtues strong men and leaders can have. In fact, kindness is a trait that both genders crave in a mate. Kindness is important, mercy is important, generosity is important, abundance is important, but none of this falls under the nice banner, which is pure weakness.

"Don't mistake my kindness for weakness."

AL CAPONE

Kindness, mercy, generosity, and abundance are all coming from positions of power and strength, not of weakness. Power and need are inverse of each other. The more power you have, the less need and vice versa. Good men are powerful; nice men are needy.

Feel absolutely no obligation to be nice as a man, but aim to be kind instead.

Aim to have manners and be a gentleman, but do not mistake kindness for weakness. To be a gentleman is to be kind and courteous, sportsmanlike and gentlemanly. This is powerful. To be rude is not necessary manly, but there are times when a good man will have to be rude and exert force either verbally or even physically to maintain his alpha position.

"The best revenge is to be unlike him who performed the injury."

MARCUS AURELIUS, *MEDITATIONS*

Be fair, be courteous, be generous, be kind, have sympathy, and have compassion, but always come from a position and vantage point of power.

Power is the ability to get things done. Never come from weakness, want, neediness, nicety, or fear. Men and women do not respect those traits; they never have and they never will.

To be a man is to be strong and powerful. To be weak and nice is an unmanly pursuit.

Being a good man is about being good at your culture's idea of manhood. If you are a man in a primitive jungle tribe, being a man means being able to hunt successfully. Being a good man in suburban America means holding down a job to support your family and fixing things around the house. If you are a single, young man, then it means being adept at interacting with women.

Being good at being a man is like filling a job description as defined by your culture's needs and wants. The jobs your culture wants done will define what it means to be a good man. A man can fail at his job of being a man but still be a good person. The word *person* is important, because it is gender neutral. What makes a good man and what makes a good woman are different things altogether, and this creates confusion for men.

> *Is manliness so flexible a concept that a community can rewrite the job description however they wish? Not if we accept any model of human nature that acknowledges differences between male and female psychology. Over the past few decades, Americans have transitioned to a service economy and educators treated boys like naughty girls with attitude problems. Males have become less interested in educational achievement, less engaged in political life, less concerned about careers, and more interested in forms of entertainment that feature vicarious gang drama—like video games and spectator sports.*
>
> *Further, if the "job description" of being a man is written in such a way that the qualities which make a good man are basically identical to the qualities that make a good woman, then those qualities are more about being a good person than anything else. It is good to be honest, just, and kind, but these virtues don't have much specifically to do with being a man. Manliness can't merely be synonymous with "good behavior."*

Jack Donovan, *The Ways of Men*

If we gender neutralize "what makes a good man" by saying "what makes a good person," this confuses men even more. The change is backwards and leads to men trying to live up to a false set of ideals or even finding meaninglessness in the distinction of being a man versus a woman. It leads to the reversal of masculine and feminine energy, men trying to act like women, and general confusion.

Women don't want other women. They want men—good men, strong men to lead them and their tribes to survival and a point of thriving.

But what happens when the man who wants to feel useful ends up feeling used? What happens when the system no longer offers men the things they really want? How long can we expect men to perform tricks like a dog for a pat on the head? How long until this neglected, kicked, starving dog turns on his master?

There is a difference between a nice man, a good man, and a man who is good at being a man. Being a good man traditionally has to do with ethics, morality, religion, and behaving productively within the framework of your civilization. Being a good man may not have anything to do with how to survive in a survival scenario. It's possible to be a good man without being particularly good at being a man. In the past, men who were good at being men sought the help of priests, shamans, philosophers, writers, and historians. Men of action needed men of words, and men of words needed men of action. The philosophers used to be warriors and the warriors philosophers; both sides needed one another as a marriage between action and abstraction. Sadly, this relationship has been lost.

> *Being good at being a man is about being willing and able to fulfill the natural role of men in a survival scenario. Being good at being a man is about showing other men that you are the kind of guy they'd want on their team if the shit hits the fan. Being good at being a man isn't a quest for moral perfection, it's about fighting to survive. Good men admire or respect bad men when they demonstrate strength, courage, mastery or a commitment to the men of their own renegade tribes. A concern with being good at being a man is what good guys and bad guys have in common."*

Jack Donovan, *The Ways of Men*

A distinction forms. To Jack Donovan, there is a good man and there is good at being a man. A good man will fit into the abstract of his morals, ethics, religion, and civilization. Then there are men who are good at being men, which fits into the framework of a survival scenario. A good man, as Jack Donovan defines it, is more like the way I define a "nice man" above.

Gangsters, criminals, pirates, thieves, and raiders are good at being men, but maybe aren't good men. I would argue that human nature knows no morals and ethics and that morals and ethics are only weapons used by one tribe to attack another tribe.

One man's terrorist is another man's freedom fighter.

Morals and ethics seem to go out the window in a survival situation or a dog-eat-dog world, so I'm not convinced that we can include them in the base definition of a good man. To paraphrase Captain Jack Sparrow, you can always trust a dishonest man to be dishonest; it's the honest ones you have to watch out for.

Nonetheless, men who are good at being men ensure the survival of the tribe, fight on the frontiers, and do their jobs. Whether for moral good or evil, they do their jobs and live their purposes as men.

As a student of human nature, I note that there are no universal morals and ethics across tribes. We often have moral standards for ourselves that are vastly different from the moral and ethical standards against which we measure our enemies.

I separate men into two camps: "good men" and "nice men." I set morals and ethics aside because they change from group to group and from situation to situation.

Donovan separates men into two camps: "good men" and being "good at being a man," which separates morals and ethics from the act of survival as a man. Using either my or Donovan's framework, there is indeed a separation between men who serve their purpose, no matter how violent or dark they must be to fill it, and the idealistic man who has been neutered to be nice, civilized, or good. Men like that would be murdered first in a survival scenario when pitted against a man who does his job—survive at all costs!

To protect the interests of the powerful people who run our highly civilized, regulated world, men and women have been mixed to discourage gang formation. The government is the reigning gang, and they don't want any rival gangs rising to compete with their power. Feminists, pacifists, members of the privileged classes know that brother-bonded men who are survival minded and good at being men will always be a threat to their power base but forget at the same time that some of these men are needed for survival of the tribe. There is a call in the United Nations to do away with outmoded stereotypes of masculinity as if Manhood was last year's fashion statement and gender can be easily switched like clothing.

To protect their own interests, the wealthy and upper classes have used feminists and pacifists to promote a version of masculinity that has very little to do with being good at being a man and everything to do with what they call a "good man," or in my words, a nice man. This version of a man is isolated from his peers, powerless, emotional, easy to manage, and tactically inept.

A man like this, who is more concerned with being a nice man, or a "good man," but is bad at being a man makes a well-behaved slave to serve the interests of his masters.

> There has always been a push and pull between civilized virtues and tactical gang virtues. However, the kind of masculinity acceptable to civilized societies is in many cases related to survival band masculinity. Civilized masculinity requires male gang dramas to become increasingly controlled, vicarious, and metaphorical. Human societies start with the gang, and then grow into nations with sports and a climate of political, artistic, and ideological competition. Eventually—as we see today—average men end up with economic competition and a handful of masturbatory outlets for their caged manhood. When a civilization fails, gangs of young men are there to scavenge its ruins, mark new perimeters, and restart the world.
>
> Jack Donovan, *The Ways of Men*

CHAPTER 5
ATTACK OF THE MAN-BOYS

What does it mean to be a man?

When you turn 18 in the Western world, you are of the age of majority, and society starts to treat you like an adult. This is confusing because age is just a number. Here are some confusing and contradictory ideas that don't really go together when it comes to age and whether or not you are a man in America:

- By 10 to 15, you grow pubic hair.

- By 12, you are in sixth grade in middle school.

- By 13 in the Jewish culture, you have your bar mitzvah and become responsible for your actions.

- By 14, historically, if you lived in a farming culture you could have been married and have already started your own farm and family.

- By 15, you can have a learner's permit to drive.

- By 16, you can have a real driver's license.

- By 17, you can join the US military.

- By 18, you can vote, rent an adult movie, and buy cigarettes.

- By 21, you can drink alcohol.

- By 25, you might be done with post-secondary school and have reached a level of competency in your career.

- By 30, in the modern world you might be married and have a family.

These ages are all over the place. They are arbitrary and do not really answer the question: when is a man a man? Certainly, at some point he is a boy and at some point he is a man, but there is no defining line anywhere when looking at the ages above.

Some people would argue that you become a man when you lose your virginity, or maybe when you go hunting and shoot your first deer. In tribal societies, boys would be cast out of the tribe into the wilderness to survive alone for some time, and if he made it back alive, he was a man.

We have no such ritual today. In fact, there are hardly any rituals left at all.

Is a man a man at 13? At 18? 25? Or 30? When is the arrival point?

I have asked myself this question for years, and since there are hardly any men's groups anymore that would practice transitioning a boy into a man, I can only say that to be a man is a philosophical choice. A boy becomes a man when he chooses to take responsibility for everything in his life. When he owns his problems, and decides to own the good and the bad and commit to becoming better every day.

You can never solve a problem that you do not take ownership of. The trouble is, most boys and men never make the decision to become an owner of their life and their problems. The opposite of owner mentality is victim mentality, and too many boys get stuck in the victim trap because our society allows for such weakness to persist. Victims get extra attention at school and from the government through food stamps and handouts. Owners get no such special treatment; in fact, owners pay extra to fund the victims' benefits.

The act of taking responsibility and deciding to become the leader of the household, leader of the family, leader at work, or leader of other men is often not taken by men these days. Thus, men remain boys.

I would argue that my own father even at age 59 has failed to make the transition into manhood because he does not own all his problems. He lives in his girlfriend's basement, owns no property, constantly struggles with money and work, and has several excuses as to why things aren't working. Real men don't make excuses; they stare their problems in the face and own them. They don't blame anyone when things don't work out; instead, they fix their problems.

There are two proven opposite mentalities in the world: the victim mentality and the owner mentality.

In the book *Tribal Leadership* by Dave Logan, there are five levels of leadership:

1) Life sucks in general.
2) My life sucks.
3) I'm great and you're not.
4) We're great.
5) Life is great.

What I love about tribal leadership is that it's a simple concept of leadership from stage 1 to stage 5. The first two levels of leadership "life sucks" and "my life sucks" are victim mentalities. People with victim mentalities do not own their lives and thus do not do well at work. They typically have trouble fitting into functioning groups and are found in prisons, gangs, and other deviant and negative environments.

At stage 3, I'm great and you're not, is where the ownership mentality starts to take over, but it's still a weak ownership mentality because the leaders in "I'm great and you're not" are out for themselves and not for the tribe. This does not help the tribe grow.

At stage 4, the tribe has the mentality "we're great." This is where leaders create other leaders. If the tribe can stay in stage 4, it will transition to stage 5, "life is great."

It's important to note that until a boy takes ownership of every part of his life, he will remain a boy. Victims—people who can "never get a break" and constantly blame others—constantly look for scapegoats to pass the cause of their problems onto.

A real man, a strong man, will always own his problems, and if he is a real leader, he will even own the problems of the tribe as if they were his own.

"Do not make excuses, whether it's your fault or not."

General George S. Patton.

Ownership is one of the missing ingredients in today's families and today's fathers. Several modern fathers never had fathers of their own, and those fathers didn't really have fathers either. The leadership is gone from individual families, which breaks down the fabric of society and divides and conquers the population.

When you look at the richest people in any country, many of these "people" are not individuals, but instead are very rich families that have been working on their wealth and influence for generations or centuries. There are very few individuals who make the list. Sure, an individual may make the list every now and then, but truly, it is a family effort and a tribal effort, a tribe with good leadership and a strong leader that is able to pass on its wealth to the next generation, grow the next generation of leaders, and overall grow the tribe.

With the breakdown of the family, with the eradication of Dad, with the family being raised by Mom only, young men today do not ever learn to suck it up and be a man. They don't learn that they must choose responsibility because their own father was incompetent, or absent.

It has been said that entrepreneurs do not choose to be entrepreneurs; instead, they have dead or incompetent parents and are forced to start, run, or grow a business to survive.

This is true for me; my parents fumbled hard with a divorce, and I became an entrepreneur by virtue of having no other options. Through the pursuit of entrepreneurship, I spent nearly $300,000 on courses, trainings, mentorships, coaches, and flying around the world to meet successful men. I met with rich multimillionaires and billionaires who taught me the lessons that I needed to know to take ownership of my life and become a man.

I drew on dozens and dozens of successful men; I studied them, devoured biographies and autobiographies on these men, listened to their lectures, attended their seminars, and came to the conclusion that real men own their problems—all of their problems. They take responsibility for everything, even things that aren't their fault. They own it all, they lead, and they at some point made the decision to become a man and own it all.

This is honorable, this is right, this is good. Both men and women crave these types of strong men in work, in love, in the family; just about anywhere men are needed, these are the type of men who are wanted by everyone.

But what do we have instead?

With the destruction of the family over the last 70 years, we have spawned a zombie swarm of man-boys scattered across the Western world. These are the toque-wearing, scarf-wearing, fake glasses-wearing, Starbucks barista, hipster men, who have a degree but can't find real jobs or meaningful work. These men often fall on the political left, complaining about the evils of capitalism, even though they ironically live a consumer lifestyle with a $1,000 iPhone, $7 designer Starbucks coffee, $300 designer jeans, drive a $25,000 Prius or Ford Focus, and have a $2,000 MacBook Pro. These men are confused; no one had the "how to be a man" talk with them.

I know these men all too well because in my university days, I used to be one of them with a left-wing victim-communist philosophy. I thought that I could complain my way to power, fight "the man" and the system, protest, and somehow make a difference by blaming my problems on other people. My father had taught me how to complain, but he didn't teach me to own my problems.

I didn't learn to own my problems until I began to study the very rich, successful, powerful men throughout history—rulers, warriors, leaders, captains of industry—and I saw a different pattern of thought.

I gave up my victim mentality and took on an owner mentality. This shifted me away from the communist political left where people complain for handouts and don't own their problems. This is not meant to be a political discussion right now in this book, but I'm showing you where this victim mentality lives in real life—on the left.

The young men of today are more educated than any other men in history, and they use less of their education than ever before. They do not have meaningful work and avoid work in general while they entertain fantasies about traveling the world and "living the laptop lifestyle as an entrepreneur." Entrepreneurs have become the new rock stars, and everyone wants to be an entrepreneur, coach, or speaker, even though these man-boys have no idea how hard it is to pull off these pursuits.

They are not winning in the game of money, so they opt for communism and the political left, which promises them the money of others in exchange for their votes.

They are not winning in the game of women, so they opt for pornography, which promises them temporary release from their desire but leave them empty spiritually.

They are not winning in the game of business or sports, so they play video games and opt out with promises of feeling a temporary victory driven dopamine and testosterone rush. But even if you win at video games, you are still a loser in real life because it doesn't translate into anything meaningful in real tribal life.

They are not winning in the game of fitness, so they opt out in exchange for intellectual superiority and the ability to hide behind internet forums, YouTube comments, and online anonymity.

They are vegans, but smoke cigarettes, which makes no sense when you consider that one is good for your health and the other is proven to kill you.

The philosophy in the minds of these men is Marxist, collectivist, communist, and socialist. "I don't own any property, so give me yours. I don't have money, so give me yours."

They are the occupy Wall Street crowd.

They are the 99% who have given up on trying to become a leader in the top 1%.

They are the anti-Trump crowd who tout success as evil, when in fact there is nothing more evil than to criticize success. If you criticize success, what does that make you?

The ideas and philosophy in their mind are the canned crap they serve up at modern universities. It is mostly cold, reheated communism heated up with a shared belief in subjectivity, relativism, and feelings over objectivity and pure reason.

Feelings and political correctness have overtaken rationality and results.

These men seek pleasure and choose the epicurean over the stoic in every way. The stoic way represented the steady and level-headed lives that were lived by the men of previous generations—when men had to fight to survive. Men on the frontier could not afford to be epicurean; there was no room for pleasure over reason and results.

They say a nation is born a stoic and dies an epicurean. When pleasure and the seeking of pleasure overtakes reason, rational thought, and results, that is the weakness that brings down empires from within. That is the weakness that disables the power and strength that we once had.

To seek pleasure over seeking ownership in life is a serious mistake, and thus, we have armies, and hordes of man-boys, like hordes of sheep, unthinking, told to think whatever was served at school.

The weakness inside these man-boys has them opting out of most things it takes to be a man: they opt out of women in favor of pornography, homosexuality, or hook-up culture; they opt out of money in favor of welfare and food stamps, minimalism, tiny house living (which is a euphemism for trailer park living); or living on a "lifestyle business" that allows them to travel. They opt out of families and children in favor of their own pleasure, lifestyle, travel, and spending. They opt out of local community in favor of the internet. They opt out of religion and God in favor of atheism, which was also served at the university with the side of communism for breakfast. Worst of all, they opt out of general responsibility and choose to play victim instead.

This is unmanly.

These are the men in the movie *Fight Club* who secretly wish to slip out of their normal lives to fight like primitive cavemen in dark, concrete, bar basements to reclaim their lost masculinity and throttled aggression.

> *"How much can you know about yourself*
> *if you've never been in a fight?"*
>
> CHUCK PALAHNIUK, *FIGHT CLUB*

The men of *Fight Club* want the tribalism, the visceral reaction of fighting and letting out all their repressed emotions that men had expressed through violence for so many generations. They want the result of being a man and want what a man is about, but there is no way to find it, express it, verbalize it, or purchase it.

You cannot purchase your masculinity, and you cannot purchase a way to be a real man. Nor can you buy achievement; you must earn it by doing the hard work. It's the only way.

You must decide to become a man, fake it until you make it, and "act as if" you are already a man. Eventually, you will become real, a real owner, a man with integrity where your word is your bond and other men and women can trust you to follow through with whatever you are required for.

In *Fight Club*, Tyler Durden is like a messiah, a Jesus, a prophet, going from town to town, setting up fight clubs and later projecting mayhem to bring down the systems and the mental prisons that have locked up and neutered the masculinity that lies dormant deep in the man-boy's heart.

Fight Club spoke to an entire generation of man-boys in the 1990s. The movie and the book were about the visceral feelings and emotions that are ripping modern men to shreds from the inside out. Men suffer and struggle in the captivity of corporate jobs and sterile environments with meaningless work and purposeless lives.

The only way to save the man-boys is to teach them to own it. Own it all and reinforce the lessons and the owner mentality over and over again with repetition.

A boy runs away from his problems, and his problems run just as fast after him. A man stays to fight and wrestle with his problems. He may not always win, he may not overcome his problems, for all men are flawed, but if he remains persistent and consistent, eventually even the hardest of problems, his biggest challenges, and his demons can be conquered.

We are all self-made in that we make daily choices that create success or failure in our lives. I had a computer science teacher who always said, "Life is about choices." He was right. Whether we want to admit it or not, we are self-made because we have made the choices that have created the sum of results in our lives. Typically, only successful men will admit that they are self-made men, and the unsuccessful men like to pass on the blame in a victim-like fashion. But the men who become successful in life recognize ownership mentality and the power of self over the environment and their decision making. We all have free will. We can choose to own our problems, or we can play the victim.

Just as primitive man had to conquer the wilderness, the elements and the land around him, the man of today must conquer himself, and the battle within to own his environment—the good, the bad, and the ugly—to truly be a man of strength, power, and value.

To be a self-made man is not about money but about the unconquerable soul of man. It's about having a fighting spirit that owns the situation no matter how good or how bad and commits to doing the necessary planning, preparations, and actions to live a better life tomorrow for himself, his woman, his children, and his tribe.

In the words of the famous general, old blood and guts, General George S. Patton, a man that the Nazis feared and who is immortalized in history as being a strong man who stood up for what was right over what was popular:

"It's the unconquerable soul of man, and not the nature of the weapon he uses, that ensures victory."

GENERAL GEORGE S. PATTON

CHAPTER 6

THE INVENTION OF
THE TEENAGER AND
DE-EVOLUTION INTO
"EMERGING ADULTS"

After World War II, the American GIs—General Issue—moved back home to America from the war in Europe. The war was long and brutal. Much life was lost on the sides of both the Allied and the Axis powers. Europe was in shambles, and America became a roaring juggernaut of industrial might. Factories that had been retooled to make tanks, bombs, bullets, and fighter planes reverted into consumer products and goods.

Women who took over the jobs in the factories moved home to look after their men and their families. The men returned to work in the factories and offices. Victory had made America more prosperous than ever. America had blown up most of the civilized world and was now the world's biggest creditor with the American dollar taking over the world reserve currency. A new world order was established with America as the center of the universe.

Oil was traded in American dollars; American culture, food, music, movies, and television were all exported as a new war effort of culture began. American culture invaded other countries for economic gain, and this made America a world exporter of not just goods, services, money and debt, but also culture.

American culture became popular around the world, and especially the music like rock 'n' roll, jazz, blues, and country all became sensations around the world. The popularity of American culture is illustrated in the song "Americano" as sung by the Brian Setzer Orchestra:

Americano

He's drivin' a jeep
But he ain't in the Army
Gets all his cigarette money
From his mommy
Dressed like a rootin' tootin'
Texas cowboy
But this lone ranger's
Never seen a horse

He wanna be Americano
Americano, Americano
He wants to drive a Cadillac
Now he's chasing showgirls
Smokin' Camels, whiskey and soda
Now he's never goin' back

He's cruisin' streets for gold
Dressed in designer clothes
Brother if you're too slow
You'd better not blink
Or you'll wind up in the drink

Wanna be Americano
Americano, Americano
Gotta buy a diamond ring
'Cause that's his baby's
Favorite thing
Okay, all right, yeah man
Wanna be American
Wanna be American

He's in the land where
Anything can happen
Reach for the stars
Grab that golden ring
Just remember he's Americano
Well watch it pal
"ause he'll take everything

He wanna be Americano
Americano, Americano
He wants to drive a Cadillac
Now he's chasing showgirls
Smokin' Camels, whiskey and soda
Now he's never goin' back

He likes that rock and roll
He's playing baseball
Loves Marilyn Monroe
A coca cola Joe
And a pizza pie to go

Wanna be Americano
Americano, Americano
Gotta buy a diamond ring
'Cause that's his baby's
Favorite thing
Okay, all right, yeah man

Wanna be American
Wanna be American
Wanna be American

Songwriters: BRIAN ROBERT SETZER, MIKE HIMELSTEIN, RENATO CAROSONE, NICOLA SALERNO

The lyrics of "Americano" show a non-American young man doing all the American things that made up American pop culture at different times in history: Coca Cola, whisky and soda, Camel cigarettes, Jeeps, diamond rings, Marilyn Monroe, rock 'n' roll, baseball, Cadillacs, and dressing like a Texas cowboy.

With all these new exports of culture, there was also a new invention brewing in America that had never existed before: the teenager.

With the advent of rock 'n' roll after World War II, America became a very wealthy country, as happens with most countries that win big wars. This newfound wealth and surplus of energy and time created a new class of citizen, somewhere between child and adult—the teenager. Never before in history had teenagers, as a separate class of citizen, ever existed.

Prior to World War II, there were children and there were adults. This was similar to Viking warrior culture in which there was no word for woman. Instead, they always referred to a woman in relation to her man. A woman was either a man's daughter or a man's wife, but there was no free woman or teenager class for Viking women.

A new role in society opened up—the teenager who enjoyed all the things in the song in "Americano"—getting cigarette money from his mommy, having fun, drinking Coca Cola, chasing showgirls, smoking Camels. This was the American teenager, and a new level of wealth and luxury was created in America that slowly led to a deferral of adulthood. In the early 1900s, before World War II, young men and women lived with their parents until they were married off at a young age, before 20 and as young as 14, and then the children became adults and left the home. There was no cumbersome middle step called the teenager—half adult, half child.

The teenager is now an 80-year-old invention and, of course, with the weakness of our society, we now have a new type of non-adult that takes place AFTER the teenage years. This new classification of citizen is called the "emerging adult."

> Starting in 1995, psychologist Jeffrey Jensen Arnett, PhD, interviewed 300 young people ages 18 to 29 in cities around the nation over five years, asking them questions about what they wanted out of life.

Despite stark differences in their social backgrounds and likely economic prospects, Arnett was struck by the similar answers he heard from his young respondents.

They shared a perception of "feeling in between"—knowing they were pulling clear of the struggles of adolescence and starting to feel responsible for themselves, but still closely tied to their parents and family.

They also reported pondering their personal identity, a theme that surprised Arnett, who thought most would have settled that question as adolescents.

Working from those interviews and examining broad demographic indicators, Arnett proposed a new period of life-span development he calls "emerging adulthood."

By Christopher Munsey
Monitor Staff
June 2006, Vol 37, No. 6
Print version: page 68

As you can see from the above excerpt, emerging adults are an invention from 1995—a relatively new invention—and this phase of life takes place somewhere between 18 and 29. As we get weaker and weaker in our society, we keep pushing and deferring adulthood later and later. It's preposterous to think that adulthood is now deferred until 25 or even 30 years old. Just a little over 100 years ago, in the early 1900s, people died in their early 40s. Nowadays you are pretty much a child until you are 30. What happened?!

Five features of emerging adults according to Arnett:

As Arnett describes it, emerging adulthood can be defined as an:

- **Age of identity exploration.** Young people are deciding who they are and what they want out of work, school and love.

- *Age of instability.* The post-high school years are marked by repeated residence changes, as young people either go to college or live with friends or a romantic partner. For most, frequent moves end as families and careers are established in the 30s.

- *Age of self-focus.* Freed of the parent- and society-directed routine of school, young people try to decide what they want to do, where they want to go and who they want to be with—*before those choices get limited by the constraints of marriage, children and a career.*

- *Age of feeling in between.* Many emerging adults say they are taking responsibility for themselves, but still do not completely feel like an adult.

- *Age of possibilities.* Optimism reigns. Most emerging adults believe they have good chances of living *"better than their parents did," and even if their parents divorced, they believe they'll find a lifelong soul mate.*

By Christopher Munsey
Monitor Staff
June 2006, Vol 37, No. 6
Print version: page 68

The emerging adult, as per the description above, seems to outline many of the problems with man-boys. This new class, this new definition of emerging adults, and I suppose, emerging men (until they are 30) is part of the problem and certainly not the solution.

> *Arnett's research shows that emerging adults want a lot out of life—*a job that's well-paid and personally meaningful and a lasting bond with a partner. *Many might be headed for disappointment, he says, noting that* most employers simply want someone who can get a job done and almost half of all marriages end in divorce.

> *"If happiness is the difference between what you expect out of life and what you actually get, a lot of emerging adults are*

setting themselves up for unhappiness because they expect so much," he says.

The unhappiness of the emerging adult is a new concept in history, and as I have said in other chapters in this book, history has never cared about the happiness of men. Men did their duty, and it was irrelevant if you were happy or not.

Through doing your duty, a man may become fulfilled instead of happy. Fulfillment often leads to happiness anyways. But to chase happiness and pleasure are a fool's endeavors that can often lead to disappointment and lack of fulfillment.

Marriage specifically has had three different ages in which every age continues to make a satisfying marriage harder and harder to obtain.

In the Victorian era, from 1837 until 1901, marriages were about utility. You had a farm or a house and needed to marry someone to help look after the house or farm with you. Happiness was out of the question. This trend of marriage continued until about the 1960s.

Post 1960s, marriage was about utility plus love. Now young people wanted someone they could love as well as work with on a daily basis. Happiness was now part of the marriage equation.

Today, marriage hopefuls seek utility, love, and growth with their partner. This is extremely hard to achieve, and such high standards for what makes a marriage are leaving scores of young people unmarried and unable to find the perfect match. Similarly, some married couples are unhappy and unsatisfied with their mates because the bar has been set too high by the new standards set by emerging adults.

Over half of marriages fail, so perhaps we need to forget about growth and love? These are subjective emotions that come and go over time and take effort to cultivate. Growth and love don't just enter the relationship by default. They take work, loads and loads of work to maintain.

As stated above, the emerging adult is looking to "find himself," and this is manifested today with a trip to Europe after high school to go backpacking and "find himself."

Sadly, finding yourself is a foolish idea. You can look and look, and look some more, but in the end, you will find nothing—because there is nothing to find.

Instead, I propose that you define yourself, make yourself, and create yourself as you go. Draw a line in the sand, claim yourself, and say: this is who I want to become. This is how I shall live today. We are human be-ings not human do-ings. Who are you to be today?

People always ask young children, "What do you want to DO when you grow up?" This is the wrong question. A better question is, "Who do you want to BE when you grow up?"

In a famous open letter, Bill Gates, the richest man in the world at one time, gave eleven pieces of advice for gradating college students:

Email Text, February 8, 2000:

Bill Gates' Message on Life

For recent high school and college graduates, here is a list of 11 things they did not learn in school.

In his book, Bill Gates talks about how feel-good, politically correct teachings created a full generation of kids with no concept of reality and how this concept set them up for failure in the real world.

RULE 1 ... Life is not fair; get used to it.

RULE 2 ... The world won't care about your self-esteem. The world will expect you to accomplish something BEFORE you feel good about yourself.

RULE 3 ... You will NOT make 40 thousand dollars a year right out of high school. You won't be a vice president with a car phone, until you earn both.

RULE 4 ... If you think your teacher is tough, wait till you get a boss. He doesn't have tenure.

RULE 5 ... Flipping burgers is not beneath your dignity. Your grandparents had a different word for burger flipping; they called it opportunity.

RULE 6 ... If you mess up, it's not your parents' fault, so don't whine about your mistakes; learn from them.

RULE 7 ... Before you were born, your parents weren't as boring as they are now. They got that way from paying your bills, cleaning your clothes and listening to you talk about how cool you are. So before you save the rain forest from the parasites of your parents' generation, try "delousing" the closet in your own room.

RULE 8 ... Your school may have done away with winners and losers, but life has not. In some schools they have abolished failing grades; they'll give you as many times as you want to get the right answer. This doesn't bear the slightest resemblance to ANYTHING in real life.

RULE 9 ... Life is not divided into semesters. You don't get summer off, and very few employers are interested in helping you find yourself. Do that on your own time.

RULE 10 ... Television is NOT real life. In real life people actually have to leave the coffee shop and go to jobs.

RULE 11 ... Be nice to nerds. Chances are you'll end up working for one.

Bill Gates—one of the richest men in the world—refuted almost everything that emerging adults believe about themselves. Perhaps Bill knows something that these young emerging adults do not?

I think Bill has a clear understanding of reality and the rules of real life. Bill's accomplishments and success speak for themselves: he is a self-made billionaire and was the world's richest man at one time. How can you argue with that?

I enjoy reading Bill's 11 rules because you can see that he is grounded in reality and does not share the idea of deferring adulthood, responsibility, and reality.

Putting off adulthood only brings poverty, weakness, dependency, unhappiness, lost time, wandering, lost self-worth, and lost self-esteem. Worst of all, it creates a person who fails to embrace reality for what it is.

Emerging adults are so busy getting "smothered by mother" that their teeth and claws have been removed by Mom and Dad.

Unfortunately, these little emerging adult bear cubs need those teeth and claws to survive in the real world.

Do not try to find yourself, for there is nothing to find; instead, embrace reality and define yourself. If you get your definition wrong, try again. Keep trying until you find something that sticks.

Every successful man in history has struggled with his identity at some point. But every man who embraces reality becomes a man of responsibility who owns his problems and makes the decision to define himself in the world. Self-definition means staking a claim to who you are and what you stand for. Throughout history men have taken ground and defended it against the elements and the violence of other tribes.

Take your ground, stake your claim against the wilderness, and fight for your self-made identity rather than going on a quest into the darkness to find something that can never be found.

Only you can define you.

In the darkness of the abyss there is nothing to find.

Claim your ground, claim your identity, and shape it over time.

A successful man makes decisions quickly and changes his mind slowly, while an unsuccessful man makes decisions slowly and changes his mind quickly.

Choose to be the successful man, no matter how much it may scare you.

CHAPTER 7
MEN SOLVE PROBLEMS; VIDEO GAMES SOLVE MEN

According to John Gray, author of *Men Are from Mars, Women Are from Venus*, men and women are psychologically wired in different ways: men are wired to solve problems, and women are wired to emote and be heard. These fundamental differences are so pronounced that metaphorically speaking, men and women appear to be from completely different planets.

Men watch football because it makes them feel like they are solving problems. A man can sit for hours of a Sunday or Monday, watching football without speaking. Even with his friends around, the men will sit in silence and watch the ball, or the puck, or the basketball, move around on the screen. The men's brains are watching the ball move around, and they are (1) in a state of nothingness—thinking of nothing and doing nothing, they are certainly saying very little and they are okay with that—and (2) feeling as though they are solving problems.

It's important to note that the men are explicitly not speaking, they are not emoting, and they are usually not conversing. They are quiet, mesmerized by the screen and solving problems in their minds.

The men are not talking while fixing up an old classic car in the garage, they are not talking if they are starting a rock band in the garage, and they are not talking if they are building a deck. The men are solving problems.

The men are not talking.

"The first rule of fight club is, you don't talk about fight club."

CHUCK PALAHNIUK, *FIGHT CLUB*

In *Fight Club*, the first rule of fight club is that you don't talk about fight club. What could be more manly than not talking about a secret club in a bar basement where men beat each other up until someone says "stop" or goes limp?

Fight Club caught part of the essence of what it means to be a man, and the story, the book, and the movie resonated with men everywhere.

Part of the key to this resonance is that the men do not talk. The fight club is men only, and no one talks about it.

If women were allowed in fight club, fight club would be talked about because women love to talk, emote, and gossip.

Men silently solve problems. Women want to talk about problems and not necessarily solve them, but they want to be heard and understood.

"People used to look out on the playground and say that the boys were playing soccer and the girls were doing nothing. But the girls weren't doing nothing, they were talking about the world to one another. And they became very expert about that in a way the boys did not."

CAROL GILLIGAN, *IN A DIFFERENT VOICE:
PSYCHOLOGICAL THEORY AND WOMEN'S DEVELOPMENT*

This is a masculine and feminine opposite and part of what makes men and women struggle to understand each other. It's also what makes the opposite sex so attractive, alluring, and arousing. The otherness, the polarity, with masculinity being defined as that which is least feminine and femininity being that which is least masculine. It's sexy, it's frustrating, it's attractive, and it works in a functional–dysfunctional way.

Watching sports stimulates the man's need to solve problems. Video games do the same. I read several studies on "how old is the average gamer?" and "how much time does a man spend per week playing video games?" The answers may shock you. The average gamer is around 30 years old and spends anywhere from 6 to 18 hours a week playing video games.

Think about that for a moment. Eighteen hours a week is pretty much one entire day per week of consciousness—assuming you sleep for 8 hours a night, a man has 112 hours of consciousness in a 7-day week with 8 hours a night of sleep. If he works 40 hours a week, that leaves him with 72 hours left in the week. If he plays video games for 18 hours of the remaining 72 hours, that is roughly 25% of his nonworking time. We didn't add in commuting time, eating time, talking to his spouse or girlfriend, etc.

So why are video games so significant and so powerful for men in today's world?

As a 31-year-old semiserious gamer myself, I can say I have experienced the instant gratification that video games provide. So many important things in life take 10,000 hours of focused effort to accomplish a degree of mastery.

Ten thousand hours is a serious investment and a barrier to entry for real achievement in life.

In video games, the games are designed for instant gratification instead; you play the game for a few minutes or a few seconds, you achieve something, and the dopamine hits your brain. Some ingenious games like World of Warcraft, which is arguably the first virtual reality world ever invented for the mass market, was released on November 23, 2004. As of October 2016, World of Warcraft had over 10 million subscribers. That's a 12-year lifespan of the game, with 10 million people still paying! At about $14.99 a month for a subscription that works out to $179.88 as annual cost for a hobby that provides so many hours of entertainment.

But what is the real cost? As a former World of Warcraft player and player of several video games my entire life from age 4 to age 31 at the time of writing, I can say the real cost is the cost on your time.

Let's say you are worth $20 an hour at your job, which is a median salary in my home country, and you play your video games 72 hours a month, that works out to $1,440 in lost opportunity cost per month. Annually, that is $17,280 per year, which is essentially a part-time job.

In my early twenties, I secretly wanted to be a pro gamer, but when the hours required to invest started to reach part-time and full-time employment hours, I quit pursuing video games as a serious hobby and now only play them occasionally.

The real cost is the cost of your time and the unmanly pursuit of taking you away from your real-life purpose and pursuit of your highest and greatest self.

Whenever I have done something great or have gone to the next level in my life, I have uninstalled and deleted all my games. The mind does not need distractions to go forward and achieve greatness in your life.

Women intuitively don't like it when their men play video games, because as intuitive sacred beings, women know deep down inside that video games distract a man from his purpose and his potential. In the eyes of a woman, a man who is not working on reaching his potential and living his purpose, which is generally his work, is unmanly and unattractive. If a man loses his purpose, he will lose his woman; she will simply find another man who is taking his purpose more seriously—this is the law of the jungle and biology.

Games like World of Warcraft are purposely engineered to time the dopamine hits first in small frequent intervals at the beginning of the game until you are "hooked," and then the dopamine and feeling of achievement becomes exponentially spaced out into longer and longer intervals.

When the dopamine hits start to take longer, the "sunk cost fallacy" takes over, and you say to yourself "I can't quit now, I've spent 50 days of my life on this, I have to keep going."

Again, when the time gaming turns into time you could spend on a part-time job or pursing a real passion or starting your dream business or vocation, these large investments of time into frivolous pleasure can ruin a man permanently over time.

Women's brains are wired differently from men's, and they do not respond to football and video games in the same way. Statistically speaking in today's world, women and men play video games in equal amounts, but women play different kinds of games; they typically are "less hardcore" gamers, and I believe they play more for the social aspect and for novelty than to satisfy the inherent brain-need obsession that men have to solve problems and not talk.

Women have an inherent need to talk, be listened to, and be heard. They want to talk to their men and have their men listen to the emoting, but they explicitly do not want their problems solved by suggestions from their man; instead, they just want to be listened to and emotionally understood.

This can be frustrating for men, who want to solve every problem in front of their faces like a puzzle addict, chess master, or crossword puzzle fanatic. To men, they are a hammer, and every problem is a nail that must be whacked down. Women just want to talk about the nail and how they feel about it; men want to whack the nail.

This is a cause of friction.

Here are some worthwhile endeavors that can be traded for a video game addiction. Note: all of these endeavors take serious amounts of time to master, whereas a video game will take nearly 5% of the time to master as a worthwhile endeavor noted below:

A list of worthwhile endeavors and the time commitment:

1) Building a business takes 2, 5, and 10 years. This business may take 10,000 hours to master, and 90% of businesses

fail in the first 5 years; 90% of the surviving businesses fail in the second 5 years. This leaves 1% of businesses surviving after 10 years. Welcome to the jungle; with such horrible odds you can see why a young man would just go for the instant pleasure of a video game and say "fuck it" to a real-world endeavor like building a business.

2) Becoming a master at an art form like music or painting with oil paints takes 10 years and 10,000 hours of practice. Again, the most complex video games take roughly 5% of that time to master. The long learning curve and delayed gratification make most men want to go for an easier route. Recently in Japan, the turntables as an instrument for DJ-ing now outsell the electric guitar. The easier it is to learn, the more people will be attracted to it. The turntables are not really an instrument in the same way a guitar is, but over time everything degrades down to the lowest common denominator and the lowest levels of intelligence. In medieval Europe, the Spanish guitar took over from the lute, which was harder to play. This has been going on throughout history. The easier the instrument, the more people will play them.

3) Becoming an athlete takes 10 years and 10,000 hours to become a master. Plus, becoming an athlete forces you to face reality, face your weaknesses, and play on your strengths. Men who do well in athletics usually do well in business because both endeavors are grounded in reality and require daily rituals and activities for success over time. Athletics brings real physical pain, muscles aching, hearts and lungs burning, and the psychological pain of fighting against your own weakness. Dealing with teams and other men is manly, but it hurts physically and psychologically with winning, losing, and hitting or not hitting your goals. Men today favor the nonphysical over the physical, simply because "it doesn't hurt." One argument is that men are evolving to a higher level of sophistication by doing less physical things, and that argument may be sound in some

ways. But the counterargument is that the lack of physical exertion in the modern man's life invites various diseases and later health problems for men. The body is like anything else, use it or lose it, abuse it and lose it.

4) To reach the highest levels in World of Warcraft only takes only 600 hours (not 10,000), which is 25 days of straight gameplay at 24 hours a day. A man who plays 18 hours a day will get to a nearly endgame level of play in only 33 weeks.

"I've missed over nine thousand shots in my career. I've lost almost three hundred games. Twenty-six times I've been trusted to take the game-winning shot ... and missed. I've failed over and over again in my life. And that is why I succeed."

MICHAEL JORDAN

Some men are afraid to make a big investment of 10 years or 10,000 hours. It's daunting, and it's scary. But the question is, how do you eat an elephant? One bite at a time!

I love the words of Earl Nightingale on pursing big goals: don't worry about the time, the time shall pass anyway. Also, Napoleon Bonaparte said, "Death is nothing, but to live defeated and inglorious is to die daily."

What does it mean to be alive if you do not reach for the things that you really want, regardless of cost or the size of the investment? God gave you big dreams and big goals, because when you were designed, he was measuring your spirit, not your wallet.

We all have 24 hours in a day.

Donald Trump, the billionaire and US president, has 24 hours in a day and so does the bum on the street. The difference is how do we use those 24 hours in a day? For purpose or for distraction?

Thirty-three weeks to master a video game, versus 555.55 weeks to master a real endeavor like sports, music, the arts, or business. Looking at the costs of becoming great in your real passions and real purposes in life shows that it's no wonder that video games are so popular in distracting men from their real purpose and work in life:

1) Games give the illusion to men of solving problems, which is very attractive to the male mind.

2) Games give an instant hit of dopamine on timed intervals to create the illusion of "fun." I can guarantee that our Warrior ancestors didn't think about fun or happiness often. They seldom had fun or happy moments, but in reality, life can be grim, brutal, and hard. Our brains can't compete with strategically timed dopamine hits of addictive games, like addictive drugs our brains get hooked on to which we can't say no.

3) The time costs of a real passion or endeavor will take nearly 10 years of real work, effort, blood, sweat, tears, time, money, and losses to achieve. This is a significant investment, and the reason why so many men never reach greatness in their lives is that they are unwilling to invest enough to get there. If a worthy endeavor such as business, sports, art, music, or anything else takes 555.55 weeks to master, which is 10,000 hours divided by 18 hours a week, this gives us 555.55 weeks to become great at a real passion. A long game like World of Warcraft, however, only takes 33 weeks of less challenging work to reach the end game, which is 5.9% of the investment. This makes rational sense why the men of today choose video games over real work.

A study some years ago with children was conducted and found to be one of the greatest indicators of success in young boys and girls. This test was called the marshmallow test.

Little children, who were 4 years old or so, were placed in a room. These children were given a marshmallow on a plate and told that if they left the marshmallow alone and did not eat it until the researcher left the room and came back some time later, the child was promised two marshmallows as a reward.

The only challenge was, the little boy or girl had to wait alone in the room with temptation itself—one delicious marshmallow.

Some children gobbled up the marshmallow as soon as the researcher left the room. Other children would sing, shut their eyes, look away, lie down, and avoid the marshmallow all together to "double down" and gain on their investment.

The children who were found to be the greatest successes as they were tracked through life were the children who had the self-discipline to avoid eating the marshmallow. On the other hand, the children who gobbled up the marshmallow in seconds were followed through life and found to not reach the same levels of success as the children who were able to defer gratification.

Deferring gratification is a major part of being an effective man.

Never before has a farmer gone to his field, planted his seed, woken up the next day, and looked out the window and said, "I don't see any crops, must be a scam!"

Farmers are some of the toughest men around, and they know that farming takes time.

Farming goes through seasons and cycles.

Farming does not happen overnight, and the discipline that we used to have to till the barren soil has become lost over time as technology and civilization offer us easier and easier gratification to feel instantly happy with our problem-solving abilities.

Again, I will reiterate that video games are an illusion, a distraction from your true purpose, just like football on Sunday or beer and chicken wings on a Tuesday. Women don't like it when men put these activities before their purpose or do these activities too frequently. Women intuitively know by using their sacred feminine energy that a man, a real man, a strong man, must be working on his purpose every day to be masculine and attractive to her, to ensure her survival, survival of the tribe, and survival of her children.

"Show me your friends and I'll show you your future."

PROVERB

Video games do not serve a man's purpose, and in that way, they are unmanly.

You can play them, just as you can drink alcohol or smoke pot to a degree, but if done too much, they can be highly destructive and can wipe decades out of a man's life that will be lost forever.

Remember, you can always get money back, but you can never get your #1 resource in your life back—your time. Women know this intuitively. Listen to the women on this one and stick with your purpose or your passion. Do not be afraid to invest more than others and hit the 10,000 hours of investment head on and full force. Ten years from now you will thank me if you stick with this piece of advice.

I have reached 10,000 hours in several endeavors, and it has made all the difference in my life, my purpose, my passion, and my results.

Stay hungry, stay curious.

Curiosity is the base ingredient for passion, and passion is the path to purpose. Stay curious, my friend.

"Which is worse: Hell or nothing?"

CHUCK PALAHNIUK, *FIGHT CLUB*

CHAPTER 8

BE STRONG BUT FLEXIBLE, BEND INSTEAD OF BREAKING

"Do not let your fire go out, spark by irreplaceable spark in the hopeless swamps of the not-quite, the not-yet, and the not-at-all. Do not let the hero in your soul perish in lonely frustration for the life you deserved and have never been able to reach. The world you desire can be won. It exists ... it is real ... it is possible ... it's yours."

AYN RAND, *ATLAS SHRUGGED*

What does it mean to be a man? Specifically, to turn from a boy who lives with his mother, in the world of women, the world of the feminine of fun, of games, of play, and then transition into the masculine world with the men, responsibility, and work?

The Spartans—some of the strongest, most revered male warriors throughout history, popularized in hit movies like *300*—were renowned as the best warriors throughout time even by modern-day special forces because of their unbelievable masculine training programs.

At the young age of 7, a boy was taken from his mother and forced into the *agoge*, a state-sponsored training regimen designed to mold boys into skilled warriors and moral citizens.

The men would beat him and leave him naked with nothing but a crimson cloak to cover his naked flesh. They would teach the boy about living behind enemy lines. He would have to sleep on the ground—a simulation for living behind enemy lines—survive in the wilderness, and steal food from his own people to survive. If he was caught stealing, the shopkeeper or his victim was encouraged to beat him mercilessly. Such was the brutal warrior culture of the Spartans. The Spartans were strong men, and we still celebrate them today.

We romanticize this male strength in movies like *300* that depict the famous battle of Thermopylae, where 300 Spartans, King Leonidas's personal bodyguards, fought to their deaths in a narrow pass of terrain and supposedly killed an estimated 100,000 to 150,000 Persians. Ancient sources claim there were up to one million Persians, but what we know for sure is that there were many more Persians than Spartans. All 300 Spartans were slain in battle, which immortalized them in history for having a "death before dishonor" ethos. The Persian emperor Xerxes was stalled enough at the battle of Thermopylae to delay his Greek invasion. As a result, Sparta was able to mobilize a real army to fight off the Persians to defend their homeland.

The Greeks had strong man stories of real strength. Marathons today are named after the Battle of Marathon, where one man, Pheidippides, ran to Athens with the news of the great victory his people had over the Persians at Marathon.

The distance he ran was about 26 miles, and he died after the run.

This is depicted in the 2014 film entitled *300: Rise of an Empire*.

These amazing stories and amazing strength show the duty and importance of a man's brutal and violent work in history and reinforce the fact that men have historically lived short, brutal lives as expendable genetic fodder for the wars of history while women have lived long, brutal lives as slaves, captured women, and sexual conquests if their men were killed in battle. We humans have a long history of brutal violence, mutilation, and enslavement of others. In the last century, we have toned such violence down in the Western world, but the violence and slavery still exist around the world today.

Hard times create strong men, and in the violent pages of history are recorded stories that were hard for both men and women. The Spartan queen in the movie *300* mentions what it takes to be a "real man" several times in the movie. She is tough as nails, killing the men who betray her husband with nothing but a short dagger and her bare hands.

The Spartan women were much tougher than the snowflake men of today. But life was so much harder in the warrior culture of Sparta.

I will not romanticize the Spartan culture. They were excellent warriors but also rigid in their thinking, to the point of Sparta's demise. They would fight to the death and never retreat. This led to a small city state of Sparta that could not really expand territory or influence but rather only hold ground and contract over time.

Sparta was hard to invade, but it could not become the mighty Roman Empire of the future because of the Spartans' rigid thinking. Sometimes strength comes from the ability to bend without breaking, but being able to flex is much stronger than being brittle and snapping under pressure.

"It is not the strongest of the species that survives, nor the most intelligent; it is the one most adaptable to change."

ATTRIBUTED TO VARIOUS SOURCES; DERIVED FROM
CHARLES DARWIN'S *ON THE ORIGIN OF SPECIES*

The hardness of the rigid warrior philosophy also led to the demise of Sparta because their "never surrender" and "fight to the death mentality" was too one-dimensional, and they started losing wars. The great warriors of Sparta eventually became irrelevant to modern warfare and history.

Is Sparta a military power today? No.

"A pint of sweat will save a gallon of blood."

GENERAL GEORGE S. PATTON

"Sweat saves blood, blood saves lives, but brains saves both."

ERWIN ROMMEL

What is a better mentality than rigidly fighting to the death is to be more like the legendary Erwin Rommel, the Desert Fox, a professional German infantryman in WWI and later a field marshal in WWII who was admired by the Allies and the Axis soldiers alike.

He was one of the most brilliant military minds in history, and both his allies and enemies knew it during his time.

Rommel was a German but not a Nazi. He was also extremely flexible in his battle plans and tactics. Hitler would want his supermen, the Waffen-SS, and his other military divisions to relentlessly fight to the death like the suicidal Japanese soldiers. Rommel would ignore those orders in favor of saving the army so they could fight again another day. A master of surprise attacks and prompt retreats, Rommel pierced through his enemies' lines by surprise, causing confusion, and then promptly retreated, drawing his enemies into kill zones of flak 88mm antiaircraft cannons that were meant to shoot down planes, but were just as good at piercing the armor of enemy tanks.

Rommel was resourceful and used whatever weapons he could find to use in unconventional ways that the enemy was never expecting. The flak 88 cannons were designed to shoot fighter planes out of the sky and thus had tinted lenses, perfect for aiming into the sun or at the hot reflective sand in the desert, and shells that pierced enemy tanks perfectly.

If an 88mm shell missed a tank, it would skip and bounce across the desert sand and mutilate forces that lay in the shell's wake. These weapons were so effective after Rommel prototyped them in the North African theatre that flak 88 cannons became standard issue on the legendary German Panzer VI, the Tiger Tank, the most feared tank of the war by the Allies.

Not a single Tiger Tank had its 10cm of front armor pierced from the front in the entire war. The Germans lost most Tiger tanks to running out of fuel and abandoned more tiger tanks than they lost in battle. The Tiger Tank had a horrible fuel economy, approximately 2.75 gallons per mile.

Rommel would push into enemy lines with surprise and deception. He even would make fake tanks of wood when Hitler would fail to send him enough material to fight the war. At one point in North Africa, Rommel had almost no tanks, and a collection of Volkswagen cars instead.

To intimidate his enemies, Rommel fashioned fake tank chassis out of wood and paraded his fake tanks in the distance of British camps and strongholds.

The British would see an overwhelming number of tanks in the distance kicking up huge clouds of sand and dust, which would terrify them into surrendering without a shot.

In the *Art of War*, the perfect warrior wins the fight without violence. Rommel embodies the skill of the perfect warrior.

In battle and in life, it's much better to be resourceful, and flexible in your thinking than to be rigid and one dimensional.

Be like Rommel instead of the Spartans. Both are manly, both do their jobs, but to be strong is also to have the ability to bend and change as the dynamics change.

Both Hitler's forces and the Spartans were losers in history for being too rigid in their thinking and fighting to the death. Both groups of warriors were incredibly strong and were the best of their time. Both succumbed to rigid thinking with not enough resourcefulness and flexibility.

If Rommel were in charge of German forces in WWII instead of Adolf Hitler, who believed his own insane ideas and was borderline delusional, America and the rest of the world would be speaking German instead of English today.

CHAPTER 9
WHAT DOES IT MEAN TO BE A MAN? JACK AND THE BEANSTALK
The Fable of Becoming a Man

There is a famous story about the transformation from the boy world to the man world, and that famous story is called "Jack and the Beanstalk."

You may know the story, but let me refresh your memory.

The story opens with a young man, Jack, who is poor and lives with his mother in their small country house. Jack doesn't have a father; it's just him and his mother. One day his mother sends Jack to market to trade in his mother's old cow, which no longer provides milk, for something better that they can use.

Jack comes home from the market and shows his mother with great joy what he traded for her last old cow—a bag of magic beans! Jack's mother is furious that Jack would make such a stupid trade, and she hits him over the head and throws the magic beans out the window and sends Jack to bed with no supper.

The next morning Jack looks out the window and sees a huge beanstalk that stretches far into the clouds. Jack starts to climb the beanstalk and ends up in a castle in the clouds.

He enters the castle that belongs to a giant. The giant bellows the famous words:

> *Fee-fi-fo-fum*
> *I smell the blood of an Englishman.*
> *Be he alive or be he dead*
> *I'll grind his bones to make my bread.*

The giant chases Jack around the castle, but Jack is able to steal three key objects from the giant: a singing harp, a golden goose, and a princess held prisoner in the giant's castle.

Jack takes the spoils of his raid, and escaping the giant, he begins to climb down the beanstalk and back to his mother's house.

The giant chases after Jack by climbing down the beanstalk after him.

When Jack gets back to his mother's house safely, he grabs an axe and chops the beanstalk down. The beanstalk tumbles over, and the giant falls to his death.

Jack, the owner of his problems, now becomes "Jack the Giant-Slayer."

Jack went up the beanstalk as a boy living with his mother, without a father, uneducated and irresponsible for trading his mother's only asset for a bag of "magic beans," a very boyish behavior indeed.

While up on the beanstalk, Jack has to face his fear and slay the giant, which represents the struggle of a boy becoming a man.

As he leaves the castle, Jack gains three pillars that serve as a base for Jack becoming a man:

The 3 Pillars of Becoming a Man

1) **The singing harp:** This represents Jack's vocation and calling in life—his work and the thing he must do to live his purpose.
2) **The golden goose:** The goose represents a way for a man to make money and support his women and his family.
3) **The rescued princess:** This represents Jack's bride—his woman and perhaps the future mother of his children.

A man without those three things is hardly a man. He might still be living like a boy.

Every man needs the three things above in his life: a battle to fight, an adventure to go on, and a beauty to win.

Jack had all three, which is why Jack's tale is a great story of what a boy needs to become a man.

Face the giant, slay your problems within, and earn the right to call yourself a man.

The 4 Parts of Being an Effective and Strong Man

"May I never be complete. May I never be content. May I never be perfect."

CHUCK PALAHNIUK, *FIGHT CLUB*

"Stop Hoping for a Completion of Anything in Life

Most men make the error of thinking that one day it will be done. They think, 'If I can work enough, then one day I could rest.' Or, 'One day my woman will understand something and then she will stop complaining.' Or, 'I'm only doing this now so that one day I can do what I really want with my life.' The masculine error is to think that eventually things will be different in some fundamental way. They won't. It never ends. As long as life continues, the creative challenge is to tussle, play, and make love with the present moment while giving your unique gift."

DEIDA, *THE WAY OF THE SUPERIOR MAN*

It is not enough to just make the transition of boy to man through your work, your purpose, and your ownership of the good, bad, and ugly of your life. In addition, a man must take care of the four parts of his being: mind, body, spirit, and emotions.

Those four parts make up a human being, and so many people just focus on the physical realm of life through their physical body, material goods, and anything tangible they can see. But the truth is, the physical realm is a "printout" or manifestation of the three invisible realms: mind, spirit, and emotions. Much like a printer prints out the words that exist inside of a text file or inside of a computer, your physical realm is a printout of your thoughts, emotions, and spirit.

The invisible manifests into the visible.

A Strong Man Must Have a Strong Mind—The mind is the central command center of your being, the consciousness that you are on this earth. Every decision you make in your body, mind, soul, and emotions at some point passes through the mind. If you lose your mind, you lose everything. When you see broken homeless people on the street, you typically see someone who has lost his mind. A strong man's mind is constantly looking for ways to improve his life and his environment by becoming better at everything incrementally. Over many millennia, men have evolved from living in caves and bashing each other over the heads with clubs to the great scholars and philosophers of our current age and beyond. A man with a sound mind will own a library of books in his home versus TVs in every room.

It has been said that rich people have big libraries, while poor people have big TVs. To become rich, you must become rich in the mind first, before you come rich in the pocket. Man's mind is the only survival tool in the wild that keeps him alive and allows him to prosper; he has no claws, jaws, large muscles, teeth, or any other survival mechanisms of the wild beasts except for his mind.

And blessed be he with such a powerful tool like a sound mind. The neocortex, the thinking brain of man, is far more advanced than any other animal brain on the planet and a great argument for intelligent design.

Why are there no other evolved animals with neocortexes or "thinking brains"? They say God made man in his image. The neocortex, the thinking mind, the connection to the future and the spiritual realm of the unseen, in my opinion, is evidence that we did not randomly evolve out of primordial ooze, and, in fact, there was intelligent design behind man and his ability to think above all other animals in the kingdom. But I digress into three types of capital that man must command with his mind.

To separate men from the cavemen of ages old who spent most of their days digging in the mud and foraging for food are three types of capital.

Capital is the difference between the rich, poor, and middle class. Capital is wielded with man's mind and always comes from man's mind.

Napoleon Hill's famous manual on becoming rich, *Think and Grow Rich,* was written in the 1930s and had the recipe for becoming rich as per his interviews with the 500 richest men in the world at the time.

Three types of capital that man must wield with his mind:

1) Real capital—cash, credit, and debt
2) Social capital—his network, tribe, brand, and social connections
3) Intellectual capital—his inventions, intellectual property, and specialized knowledge that makes the base of his wealth

A man's mind will give him his social class in society; however, it is not always the smartest man with the highest IQ who wins in society. Instead, it is the man who uses what he has in the best way who wins and commands the capital he needs to see his dreams and plans come true.

A woman may gain social class through her body, her genes, her DNA, and her ability to reproduce with a powerful man and provide children to him and pass on great genes. But a man's social class is always derived from his capital: real capital, social capital, and intellectual capital.

A man's capital is what gives him a dominant or submissive position in the tribe and ensures his survival as a man and the survival of his woman and his offspring. A man derives his class from the quality and amount of his three types of capital. As a man, you always want to be moving up to a better class or a better caste. A man's social position is his power; his capital is power, ability to do things.

Power is manly.

A Strong Man Must Have a Strong Body—Throughout history we have had several ages, including the hunter/gatherer age, when men would hunt and women would gather. We were roaming bands of nomads living off the land. Physical strength in the hunter/gatherer age was essential for killing animals, fighting off other tribes and internal tribal enemies, and carrying back the dead carcasses of your prey to your tribe and family. In the agrarian age, which was an age of farming, big strong muscles were needed to plow the soil and plant the harvest. You had to be physically big and strong to survive on the farm. This applied to both men and women because farming was hard work every day, and life was generally hard.

We then entered an age of industrialization when the tribes turned from small tribes into big national super tribes, and men became specialists working in offices and factories. The muscles meant less than in the agrarian age, and today we are in the information age when muscles are irrelevant to our immediate survival.

Still, in the modern world, man must be physically strong enough to do his work and be the leader of other men. Physical presence is important.

The rapper known as 50 Cent grew up in the hostile environment of lower-class America. He had to get big and strong to have an intimidating presence to ensure his survival while dealing drugs.

It never hurts to have a strong presence. It has been said that when people are choosing to be led or buy from a man, subconsciously they are thinking, "Would I step into the trenches of a war with this man? Would he help me survive or not?" If a man has a strong presence of a leader, which includes physical strength and height, then these qualities give him power in the tribe to command, influence, and lead. With a commanding presence, he can become the leader of other men, which is always important throughout the ages.

Physical strength and health are also important today to live long enough to raise and protect your family. Life spans at the time of writing for men are currently in the 82–87 year range and in the next few decades will likely surpass the 100-year mark. In the early 1900s, men only lived to be about 45 and then died. A man must be strong enough to carry out his responsibilities to his family, his woman, and his tribe. In today's world, he must live long enough to provide the economic protection and security for his family after he dies through insurance policies, investments, real estate, or just cash. Such is the legacy of being a man.

A Strong Man Needs a Strong Spirit—A man must be spiritually mature to do what is right, observe the physical and metaphysical laws of the universe, and have a relationship with God and the divine.

> *"You are a little soul carrying about a*
> *corpse, as Epictetus used to say."*
>
> MARCUS AURELIUS, *MEDITATIONS*

A true man makes a study of the spiritual realm to see the unseen and practice faith, usually through practiced religion. There is a general belief in today's modern world that religion is a dirty word.

I think this is a wrong idea because what organized religion brought to the table in the past was a system in which man could study the spiritual realm and learn in an organized way. People today claim to be atheists, agnostics, or just spiritual, as they are taught in the universities and school systems to think.

There has been a societal attack on religion in the last 70 years, and I think that we as a people are spiritually losing today because of the loss of religion.

Atheism is the most expensive religion because it denies the facts and laws of the spiritual universe. Physicists today claim that there are 11 dimensions of reality, but we can only see and sense 4 dimensions with our primitive senses—forward/backward, side to side, up and down, and the time continuum.

So what is in the other 7 dimensions?

The other 7 dimensions contain things we cannot see with our senses. Unseen invisible forces are just as powerful as seen forces. The spiritual realm is the realm of unseen forces. Inside a seed is a mighty oak tree. Though the tree is unseen, faith knows that the tree can come forth with watering and care. We cannot sense the tree today, but the information for the tree is contained in the seed, inside the spiritual realm, the realm of the unseen. To deny the spiritual realm is a major mistake that men make and that limits their true creative potential in this life.

A strong man will obey physics and the laws of the spiritual realm. If man lives by these laws, they will be able to serve man in the realm of the "unseen" and bring things that are bigger than the man into his life.

This is extremely important and is discussed in major books such as Napoleon Hill's *Think and Grow Rich,* which is really about command of the spiritual realm—infinite intelligence (a secular word for God)—to manifest as real riches.

The spiritual realm is a missing ingredient in today's world for a man to be become greater than he is.

Study the spiritual realm, master it, and be able to manifest reality and bend reality to your will.

Such is the power of having a neocortex and being the only animal on earth able to understand and connect to the spiritual realm: truly a gift from our creators and the intelligent design behind humanity, as no other animal on this planet has this gift.

To deny yourself of the spiritual realm is the same as denying the existence of your body, mind, or emotions. You cannot see your mind or emotions, but you know they exist. The same is true for the spirit and the spiritual realm.

A Strong Man Is Emotionally Strong—Emotions are another perilous topic for men in the modern society and expectations of what a man is.

When I was young, around 17, I only acknowledged my mind and body as my father, mother, and primitive school system taught me. They left out the spiritual realm and the emotional realm, and I failed to know the existence of those two unseen realms until much later in life.

A man's emotions are vitally important, as human beings typically make all decisions on emotion, but justify their decisions by logic. A man's emotions serve like a software program between his mind and his spirit, and emotions can be both tremendously creative and tremendously destructive if not handled correctly.

Most men are taught nothing about their emotions—how to feel, how to love, how to be angry, how to let the dark emotions be felt and released.

This is sad and has horrible side effects on a man's mental and physical health over time.

I can speak from experience. I have repressed all sorts of emotions from my teenage years and am likely still dealing with the side effects of those repressions today at 31. Getting professional help on your emotional issues is huge for your mental, physical, spiritual, and emotional health.

A strong man's mind, as is suggested by stoic philosophy, must be ruled by reason and not emotions, able to keep his emotions in check but still feel. A stoic can feel emotions and can enjoy emotions and pleasure, but he is not ruled by emotions.

Stoic philosophy is a strong man philosophy that is nearly always in place when a nation is born, specifically born out of war like Rome or America. A nation is born a stoic and dies an Epicurean. Where a stoic focuses on reason, an epicurean focuses on pleasure alone.

We are living in an epicurean time in the modern world where emotions and pleasure are getting out of control. Reason has been lost on several important societal topics: money, sex, religion, and politics.

Living in modern civilization is a hostile place for man, his mind, body, soul, and emotions. Several authors, writers, and thinkers throughout history have claimed that if a man stayed in city life long enough he would go insane.

I think this is true and is based on reality.

One way to fix the problems of civilized life is to unplug from it and go without food and live on only water, to fast alone in nature.

To fast is to not eat and to only drink water.

Nearly all religions of the world practice some form of fasting to rebalance the mind, body, soul, and emotions.

Nearly all ancient medicine used some form of water fasting to heal sick people. Hippocrates, the ancient Greek medicine man, of whom all modern doctors take the Hippocratic oath "do no harm," used to make his patients fast. In the words of Hippocrates, "to feed a sick man was to feed his illness."

That is an unspoken part of the Hippocratic oath today. I practice fasting once a year for a long period of time. Last year I spent 30 days in the jungle in Costa Rica fasting on water alone. I lost 68 pounds and calibrated my mind, body, soul, and emotions. I came home to civilization afterwards and began fixing the problems with my business and my life, as I was able to gain perspective on things I could not see.

This last year I only spent 18 days fasting in the jungle, but I have had major spiritual revelations from that time. In fact, in less than 30 days after returning to civilization, I have written two full books, and I will produce three published full-length books this year.

The power of fasting to rebalance a man is usually combined with prayer and was used by powerful men such as Aristotle, Socrates, Jesus, Mohammad, Ghandi, Moses, Marcus Aurelius, and many others. These men would fast for up to 40 days on just water, and this was a major source of their spiritual power, clarity, and reasoning.

Fasting also has major regenerative health benefits and can cure most diseases, especially chronic ones, and can even destroy tumors. I am not a medical doctor, and medical doctors do not endorse fasting because there is no money to be made—fasting is free to any man. That is why modern medicine does not promote fasting: drugs, surgery, and chemotherapy are major cash cows for the multitrillion-dollar medical industry. Fasting has $0 of profit in it, and thus it's a secret in today's medical world. Do not take my words on the benefits of fasting; do your own research!

WARNING: If you want to try fasting, please do it with a professional and with medical supervision. You can hurt yourself if you do it wrong and even die if done improperly, so please fast with professional help, especially on fasts longer than 2 to 3 days.

CHAPTER 10
GREAT EXPECTATIONS
Why It Is Your Duty to Become
a Rich and Powerful Man

*"He is richest who is content with the
least, for content is the wealth of nature."*

SOCRATES

I had the pleasure of going out to dinner with a good friend of mine one night in Ottawa, Canada. My friend was a fantastic public speaker and ran a successful coaching and corporate training practice. My friend is one of the best public speakers I have ever seen, a very manly quality indeed.

In the ancient world, all men were judged on their masculinity by their ability to speak to a group of other men and their oration ability. Today we are no different. Men who speak to groups of other people are some of the highest paid people in the world.

My friend was struggling with the conflict that many men feel between putting more time in at work and spending more time with his kids and family. He had reached a degree of success and a high income. I didn't ask him what his income was, because it didn't really matter. He felt as though he had to be around for his kids.

He loved his kids and wanted to be a good father. His assumption was that he had to be around the house all day to "be there" for his kids.

On the other hand, he told me that if he "pushed it" this year, he could make a million dollars. But he was struggling with the idea of sacrifice between a million dollars in the bank at the end of the year and his time away from his children—a noble dilemma.

I listened to his dilemma and then looked at him straight in the eye over a fancy upscale dinner and said, "You have to make the million dollars. You must."

To me the answer was clear: let me explain my logic.

I am not a father at the time of writing, but I do know the role that a father plays in a household. I got to learn firsthand about what a father is *not* from my own parents and my own parents' divorce.

My own father failed to provide money and income for our family in the way that my mother wanted. This forced my mother into the masculine role of being the breadwinner in the home; it reversed the feminine and masculine energy in the relationship, depolarized the sexual attraction, and made my mother lose respect for my father as a man.

I got to watch my father struggle with his "business"—and I use that term loosely because he earned the same amount of money from his business for 16 years straight. His company had debt that my mother had to support and cosign for. This scared her and her middle-class conditioning—the middle class hates debt.

She was making $80,000 a year when she told him she wanted a divorce. He was lucky if he was bringing home $30,000. The same amount of money he had made since 1985 when he had a corporate job before I was born, except this was 2005. Thirty thousand dollars over a 20-year time span was worth less than in 1985.

This displacement of power, especially economic power, and the reversal of the masculine and feminine polarity pissed my mother off. It violated her as a woman and violated my father as a man; he couldn't play his role.

> "Let me tell you something. There is no nobility in poverty. I have been a rich man and I have been a poor man. And I choose rich every fucking time. Because at least as a rich man, when I have to face my problems, I show up in the back of a limo, wearing a $2,000 suit and a $40,000 gold fucking watch! And if anyone here thinks I'm superficial or materialistic, go get a job at fucking McDonald's, 'cause that's where you fucking belong! But before you depart this room full of winners, I want you to take a good look at the person next to you. Go on. Because sometime in the not-so-distant future, you're gonna be pulling up at a red light, in your beat-up old fucking Pinto, and that person's gonna be pulling up right alongside you in their brand new Porsche. With their beautiful wife by their side, who's got big voluptuous tits. And who're you gonna be sitting next to? Some disgusting wildebeest with three days of razor-stubble, in a sleeveless muumuu, crammed in next to you in a carload full of groceries from the fucking Price Club. That's who you're gonna be sitting next to! So you listen to me and you listen well. Are you behind on your credit card bills? Good, pick up the phone and start dialing! Is your landlord ready to evict you? Good! Pick up the phone and start dialing! Does your girlfriend think you're fucking worthless loser? Good! Pick up the phone and start dialing! I want you to deal with your problems by becoming rich!"

Jordan Belfort played by Leonardo DiCaprio in *The Wolf of Wall Street*

Back to my friend and his million-dollar dilemma. "So," I said to him, "if you have the opportunity make a million dollars this year, *you must do it.* You might not always have the opportunity in your life to make that kind of money! If your business is relevant right now and you have the chance, then take it! Most men don't get that kind of opportunity ever in their lives. Make as much money as you can in the fastest way possible. Sacrifice a few years of your life to live in ways people won't, to live the rest of your life in ways that people can't. Your kids, your little girls will look back on their father and thank you later in life for your sacrifices and your duty that you carried out so they can live comfortably. It doesn't have to be forever, but if you have the opportunity, you must seize it!"

"The reason a lot of people do not recognize opportunity is because it usually goes around wearing overalls looking like hard work."

THOMAS A. EDISON

The fact of reality is, making $1,000,000 a year in speaking, coaching, and consulting is still not easy or guaranteed. I know because I have built my own company to that point and beyond. It's a struggle, it's difficult, it's scary, it challenges you, and leaves you on the edge of survival. It's something most people don't have the balls to do because running a business is like riding a lion:

"Being an entrepreneur is like watching a man ride a lion.

People look at him and think, *This guy's really got it together! He's brave!*" says CEO Toby Thomas. "And the man riding the lion is thinking, How the hell did I get on a lion, and how do I keep from getting eaten?" The truth of the matter is that my friend may or may not actually be able to make $1,000,000 in a year. It's a lot harder than it looks, and it takes tremendous effort. My work ethic to reach income levels like that and beyond has taken me working "two days" for every working day for 5 days a week for 10 years to achieve that level of income. I have always had at least two to four jobs, even when I was broke. I always had side hustles or other endeavors or businesses to earn money. I learned the immigrant hustle from my immigrant father.

However, I will take my friend's statement at face value. Let's assume he can make his $1,000,000 in a year. If he can do it, he must try. He must ride the lion and be the man who can seize everything that he and his family might want. Even if he only gets half, he's still a major success, even at a quarter of a million dollars, he's a top 1% income earner in Canada, even at half of a quarter ($125,000) he's above the top 1% income for his age.

Shoot for the moon and you might end up among the stars.

I believe success is your duty. Economic success is your duty. I also believe that a man should strive to become as rich and powerful as possible so that he can protect himself, his family, his wife, his children, and his tribe.

As $100,000,000-man Grant Cardone says: success is my duty and my responsibility. Cardone has disclosed on several occasions that his new goal is to be a billionaire, essentially 10 timing what he claims to be his current net worth of around $100,000,000. The person who suggested that he become a billionaire was his wife. Now, what are you going to do with a billion dollars? The answer is probably *nothing*, but making a million or a billion is not about the money, it's about the achievement, it's about hitting your potential, finding meaning and purpose in your work and working as hard as you can to reach your goals and your potential. Your women, your children, your tribe, will appreciate your success, and you will be able to give your family the things that only a rich and powerful man can afford.

"Don't be a little bitch."

GRANT CARDONE

I find it interesting that Cardone's wife, actress Elena Lyons—now Elena Cardone—was the one who saw her husband's potential and said to him, "Why aren't you a billionaire yet?"

In Napoleon Hill's *Think and Grow Rich,* Hill talks about the importance of the right woman for a man, and specifically a man's wife when well matched and married can be the source of his power and his genius. Women have an amazing intuition about men, and they can see potential and intuit all sorts of distinctions that men cannot see.

Such is the divine feminine power of being a woman; men lack such intuition or life-giving sexual power.

If Cardone were a bachelor, or without such a great woman, maybe he would be lazing around on the golf course, slacking off and squandering hitting his potential. Cardone admits that he reached a point of comfort before meeting his wife, and he was slowing down and playing too much golf.

Comfort is a killer to success and your ultimate potential.

A woman always wants to see her man hit his potential and become the best version of himself. The pursuit of greatness in a man's work is manly, and women love to see their man push for greatness—it's a turn-on for them. All women love ambition in a man, especially the man they choose.

Cardone also has two young little girls, Sabrina and Scarlet Cardone. These little girls are young, under 10, and in Grant's books he mentions that he only spends one to two hours a day of quality time with his kids, and that's all they want. I think Cardone is right in this statement.

Do your kids *actually* want to see their father all the time? Do they want their dad for more than an hour a day? Probably not. Kids have their own things to do; they don't want to hang out with Dad for more than an hour to two of quality time per day. This makes great sense. When I was a kid I wanted my father's support, but I wasn't attached to him every hour of every day. In fact, I wanted him to go away and leave me to whatever I was doing most of the time.

There is an effeminate, unmanly idea that you must be home all day all the time to dote on your kids and essentially be a stay-at-home husband. This is backwards; my father did it, and it pissed my mother off because he wasn't filling his purpose and reaching his potential. When my father cried and begged my mother on his knees like a dog for a second chance in the family, my mother laughed and ejected him from her life. She was done with him. He wasn't filling his role as a man, and instead of him, she chose nothing. She chose to be single and have a dog instead. Tony Robbins says that if you want love and connection but can't communicate well enough for humans, get a dog instead.

Women are ruthless with a man who doesn't hit his potential. They appear to be the softer and nicer of the sexes, but make no mistake, women are ruthless with a man who is not producing. Female power and sexual power are like money. The second there is weakness or neediness in a man, the money is gone, the power is gone, and so are the women. This is a cruel fact of life, and some women may disagree with my statement here.

"Only women, children and dogs are loved unconditionally. A man is only loved under the condition that he provides something."

CHRIS ROCK, *COMEDIAN.*

But ask yourself: all things being equal, would your woman prefer you to be rich or poor?

All things being equal, I'm sure she would pick rich every time and you hitting your potential every time!

Women have great expectations for their men and want a man to fill his purpose and become the best version of himself.

They are generally not attracted to a stay-at-home dad; nobody really wants a stay-at-home dad—men or women alike. Stay-at-home dads are avoiding their potential and can appear to be untrustworthy because they have forsaken their purpose and their work and have slipped into feminine energy and the feminine purpose of family and the home. This is confusing to both men and women. No offense to you if you are a stay-at-home dad, but it is a strange gender reversal that is not really respected by men or women, and I will just say that it will lead to problems down the road at some point when the biology of your woman catches up to her and says, "What the fuck?! Why is he just hanging out at home all day? This is not a turn-on."

Men throughout history have been absent from the home on long work adventures. If you were a Roman soldier, you would campaign in war for 5 or 10 years at a time, and when you came home from war your kids would be grown up. The Roman soldiers weren't at home being stay-at-home dads. They were out defending the empire, and the women took care of the house alone for years.

Great Expectations by Charles Dickens illustrates a young man's desire in the 1800s to be rich and powerful. In *Great Expectations*, Pip is the poor stepson of a blacksmith named Joe. His sister, Mrs. Joe, is cruel to both Pip and Joe. Pip is the protagonist in the classic Dickens novel (and the novel is damn long because Dickens was paid per word by his publisher). Pip is set up to meet and fall in love with the beautiful Estella by a rich and evil old woman named Miss Havisham. Miss Havisham was not born evil or twisted, but rather she was destined to marry a man and on her wedding day, her groom didn't show up to the wedding, and she was left alone in her wedding dress, with her wedding cake and a broken heart. She was so heartbroken that she stopped all the clocks in her house at the moment she was supposed to get married. Because her heart was broken, she made it her mission to destroy the hearts of men. Enter Estella, her gorgeous young stepdaughter. Estella is an angelic young girl, selected by Miss Havisham to be her weapon against the hearts of men as she raises the beautiful young upper-class Estella to become a maneater.

maneater as per Urban Dictionary:

> An irresistible woman who chews and spits out men after using them for some sort of gain—be it *sexual*, financial, or psychological.

When Pip first lays eyes on Estella in Miss Havisham's garden, he falls madly in love with her, but he realizes the only way he will ever become a man in her league is to become a rich and powerful gentleman. He realizes that he cannot have the upper-class Estella when he is just the lower-class son of a blacksmith. Pip makes it his mission to become a gentleman to win the girl.

The opening of the book has Pip wandering the local graveyard visiting his parents' graves, and he stumbles upon an escaped convict hiding amongst the tombstones. The convict threatens Pip and demands "wittles," which are little morsels of food, and a file to break his chains. Pip as a young boy is terrified and goes to Joe's blacksmith shop to find a file and food for the convict.

When Pip returns to the graveyard, he is ambushed by a second convict before he finds the original convict. Pip hands the food over to the beast of a man and mentions the second convict. This disturbs the first convict, but he devours the food mercilessly, cuts his chains, and escapes.

Four years into his apprenticeship, a mysterious benefactor allows Pip to escape his vocation as a blacksmith and move to London to realize his dream of becoming a gentleman. As a young man, Pip believes his benefactor is Miss Havisham, Estella's adopted mother, and he believes that she is benefiting him to make him desirable for her daughter. After moving to London, Pip's benefactor remains unnamed, and Pip is unwise to spend his gifted money before he comes of age at 21. His legal guardian, a lawyer named Mr. Jaggers, points out the difficulties that Pip is creating for himself, but leaves Pip to navigate his own life.

At age 23 Pip's benefactor appears in person, and it is the convict he met in the graveyard as a boy. He learns the convict's name is Abel Magwitch, and this shatters Pip's hope that he is meant for Estella, and Pip feels disgust, as he knows nothing about what type of criminal this man is. Despite his feelings of disgust and disappointment, Pip's sense of duty that compels him to help Magwitch is a sign of his inner goodness, just as he had at the age of 7 in the graveyard. After Magwitch dies, the Crown confiscates his fortune, and Pip at 23 learns that having material possessions such as good clothes, well-spoken English, and a generous allowance do not make him a gentleman.

Pip falls ill for several weeks, and his old mentor Joe the blacksmith comes to care for him until he is strong enough to walk. After Joe leaves, Pip goes home to find Biddy, the good and virtuous girl he should have married, is now married to Joe instead. Without any money or any skills or profession, Pip is struggling to find his place in the world. Herbert Pocket, Pip's friend, suggests that Pip get a job at the firm where he works in an office in Cairo. Pip gets a job as a clerk, Herbert marries his fiancée Clara, and Pip lives with them as the third wheel. There is irony in this reversal because Pip used his financial gift at 21 of 500 pounds to get Herbert a job with the new firm. Now that Pip has lost his funds, he asked Miss Havisham to pay the money owed, and she does. Joe, in a very manly way, ends up paying for the rest of Pip's debt and money that he is unable to pay.

Eleven years later, Pip comes home to England to find Joe, Biddy, and their new children. He walks the land and finds Estella, and both of them are changed from their experiences in life. After they reconcile, they hold hands and Pip sees nothing that can part them again.

True power, true riches—the things that Pip desires to win Estella—are fake. Pip is a fake, and he realizes that fine words and fine clothes do not make him a gentleman.

"True power is earned, not inherited."

GENE SIMMONS

Ironically, Joe the blacksmith is the real man in the story of *Great Expectations*. He is neither rich nor powerful in a big way, but he is rich and powerful relative to his potential in spirit, character, integrity, hard work, real cash in the bank, taking care of his women, his family, and his children. He proves that rich and powerful starts with a man's character, not his bank account.

Joe is the master of his domain, the king of his domain. That is what a man must be. He may not be the most rich or powerful in the world, but he has control and power over his domain. He is the king of his own house, no matter how large or small.

Pip was living a lie. His wealth was a lie, his status was a lie, and the man who was his benefactor was a convict financing him on stolen money. Contrary to popular belief, the clothes can never make the man. The man, the power, and the wealth are only a derivative from the virtues within a man's spirit.

Pip's spirit is rotten and thus, he gets a rotten result. Joe's spirit is strong and virtuous, and he ends up with the young virtuous girl that Pip should have married, a happy family, and money to bail Pip out of his debts. Strength that is earned from real struggle, real hustling, real grinding, and real value is lasting and infinite as long as your character is good. A man who has no substance, or a man who utters words that are baseless in reality is a liar, and to be a liar is to be unmanly.

Women can lie. Feminine energy is chaotic like a stormy ocean, and a man may not always get truth from his feminine woman. For example, a woman who says "I'm fine" is never "fine." Fine in the female language means explicitly "not fine." The words do not match the actions, emotions, and feelings, and this is okay in the world of feminine energy.

Welcome to feminine energy; feminine energy can lie. But for a man to lie is unmanly. Masculine energy, unlike feminine energy, is focused in a linear direction; it's direct, and a man who lies to his tribe threatens the survival of the group. A woman's lies, especially lies made to other women, do not traditionally threaten the survival of the group. Her lies are often frivolous and fun. This is feminine and acceptable to the tribe because these lies are nonthreatening and usually trivial. The difference between masculine and feminine energy is what allows women to lie acceptably, but men cannot lie without violating their masculine energy.

Pip was a liar. His wealth was a lie, his status was a lie, and he was not powerful or manly or the master of his domain.

"People think that a liar gains a victory over his victim. What I've learned is that a lie is an act of self-abdication, because one surrenders one's reality to the person to whom one lies, making that person one's master, condemning oneself from then on to faking the sort of reality that person's view requires to be faked...The man who lies to the world, is the world's slave from then on...There are no white lies, there is only the blackest of destruction, and a white lie is the blackest of all."

AYN RAND, *ATLAS SHRUGGED*

It is your duty to reach your potential as a man, and you should strive to be the master of your domain and be as rich and powerful as possible. If you can make a million or a billion dollars—do it! Seize the opportunity right now; not every man has the chance or the ability to pull off such a feat for himself and his family.

It is your duty to reach your potential in power and money, whatever that potential may be. Everyone loves a man who strives to be better today than he was yesterday. But most importantly, your wealth, power, and ability to be the master of your domain must come from your own inner strength and your own inner virtue. Lying is unmanly, threatening to the tribe, and violates your masculine energy. Be virtuous and good in your pursuit of your potential, riches and power, for:

> "A tiger can smile
> A snake will say it loves you
> Lies make us evil."

Chuck Palahniuk, *Fight Club*

PART II
SEX, WOMEN, CHILDREN, AND FAMILY

"If you tell a beautiful woman that she is beautiful, what have you given her? It's no more than a fact and it has cost you nothing. But if you tell an ugly woman that she is beautiful, you offer her the great homage of corrupting the concept of beauty. To love a woman for her virtues is meaningless. She's earned it, it's a payment, not a gift. But to love her for her vices is a real gift, unearned and undeserved. To love her for her vices is to defile all virtue for her sake—and that is a real tribute of love, because you sacrifice your conscience, your reason, your integrity and your invaluable self-esteem."

AYN RAND, *ATLAS SHRUGGED*

CHAPTER 11

WHAT WOMEN WANT

"By all means marry; if you get a good wife, you'll become happy; if you get a bad one, you'll become a philosopher."

SOCRATES

When a man types "what women want" into Google, he gets about 5,900,000,000 results. 5.9 billion results—yes, that is billion with a "B."

There is only one thing that women really want, not 5.9 billion things!

To give you some perspective on the number of ideas on what women want, if you type "porn" into Google you only get about 471,000,000 results.

There are roughly 12 times more ideas about what women want than there are porn results on Google. Think about that for a moment: The top of the Google crap-heap of the 5.9 billion results on "what women want" is a movie entitled *What Women Want* with Mel Gibson. In the movie, Gibson's character has a freak accident, after which he is able to read the minds of women. He also waxes his legs in the movie, wears pantyhose, and does a whole bunch of other strange things, including electrocuting himself in a bathtub with a blow-dryer. The movie sounds stupid, because it is stupid, and has nothing to do with what women *actually* want.

"Don't believe everything you read on the internet."

ABRAHAM LINCOLN

I assure you, women do not want the movie *What Women Want*. Instead, I will refer to a half-a-millennia-old story by Geoffrey Chaucer who died in the year 1400. In Chaucer's story, *The Canterbury Tales*, there are several characters who are on a pilgrimage, and each one of the characters tells a story.

One of the character's name is the Wife of Bath.

The Wife of Bath was a professional wife, as up until about 1900, a professional wife was a real career for a woman. Women were either wives or prostitutes—those were the only jobs for women. The Wife of Bath had grown wealthy by marrying and remarrying a collection of men, all of whom died. Each time a husband died, she grew wealthier.

The Wife of Bath is an experienced woman and tells the story of what women really want.

In her story, there once was a knight, a handsome knight who was riding through the countryside.

This knight comes across a beautiful virgin in the countryside, and he thinks she is beautiful, so he rapes her. The knight continues on his journey after the rape and ends up in the local town where the girl who was raped has told the queen about the knight who raped her.

The queen orders the knight into the court and holds him on trial. He is found guilty, and the queen is prepared to sentence the knight to death unless he can find out "what women truly want." The knight has one year to solve the mystery of what women want, or he will be put to death by the queen.

The game is on.

The knight searches far and wide asking everyone he can in the kingdom about what women want.

Some people claim that women want money, women want family, women want children, women want all sorts of answers that do not seem to be better than the last one.

Finally, the knight is running out of time, and he meets an old disfigured beggar witch in the street, and she says, "Sir knight, I know what women want."

The knight is intrigued and asks the beggar witch, "What is it that women truly want?"

The beggar witch withholds the information but makes a deal with the knight. She will tell the knight what it is that women truly want, and in exchange if she is correct, the knight shall marry her after he is saved from the queen.

The knight is growing desperate, so he agrees to the beggar witch's bargain right before his second trial. The old woman whispers into the knight's ear as to what it is that women truly want.

The knight arrives in court, and the entire kingdom is at the trial waiting to see if the knight has learned his lesson or not.

The queen asks the knight, "So, sir knight, what is it that women want?"

The knight proudly walks into the middle of the court and gives the court the answer that the beggar witch passed on to him.

The queen is stunned at how good the knight's answer is and pardons him for his crimes. She had never heard such an answer before.

As the knight turns to leave the court, the beggar witch appears out of the audience and tells everyone that it was she who helped the knight and reveals the bargain he had made with her for marriage.

The queen asks the knight, "Is this true?"

The knight sighs and says, "Yes, it is true."

And so the wedding is to commence.

The knight walks down the aisle at the wedding to meet his bride, follow through with his word, and marry the beggar witch. She is ugly and foul smelling, and he does not want to kiss her. The knight does everything he can to avoid the old woman, but finally on their wedding night he is in bed with the old beggar witch, and he is avoiding his husbandly duties of consummating the marriage.

The beggar witch wants the knight to kiss her and take her as his bride officially by consummating the marriage with a kiss and with sex.

The knight is disgusted and avoids her in bed, trying to avoid her at all costs.

But finally, the witch asks sweetly, "Please, sir knight, won't you kiss your new bride?"

She leans in for a kiss. The knight realizes he is never going to get out of this situation without kissing her, closes his eyes, and leans in to kiss the witch.

In the moment of his obedience, upon kissing the witch, she transforms into a beautiful young maiden, and the knight and the young maiden live forever happily ever after.

So what is it that women truly want? What was the secret that the beggar witch gave to the knight to impress the queen and save his life?

What do women truly want?

The answer is "mastery over their men."

The knight was a criminal for taking the virgin at the beginning of the story against her will and was punished by the queen in return.

In the end, however, the knight was rewarded for yielding and giving mastery over himself to his wife, the old beggar witch, who happened to transform into a beautiful young maiden for him to enjoy.

It's a simple story, but it's a powerful story at the same time.

What do women want? Mastery over their men.

To make a woman happy, she wants a real man, a strong man to have mastery over.

Chris Rock, the famous comedian, used to say, "Men see something they want and say, 'What do I have to do to get me that?' Women see something they want and say, 'Who do I have to get to get me that?'"

In the medieval times, the only person who could tell the truth was the court jester. Today, it is comedians like Chris Rock who tell us the truth.

Women want mastery over their men, but they want real men, strong men, not man-boys and not effeminate men who do not take responsibility and ownership over their lives.

Attraction, polarity, and sexual excitement lie in the denial of what she wants. She wants mastery over a strong man, and to create attraction a man must deny her such mastery to create tension, while still creating enough release through moments of temporary mastery. Such is the tension and push-and-pull nature of polarity and attraction.

If a man is to give in to his woman and give her full mastery, he could depolarize the attraction and be a guy she can "walk all over." This is not what women want. Women want mastery over the most powerful man they can find, the tribal leader. If you give in to her, you are socially beneath her, and that will serve as proof that you are not the tribal leader. She will set out to find a new leader and a stronger man to master. This is unfair, this is cruel, but this is life and biology. In many ways we are no better than the apes.

Contrary to popular belief, Women do not want to be #1 in your life; instead, they want to be #2 after your purpose. Your purpose grounds you in masculinity and makes you attractive to women.

CHAPTER 12

HOW TO LIVE YOUR PURPOSE AND GIVE WOMEN WHAT THEY REALLY WANT

"Life is never made unbearable by circumstances, but only by lack of meaning and purpose."

VIKTOR FRANKL

Rule #1: She Doesn't Really Want to Be Number One

"A woman sometimes seems to want to be the most important thing in her man's life. However, if she is the most important thing, then she feels her man has made her the number one priority and is not fully dedicated or directed to divine growth and service. She will feel her man's dependence on her for his happiness, and this will make her feel smothered by his neediness and clinging. A woman really wants her man to be totally dedicated to his highest purpose—and also to love her fully. Although she would

never admit it, she wants to feel that her man would be willing
to sacrifice their relationship for the sake of his highest purpose."

DEIDA, *THE WAY OF THE SUPERIOR MAN*

A man must never sacrifice his purpose for his woman because to do so would debase him as a man, force him into feminine energy, which is of the family, and force his woman who typically wants to be feminine into the masculine role of work. A man's value comes from his dedication to his purpose at all costs, and women find this very sexy. It allows them to relax, live in their feminine energy, and "feel like women." In so many romance movies, you will see the female protagonist say, "You make me feel like a woman," which is a woman allowing herself to feel feminine relative to a man being masculine and living his purpose.

Contrary to the popular narrative of today, the homogenization of genders is unfavorable with men and women when it comes to sex and attraction, which is fundamentally based on inequality and complementary and reciprocal opposites. Sexual attraction and energy come from opposite forces colliding, not so much from a sterile, homogenous, government-mandated, gender-neutral slogan. Men and women have attraction through the oppositeness of their masculine and feminine energies. It's not about gender-neutral people and their gender-neutral energy; there is no sexual tension in that.

Rule #2: Your Purpose Must Come Before Your Relationship

"Every man knows that his highest purpose in life cannot be
reduced to any particular relationship. If a man prioritizes
his relationship over his highest purpose, he weakens
himself, disserves the universe, and cheats his woman of an
authentic man who can offer her full, undivided presence."

DEIDA, *THE WAY OF THE SUPERIOR MAN*

If you make your purpose second to your relationship, you will have gender neutralized yourself and, in a sense, made yourself into a woman. Women do not want other women; they want men, and the strongest men they can find. They want the tribal leader, the alpha, and for you to put your relationship first before your purpose disqualifies you from being the leader of the tribe, because women intuitively know that no tribal leader would put her whims before the purpose and survival of the tribe.

Rule #3: What She Wants Is Not What She Says

"Sometimes a woman will make a request of her man in plain English, not to get him to do something, but to see if he is so weak that he will do it. In other words, she is testing his capacity to do what is right, not what she is asking for. In such cases, if the man does what his woman asks, she will be disappointed and angry. The man will have no idea why she is so angry or what could possibly please her. He must remember that her trust is engendered not by him fulfilling her requests, but by him magnifying love, consciousness, and success in their lives, in spite of her requests."

DEIDA, *THE WAY OF THE SUPERIOR MAN*

In spite of your woman's requests, you must stick to your purpose, which usually is your work. She might ask you to put her first or her needs first, but this is a gambit, a ploy to see if you are weak enough to be subordinate to her. Contrary to popular belief in our current society, women do not want to be biologically equal with their men. They want a man who is the tribal leader and stronger than them. For her man to succumb to her every whim and to put her purpose first violates what she wants. She will be unhappy to find out that her man is not the tribal leader after all and will seek to find a better man if you violate your purpose.

Rule #4: Women Are Not Liars

"Keeping your word is a masculine trait, in men or women. A person with a feminine essence may not keep her word, yet it is not exactly "lying." In the feminine reality, words and facts take a second place to emotions and the shifting moods of relationship. When she says, "I hate you," or "I'll never move to Texas," or "I don't want to go to the movies," it is often more a reflection of a transient feeling-wave than a well-considered stance with respect to events and experience. On the other hand, the masculine means what it says. A man's word is his honor. The feminine says what it feels. A woman's word is her true expression in the moment."

DEIDA, THE WAY OF THE SUPERIOR MAN

Feelings come and go, emotions are fluid, and reason and clear thinking are direct and often concrete. When a woman emotes, she is saying what she feels, and feelings are not usually well thought out. She is not lying; she is being emotionally expressive. Men will be frustrated listening to what women say—what she says is not what she means. What men say is what they mean. But a woman says what she feels, and her feelings are fluid and can appear to be crazy over time. As the masculine one in the relationship, just stick to reason, stick to your purpose, and let the emotions blow over like a storm. She wants you to be the rock and the stable one, while she can emote and be a little crazy.

Rule #5: Her Complaint Is Content Free

"Women are always wanting divine masculine presence in a man, regardless of their specific complaint or mood. A man should hear his woman's complaints as warning bells, and then do his best to align his life with his truth and purpose. However, if he believes in the literal content of her complaint, he will immediately go off course, for the content reflects her present

mood more than a careful observation of his tendencies over time. Her complaint should be valued as a reminder to "get it together," and perhaps as an indication as to how. But more often than not, the specifics of her complaint do not describe the real, underlying action or tendency that needs to be changed."

DEIDA, *THE WAY OF THE SUPERIOR MAN*

A woman's complaints are not actually about what she says. A man must use a woman's complaints to recheck his purpose and make sure he is on course with his truth. What she is complaining about is often not the root cause of the problem. "You play too many video games" might mean "You aren't doing well at work, why don't you get it together instead?" A man must not try to decode all of these complaints and again stick to his purpose and get back on course to make his woman truly happy.

Rule #6: She Wants to Relax in the Demonstration of Your Direction

"A woman must be able to trust you to take charge if she relaxes her own masculine edge. This is true financially, sexually, emotionally, and spiritually. The man doesn't have to actually do all the work, but he must be able to steer the course if his woman is going to relax into her feminine without fear."

DEIDA, *THE WAY OF THE SUPERIOR MAN*

Again, contrary to what we are told in schools and societies, women want to relax in the presence of the masculine. They don't want a democracy where everyone has a vote. To be feminine, she doesn't want to have to make the decisions. That is the masculine energy's job. Feminine women want the man to make the decisions and be direct so she can relax into feminine energy. I remember when I used to take my ex-fiancée to a restaurant we both liked called Spaghetti Factory. If I picked her up and asked her where she wanted to go, we would mutually decide on Spaghetti Factory, and she would be mad that I didn't plan anything. But if I called her in advance, told her to dress up and I was going to take her for dinner to surprise her, made reservations and still went to the same Spaghetti Factory, she was happy because I made the masculine decision that she craved and had thought about her in advance. Women want the decision of the man to protect her so that she can relax into the feminine. She does not want to be equal voting decision-making partners as our society would now suggest.

Rule #7: She Wants the "Killer" in You

"Among many other qualities, a woman wants the 'killer' in her man. She is turned off if her man is afraid and wants her to kill the cockroach or the mouse while he stands on a chair and watches. She is turned off if her man wants her to get out of bed in order to check out the strange sounds in the house to find out if a burglar made the noise. Fearlessness, or the capacity to transcend the fear of death for the sake of love, is a quintessential form of the ultimate masculine gift."

Deida, *The Way of the Superior Man*

Women love killers. The human race is violent, and violence is part of who we are. To lead the tribe, usually the alpha male leader must make life-and-death decisions. Male leaders throughout history have often been ruthless killers, and it's no surprise that women love the killer instinct. If you can handle the killing, she can handle being a woman. If you can't handle the killing, maybe she will have to handle it, and that will piss her off. She will leave and go find a man who will kill for her instead. Have that killer instinct, have the edge, pull the trigger, and make the decision to own your purpose and be a man: this is what women crave.

Rule #8: Never Change Your Mind
Just to Please a Woman

"If a woman suggests something that changes a man's perspective, then he should make a new decision based on his new perspective. But he should never betray his own deepest knowledge and intuition in order to please his woman or 'go along' with her. Both she and he will be weakened by such an action. They will grow to resent each other, and the crust of accumulated inauthenticity will burden their love, as well as their capacity for free action."

DEIDA, *THE WAY OF THE SUPERIOR MAN*

To change your mind for a woman is to make her the tribal leader, and that's not what she really wants. She wants you to be the leader so she can enjoy her own feminine energy and be free from the responsibility of being masculine. If she changes your mind about something, then make a fresh decision based on new information. This is normal negotiation practice, but you must be careful not to be the beta to her alpha. Again, that compromises the man's position as the tribal leader and makes your woman unhappy.

On the chessboard, the queen is the most powerful piece. She's the most influential and the most dangerous piece in the army. The king is a bumbling fool who is fragile and can only move one square at a time. This relationship between the chess queen and the chess king illustrates the power of women in reality.

When men and women pair bond and consummate a marriage, the man absorbs some of her traits, and the woman absorbs some of his traits.

They say that when a man is in love with a woman, she becomes his weakness, and when a woman is in love, he becomes her strength. This is called the exchange of power, and women want a powerful man to exchange her sexual and reproductive life-giving energies for his strength, masculine power, and energy.

There is an exchange of energy, and traditionally it has been money for sex and sex for money. Even in Chaucer's time in the 1400s, several of his writings and stories observed the money for sex exchange between men and women. In reality, we can replace money with power. Power for sex and sex for power.

"Female sexuality is power"

GENE SIMMONS

Or beauty for power and power for beauty.

"Being powerful is like being a lady. If you have to tell people you are, you aren't."

MARGARET THATCHER

In any event, women want power. The power comes from her man, her king, and makes her the most powerful piece on the chessboard.

"Everything in the world is about sex except sex. Sex is about power."

OSCAR WILDE

It's fitting that Robert Greene, the author of the bestselling book *48 Laws of Power,* also wrote a book on the art of seduction. The book was all about sexual exchange between men and women and had strong undertones of power throughout. Greene's other hit books have been *33 Stratagems of War* and *Mastery,* which also revolve around power and sometimes sex as power.

There you have it: power, war, seduction, and mastery all perfectly situated together as related studies. All of Greene's books are excellent, but they contain similar anecdotes and similar lessons. To wield power and to wield seduction are not that different, which become obvious as you can read through his published books.

So, what do women really want? Mastery over their men, and not just any men—the tribal leaders, the powerful men, the men with money, the men with the ability to do things. They want to exchange their power, their sexual power, their reproductive power in exchange for real power in the real world.

The woman will become the man's weakness in this exchange, and he will become her strength. More women are interested in this "Strong Man" book because they want their own men, the men they are exchanging their sexual energy with, to be stronger and more powerful and to serve their own whims and agendas. This idea makes sense and is justified. A woman is only sexually attractive until a certain age, and as Ben Franklin says, "When a woman grows to be less handsome in appearance, she must focus on becoming a good woman."

Women have a peak sexual value at around age 20. This has been proven with studies conducted by dating websites like Match.com in which men aged 18–70 chose women's pictures and profiles who were aged 20 to be the most attractive.

Women, on the other hand, typically chose men their own age until they reached age 45 and older, on which at every age after 45 they still chose a 45-year-old man.

The genders of men and women have inverse sexual values. A man has low sexual value at age 20 and peaks his sexual value at age 45. His sexual value is derived from "K" value, which means "Carrying capacity" in German reproductive studies. Carrying capacity is about resources and how can he provide to ensure the survival of his children. A 20-year-old young man has low carrying capacity, whereas a man who is 45 has peak carrying capacity and can even support a first or even second family, which explains the biological urge for a man to have a midlife crisis (run away from his aged wife with his hot young secretary) and start a second family. His carrying capacity is high; he can afford it.

Women, on the other hand, peak at high sexual value at age 20 with high "R" value, which is reproductive value, and their value slowly declines until age 45. Reproductive value declines in both men and women as they grow older because R value is based on physical traits. When you see young sexy people at the club with toned muscles, sexy outfits, perfect hair, healthy tanned bodies, thin bodies, tight bodies, and looking gorgeous, that is an R-value environment. No one is considering the carrying capacity of anyone in the nightclub. Instead, everyone is just looking at the physical replication value, and that is how value is judged in that environment.

Interestingly, this all has to do with reproduction and children, where a 20-year-old woman has youth and beauty on her side and is able to reproduce several children in a healthy way. Her "R" value or reproductive value is very high at 20. On the flip side, a man's value comes from his "K" value, which is his carrying capacity. It comes down to money, power, and economics, and a man who has survived until age 45 is a proven commodity in the sexual marketplace. He has theoretically raised his first family at 20 and is ready for his second family at 45. Thus, the built-in software for the male midlife crisis. Amazingly, young women still find 45-year-old men attractive. Even if the man has kids, he is a proven sexual commodity and able to reproduce and carry his second set of offspring with resources until they are old enough to be adults. This proven abundance of resources is very attractive to women.

Conversely, a 45-year-old woman with kids is not attractive to men, because men are looking for "R" value, reproductive value, and a woman at 45 has very little ability to produce more children when compared with a young, beautiful, fertile 20-year-old. Furthermore, if she has kids from another marriage or relationship, she is deemed to be less attractive than a woman without kids. Men of high value do not want to raise another man's kids.

Is this a double standard?

Yes!

Is it unfair?

Yes!

However, this is the reality of life and the way biology was designed for our survival of the human race.

This explains why older men are frequently with younger women.

In Canada, where I live, men statistically marry women 5 years younger than them, which is standard in this culture.

Statistically speaking, a man can marry a woman up to 9 years younger than him, and the chances of divorce are not too bad. If he marries a woman 10 years, 15 years, or 20 years older, the stats for divorce start to become perilous, and the marriage is unlikely to work out.

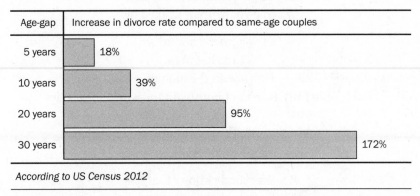

Divorce Rate Based on Age Gap

Age-gap	Increase in divorce rate compared to same-age couples
5 years	18%
10 years	39%
20 years	95%
30 years	172%

According to US Census 2012

As far as women marrying younger men, the maximum age gap for older women and younger men is only 2 years. If the man is any younger than 2 years, the stats for divorce become unfavorable indeed.

Women want the exchange of sexual power with strong men, tribal leaders, and alpha males. They want to take ownership of these men, much like the queen on the chessboard, and want to use his power, his resources, and his money to serve her offspring and her wishes and dreams. This is what women want. Is it cold? Perhaps. Is it right or wrong? Who knows. But what it is, is the reality of the sexual marketplace and if you are a young man wishing to do well in the sexual marketplace, you might as well understand what women really want and fill the need; otherwise, you will be singing the "young man blues."

Young Man Blues

As performed by The Who

Oh, well, a young man
Ain't got nothin' in the world these days
I said a young man
Ain't got nothin' in the world these days

Well, you know in the old days
When a young man was a strong man
All the people, they'd step back
When a young man walked by

But you know, nowadays
It's the old man
He's got all the money
And a young man ain't got nothin' in the world these days
I said
Ain't got nothing
Got sweet nothing

Everybody knows that
Everybody knows that
Everybody knows that a young man ain't got nothin'Ooh, yeah
Everybody knows that a young man ain't got nothin'
In the old, in the old days
Oh, in the old days
Everybody stepped back when a young man walked by
They stepped back

They stepped back
They stepped back
They stepped far, far back, yeah

Have pity on the young man
They ain't got nothin' in the world these days, I said
They ain't got nothin'!
They got sweet fuck-all!

CHAPTER 13
WHAT MEN WANT IN WOMEN

"Falling in love is not a choice.
To stay in love is."

UNKNOWN

When I was younger, my mother used to give me advice on choosing a woman. She would say, "Marry your match."

My father would say, "Find a smart girl from a good family."

Those are both still good pieces of advice as I type this book out at age 31.

I think they are still both relevant in today's world.

Being a man and selecting a woman is a hard job these days. Just as choosing a strong man out of a population of weak men has made finding a good man hard for women, the opposite is true as well. To find a virtuous woman, a good woman, a "smart girl from a good family," is equally hard in a sea of broken people and broken families.

I have thought about my parents' advice on women for several decades now, and I think my father is 100% right. "A smart girl from a good family" is bang on. We learn so much from our family of origin, and if you want to know the fruits, just examine the roots. As said in the Bible, "A good tree cannot produce bad fruit and a bad tree cannot produce good fruit."

"The apple doesn't fall far from the tree" is a secular version of the same idea.

Both women and men take on the traits of their families. The relationship that your potential woman has with her father is one of the biggest keys to her relationship with you.

Typically, a daughter's relationship with her father will give a man hints as to how his future relationship will be with her. The reverse is true as well; how men treat their mothers is usually how they will treat the woman they love.

Children learn how to love from watching their parents' relationship; if the parents fight and scream, they become fighters and screamers. If the parents are openly affectionate, then the children learn to be openly affectionate.

Examining the parents of your potential woman is one of the most important things you can and should do before making a major commitment to her.

My mother's advice to marry my match is, according to her, from the *Odyssey*. The *Odyssey* is the story of King Odysseus, an eponymous strong man has married the strong woman Penelope. Although Odysseus is lost at sea for 15 years after fighting the Trojan War, Penelope remains strong and faithful by staving off the line up of suitors who want to take her hand to replace Odysseus as king.

After pondering my mother's advice for nearly three decades, I think that "marry your match" is somewhat true. King Odysseus and Queen Penelope are both evenly matched in that they have strong spirit, but they are not really equals in any sense.

Odysseus goes out and fights wars, and Penelope stays home and looks after the house. I would edit my mom's advice to give to young men to say, "Marry your complement and your reciprocal." Whatever you are, marry the complement, the equal opposite of what you are.

When two people are the same, when two people are equal, one is not needed. This is one of the glaring problems with marriages today. Men and women are too equal, too homogenous. The man does not need the woman, and the woman does not need the man. There is nothing exclusive or special about either sex today.

In past history, especially pre-1940s, men had specific roles to play and so did women. The roles were mutually exclusive, and a man desperately needed a complementary woman and a woman desperately needed a complimentary man.

As per statistics published by Randy Olson in the *Washington Post*, we can see 144 years of marriage and divorce in the USA, and some of the trends in number of marriages and number of divorces.

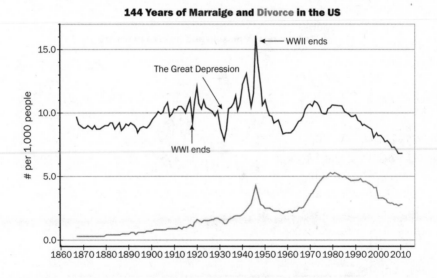

144 Years of Marraige and Divorce in the US

First, you can see that the common generalizations are true. As the chart shows, marriage rates have declined steadily since the 1980s. Today they are lower than any other time since 1870, including during the Great Depression. However, divorce rates today are actually slightly down compared with the 1970s, '80s, and '90s on a per capita basis.

In addition, you can see that events like World War I, World War II, and the Great Depression all had a significant impact on marriage and divorce rates.

Couples rushed to the altar before the wars started, as well as at their conclusion. As Olson notes, divorces also spiked after the conclusion of WWII, perhaps because some couples who had married rashly before the war realized their differences.

The chart also shows an obvious drop in marriage rates during the Great Depression of the 1930s. Fewer jobs and less economic stability appear to be a popular reason for not forming new families—a trend we also saw during the Great Recession.

This second chart shows the raw counts for marriages and divorces (not adjusted per capita, like the first chart):

As Olson writes, the second chart makes clear that the dip in marriages and divorces in the 1960s that you see in the first chart is due in part to the post-war population boom. A surge in Baby Boomers in the 1950s

and 1960s greatly increased the population; since the Boomers were almost all too young to marry, the per capita marriage rate declined. Once the Boomers got old enough to tie the knot, marriage rates rose back to pre-WWII levels.

> "Many marriages would be better if the husband
> and wife realized they were on the same side."
>
> ZIG ZIGLAR

The chart above, with the raw numbers of marriage and divorce not adjusted for population, shows the real story that is happening in raw numbers. We must remove the rash of marriages during WWII, as people just wanted to have sex before the war. The only way to have sex was to be married back then.

The 1960s signaled the beginning of the decline of men, the decline of the family, the upswing of feminism, and really the mass degradation of our societal fabric. What is also true from the raw numbers is the current decline of marriages in raw numbers as men are "opting out" of women all together, divorce is trending down as well, but it's in direct correlation with the downtrend in marriage.

When men and women were complementary, certainly in the 1940s and prior, the data are clear. Marriage worked in a functional way, there were families, there were children and population growth, and we had strong men. America was so strong back then it could win two world wars in a row and become the industrial giant of the world. It became the dominator of the world through owning the world reserve currency, had a currency backed by gold, and entered a golden age in history.

The hard times of WWI, the Great Depression, and WWII created strong men. The family was needed, men were men and women were women. Since 1960, we have seen the major declines of strong men, family, and desirable women. As the graph suggests, we are seeing a decline back into hard times, which will bring back strong men, families, and a need for women to learn how to be desirable women again instead of women who operate as worse versions of men.

"Some of us (women) are becoming the men we wanted to marry."

GLORIA STEINEM

You want your reciprocal, not an equal. You want complementary, not the same. Both men and women know in their hearts and in their emotions that they all want a reciprocal and a complement, not an equal. Allow me to explain why.

The basis of all attraction is a polarity of energy as illustrated in a wonderful book that I recommend for men and women anywhere entitled *The Way of the Superior Man* by David Deida.

Deida has studied and, I would argue, mastered the study of what makes a man's essence and what makes a woman's essence. The way he explains masculine and feminine energy is so clear that it explains every one of my failed relationships and even my parents' failed marriage. Whenever I see a relationship failing between a man and a woman, or even a same-sex couple, what you see with the loss of attraction is the loss of polarity.

The following is an excerpt from *The Way of the Superior Man*. He can explain masculine and feminine energy and polarity better than I ever could:

> Your sexual essence is always attracted to its energetic reciprocal. Masculine men are attracted to feminine women. Feminine men are attracted to masculine women. Balanced men are attracted to balanced women.
>
> About 80% of all men have a more masculine sexual essence. These men, of which you are probably one, are attracted to all things feminine. Not just feminine women, but anything with feminine energy, anything which is radiant, alive,

enlivening, relaxing, and moving. Feminine energy gets you out of your head and into your body. Music, beer, nature, women, they are all forms of feminine energy.

It is not just a visually gorgeous woman who attracts you. If a woman is free and radiant in her feminine energy, you are probably attracted; sometimes more attracted, sometimes less attracted, but always attracted, at least enough to steal a glance at her form. This attraction is not only natural, but healthy. It is a sign of polarity, the same kind of natural flow of polarization by which electricity flows between the positive and negative poles of a battery. It's nothing to be ashamed of. It's why there are men and women. The nature of nature is polarity, from the magnetism that flows between the north and south poles of the earth, to the attraction that flows between your masculine core and the feminine radiance of a woman.

If you feel uncomfortable with your attraction to women, you are probably uncomfortable with your own masculine essence. If you feel it is demeaning for a woman to be the "object" of your polar attraction, then you have probably disowned your masculine core. You have energetically emasculated yourself by condemning and suppressing your native desires. You are negating your sexual essence, rather than being at home with it.

Any negative attitude you have about your attraction to women is a sign of fear; somewhere along the line you learned that such attraction was "bad" or "evil." Your attraction to women, all kinds of women, is natural, normal, and beautiful. In fact, it is an aspect of the same desire that will ultimately lead you toward spiritual freedom.

If you are a man with a masculine sexual essence, you will always feel sexual polarity with anyone who animates feminine energy. You may feel this attraction many times a day, with many women. Enjoy it. Women are a blessing! The feminine, even in the non-human forms of a lush tropical

island, a cold beer, or your favorite tune, could make the
difference between dreariness and ahhh-ing in ecstasy. Our
acceptance of sexual attraction, even with music and places,
is at the root of our capacity to experience bodily pleasure.

About 80% of men have a masculine essence, and to make men and
women the same by social constructs or new social rules that homogenize men and women is somewhat evil. It takes the good and sacred
things that make women away, and it neutralizes men and makes both
sides unnecessary to the other.

At their cores and essences, men and women are very special. The
masculine and feminine essence is the energy that makes each side
attracted to the other.

The polar otherness of women is what men find to be sexy and attractive. Like magnets, men and women crave that otherness. Just as Jack
Donovan wrote, "Masculine is what is least feminine and feminine is
what is least masculine." These two energies are the opposites of a spectrum, not equals on a spectrum, but reciprocal and complementary
forces.

Imagine what would happen if we tried to depolarize the earth or
depolarize positive and negative electrical charges. The basic forces
that make the world work would cease to work. The same applies to
men and women and attraction.

Choose a Woman Who Is Your Complementary Opposite:

If a man is very masculine by nature, then he will be
attracted to a very feminine woman, who will complement
his energy. The more neutral or balanced he is, the more
balanced he will prefer his woman. And, if a man is more
feminine by nature, his energy will be complemented by the
strong direction and purposiveness of a more masculine
woman. By understanding their own needs, men can learn
to accept the "whole package" of a woman. For instance, a
more masculine man can expect that any woman who really
turns him on and enlivens him will also be relatively wild,
undisciplined, "bonkers," chaotic, prone to changing her

mind and "lying." Still, from an energetic perspective, this kind of woman will be much more healing and inspiring to him than a more balanced or neutral woman who is steady, reasonable, "trustworthy," and able to say what she means in a way he can understand.

You have probably met a woman who seemed fantastic, only to discover she has some emotional weirdness that you don't really want to deal with. She seemed incredibly sexy, but also a bit "bonkers" or crazy, saying one thing one moment and another the next. You have probably also met some very reasonable and trustworthy women who don't seem to constantly change their mind and, in fact, with whom you could have good conversations that don't end up frustrating you. Although you may love these women and enjoy spending time with them, they don't arouse your passion as much as the women whose words you wouldn't trust to remain true for an afternoon, but who move their body in a way that drives you wild.

"Why can't a woman be more like a man?" many men have wondered. But, of course, it is precisely those ways in which a woman is least like a man that most attract you sexually, if you have a masculine sexual essence. A woman's feminine shine, the energy that moves her body, her utterly refreshing spontaneity and mystery, not to mention her delightful smile, are what attract you. And the more feminine a woman is at her core, the less she is likely to evidence strong masculine traits, such as speaking clearly and unequivocally about thoughts and desires, rather than primarily expressing her feelings of the moment.

A woman with a more feminine sexual essence will say she loves you one moment, and then, when you have done something you are not even aware of, she will say she hates you. This is the beauty of the feminine; to her, the masculine grid of words and events is less relevant than the fluidity of relationship and feeling. Thank God for such women, who make no apologies for their oceanic depth and riptides of emotion.

You are always attracted to your sexual reciprocal. So, if you have a more feminine sexual essence, you will be attracted to a more masculine woman. You have probably seen men and women in couples like this. The man is more radiant and lively than the woman. The woman is more commit-ted to her direction in life than the man. The relationship is more important to the man, whereas the woman likes to be left alone much of the time. These are signs of a relationship where the man has a more feminine essence and the wom-an's essence is more masculine.

Other men, with more neutral sexual essences, prefer women who are also more neutral, neither particularly masculine nor feminine. This kind of couple can talk about anything, and they like talking about everything. They share hobbies, friends, even career goals. Though equally loving, this kind of couple is usually less sexually passionate than highly polarized couples. It would be unusual to hear about this kind of neutral or balanced couple yelling at each other, throwing pillows, wrestling each other down to the floor, and passionately making love right there and then.

Through lack of understanding, you might have depolarized yourself and your partner into a relationship that seems neutral, but actually isn't. Only about 10% of couples are actually the neutral or balanced type in their true essence. Another 10% of couples are made up of a feminine man and masculine woman. But if you are like 80% of couples, you have a masculine sexual essence, and your woman has a feminine one. That is, her feminine way frustrates you, drives you crazy, inspires you, or turns you on, more often than she is simply your sexually neutral buddy.

The false neutralization, or depolarization, of relationships is one of the main reasons that couples break up. The reju-venative charge of sexual loving becomes weak, while all the things that irritate you and your partner remain just as strong as ever. The secret is not to try to change your woman's irritating feminine ways, but to help cultivate the depth and rejuvenative power of her feminine blessings.

If you are like most men, you have probably minimized your appreciation of the full spectrum of your woman's feminine energy by numbing yourself to the aspects that most irritate you. For instance, she doesn't drive you crazy anymore because you've learned not to take her too seriously. Perhaps you have learned to seem attentive while not really listening to her endless chat. Or, maybe you have learned to give her a daily dose of affection as a way to quell her ongoing need for more intimate time than you really want to spend with her.

This is the wrong approach. The feminine is an infinite source of love, inspiration, and power, both physically and spiritually. Feminine women are connected with the elements of nature in ways that more masculine people, such as yourself, usually aren't. Feminine women may seem wild, untrustable, or even irresponsible from a man's perspective, but such women are simply free of the masculine need to live in a world governed by reason and control

So, choose a woman who is your complimentary opposite, which for most men means a more feminine woman. It is only a feminine woman who can give the gifts that you, as a masculine man, need. Along with these gifts, however, come the relative chaos and emotional weather storms that most men dread. Realize these are aspects of the same energy that turns you on. In fact, you can learn to be turned on by her dance of anger as much as by her slinky purr. This capacity is one of your gifts to her. You can learn to stand free and strong no matter what emotion she displays. You won't leave, turn away, or dissociate in disgust. You can meet her enormous energy and stand full, loving her through the storm, embracing her complete feminine power, dark and light.

Deida, *The Way of The Superior Man,*

Instead of sameness, focus on reciprocals and the complementary, which is what has held the human race together since the beginning of time. Even if you are a feminine man or an energy neutral man, still look for your reciprocal, your opposite, the other half—not the same half!

The exchange of feminine energy, which is manifested as youth, beauty, and sex for masculine energy—power, status, and survival—is the precise collision of energy that is able to create life. The energy is reciprocal and opposite, and as man you need to understand to maintain your masculine position so that your woman can stay feminine.

When men slip into feminine energy, it forces a woman's energy to flip upside down into masculine energy in the relationship. Women can tolerate this temporarily, but not for long. Eventually she will be pissed off with taking on your roles, and she will lose all attraction to you. I witnessed this firsthand in my parents' divorce. My father fell out of the masculine energy when he failed to produce at work and he focused on the home, which kept him away from his masculine purpose—his work. This forced my mother to step up as the breadwinner, and she hated filling this masculine role. She filled the masculine role for 20 years, and then she said, "Fuck this" and got rid of my father and his weakness. We live in a society now full of weak men who do not understand polarity, and the women hate it. Women want to be women; they want to be feminine and enjoy their divine energy. When men fail to be masculine and live their purpose, which usually is doing their work and earning the trust of the tribe, women get pissed off and go on man-killing rampages.

The exchange of reciprocal power is what gives men and women power as a unit: she becomes his weakness, and he becomes her strength. Such is the exchange of power in a relationship, and to stay with this exchange of power, men must stay masculine and women must stay feminine to keep the magnetism and the togetherness.

> *"You will only be happy in intimacy if you choose a woman who is your sexual reciprocal as a partner."*
>
> Deida, *The Way of the Superior Man*

CHAPTER 14
FUN WOMEN VERSUS MARRIAGEABLE WOMEN

"Life is really simple, but we insist on making it complicated."

CONFUCIUS

As a man, you will always struggle when it comes to women with "what you want" and "what you need."

The Universal Hot vs. Crazy Matrix—a Man's Guide to Women is a popular viral video on YouTube in which a man in his 40s is giving advice to young men about selecting a woman.

Link: https://www.youtube.com/watch?v=vwbKYcBdVyk

The Hot Crazy matrix really explains a man's struggle between "what he wants," which is usually hot-attractive women, and "what he needs," which is usually wife material and un-crazy women.

Such a balance is the minefield that a man must navigate when choosing a woman to be his partner in life. Does he lean more towards the sexual polarity of hot and crazy women who will excite him with unpredictable sexual energy and take the risk on the crazy side? Or does he go for a less hot, less crazy woman whom he can actually build a life with? Every man struggles with this question at some point, and this is why the Hot Crazy matrix has gone viral. It's humorous, satirical delivery of an otherwise cold hard truth about men and women.

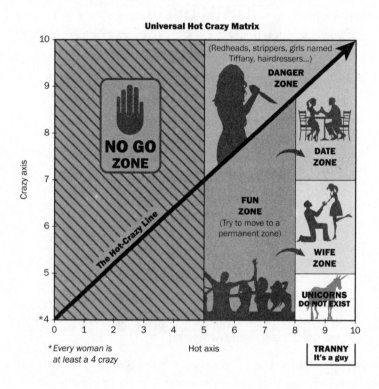

The Hot Crazy matrix is a two-axis chart with crazy going from a scale of 4 to 10 on the y-axis, because all women are at least a 4 crazy, and the hot axis from 0 to 10 on the x-axis.

As a rule, men will not date a woman who isn't at least a 5 hot and above the "hot crazy line" that creates the "no go zone." Men do not date women who are not at least a 5 on the physical attractiveness scale.

Above the "hot crazy line" is the "danger zone." This is the zone so many men get trapped by going for "what they want instead of what they need." In the video, the man explaining the danger zone gives examples of danger zone women: redheads, strippers, girls named Tiffany, and hairdressers. These are the women whom men usually lust after, and they are so hot that they can get away with being dangerously crazy.

I personally have dated several women in the danger zone, and for a long time I was addicted to the danger zone. I would classify myself as a highly masculine energy man, so I usually go after women who are very, very feminine, highly attractive, and thus, danger zone crazy.

This is dangerous, living on the edge; it's fun, it's exciting, but building something of lasting value with these women is almost impossible. These women are like fast money: easy come, easy go. Be careful if you are going to play in the danger zone; it doesn't really work well for most men in the long run. Very hot, very crazy women are a liability. They are so hot that every single guy who sees them in person or online is constantly hitting on them. In addition, their crazy side makes them unpredictable. This is generally a bad combination for a stable, long-term relationship, but it sure is fun in the short term. Beneath the danger zone is the fun zone, women who are not that hot and not that crazy. You likely will date these women and have "fun" with them, but you won't pursue them that passionately because they just simply aren't that hot. You know you can do better.

When you look at the date zone you have women who are a 7–10 crazy and an 8–10 hot. These are the women you date long term and get to meet your family, friends, and parents. The holdback is they are just a little bit too crazy for wife material.

The wife zone is where you want to get to, 5–7 crazy and 8–10 hot. It's important to note that your wife might not be the hottest girl you ever date, but that's a good thing. It's normal for men to have a slightly less hot wife in exchange for a much more stable and less crazy woman. To illustrate the point, check out this famous article in which a JP Morgan CEO responds to a very pretty girl's request to marry a rich man. The pretty girl notices that rich men often do not have the prettiest of wives, which I believe to be true.

A reply from CEO of J.P. Morgan to a pretty girl seeking a rich husband

A young and pretty lady posted this on a popular forum:

Title: What Should I Do to Marry a Rich Guy?

I'm going to be honest of what I'm going to say here.

I'm 25 this year. I'm very pretty, have style and good taste. I wish to marry a guy with $500k annual salary or above.

You might say that I'm greedy, but an annual salary of $1M is considered only as middle class in New York.

My requirement is not high. Is there anyone in this forum who has an income of $500k annual salary? Are you all married?

I wanted to ask: what should I do to marry rich persons like you?

Among those I've dated, the richest is $250k annual income, and it seems that this is my upper limit.

If someone is going to move into high cost residential area on the west of New York City Garden(?), $250k annual income is not enough.

I'm here humbly to ask a few questions:
1. Where do most rich bachelors hang out? (Please list down the names and addresses of bars, restaurant, gym)
2. Which age group should I target?
3. Why most wives of the riches are only average looking? I've met a few girls who don't have looks and are not interesting, but they are able to marry rich guys.

4. How do you decide who can be your wife, and who can only be your girlfriend? (my target now is to get married)

Ms. Pretty

A philosophical reply from CEO of J.P. Morgan:

Dear Ms. Pretty,

I have read your post with great interest. Guess there are lots of girls out there who have similar questions like yours.

Please allow me to analyze your situation as a professional investor.

My annual income is more than $500k, which meets your requirement, so I hope everyone believes that I'm not wasting time here.

From the standpoint of a business person, it is a bad decision to marry you. The answer is very simple, so let me explain.

Put the details aside, what you're trying to do is an exchange of "beauty" and "money": Person A provides beauty, and Person B pays for it, fair and square.

However, there's a deadly problem here, your beauty will fade, but my money will not be gone without any good reason. The fact is, my income might increase from year to year, but you can't be prettier year after year.

Hence from the viewpoint of economics, I am an appreciation asset, and you are a depreciation asset. It's not just normal depreciation, but exponential depreciation. If that is your only asset, your value will be much worse 10 years later.

By the terms we use in Wall Street, every trading has a position; dating you is also a "trading position." If the trade value dropped, we will sell it, and it is not a good idea to keep it for long term — same goes with the marriage that you wanted. It might be cruel to say this, but in order to make a wiser decision any assets with great depreciation value will be sold or "leased."

Anyone with over $500k annual income is not a fool; we would only date you, but will not marry you. I would advise that you forget looking for any clues to marry a rich guy. And by the way, you could make yourself to become a rich person with $500k annual income. This has better chance than finding a rich fool.

Hope this reply helps.

signed,

J.P. Morgan CEO

Source: https://www.wallstreetoasis.com/forums/a-reply-from-ceo-of-jp-morgan-to-a-pretty-girl-seeking-a-rich-husband

Also found on several other websites.

And thus, there are two categories left, the unicorn zone, below 5 hot and 8–10 crazy, which the man explaining the hot crazy matrix claims does not exist. What is unexplained in the hot crazy matrix is that feminine energy is what drives the "craziness" on the crazy axis, and the men in the video explains that "unicorns" with 8–10 hot and below a 5 crazy do not exist in nature. Feminine energy is too abundant, too crazy, and to have a hot, depolarized woman who is more masculine than feminine leads us into the next category.

Lastly is the tranny zone, below 4 crazy and 8–10 hot, which makes sense because she really is a "dude disguised as a woman," so we are back into predictable masculine energy and the feminine energy is gone.

> *"Women want the most alpha male out of the 50 men they know, and men want the hottest woman he can tolerate."*

STEFAN AARNIO

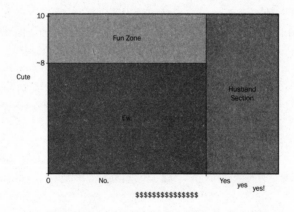

When the hot crazy matrix is reversed to a woman's perspective on choosing a man, it's much simpler because men are much simpler.

The two axes for women are cute (physical attractiveness) and money, which represents power in today's modern world.

Women have a large no-go zone, under 8 cute and no money. So there really are only two options for women:

1) The fun zone full of cute guys with no money. Think of the club, the DJs, pretty boys, the dudes who lift weights all day and go tanning. These men are temporary distractions for women; they are fun, but women know that they are not long-term stable options.

2) The husband zone, which is after a certain amount of money, and it doesn't matter if you are cute or not—think of gold diggers. If you are rich and powerful enough, it doesn't matter how cute you are. Some people might think this is sad, but why be sad? It doesn't really matter. Women are exchanging their limited sexual and life-giving force for power, which in today's world is money. It's a trade. Why not get the best trade for what you have? This seems rational; we all want to negotiate the best deal for ourselves.

This chart fits in perfectly with feminine energy wanting masculine energy. A man's purpose is his work, which creates money, and women want a purposeful man. Sure, they can have fun with a pretty boy and have some sex and go on trips, but ultimately women want a man with a strong purpose who is living his values and has reached a point of success to support her and her offspring. This is completely natural biologically. A man who is living his purpose, doing his work, and monetizing that work properly will of course have money. He may not have all the money in the world, but he can be the master of his domain and have enough money to be a long-term stable partner.

CHAPTER 15
ON SELECTING A WOMAN

"Show me the woman he sleeps with and I will tell you his valuation of himself. No matter what corruption he's taught about the virtue of selflessness, sex is the most profoundly selfish of all acts, an act which he cannot perform for any motive but his own enjoyment—just try to think of performing it in a spirit of selfless charity!—an act which is not possible in self-abasement, only in self-exaltation, only in the confidence of being desired and being worthy of desire. It is an act that forces him to stand naked in spirit, as well as in body, and to accept his real ego as, his standard of value.

He will always be attracted to the woman who reflects his deepest vision of himself, the woman whose surrender permits him to experience—or to fake—a sense of self-esteem. The man who is proudly certain of his own value, will want the highest type of woman he can find, the woman he admires, the strongest, the hardest to conquer—because only the possession of a heroine will give him the sense of an achievement, not the possession of a brainless slut."

Ayn Rand

I have formatted this section into a checklist that you can use to evaluate any woman on key points that are important for a valuable long-term relationship.

☐   What are her top 10 values vs. what are your top 10 values? Do you share the same values? Happiness is living your values. If you have a mismatch of values, happiness will be difficult to achieve long term.

☐   Do her virtues match your virtues in kind and magnitude? If you are opposites maybe you have different virtues; in that case, are her virtues equal opposites to yours? Virtues are the intrinsic good in a woman; vices are the opposites of virtues. Choose a woman with virtue and value besides her body and sex. You can get sex and a hot body anywhere, but virtue is hard to find in today's unvirtuous world.

☐   Do you have compatible beliefs on money, sex, religion, and politics? These are usually explosive topics that can create serious friction if they are not compatible.

☐   When you do have sex with her, how good is the sex? Good, great, best? Is it epic sex that you will talk about in the old folks home after you have lost your mind and can only remember the epic sex you used to have? If you haven't had sex with her, will you ever get to know before you marry her? We live in a "try before you buy" culture today, and sex is important; know what you are getting into. Note: the women that I have had the best sex with were bad choices for long-term partners; you certainly don't want to base your decision on sex alone, but 8/10 sex minimum is where you want to be. Women who give you 11/10 sex are dangerous, and you are playing with fire; just like the hot crazy matrix, 11/10 sex is in the danger zone.

☐   Have you met her mother? Do you think her mother is attractive? She will look exactly like her mother in 20–30 years. Are you okay with that?

☐ Do you make more money than her? Having your woman making more money than you will be a constant source of friction in your relationship, and she will emasculate you and beat on you if that problem persists. If she earns more, can you increase your earnings? You might need to go for a woman who makes less money because women biologically hate making more money than their men. I think this is a real factor that people try to deny in today's world. Make more money than your woman or you will be emasculated.

☐ Does she push and inspire you to do better in your purpose? A woman of higher value will push you towards your own higher value and make you into the best version of yourself. A woman of lower value will drag you down to her level. Aim for a woman of higher value to push you towards optimal greatness.

☐ Are you older than she is? Statistics show that men have greatest success staying married to a woman no more than 9 years younger, and women have success in staying married as long as their man is no more than 2 years younger. Obey these rules for the lowest chances of a divorce. Couples of the same age have the lowest chance of divorce.

☐ Do you connect in the 4 parts of being a human—mind, body, spirit, emotions?

☐ Can you live with her weaknesses? No one is perfect. Embracing the weaknesses of another person is a huge part of any successful relationship, whether in love or business.

☐ If you want children, does she have the ability and affinity to be a mother? Is she the appropriate age to bear children if you want them? What is her education level? Your children's education typically will not surpass the mother's education level. If she is uneducated, so will your children be. If she is highly educated, so will your children become. What are your values on education?

Young Women Offer You a Special Energy

*"In general, youth in a woman bespeaks radiant, unobstructed,
and refreshing feminine energy. A young woman tends to be
less compromised by masculine layers of functional protection
built up over years of need. Traditionally, young women were
understood to offer a man a particularly rejuvenative quality
of energy. Older women may maintain, or even increase,
the freshness and radiance of their energy, but it is rare."*

DEIDA, THE WAY OF THE SUPERIOR MAN

☐ If she already has children, are you willing to take on her children and be a stepdad? Personally, I will not take on anyone's children unless (1) it turns out I'm infertile, or (2) perhaps I would consider a highly virtuous and faithful widow with children. Women who have children from divorce or other relational problems are disqualified for me. They couldn't hold it together with the other guy, so how are they going to be different for you? Can you deal with other people thinking you are a cuck for looking after her kids? It's a noble idea to look after someone else's kids, but nice guys finish last.

Allow Older Women Their Magic

*"Men should support older women in their wisdom, power,
and intuitive and healing capacities. Men should not
degrade older women by demanding or desiring them to be
like young women. There should be no such comparison.
Each age of woman has its own value, and the transition
from superficial shine to deep radiance is inevitable."*

DEIDA, THE WAY OF THE SUPERIOR MAN

☐ Does she have the ability to complement you and offset your weaknesses and downfalls?

☐ Is there evidence that she is a strong woman with an ability to be loyal and stick through hard times? Will she abandon you if things get hard? If she has divorced parents, divorce is an option in her mind. If Mom and Dad are still together in her family, divorce does not exist in her mind, and she is more likely to "work it out" with you rather than jump straight to a divorce.

☐ Does she have a high degree of pedigree? Was she well bred? Who are her parents? Are they drunk losers beating each other up in a dark alley somewhere or are they reasonable people who have raised a good daughter? Does she even know who her parents are? This is a major question in the modern world. A lot of men and women don't know one or either parent well.

☐ Does she have a relatively similar background and upbringing as you? This is important because it determines what is "normal for her" and "normal for you." People always revert back to whatever they think is normal. If she came from a house with yelling, screaming, beatings, and drinking, she will want to recreate "the normal" in your home. If she came from a nice family that was civil and loving, she will bring that normality into your home. What is normal for her? Does it match your normal?

☐ Does she remind you of your mother? Men are always trying to marry their mothers, because your mother represents the original and perfect woman in your mind. Mother was first; mother is the perfect archetype; does she match your idea of Mom?

☐ Does she have a history of relatively low emotional pain or trauma and a low number of sexual partners? The more pain and trauma a woman must deal with, the more damage and baggage you must deal with. A long history of sexual partners also brings much more damage to the table. Do you want to be dealing with damage control all day? Or would you rather work with a clean slate?

The million-dollar question: are we really meant to be with one woman forever? Does marriage really make sense in today's world?

Are we really meant to be with one woman forever? This is a tough question to answer. As a man you will always want more than one woman; that is the nature of being a man. There are four parts to a human being—physical, mental, emotional, and spiritual—and I think that when you consider staying with one woman forever, it violates our animal urges in the physical, mental, and emotional realms. If we let those parts of us decide how to live our lives, then we will want and act on having multiple women.

However, I believe the true benefits and value from having a deep relationship with one woman over time feed the needs of the spirit and the soul. Going deep with one woman is what will enrich your life the most and give you the most power with the least amount of problems. This is why the religions of the world promote monogamy; there is power in it, spiritual power that brings physical power, mental power, and emotional power as well. It also brings healing powers through the battery effect when love, sex, and adoration are mixed.

On the secular side, *Think and Grow Rich* by Napoleon Hill suggests that much of man's power comes from the power of love for his woman. Not his harem.

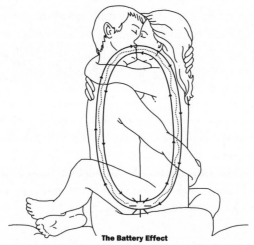

The Battery Effect

When two people have sex within adoration/love the heart opens, and the energy between both of them give and receive. This transfer of energy can transmute emotional trauma, unlock information within your DNA, align you with your higher self, and bring pleasure all at the same time. Instead of feeling drained afterwards, you glow feeling replenished on a spiritual, physical, and mental level.

"Marriages, not blessed with the eternal affinity of love, properly balanced and proportioned, with sex, cannot be happy ones—and seldom endure. Love, alone, will not bring happiness in marriage, nor will sex alone. When these two beautiful emotions are blended, marriage may bring about a state of mind, closest to the spiritual that one may ever know on this earthly plane.

When the emotion of romance is added to those of love and sex, the obstructions between the finite mind of man and Infinite Intelligence are removed.

Then a genius has been born!"

Napoleon Hill

From firsthand experience, the most successful times in my life have either been (1) in a committed loving relationship with one woman, or (2) single and celibate.

The least successful times, the times of loss, the times of confusion, the times of stagnant or going backwards in my life came from times of multiple women and multiple girlfriends.

You can live your life any way you want. You must choose what is most important in your life: your purpose or your pleasure. Sticking with one women whom you love for sex, love, and adoration mixed together will bring you to levels you could never imagine, while loveless sex unto itself is draining. It's best to know your purpose and have yourself defined before you start complicating your life with other people, especially women.

"To say 'I love you' one must know first how to say the 'I.'"

Ayn Rand, *The Fountainhead*

Perhaps try both and decide for yourself. Just like touching a hot stove to know that it burns, to learn firsthand is sometimes best.

You decide; it's up to you.

"Love is blind, they say; sex is impervious to reason and mocks the power of all philosophers. But, in fact, a person's sexual choice is the result and sum of their fundamental convictions. Tell me what a person finds sexually attractive and I will tell you their entire philosophy of life. Show me the person they sleep with and I will tell you their valuation of themselves. No matter what corruption they're taught about the virtue of selflessness, sex is the most profoundly selfish of all acts, an act which they cannot perform for any motive but their own enjoyment—just try to think of performing it in a spirit of selfless charity!—an act which is not possible in self-abasement, only in self-exultation, only on the confidence of being desired and being worthy of desire. It is an act that forces them to stand naked in spirit, as well as in body, and accept their real ego as their standard of value. They will always be attracted to the person who reflects their deepest vision of themselves, the person whose surrender permits them to experience—or to fake —a sense of self-esteem ... Love is our response to our highest values—and can be nothing else."

AYN RAND

CHAPTER 16
HYPERGAMY
Everyone Wants to Trade Up.

"He who is not contented with what he has, would not be contented with what he would like to have."

SOCRATES

Sexual Market Value: The Market for Promiscuity by: Stefan Molyneux

https://www.youtube.com/watch?v=8J59XD9x_Vc

One Sunday afternoon I put on an episode of Freedomain Radio with host Stefan Molyneux. A young couple, Mathew and Christina, called in for some theoretical advice about their relationship. Christina wanted to practice polyamory, which means she wanted to be in a relationship with Matthew but also let other men have sexual access to her. Their question to Molyneux, modern philosopher and adept debater, was, "Why be restricted to just one relationship?"

This interview shows the state of confusion that young generations have around sex, love, marriage, kids, and what a family really means. We used to have systems through religions and protocols for how to start a family. This interview represents a complete destruction of what has been proven to work, committed man-woman relationships, and this interview perfectly illustrates the horrors of what happens when weak men like Mathew are put into positions of decision-making power while hot and crazy women like Christina stomp on the bleeding mess that was once his heart. This interview is the disaster that we are living today in the Western world when it comes to dating, marriage, and family:

And thus the debate began:

> S: So (Christine), Mathew might not be enough for you (sexually and as a partner)?
>
> C: Yes.
>
> S: Well, if I had the best meal I could have, I'm not saying I want to go to another restaurant, right?
>
> C: Well, the next day I don't want to eat the same thing, yes...
>
> S: We are talking about sexual activity here, right?
>
> *(Christine skirts around the answer of the question by saying "emotional and sexual intimacy.")*
>
> S: Of course, Mathew isn't (saying you) can't have any (male) friends?
>
> *(Christine is indeed wanting to have sex with other men besides Mathew.)*
>
> S: Forget about friendship, we are talking about sexual access. That's where monogamy usually shows up.

Molyneux continues to interview the couple for one-and-a-half hours, and they debate whether Matthew should allow Christine to have extra men for sex on the side. Christine's argument for wanting extra men has some holes in it, and as time passes and Stefan explores their argument, Christine's logical argument for wanting extra men starts to implode on itself.

Christine is being evasive about her motives but claims she wants to see other men besides Mathew. Mathew says he loves Christine and thinks she's great and doesn't want her to see other men but will support her in doing so.

S: Do you want to have kids one day?

(Both say "yes we do.")

Molyneux then drills down on the downsides of having multiple men coming over to fuck Christine while Matt is in the same house looking after the kids.

Molyneux explains that child abuse rates go up 30–32 times with weird nonbiological stepfathers or unrelated boyfriends in the house. The taboos of incest aren't there.

Other outside men besides Matt don't want to have sex with Christine while the kids are watching *The Little Mermaid*.

Matthew and Christine go on with some half-baked argument that Christine fucking multiple men on the side will somehow enhance and enrich the children's lives by having multiple fathers.

Christine wants to stay with Matthew to mitigate her sexual downside, but she wants to explore other men for potential sexual upside at the same time.

Molyneux takes no bullshit: "No, this is about sex. You want to have sex with other men, not have other people in your life ... There must be some mismatch. Matthew, you must feel that you have to compromise to keep your value with Christina. If Christina were like that with me (wanting extra sexual partners in a monogamous sexual relationship with me), I would say, "No, not like that, not in a million years ..." Matthew, the only reason why you are considering this is because you feel you aren't bringing enough to the table, so you feel you have to bring other penises to the table just to keep her interest. I'm sorry for being so blunt and that other people haven't told you this, but that's what you need to hear!"

M: How do you know it's not in my interest?

S: For your woman to have sex with other men?

M: I have been considering it.

S: There is an imbalance of sexual attraction here. You are reaching too high up the scale of feminine attractiveness, and you are willing to let her sleep around to make up for your own lack of attractiveness ... Do you think that if you were Brad Pitt she would say, "But I really want to bang some guy from high school?" There must be some mismatch! Matthew if you are willing to consider something that goes against your sensibilities and goes against what you want ... that is why you must feel that there must be some compromise to make up for your lack of sexual attraction.

(imagine) She's walking out the door ... for a sex weekend with some other guy; and you know it; and your kids are asking you: "Daddy, where is Mommy going?" How is that not a terrible fucking day?!?!?!??

On what planet is that not the worst thing ever?!?!?

Sorry, Mom's off chasing penis. I hope she'll be back; she probably will. Let's go play hide and go seek ... How is that not a terrible day?

M: What if he's my best friend?

S: He ain't your best friend if he's banging your wife. I don't even know why I need to say these things. But I guess I do, because he knows it's going to fuck up your life. He knows it's going to make your children cry, he knows it's going to break your heart, he knows it's going to crush your heart like a meteor from hell on an ant ... which still has more testosterone than you apparently ...

So there's no friend on the planet that says "love you, Matt," and now I'm going to express it by bending your wife over the sink ...

M: Well, it sounds like you have an idea of what polyamorous relationships are ...

S: No man, let's get back to this, sorry to do this to you, don't give me this theoretical crap, you're just thumbing through a dictionary of abstract defensiveness ... that man is a bad man, he's willing to destabilize a family just to get his rocks off, he is not a quality individual. There are plenty of guys out there who will have sex with a woman who doesn't have kids and doesn't have a husband ...

S: Her having sex with other men, how is that a benefit to you? Forget what she wants, forget what she needs ...

M: It's not about me, it's about the children ...

S: Oh, my god, do you have an identity? Do you not know what is good for you? Explain to me what is good for you for your wife to have affairs? ... The things I have to say in this show are incomprehensible to me ...

You know I can see pictures of both of you? We aren't going to publish these, of course. What would you rate her on a 1–10 attractiveness scale?

M: We each thought we were a 6 and the other was an 8?

S: It's not true ... physically she is more attractive than you, she's very *attractive*, she has youth and fertility and more sexual value than you do; you are just starting out in life. You have to make up your 7 to her 9 by offering her penis on the side ... "Does me plus extra penis equal a 9"?

M: Are you saying you want to join our circle? ...

S: There is no amount of money you could pay me to join your circle ... you are like a short guy and she doesn't date short guys. But if you stand on a couple of extra penises, then are you tall enough? Could you date her if she gets extra penises on the side? ... So, what you are saying is me plus option penises equals equality in this relationship?

S: You need to have the confidence to say that you will "not concede to a position in a relationship that is going to hurt me ..." If she really cared about you, she would say, 'Okay, it's off the table, because I don't want to hurt you ..." but I'm telling you man, think of her at 250 pounds ...

M: right ...

S: Do you really think at 250 she would say I really want to date you, but I want to date other guys.

M: Actually, I don't think she'd be able to get sex ...

S: You don't think that 250-pound women have sex? Are you kidding me? ... What you are saying is you wouldn't be with her if she were 250 pounds?

M: No, I'm not saying that.

S: So what you are saying is that even if she were 250 pounds she would be able to demand extra penis on the side? And you would be okay with that? ... You can do better than to offer up your future heartbreak to only date a woman ... there's something called the shit test. Have you heard of that phrase?

M: Oh, yeah.

S: This is a shit test.

M: Yeah, and actually ...

S: She's reaching under your kilt and she's trying to determine if you have peas or bowling balls under there ... unfortunately you came out peas. It's a shit test! She's giving you an outlandish request in order to gauge how in lust you are ... (what she is saying is) ... my outlandish requests measure the value of my vagina, measure the value of my prettiness... when a woman is wearing a very expensive purse or very expensive shoes, or she's wearing all in white, what she is saying is "hey this is what my vagina is worth," this is what my eggs are work at market ...

You don't have the money to buy her stuff, so she gives you outlandish requests, and if you concede to them it gives her a glow of value, and it's exactly what nature intends people to do , which is to gauge their sexual market value and to get the highest value possible.

So, if you allow her to have sex with other guys, it's because she is that attractive that you are willing to offer her up to other guys just to get a slice. And that gives her value and pleasure ...

The shit test is ... I wonder what my eggs are worth? ... I wonder how much power I have over him... he's willing to share me with other men just to be with me, damn I must be hot! It's like the (hot) crazy (matrix), ... if you are crazy and guys still want to be with you, you must be really hot. You can be random, you can be mean, and guys still come swarming back, (saying) "that be hot baby," and so these outlandish requests translate into "how attractive am I?" ... It's something you listen to patiently and say "not in a million years, honey... you are looking for the spineless guy down the street who is going to pant after you like a puppy dog ..."

M: I have some introspection to do...

S: Sorry, Christina, talking about you like you weren't here. I'm doing my best to bring happiness to you guys, if you can commit and have more empathy to what you guys actually need.

<<Dead air, no response from Christina ...>>

S: Is she off the air?

C: Thank you.

<< End of the call >>

I put that transcription of Molyneux's show on YouTube in this book to painfully illustrate a point. It was painful the first time I watched that video. In fact, I watched it twice because I couldn't believe the nonsense coming out of Matt's mouth.

I listened to it a third time as I was transcribing it for this book, and it's unbelievable to see how spineless, how lost, how weak, and how dumb Matt is. This man is a weak man and a major cuck. It's hard to listen to.

Urban dictionary defines cuck as: a man who is desperate for acceptance, approval, and *affection* from women. This desperation has led to the compromise of his beliefs and values, the desecration of his dignity and self-worth, and his inability to stand up for himself and what he deserves as a human being, e.g., loyalty, fidelity, and honesty in a romantic *relationship*.

Example: I know John has always wanted a girlfriend, but since he and Mary started dating he's become a cuck. She spends all of his money and flirts openly with other men. I can tell it bothers him, but he's so afraid of losing her that he doesn't say anything.

Cuck is short for cuckold. A *cuckold* is the husband of an adulterous wife. In evolutionary biology, the term is also applied to males who are unwittingly investing parental effort in offspring who are not genetically their own. The word *cuckold* also derives from the cuckoo bird, alluding to its habit of laying eggs in other birds' nests.

The interview with Matt and Christina is a painful display of where we have come to in society where weak men will become cucks and give their female sexual access up to their enemies and be okay with losing sexual exclusivity. A cuck may desire sexual exclusivity with his woman and usually agrees to abstain from pursuing other women. Matt is horribly emasculated by Christina, confused, trying to be "nice," and his woman, Christina, is destroying him with no recourse.

Women destroy weak men; they do not want weak men. They do not tolerate weak men. This interview with Matt and Christina is a perfect example of a woman walking all over and destroying a weak man's mind, body, soul, and emotions. She is publicly destroying him and his happiness and is doing it mercilessly without even realizing what she is doing.

We have entered a cuck culture; the end of a civilization.

In the movie *Braveheart*, William Wallace, played by Mel Gibson, is subject to a law in medieval Scotland where newlywed women would have to have sex on her wedding night with the English lord. This was a form of violence and genocide against the Scottish people.

After a few generations, the Scotts would be bred out, and the English would be even genetically and politically dominant, effectively removing purebred Scottish people from the population and utterly dominating the conquered tribes.

This has happened several times in history where a tribe loses a war and the men are killed, the women are assimilated by the stronger tribe through rape while the children are made to be slaves.

Cuck culture is the epitome of weak men, and no strong man would ever stand for such unreasonable demands by his woman. A man with confidence would walk out, he would say no, or he would do what William Wallace does in the movie *Braveheart* and brutally slaughter every last Englishman he could find and go on a rampage across the country killing, torturing, mutilating, and dominating his enemies until they are all dead or he dies in the process. Eventually William Wallace is captured, tortured, disemboweled alive, and killed, but at least he took death before dishonor. He did not allow himself to live as a weak cuck man.

What we are really seeing in the debate with Stefan, Christina, and Matt is a phenomenon called hypergamy rearing its ugly head.

hy·per·ga·my
hī'pərgəmē/
noun

> the action of marrying a person of a superior caste or class.

As per google

On Wikipedia:

> *Hypergamy* (colloquially referred to as *"marrying up"*) is a term used in social science for the act or practice of a person marrying another of higher caste or social status than themselves.

> Studies of heterosexual mate selection in dozens of countries around the world have found men and women report prioritizing different traits when it comes to choosing a mate, with men tending to prefer women who are young and attractive and women tending to prefer men who are rich, well-educated, ambitious, and attractive. Evolutionary psychologists contend this is an inherent sex difference arising out of sexual selection, with men driven to seek women who will give birth to healthy babies and women driven to seek men who will be able to provide the necessary resources for the family's survival. Social learning theorists, however, say women value men with high earning capacity because women's own ability to earn is constrained by their disadvantaged status in a male-dominated society. They argue that as societies shift towards becoming more gender-equal, women's mate selection preferences will shift as well. Some research support that theory, including a 2012 analysis of a survey of 8,953 people in 37 countries, which found that the more gender-equal a country, the likelier male and female respondents were to report seeking the same qualities as each other rather than different ones. However, Townsend (1989) surveyed medical students regarding their perception of how the availability of marriage partners changed as their educational careers advanced. Eighty-five percent of the women indicated that "As my status increases, my pool of acceptable partners decreases". In contrast, 90 percent of men felt that "As my status increases, my pool of acceptable partners increases."

And thus, hypergamy in the simplest sense is "looking to get a better deal."

Matt and Christine are an example of hypergamy because Christine is trying to limit her sexual downside of possibly losing access to Matt's resources by taking a less than ideal relationship with Matt. But she also wants to be open to the benefits and upside of access to a better man with more resources in case a stronger man comes along. She is not convinced that Matt is the best deal for her reproductive eggs, and she is trying to hedge her bets and play the best of both sides—limited downside with Matt, unlimited upside with Mr. Right if she can find him.

Matt, on the other hand, thinks Christine is as good as it's going to get. She's a 9 on the attractiveness scale, and he's a 7. Thus, Christine is not done shopping and is looking to take an option on Matt, but she will not commit to buying him today while she shops the store for a better deal. Matt is in her figurative "shopping basket," but she is willing to put any number of men in her "shopping basket" until she gets to the checkout at which she will throw out the men she doesn't want and attempt to keep the best man.

The real question is, when she gets to the checkout, will the best man still want her?

In order for a woman to flip the female circuitry in her brain and deem you an acceptable mate, she will need to see evidence that you are an alpha male:

1)   You are the leader of men in your tribe.
2)   You are desired by other women.
3)   You are the protector of your loved ones.

If you can flip those three switches in a woman's mind and subtly prove that you are those three things, then she will be open to having sex with you. In the case of Matt and Christine, Matt is clearly not the leader of men, and it appears that he is not desired by other women; however, he seems to want to protect his loved ones. So, he scores 1/3 on the suitable mate test above, and Christine is looking for a man who is more alpha than Matt.

One of the major struggles with sexual power is trying to balance it in a fair way. Sexual power between men and women is perpetually unbalanced. It is either the man with multiple women, in which the man has all the sexual power through choice and options with multiple women, or the woman has exclusivity with the man and has all the power because she controls the limited amount of sexual supply, aka access to her vagina.

In the case of Matt and Christine, the exclusivity that Matt desires puts Christine into the power position. If Matt had multiple women, he would have the power.

The power is never balanced when it comes to sexual power, but the best configuration is for the man and woman to be exclusive and the woman be slightly better than the man in sexual value so that he must be on his best behavior at all times and treat her well. This arrangement is the romantic love that makes Disney movies and happily-ever-after moments. The man striving for a slightly better woman, not a woman two leagues above him, just slightly better so it costs him some pain and effort to acquire her.

In relationships where the woman is of lower sexual value, the man will torture the woman by cheating on her, treating her badly, forgetting about her, never calling her, etc. I know both sides too well from personal experience. I have lived on both sides of the fence. I have been the one with no sexual power with a hotter woman than me, and I have also been the higher value man torturing multiple women who want to be exclusive. I'm not proud of either position. It simply is a troublesome fact of male and female sexual power.

Hypergamy comes from the emotion of always wanting to get a better mate.

Hypergamy for women means getting typically an older man with more power and more wealth and resources to protect her and her potential offspring.

Hypergamy for men usually means getting a much younger, hotter woman, a better woman, perhaps a woman of higher class and status as well. As I age and acquire more power and money, I also get better access to better women. Life at 31 for a man is much better than life at 21. A man's sexual access goes up until age 45.

The modern world of Tinder, Facebook, Instagram, text messages, and social media have exposed previously solid relationships to the perpetual threat of hypergamy. If you are a man and you are dating a woman, there is an unlimited number of other men texting your woman, liking her photos on Facebook, or even worse if she has a Tinder account, you are exposed to an unlimited number of upside for your woman, and hypergamy is secretly in full force effect. She's looking to trade up, and the same can be true with a man quietly looking for a better deal on social media or dating apps like Tinder.

Hypergamy is evil in nature. Rather than just telling your woman that she isn't good enough for you, or her telling you that you aren't good enough for her, one or both of you carry on in this perpetual state of trying to trade up. You could either (1) become better to meet each other's needs, or (2) break up instead of engaging in hypergamy. It's dishonest to the core, and such is the dating world we live in: cuck culture and rampant hypergamy. Both are signs of weak men taking over the landscape.

Weak men frustrate women in dating and relationships. There is nothing attractive about weak men, and weak men are frequently victims to cuckolding and hypergamy by much stronger and more powerful men. As normal, throughout this book, I keep showing historical evidence where weak men are taken violently by much stronger men. This is true in money, sex, religion, politics, violence, and war. Nowhere is it good to be a weak man. You must be a strong man to survive the brutal effects of tribal competition for your own survival and the survival of your genes.

Stop Hoping for Your Woman to Get Easier

"A woman often seems to test her man's capacity to remain unperturbed in his truth and purpose. She tests him to feel his freedom and depth of love, to know that he is trustable. Her tests may come in the form of complaining, challenging him, changing her mind, doubting him, distracting him, or even undermining his purpose in a subtle or not so subtle way. A man should never

think his woman's testing is going to end and his life will get easier. Rather, he should appreciate that she does these things to feel his strength, integrity, and openness. Her desire is for his deepest truth and love. As he grows, so will her testing."

DEIDA, *WAY OF THE SUPERIOR MAN*

In nature, human men who are cucks are genetically dominated by alpha males and their tribal leaders. In the world of lions, an alpha male lion is the opposite of a cuck. When he takes over a territory, he kills all the cubs to keep the competition down. A cuck man nurses the children who aren't his own and spends his life and resources to raise another man's genes. We are living in a cuck world now; the big strong alpha male lions are gone.

Cuckoldry and hypergamy are signs of the decline of a strong culture to a weak culture. If the men are weak and are allowing sexual access to their women by other men and other tribes into their gene pool, this spells the end of the tribe as we know it. In the case of medieval Scotland as depicted in the movie *Braveheart*, this was planned genocide and one way to completely wipe out a tribe from the face of the earth. Breed them out of existence so they can never rise again.

If you are a man and your woman wants to try some cuckold behavior, just refuse. Walk out the door; tell her no way. When I was younger I was engaged to a very pretty girl, and she "wanted to try other men." I let her, and it was a massive mistake in my life that brought immense pain, suffering, and heartbreak. It was a cuck move, and I will never do it again. I had the freedom of sexual access to other women in exchange, and I exercised it to the fullest of my ability with several women, but the emotional destruction of knowing the woman I loved was with another man nearly ruined me. It was paralyzing to my mind, body, soul, and emotions. I do not wish the sick feelings I felt twisting in bed on a night where I knew she was with another man. I was psychologically and spiritually connected to her through a thin thread across the ether, and I knew exactly what was happening and when it was happening. The emotional pain was unbearable.

Never allow yourself to succumb to such unmanliness, such weakness; be the man, be the leader. When your woman suggests some cuck bullshit, throw it out the window. Either the bullshit goes, or you go. Don't allow yourself to fail any of her shit tests or feminine nonsense that she thinks is a good idea in the moment. Be masculine, use reason and logic, and don't allow the inmates to take over the asylum.

As far as hypergamy, again, don't let it in. If you are with a woman, be with her all the way. I have new policy—only date women I can marry. This really changes the game. You need to go for a woman who is a great deal, not a good deal, as good is the enemy of great.

Do not waste your time with inferior women or women who are looking to trade up every two minutes. Do not allow yourself to become a weak cuck-man of today; instead, become strong, draw the boundaries and stick to your positions. Strong men have always drawn the boundaries and stuck to their positions when taking new territory or fighting the wilderness, do the same in your relationship with your woman. The survival of you and your tribe depends on it.

CHAPTER 17

WHY MANIPULATION AND PICKUP ARTISTRY NEVER WORK IN THE LONG RUN

"The most beautiful people we have known are those who have known defeat, known suffering, known struggle, known loss, and have found their way out of the depths. These persons have an appreciation, sensitivity, and an understanding of life that fills them with compassion, gentleness, and a deep loving concern. Beautiful people do not just happen."

ELISABETH KÜBLER-ROSS

I n 2005, Neil Strauss published a life-changing book for men around the world called *The Game: Penetrating the Secret Society of Pickup Artists*. The book peeled back the veil on a world of men who were meeting in online chat rooms and forums to dissect the female mind and discuss "how to pick up women." These men called themselves pickup artists.

I remember buying *The Game* when I was 23, and I read it in one sitting. I recall staying up till 6:00 a.m. one morning, my eyes bleeding as if I had been doing drugs or heavy drinking. I'm not a drug user, but Strauss's book on how to pick up women was drugs for my mind, and I could not believe the godly powers that these highly skilled PUAs (pickup artists) had over women.

These men had meticulously mapped out the female mind; they knew all of the triggers, the social responses, the statistics of how long it took for a woman to sleep with you—7 hours, by the way. How many times would she have to IOI (indications of interest) you before you could kiss her. The book was fascinating, and I tried almost everything in the book in the real world—and it all worked like magic!

The story in *The Game* was of Neil Strauss and his entry into the world of pickup artistry. He met one of the gurus of the industry—a man named Mystery. Mystery is the best pickup artist out there. Neil learns from Mystery, David DiAngelo (real name Eben Pagen), a guy named Tyler Durden, and an entire slew of men who pick up women for sport.

These men are addicted to "the game," and part of it is really cool and fascinating that these men can play women like a Stradivarius violin, but eventually the music stops and the dark side of PUA is exposed. As the story goes on, you start to see these pickup artists have major problems in their lives. They move into a mansion in LA called "Project Hollywood." The men fall in love with certain women, other men have horrible breakups, most men are "found out" by their girlfriends that they aren't as cool or interesting as they were made out to be in their PUA routines, and somehow the coolness of pickup artists starts to unravel like a mummy.

The plot of the true story continues into a death spiral as the men who practice pickup artistry seem to go through the same in a predicable sequence:

1) Nerdy guy can't get women but wants women.
2) Nerdy guy signs up to become a pickup artist.
3) Nerdy guy learns a few routines, and of course exploiting women's brain mechanics for easy sex works just like turning the lights on with a light switch—mechanics are mechanics.
4) Nerdy guy has lots of sex, maybe too much sex. Nerdy gets a girlfriend way out of his league for a short while.
5) Nerdy guy is "found out" to "not be that cool after all" by his girlfriend who he is now falling deeply in love with.
6) Girlfriend leaves nerdy guy.
7) Nerdy guy collapses emotionally.
8) Step 4, 5, 6, and 7 might repeat a number of times while Nerdy guy rips a massive emotional and spiritual hole inside of himself that he tries to fill with more women. By trying to add more women, he creates a bigger and deeper emotional and spiritual hole. This continues until Nerdy guy cannot take it anymore. Nerdy guy is out of energy and out of money crawling around at the rock-bottom point of his life, thinking suicidal thoughts and becoming consumed by the massive hole inside of himself by the loss of the love of his life, his fake girlfriend that he acquired by fake PUA techniques.
9) Nerdy guy quits PUA and turns to spirituality or religion to repair the massive hole in his heart and spirit. If he does the work, he will find himself and his character and stay out of the PUA lifestyle.

It was shocking to read that book and see the pattern happen over and over again to the different pickup artists.

I started to implement the PUA techniques in real life, and lo and behold, they work. Women's minds and men's minds have mechanics and built-in architecture that can be exploited and manipulated for getting what you want. This is true in sales and negotiation (which I have written books about) and also in "picking up" women. I started to go out with different women every day, date after date. I would end up with eight girlfriends at once and start to live a degenerate life where they would all fall in love with me, but I was emotionally unavailable and incapable of opening my heart to any of them. I had a small hole in my heart and spirit that suddenly ripped open and became a massive and fatal wound.

I hurt a lot of women in that phase of my life, and I'm not proud of it. If I could take it back, I would, but I was young and stupid, and I thought that a few techniques or a cool veneer would change my life. Alas, veneer is just veneer. Learning techniques doesn't change who you are; it's just veneer—a thin veil of bullshit that gets pierced by the truth so easily.

Years later, Neil Strauss released the 2015 sequel to *The Game*, called *The Truth*. I loved the original book, so I bought Strauss' second book online ready to be entertained and enthralled by whatever Neil was going to show me 10 years later after his first adventure.

What I read in *The Truth* was disturbing and struck me in the deepest places of my heart.

Strauss was seriously fucked up at this point in his life and was going to therapy after therapy for sex addiction. He had trouble pair-bonding with the woman he loved. He was going to orgies and all sorts of kinky girlfriend/wife-swapping parties, and he kept trying to increase his insatiable need for sex and pickup manipulation.

The PUA lifestyle had penetrated through his flesh and into his soul. Neil had become lost in the game and, like an alcoholic spiraling out of control, he couldn't get out. He couldn't look at a woman without fantasizing about fucking her in the most demeaning of ways. The woman he should have loved and perhaps married left him, and he was left alone in a barren wasteland of orgies and increasingly fucked-up perverts who were wife swapping, girlfriend swapping, and participating in all sorts of weird group sex. Neil tried polygamy (dating multiple women almost like starting a harem like the ancient kings of the world) on many occasions. He tried having extra women on the side. He was searching for the alchemist stone that could turn lead into gold—or in Neil's case—one decent woman into multiple pornstar-style-sex-orgy-cum-swapping-nymphos just like the kings of forgotten times.

Neil wanted to be the modern king, like the king of the ancient world, with an "all you can eat buffet" of hot women ready to pleasure him all the time. The only problem was, Neil wasn't an ancient king who could rule with brutality, violence, a standing army, and other things that a king would need to enforce his power over a harem of multiple women (and competing men). Neil was just a normal nerdy, shrimpy guy from the United States, nothing special, just a regular Joe. Neil was not a medieval king, so how could he pull off a harem of women? The answer is, he couldn't and unless you are a medieval king, neither can you.

None of this bullshit worked. He was constantly falling out on his ass and wiping out emotionally and spiritually. He floated in and out of rehab, repeating the same mistakes over and over again. I felt bad for my pickup artist idol; his story was painful and showed how dark things could get if you took your PUA game too far.

I also started to feel badly for myself. I was a player, I had too many girl-friends, I was making the same dumb mistakes Neil was, and reading his story brought clarity to my own life. Neil's addiction to women and sex was like an alcoholic who was drinking beer for breakfast. By reading the story of this beer-for-breakfast alcoholic, I began to understand my own addictions.

Pickup artistry doesn't really work in the long term and here is why:

1) It's a system based on manipulation of the mechanics of the human mind. People who are manipulated into doing something are just as easily manipulated out of something. As a professional salesman, I know that if I have to manipulate someone into a sale, I will have a refund, a complaint, and although I have the tools and techniques to manipulate, it is unethical to manipulate someone into a sale because they will jump out just as fast. This is seen with pickup artistry all the time.

2) When you run out of "routines" and ways to entertain women, they will get bored and go somewhere else. Routines are routines. You are not a monkey in the circus. You are not as cool as you appear to be when you are running a PUA game, and when the hot women out of your

league realize that you are way below their league and you are just showing them some temporary cool shit, but you are intrinsically uncool, they will abandon you for a guy who actually has his life together.

3) Pickup artists usually get themselves into a situation of too many women and thus too many choices. Too many choices mean no decision at all, and they go through scores and scores of women hurting themselves and the women in the process. This is just plain stupid. It's like going to a buffet and taking a bite of everything and then spitting it back out into the buffet so both the piece you ate is spoiled and the buffet is spoiled for everyone else as well.

4) PUA distracts men from their real purpose in life and wastes their sexual energy. So many PUAs are losers who have no money, no jobs, live with their mommies and aren't real men. They simulate real men, look like real men, interesting men in fact, they talk cool, act cool, but are 35 and still live with Mommy. This is like being cool on the internet. To some you appear to be cool, but you are still a massive loser in real life.

5) PUA wastes a man's sexual energy, his creative energy that keeps him from reaching his creative potential, and takes his real drive out of life, as he is addicted to the drugs of bedding new women as often as possible. This is a rush, and the chase is more important than the kill. I know first-hand and have been addicted myself. It's an evil cycle, and a man can get stuck addicted to the chase like a drug fiend. This is a bad cycle to get into—avoid it.

6) Many PUAs get stuck in a cycle of a pornography addiction as well as a video game addiction with an internet forum addiction, and these addictions sap the remaining energy out of this poor struggling man so he is again stuck in another cycle of addiction. They are like the dopamine rat that is pushing the button on the wall that releases dopamine in his brain until he is so exhausted he dies. We, as men, are limited creatures when it comes to addictions to pleasure. We are no better than that rat if we allow ourselves to stoop a rat's level.

7) PUA doesn't prepare a man for an actual relationship with a woman. It's all about the sale, the marketing, the negotiation but not about the product—you! You are the product! Rather than personal growth and improvement, you are sacrificing your own betterment by merely working on flimsy routines and magic tricks. You become like a dancing monkey in the circus because dancing monkeys in the circus practice routines. Instead of a monkey, you are a man and should be working on becoming a better man every day and increasing your real value, not fake value. Women focus on makeup, hair, fake eyelashes, shoes to firm up their butt and legs, clothes to drape their bodies, and other fake things to make them more appealing. Don't succumb to that level where you are only working on routines and a shallow exterior. Go deep on yourself. It's more important to you as a man, your purpose, your masculine essence and to your woman and to your tribe in the long run.

"Not my monkey, not my circus."

POLISH PROVERB

I know these problems because I have experienced them firsthand myself. I have also read the stories of Neil Struass, who had much bigger versions of the same problems.

"Whenever you are about to find fault with someone, ask yourself the following question: what fault of mine most nearly resembles the one I am about to criticize?"

MARCUS AURELIUS

In my own life, while I was dating too many women, there was one girl I wanted to have a relationship with. In the perfect vision of hindsight, she was paranoid about the other women I was seeing, and rightfully so. Some of these women were hot and crazy, and she was worried that they would show up and attack her in some way. I now understand her feelings; it's totally normal. People do crazy things when they are in love. I even got rid of the other women on two occasions, all of them, but she didn't trust me anymore, and I probably deserved it.

In the end I lost her, the one girl I wanted. I lost two years of my life and was left lonely, heartbroken, and still unable to learn my lesson. I had chosen her, but she didn't choose me because of who I had become by chasing women, debasing my purpose, and feeding my addictions for the rush and the chase of pickup artistry.

Choose a Woman Who Chooses You

"If a man wants a woman who doesn't want him, he cannot win. His neediness will undermine any possible relationship, and his woman will never be able to trust him. A man must determine whether a woman really wants him but is playing hard to get, or whether she really doesn't want him. If she doesn't want him, he should immediately cease pursuing her and deal with his pain by himself."

DEIDA, *WAY OF THE SUPERIOR MAN*

Today, as I type this, I'm 31, and I see families and married people around me. I see my married and successful business coaching clients raising children with good wives. I think to myself, "I should be doing that too right now. I would like to be married with kids right now." But my actions have spoken louder than words.

I got caught up in the PUA trap, and thus I am not where I want to be in my personal life with women right now. As I type this I am single and celibate, staying away from women for a very long time. It has given me clarity on the situation, and I own my mistakes.

The thing about making mistakes is you always think you are doing the smartest and best thing at the time of your transgression. Afterwards you get to learn the lesson if you choose to accept it.

"A man has only one escape from his old self: To see a different self in the mirror of some woman's eyes."

CLARE BOOTHE LUCE, *THE WOMEN*

If you own your mistakes and own your situation, that is the only way you can really learn and move forward.

"You can never solve a problem you do not own."

UNKNOWN

So here I am, eight years after studying PUA, kind of fucked up, emotionally unavailable, failed with the last girl I really wanted, fasting my sins out in the jungle, and typing this book out in a moment of clarity. Would I study PUA again? I'm not sure; it is a highly seductive subject, a dark art with untold power to a young man who wants women and sex (which is all young men).

When I consider my time studying PUA and having too many girlfriends, I realize that it has caused an incalculable amount of damage. I feel as though I should be married to a woman I love right now and maybe even have some kids. I feel that those things greatly enrich a man's life, empower him, and bring him to higher levels of performance in every way when done right. I see the evidence all around me. As a successful business and real estate coach, my best performing clients are married men with kids. These men are stronger, smarter, and generally perform better at work and at home. Their family, their wife, and their kid, strengthen their power and purpose in life. I see it every day, over and over again. These men have more power, more resolve, more energy and strength than single men or men who are dating but not married. The source of a happily married man's power is his wife. She heals him, fixes him back up through the battery effect, and sends him back out into battle.

I played with fire, and I got burned. Do I blame Strauss and Mystery and all the other guys I studied? Hell no, I own it. It was interesting; at times it was fun. It's not their fault; many of them had similar spiritual awakenings through the pain and suffering of the PUA journey. Would I recommend studying PUA to young men?

No.

Instead, work on your divine masculine essence—your purpose—and women will be attracted to your real value by default. They will stay with you because of the real value you have as a man. It's a simple concept; increase your real value and you will attract real value in return.

I have always practiced this in my business, but not in my personal life. I own it, and I'm changing it. Writing this book on what it takes to be a strong man is part of the catharsis and recovery from the mistakes I made studying and succeeding in PUA.

PUA is a zeitgeist—like Donald Trump as president—it's a sign of the times. PUA as a popular movement for men comes from masses of young men not having fathers to teach them about women, sex, and the courtship of women, marriage, and families.

> *"The opinion of 10,000 men is of no value if none*
> *of them know anything about the subject."*

> MARCUS AURELIUS

In times long past, in times of strong men, fathers would teach their sons how to love women, how to be chivalrous and a man of real value who can attract a woman based on his real value and keep her with real value. The fathers are gone, so we have PUA instead. With the fathers being gone from society, I have written this book to be "Dad in a box" to Peter Pan and the Lost Boys who are looking for answers to the hard questions in life: what does it mean to be a man?

My own father didn't teach me anything about "getting women," so I looked for what I could find. I did my best with what I thought was the best. PUA, like so many popular ideas today, is wrong and leads only to weakness, waste, pain, and misery. The good side of weakness, waste, pain, and misery is that if you learn from your mistakes, you can find strength, resourcefulness, pleasure, and joy. I am learning as all men must—slowly and painfully. I just couldn't find someone to help me or the instruction manual on how to live. This book is to serve as an instruction manual for you on the fastest path to male success in life.

My very religious friends warned me of evil when I started to study PUA, and some even claimed it was satanic. I thought that was a little extreme and shrugged it off. Is PUA satanic? I don't know, but it certainly is a waste of time, effort, energy, and money when compared to using the same resources to increase your real value as a man through personal development, going to work, and owning your shit—these are the real things that women want in men!

There are real things in life, and there are fake things in life. PUA is fake. The men who practice it are fake, the women who fall for it are fake, and in the end, the public display of fakeness is of no real value to anyone. Being a man is about bringing real value to the table. Little boys can be fake, girls can be fake, women can be fake, but not men and certainly not strong men. You have to be painfully real with yourself, your woman, and your family and tell the truth for what it is, no matter how bad it might be. This is manly, and both men and women respect a man who says it like it is.

PUA is a door to sin, and sin is a waste of energy. I'm not making a moral or ethical judgment here; it simply is a waste of your resources as a man. You only have so many resources in this life—time, effort, energy, money, breaths, heart beats, and orgasms. Don't waste your life on fake things that don't matter. Focus on your purpose, your work, and the real value you bring to the table every day. Just as I learned in business: money chases value. The same applies to women; women chase value. Become valuable—really valuable—and you will have your choice of women, better women, real women of value.

The trouble with being human, however, is that no matter what you know in advance, no matter what warnings you have, we all must touch the hot stove and get burned to know that the stove is really hot. We never fully take in the words and experiences of others or fully learn until we experience the pain firsthand.

They say that through sin we become pure; growing through your sins is what it means to be human.

> *"God, grant me the serenity to accept the things I cannot change, the courage to change the things I can, and the wisdom to know the difference."*

REINHOLD NIEBUHR

"*Man looks in the abyss, there's nothing staring back at him. At that moment, man finds his character. And that is what keeps him out of the abyss.*"

LOU MANNHEIM, *WALL STREET*

CHAPTER 18
RAMPANT HOMOSEXUALITY
The Pink Elephant in the Room

"Without women, men have no future."

JACK DONOVAN, *THE WAYS OF MEN*

"Under normal conditions, in their natural habitats, wild animals do not mutilate themselves, masturbate, attack their offspring, develop stomach ulcers, become fetishists, suffer from obesity, form homosexual pair-bonds, or commit murder. Among human city-dwellers, needless to say, all of these things occur. Does this, then, reveal a basic difference between the human species and other animals? At first glance it seems to do so. But this is deceptive. Other animals do behave in these ways under certain circumstances, namely when they are confined in the unnatural conditions of captivity, the zoo animal in a cage exhibits all of these abnormalities. Clearly, then, the city is not a concrete jungle, it is a human zoo."

DESMOND MORRIS, *THE HUMAN ZOO*

In zoologist Desmond Morris' book *The Human Zoo*, Morris proves that when the density of any animal, rats, monkeys, mice, or humans increases past a certain number, the percentage of homosexual pair bonds increases.

As Morris says, we do not live in a concrete jungle; we instead live in a human zoo. In the human zoo, Morris explains that in a low population density environment, men and humanity do not experience the pressures of being in captivity. This brings on homosexual pair bonds, self-mutilation, masturbation, murder, attacking their offspring, stomach ulcers, fetishes, or obesity. These are problems that plague our cities today. The higher the density of the city, the worse the problems.

Animals live in natural habitats with a certain population density they need to live and feel free, and so do humans. As Morris points out,

> Despite the pressures, however, the benefits (of captivity in a zoo) are great. The zoo world, like a gigantic parent, protects its inmates: food, drink, shelter, hygiene and medical care are provided; the basic problems of survival are reduced to a minimum. There is time to spare. How this time is used in a non-human zoo varies of course, from species to species. Some animals quietly relax and doze in the sun; others find prolonged inactivity increasingly difficult to accept. If you are an inmate of a human zoo, you inevitably belong to this second category. Having an essentially exploratory, inventive brain, you will not be able to relax for very long. You will be driven on and on to more and more elaborate activities. You will investigate, organize and create and, in the end, you will have plunged yourself deeper still into an even more captive zoo world. With each new complexity, you will find yourself one step farther away from your natural tribal state, the state in which your ancestors existed for a million years.

Another factor that has contributed to the feminization and homosexualization of men has been the removal of the needs for daily survival. In a small, low-density, tribal environment, every man and every woman was a "food getter" and spent most of their time and energy each day getting food. Now, however, the problems of survival are almost nonexistent.

In *The Way of Men* by Jack Donovan, he explains that the frontiers of survival, the edge of danger and no danger, are so far removed from the cities now that men, women, and society as a whole no longer even consider the basic factors of survival. There are no lions, tigers, or bears invading and threatening the tribe, we are sheltered from the elements, there is an abundance of food, we have more entertainment and distractions than ever, and there is an abundance of excess time and energy.

So what does man do with his spare time and energy? If he does not have a strong work ethic and purpose in life, usually a man will turn his energy inward and become self-destructive through engaging in all the things mentioned by Desmond Morris in the opening of this chapter.

"The story of modern man is the story of his struggle to deal with the consequences of this difficult advance (to an abundance of time and energy in modern civilization). The picture is confused and confusing, partly because of its very complexity and partly because we are involved in it in a dual role, being, at the same time both spectators and participants."

DESMOND MORRIS

I had a coach once who said that if you are a pickle in a pickle jar, you could not read your own label. That is why we all need a coach to show us our blind spots. Morris points out that we are blind because of our dual role: being both spectators and participants in this changing way in which men and women live. It's hard to discern causes and effects of things when you are indeed a pickle inside of your own jar and cannot read your own label.

To be clear, what men and women do in their own bedrooms is none of my business. I am not for or against homosexual relationships or marriages or families; it's none of my business.

However, the reason I am writing on this is because this book is on being a man, and a popular choice for young men today is to be gay. You might say or think that being gay is "born this way" and not a choice. You may believe that sexual preference is hard coded into a person's DNA or "just who he is." That may be true. However, what I believe to be true about all of humanity is that we have the power of free will to choose how we live our lives. We do not leave things to chance and always have the final say in all decision making; we can own our problems and deal with them in our own way.

Some people react to problems emotionally, which is weak. Emotions are frequently wrong, and when emotions go high, intelligence goes low. The proper way to deal with problems is to pause, think, and respond in a rational way. Responding is much different from reacting. Responding allows you to think and use the power of reason and your mind, whereas reacting lets your emotions take over—your emotions are usually false.

To be clear, throughout history, any society that has had a high enough density of humans has always had homosexual men and women. How society dealt with and responded to those relationships, however, has been different throughout history.

The Kinsey Scale—Are We All Gay?

In the 1940s and 1950s, a man by the name of Alfred Charles Kinsey was the first official researcher in America to consider the sexual behaviors of human beings and treat the subject as a science. Kinsey was an American biologist, professor of entomology and zoology, and a sexologist, which was new in 1947. He founded the Institute for Sex Research at Indiana University, now known as the Kinsey Institute. He is best known for his work *Sexual Behavior in the Human Male* (1948), and *Sexual Behavior in the Human Female* (1953), also known as the Kinsey

Reports, as well as the Kinsey scale. Kinsey's research on human sexuality, foundational to the field of sexology, provoked controversy in the 1940s and 1950s. His work has influenced social and cultural values in the United States, as well as internationally.

> Source: https://www.kinseyinstitute.org/about/history/alfred-kinsey.php

Kinsey wrote that

> males do not represent two discrete populations, heterosexual and homosexual. The world is not to be divided into sheep and goats. It is a fundamental of taxonomy that nature rarely deals with discrete categories ... The living world is a continuum in each and every one of its aspects. While emphasizing the continuity of the gradations between exclusively heterosexual and exclusively homosexual histories, it has seemed desirable to develop some sort of classification which could be based on the relative amounts of heterosexual and homosexual experience or response in each history [...] An individual may be assigned a position on this scale, for each period in his life. [...] A seven-point scale comes nearer to showing the many gradations that actually exist.

Kinsey, et al. (1948). pp. 639, 656

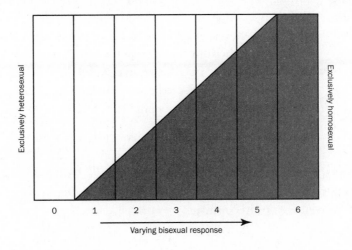

At the time of his research and writing, Kinsey was ridiculed, attacked, and challenged for his findings on the human animal. Kinsey threatened the popular view of his time and thus was dangerous. In 1948, to talk about homosexuality in an open way as he did or to suggest that there was a scale and that everyone was "a little bit gay" was extremely threatening in a very religious, intolerant society like America. America is much more tolerant of these ideas today.

The Kinsey scale shows 0 to 7, with 0 being exclusively heterosexual responses and 7 being exclusively homosexual responses. This was a new and threatening idea in the 1940s and 1950s, and today we take it for granted in the modern world.

When I grew up in high school, the popular idea in the school system was that 10% of the population is gay; that is a significant number of people in a modern country or population. It's hard to determine what percentage of the population has been traditionally gay, as there is not a lot of statistical data to measure the validity of the gay 10% throughout history. But what we do know is that sex, sexuality, and homosexuality have always existed on some level as long as humans have had enough density to support it. What has changed are our attitudes towards sex and homosexuality.

In some ways, homosexuality is like illegal drugs, prostitution, bootlegging, pot smoking, hit men, and other "illegal activities." I put "illegal activities" in quotes because in several countries around the world, especially intolerant countries ruled by strong men, homosexuality is illegal, underground, something that happens, but people don't talk about. Several countries ruled by a strong man mentality—specifically Muslim countries where it is manly to be angry to show dominance, act violent, and rule with an iron fist—openly kill, torture, and mutilate homosexuals.

Slavic countries in Eastern Europe and Russia openly admit, "We don't have gays, we kill them." I have heard that line said firsthand from several immigrants I have met from Russia, Croatia, Serbia, Albania, and other Eastern European countries.

Is it right to torture and kill people? No, but it happens every day around the world in places where life is much harder than in the Western world.

It's confusing for young men to have the option of homosexuality. I remember when I was in my teens and confused. My mother told me that men just like all women sexually. This turned out be false information. I have a type of woman that I'm sexually attracted to, as most men do. That type of woman sexually turns me on more than anything else, and women who don't fit my type I'm not really interested in.

Since I tried dating women I wasn't interested in, and the premise from my mother was all men like all women sexually, I thought I was gay for a very brief period until I realized, "I'm just not into this specific woman," which turned out to be true.

We all have personal tastes and flavors, and I have taken some mild tests online and scored "exclusively heterosexual" in my late 20s.

Could all of this change throughout life? Kinsey claimed that as he grew older, he moved from "exclusively heterosexual" to more in the middle of hetero and homosexual. That could make sense; your sex hormones change throughout life, and your testosterone and estrogen balance out. People change as their hormones change; it makes sense.

What is confusing for young men in the cultural narrative is the way that homosexuality is sold today. It is overrepresented in the media, in schools, in public education, and in universities. Thus, there is some danger of overrepresenting that way of life. What I believe to be important is to see things for what they are—no more, no less.

"The first rule is to keep an untroubled spirit. The second is to look things in the face and know them for what they are."

MARCUS AURELIUS, *MEDITATIONS*

Are we born gay or made gay? Or is man just "prison gay"?

These questions have been asked throughout history. Are we born gay or made gay? Or do we choose it? This is a tough question to answer because it is somewhat subjective and somewhat objective.

The popular narrative in Western society currently is that to be gay is to be "born this way." At other times in Western history it was a choice. I am an exclusively straight man, so it's tough for me comment on this, as I have not walked a mile in an exclusively gay man's shoes. But what I do believe is that every decision in life always has an element of choice and reason.

Yes, there are preferences, yes there are tastes, and I prefer a specific type of woman that I'm not going to discuss in this chapter. Tastes are highly subjective because, as Warren Buffet says, "taste is personal, you put a Snickers bar in your mouth, that's highly intimate. You don't want to take a risk with something else." Buffet is right; taste is intimate and personal, especially when you are going to put a Snickers bar in your mouth. Your mouth is an intimate place, and you choose what to put in there!

What is a fact, however, is that when the density of men goes up and there is a lack of women, men revert to becoming homosexuals or "prison gay."

Men who are prison gay are men who wouldn't be gay with women around, but there are no women in prison. There are no women in prison, and the men are in a high-density living environment, and they need to get sexual release somehow. A man generates hundreds of millions of sperm a day and loads of testosterone; he has to get a release somehow.

This is seen in militaries, submarines, and high-density cities like New York City. This behavior is shown and proven in rats, as Desmond Morris points out in his book *The Human Zoo*.

> So density of men, lack of women can create a homosexual environment, making that lifestyle a product of an environment and naturally occurring in unnatural environments. If humans had enough space, enough fresh air and the perils of daily survival, I would estimate that homosexual

pair-bonds would virtually nonexistent as Desmond Morris Claims. Human density and the pressures of living in high human density create more homosexual pair-bonds. Without density, this is not seen in nature as Morris writes.

Forget Homo or Hetero, What about Just Sexual?

Ancient Greece and Rome had a totally different view of sex than we do. The ancient Greeks and Romans did not have a concept of homosexuality as we do today; instead, they were just sexual. There was no concept of homo or hetero.

This same mental attitude towards sex is shown in the modern world with "gay porn stars," several of whom are not gay in their personal lives, but only on screen. They prefer women, but enjoy rubbing their penises for pleasure (like all men do) and claim that they are just sexual and not homo or hetero. That is the same way that the ancient Greeks or Romans used to view sex—neither homo nor hetero. That idea of just *sexual* without homo or hetero, I believe, makes the most sense when looking at sex for humanity.

For a man, sex is mechanical; if you rub his penis enough, he will ejaculate. A robot could be rubbing it, a sex doll, a woman, a man, a dog, a cat, a sheep, a goat—I don't think it matters too much what or who is rubbing a man's penis as long as it's getting rubbed. Throughout history men have had sex with just about anything; this is illustrated in Jared Diamond's book *Guns, Germs, and Steel*, where he believes that Europeans inherited their plagues and nasty diseases from sex with livestock. If men and humanity are just sexual and like rubbing their penises generally, then this makes sense.

Women, on the other hand, I believe, have a more emotional, mental, and spiritual connection to sex, and they do not have this "penis rubbing" phenomenon that men have. I also believe that women have been traditionally conquered by powerful men in history. In small tribes, the king or the leader would have sexual access to 50% of the women. In a tribe of 150 people, that's nearly 37 sexual consorts, assuming 75 males and 75 females. This sexual and genetic dominance over the group is still seen today in polygamist colonies, and smaller tribes around the world.

In ancient Greece and Rome—strong warrior cultures—a man was a man; he had a wife, children, a family, and maybe a little boyfriend on the side and maybe even a girlfriend too. Sex was sexual, not homo or hetero. But the Greeks and Romans understood something that we are missing in today's modern world when it comes to homosexual pair-bonding.

The Greeks and Romans had a great need for children and families because they had strong societies, warrior societies. They needed men, warriors, and children to assert their dominance as empires. The Greeks and Romans, although they allowed homosexual activity to take place "on the side," did not encourage for exclusive homosexual pair-bonds, which are explicitly destructive to a society.

In the ancient world, the Greeks and Romans would make a man "grow up" out of boyhood and marry a woman; that was pretty much nonnegotiable. As a rule, if the newly married man had an older boyfriend, the relationship had to stop when he got married, and now the newly married man could get a younger boyfriend "on the side."

What's important to look at with the ancient Greeks and Romans is that they had what I would call "functioning homosexuality" in which the men of the day were husbands, fathers, warriors, leaders, philosophers, orators, and from time to time would enjoy sex with a little boyfriend or little girlfriend. Julius Caesar would dominate his enemies by first having sex with his enemies' wives and then having sex with his male enemies as well. This was how you showed how tough and manly you were in the Greek and Roman days. But it was not homo or hetero; it was just sexual. You rubbed your penis and got off. Society had its own set of rules around families, women, and raising children, and those societies were able to function and rule the world much longer than our American empire will last today. This system functioned, it worked, it was strong, and it was intolerant of exclusively homosexual pair-bonds.

What we have today is different from the functioning homosexuality of the Greeks and Romans where there were mother-father families, women as wives, and children being born with strong fathers to teach men how to fight, philosophize, lead, and be men. Instead, we have a nonfunctioning boy-type homosexuality that generally leaves women out of the equation. This is creating a new set of problems for our Western world.

As Jack Donovan (who is an openly gay man) is quoted at the top of this chapter as saying, "Without women, men have no future." An exclusive group of homosexual men, a gang with all male pair-bonds has no future, no way to reproduce, no way to step out of boyhood and into women, family, and children. It's a gang of boys, and without women they are extinct.

So why are the religions of the world so violently against homosexuality? Religions and intolerant strong societies of the past have killed homosexuals to send a violent message to young men about "how to be a man." Why is homosexuality so bad for religions?

First of all, the Romans and Greeks were pagans, and religion in general follows the governing style of the society. It was a world ruled by several city-states. For example, the ancient Greeks had several gods who ruled over local city states such as Athens, Sparta, Phrygia, and Macedonia. This was philosophically different from an empire mentality. Many city-states, many gods, many voices, many ideas. This city-state mentality is different from an empire or one ruler mentality.

An empire is ruled by one king or one emperor. That creates monotheism—one god—in religions such as Christianity, Judaism, and Islam. Those are the ruling religions of today, and our countries and empires are ruled by one figurehead of an empire instead of a city-state. A one figurehead society adopts a one-god religion to work with the power structure and messaging of ruling over the people.

The third type of religion is totalitarianism, which happened in Nazi Germany and Communist Russia, and to a point in Imperial Japan in World War II. These societal setups create the state and the ruler of the state as a religion unto itself, and there is "no god" in these totalitarian regimes outside of the state and the figurehead of the state who is a god unto himself.

So we go from paganism to monotheism to atheism based on the power structures of our societies. The more the power is consolidated, the fewer gods there are until there are literally no gods, as in an atheist society where the state has become god instead.

What I believe happened in history a long time ago could happen again in the modern world. Long ago, likely in the desert somewhere near the base of all religions, the early human tribes probably had a major catastrophe with a lost generation.

I am convinced that there was a lost generation in Western history caused by an entire generation of men who decided to say "fuck it" to the responsibilities of women, family, and children and instead choose a life of pleasure as a sodomizing homosexual. The men of this generation formed exclusively homosexual pair-bonds and opted out of women and families all together.

That one generation was devastating to that civilization because the men opted out of the reproduction pool, which left a generation of unmarried women. The lack of families created a lack of offspring, and I'm convinced that this ancient civilization either (1) wiped themselves out by having no offspring or (2) nearly wiped themselves out and were conquered by outside tribes. Either way, the lesson was extremely painful at some point in history, and as I type these words, our modern world is trending in the way of the grim story I laid out for you above. In the biblical texts there is the story of Sodom and Gomorrah that faced the destruction of fire and brimstone as the people in those cities practiced homosexuality and thus the word *Sodomy* or *Sodomite* comes from the city of Sodom and means sexual crimes against nature such as: homosexual sex, anal sex, oral sex, or bestiality.

To allow for exclusively homosexual pair-bonds is to begin to depopulate and destroy a society from within. Men choosing other men over women leaves a group with no future, no women, no families, and no children. This is a plan for depopulation and self-inflicted extinction.

We are in a time when birth rates are negative; it takes 2.1 or 2.2 children to keep our population level and population growth at 0. Currently in Canada, where I live, we have a birth rate of 1.2 children per couple. This is a negative birth rate, and we will go extinct eventually because we cannot replace our own people. Consequently, we import people from around the world, some of whom are compatible with our way of life and others who are incompatible or are even hostile to our way of life. The new people, the immigrants who move in from Islamic countries, for example, have 8 babies to our 1.2. We will be bred out of existence, much like the end of Sodom and Gomorrah, who went extinct in desert long ago, which served as a warning to the religions of the world against exclusively homosexual pair-bonds.

The promotion of homosexual pair-bonds in a "nonfunctional way," which excludes women, children, and the traditional family as we have today, was likely a poison that utterly destroyed some groups of people in ancient times. And thus, the reigning religions of the world are against homosexual relationships. They know what happens if "every man decided to be gay and opt out" and know that it spells explicit self-destruction of the tribe.

If rampant homosexuality can wipe out a tribe, then is it right or wrong in a rational sense?

"If it is not right do not do it; if it is not true do not say it."

MARCUS AURELIUS, *MEDITATIONS*

This is not an emotional argument; remember, being a man is not so much about your feelings and your happiness. It's about your work, your duty, and doing what is right for the tribe and tribal survival.

"Do your duty as you see it and damn the consequences."

GENERAL GEORGE S. PATTON

History has never cared about the happiness of men or the fulfillment of men, or men's dreams or feelings. Men have usually lived short, brutal lives that end in violence and death at the service to the tribe or defense of the tribe against an enemy. Your dreams, your happiness, and your feelings are not really what being a man is about. Little boys, little girls, and women can focus on being happy and dreaming; men usually must do the violent, dangerous, and hard jobs of the tribe, which are usually unhappy and brutal work.

Being a man is doing your duty to the tribe, which usually means doing your work and leading, protecting, and gaining the trust of the other men and women in the tribe.

Throughout history, men have been expendable. The male seed and males of the species have been sent into wars and killed wholesale, *en masse* in huge scores, because one surviving man could repopulate the tribe or the group easily. After all, a man produces hundreds of millions of sperm a day while a woman's body releases one egg a month. If that egg is fertilized, it takes 9 months to grow a baby and nearly 12 to 18 years of child-rearing to get the child to become self-sufficient.

Reproduction has always been a greater risk for women, and thus women have always been held in higher value and were exempt from wars, because you needed each and every womb to repopulate the tribe. The wombs were important to repopulate the lost soldiers, the lost men who died defending the tribe. The sperm and testicles were not needed, so they were sent into bloody, violent combat.

These biological facts have thus created short brutal lives for men throughout history and long brutal lives for women. Women have traditionally led long brutal lives because after losing a war, the men would be killed in battle, and the women would be raped and thrown into sexual slavery—real slavery—along with their children as a conquered tribe.

These words sound harsh, but we have to remember that every human empire was built on slaves and conquered people. I would even argue that slavery still exists in Africa and in the prisons of America where mostly black men have their voting rights stripped from them when they enter the prison system, and they are not paid for their labor while they work for private corporations in the fastest-growing housing sector in the USA. The United States is a small minority of the world's population (5%), but it represents nearly 25% of the world's prison population. I would also argue that minimum wage and minimum tipping wage in America are also forms of slavery, because if you work the whole year and own nothing at the end of the year to show for your labor, you are a slave. Recently in 2017, in none of the 50 states in the USA can someone rent a two-bedroom apartment on minimum wage earnings. Tell me that is not modern economic slavery? So is it right or wrong to be homosexual in the rational sense in the modern world?

Earlier in this book I outlined right and wrong as, "If everyone did it, would the world, would the tribe be able to survive?" What if everyone stole, murdered, got drunk, became addicted to drugs, was a pedophile, or was a rapist? The world would certainly fall apart.

If everyone decided to say "fuck it" to the opposite sex and opt out of families and babies, we would be wiped out as a tribe within one generation.

By this definition, nonfunctioning, exclusive homosexuality pair-bonds are wrong. If we adopted the Greek or Roman way of homosexuality, perhaps it could be right because we could maintain our society and our birth rates and keep women involved in families and reproduction.

The new question becomes, if we do not promote "functioning homosexuality" today as the Greeks and Romans had, where women, children, and families were still part of the equation, then do exclusively homosexual families work? Can two men raise some adopted kids and afford them all the benefits they would get from having both a man and woman raising the children?

There isn't much data on this, because it's a relatively new idea in the Western world. Gay marriage has recently been supported by the governments of Canada and the USA, and that makes sense from a property and law standpoint.

But can two guys or two girls really raise adopted or surrogate children as well as real biological men and women?

Let me first say that there is no prerequisite for any heterosexual couple to have sex and create a child. And thus, we have many stupid people and unqualified people raising children, abusing them, and essentially fucking them up very badly. So I'm not sure that heterosexual couples have a great track record anyways.

In fact, when thinking about it further, I'm amazed that the gay population has fought so hard to have same-sex marriage, because marriage has a horrible track record for divorce and pain in the modern world with over 50% of heterosexual marriages ending in divorce. I'm not sure why the homosexual population would really want to participate in such a badly set-up union between "God and the government," but hey, it's a free country. You can fight for your rights, no matter how shitty those rights are, especially in the world of failing marriages and divorce.

From my own personal observations about the homosexual population, gay men are generally high-quality men—educated, wealthy (or at least comfortable), smart, good looking—and likely would make a great set of two dads raising children. I'm not sure what the consequences are of having absent women or mothers in the house or the divine feminine energy, but I would say that two high-quality men could probably raise children effectively and better than some of the mid- and bottom-tier heterosexual couples.

The track record for parenting isn't too hard to beat; people mostly suck. Three men raised three little girls on the hit TV show *Full House*, so why not? Although *Full House* was fantasy and indeed a TV show, it could work in theory.

The downside, however, is that women are left out of the equation, and this is where the destruction lies: what do you do with all of these unmarried women?

The modern problem of homosexuality is that two generally high-quality men are lost from the reproductive gene pool. This means two women are lost from the reproductive gene pool who are likely high quality in a socioeconomic way as well. Two families are lost, and at least four children are lost by virtue of never being born in the first place. This is almost like a wholesale abortion of a future generation and could be more destructive to a society and population than a nuclear bomb if practiced on a large enough scale.

The argument so far is: there is nothing wrong with wanting to be gay, but it general is unmanly because you are not looking after the women or children of your tribe, and this creates problems on a big scale.

These issues are compounded by the fact that homosexuality in today's world is trendy, powerful, and cool in the media and the popular narrative of society. It looks fun; they have parades and gay cruises where everyone is scantily clad in underwear and dances all night while having sex and drugs around the clock.

It's a party, and everyone wants to join the party. It's promoted, it's a minority with a lot of power, and I would argue that it's a little dangerous to promote such a lifestyle to men who are "on the edge" of gay or straight and thinking about opting out of women all together. It's not so much harmful to the men, but very harmful to the women, to families, and to children. The issue of homosexuality and women, children, and families is not really spoken about in the popular narrative of society, where emotions have taken over all thinking and reason.

The risks and issues of nonfunctioning homosexuality are still discussed in the churches and religious institutions, but nowhere else. Homosexuality could turn out to be a major disaster down the road for our population, culture, society, and way of life. It could bring a very hard time upon us where the majority of our good and well-built countries become the minority and we enter a steep decline, violent invasion, or brutal enslavement by other intolerant groups. Rome fell and entered into a 1,000-year dark age, so could it happen again? Absolutely!

Who could these intolerant groups be? As Rome became tolerant it fell to intolerant barbarians from the north. Who could the current barbarians be for America? Perhaps Islam? Perhaps Russia? Perhaps China? Perhaps third-world African nations? All of the places I listed above are generally intolerant groups of people relative to tolerant America and certainly do not celebrate homosexuality as a virtue. Most of the groups above oppress and kill homosexuals just as the barbarians of the north killed and brutally murdered the soft Roman men who watched gladiator games all day and participated in feasts and orgies all night.

Homosexuality also offers benefits in that men can work with their own gender as opposed to dealing with the complexities of a different gender—women, who are wired completely differently from men, and this can be seriously frustrating to a young man.

Today, homosexuality is offered as yet another opt-out tool for men to opt out of women, families, children, and the duties of being a real strong man.

So the last question is: is it manly to be gay?

I believe that the answer is: it depends. The Greeks and Romans practiced a very manly version of sexuality and homosexuality that I would argue is very secure and functioning compared to what we have today. I think they practiced sex in a healthy and manly way, and they performed their duties as men, included women, had children, mentored and raised them, and had a boyfriend on the side. It was manly because the men performed their duty to the tribe.

What we have today is more like a boyish version of homosexuality. Another Peter Pan escape, another way to opt out of the true responsibilities of life. You see men marrying men, getting two dogs instead of two kids, and using all their purchasing power and expendable income on lifestyle, trips, cruises, drugs, alcohol, material possessions, cars, houses, and whatever else they desire. They have opted out of their manly duties: taking care of a woman, reproducing natural children, raising the children, mentoring the children, and creating the next generation and real value for society. This type of arrangement is not sustainable and is most damaging to women. I would say that the way homosexuality is practiced and promoted today is unmanly and boyish. The Peter Pan version of homosexuality fails to be manly when compared to the ancient Greek and Roman style of homosexuality where a man could be strong, serve his duties to his tribe, and still have a little fling with his boyfriend on the side.

"Everything can be taken from a man but one thing: the last of the human freedoms—to choose one's attitude in any given set of circumstances, to choose one's own way."

VIKTOR FRANKL

CHAPTER 19
HOW DO YOU CHOOSE A GENDER FROM 63 GENDERS? WHAT ROLES DO WE PLAY?

"If you don't get what you want, you suffer; if you get what you don't want, you suffer; even when you get exactly what you want, you still suffer because you can't hold on to it forever. Your mind is your predicament. It wants to be free of change. Free of pain, free of the obligations of life and death. But change is law and no amount of pretending will alter that reality."

Socrates

In the Western world today at the time of writing, there are now 63 genders. For a very long time in history, there have been only two: men and women. Instead of two flavors of ice cream—chocolate and vanilla—we are now sporting 63 obscure and minority flavors of ice cream, and I'm not sure if anyone can name all 63 flavors. I cannot even come close, and I would venture to say that a PhD in gender studies would need to look at a chart to name all 63 genders. Does anyone really understand all 63 genders?

If you Google "how many genders are there?" you will find some sources claiming 33 genders, some claiming 63 genders, and some claiming hundreds of genders. Quora lists 112 genders.

Why can't we just have men and women? Mom and Dad? Everything used to be so simple?!

So how many genders are there? And how do we choose our gender out of 63 varieties?

This is like asking how many shades of gray there are between black and white?

No one can really say, but all know black and we all know white.

Only in today's world, with the frontier of survival so far away from home in our cities and civilizations, would we consider having 63 genders. In societies that spend most of their time and energy on survival and "food-getting," there is no time to even consider anything outside of men and women; survival is too important, and the tribe must survive and replicate to keep on going and self-perpetuate.

Throughout history there have always been men and women, and they were reciprocal; they fit together like puzzle pieces, and they each played a role. Men had a specific role, and they did what was required of them. They may or may not have been happy or satisfied with their roles, but it didn't matter. The men did their work. The women had a role as well, and no one asked them if they were happy or if their dreams were being fulfilled. They played their role and did their jobs, whatever those were at the time. When survival was a constant consideration, men and women simply did their jobs and what it took to survive and perhaps thrive in the hostile environment around them.

Today's environment is too friendly and is explicitly not hostile, so man with his infinite creativity has turned his creativity inward to create 63 genders that are somewhat meaningless and unnameable to the average person.

Roles are important to make groups of people function. In the group, everyone has a role that makes sense and ensures the survival of the species.

Below are some groups that have strongly defined roles to function and perform whatever is important to the group's survival.

Imagine an orchestra where everyone played whatever notes they wanted, whenever they wanted, with no specific instrument players and everyone switching instruments all the time. The music would sound terrible, and the orchestra would sell no tickets and make no revenue because of the cacophony of bad and evil sounds. Eventually this group would go bankrupt and cease to exist if it could not produce music to entertain an audience or any ticket sales.

Imagine a hockey team with no positions—no defense, no offense, no goalie, no center, no left wing, and no right wing. The players would skate around aimlessly, and this team would lose every game to more organized teams and never make the playoffs.

Imagine an army with no ranks and no roles. This army would certainly be wiped out by better organized armies, and the army without roles would cease to exist.

Imagine a company or corporation where everyone did "whatever they felt like" every day. The company would quickly run out of money and go out of business.

This book exists to ask the question, what does it mean to be a man?

The idea of 63 genders is so out of left field relative to "what does it mean to be a man?" that I'm not sure the two topics are compatible.

What does it mean to be a man is a simple question looking to simplify the overcomplicated, feminized, gender-neutral definitions of what a man is. Where a man has been homogenized into a "person" instead of a man.

The prospect of 63 genders dilutes the idea of men to the point of meaningless complexity. The book of Genesis in the Bible describes the Tower of Babel. In the story, people conspire to build a tower so high that it will reach God. Seeing this, God confounded their speech, making the people speak many different languages. With the words of others no longer coherent, humanity could not communicate to finish the tower. They could not function together and had to be scattered across the earth.

Part of the problem and the reason why I wrote this book in the first place is that it is nearly impossible to define a man in today's Western world with the junkyard of ideals that are imposed on a simple creature like a man. Sixty-three genders, or the need to have 63 genders, further destroys the simple idea of what it means to be a man and fragments the idea into pieces that are very difficult to put together in a functioning harmonious way.

Are 63 genders even enough? What about 120? What about 500 genders? When do we say "enough is enough" and that we have discovered all the genders?

When I was young in school in the 1990s, we had nine planets in the solar system. Pluto was the most distant planet in the solar system. Then one day when I was older, Pluto was no longer a planet according to "science." I have recently heard that Pluto is now a planet again— apparently, Pluto's official planet status is still up for debate, but I don't really care that much to keep track of its official status.

The Pluto approach to planets is confusing. The Pluto approach to genders is also confusing. When you split into 63 genders the question shifts from what is a man to what is a gender? We are now heading down the road to utter meaninglessness. Just like the Tower of Babel, where people could no longer communicate in a meaningful way, we live in a Tower of Babel world where there are so many subgroups and minorities with power and media channels that it seems that there is not one coherent message anymore. This is confusing to simple people trying to answer, "what does it mean to be a man?"

We explored homosexual and heterosexual men and deduced that men are just sexual and that homosexuals were either functioning in their roles of men or not functioning as men but as boys instead. That makes sense. Just like the men who are avoiding their manly duties of getting married to women and starting families but are playing boyish videogames all day and indulging in porn.

But when you open the game up to 63 varieties of sub-men and sub-women, the question of what does it mean to be a man becomes almost impossible to answer.

The complexity of 63 genders takes us further away from the simple truth and functionality that there are men and there are women, and they have simple attractive roles to play that are complementary and reciprocal. They form a unit that can have children. They can reproduce, and this is how humanity has been able to grow and prosper from small tribes of a few people into the 7 billion people of today who are all surviving and living because of men and women.

An extreme minority of people would define themselves as one of 63 genders, and extreme minorities are just that—extreme minorities. They should not be given the same power of majorities because they simply are a minority.

If something is complex, it means you don't understand it. I would argue that no one understands a system of 63 genders, and therein is where a lie must exist. I would even challenge a "gender studies" professor to name all 63 genders by heart, and I would love to see all 63 named from memory without reference materials by a gender studies professor.

On a side note, the Hungarian government recently abolished the subject of gender studies entirely in their universities, citing that it had no real value in the job market and that gender studies were taking away important resources from other university programs and failing to give students anything of real value. http://www.foxnews.com/world/2018/08/11/hungarys-populist-government-abolishes-gender-studies-courses.html

Everyone understands a two-gender system—everyone had parents as a prerequisite to being born, a sperm and an egg, a Mom and a Dad. Mom and Dad had sex, which created life, and you were born out of that! The concept makes sense. The man does certain things, the woman does certain things, this system is simple, it's repeatable, it can reproduce and self-replicate because that is how we were designed.

Success is repeatable. Men and women with roles is the most repeatable proven system in history. The Tower of Babel fell apart because the people could not form a coherent unit. Are we becoming the Tower of Babel today when it comes to gender?

Recently we have violated this repeatable, successful, reproductive, and self-perpetuating system. As a consequence, our tribe will suffer when we encounter a tribe of intolerant and violent barbarians much in the way that the tolerant and weak Rome was sacked by the primitive intolerant Germanic tribes. Who could these barbarians be? Simply look at the "more primitive" barbarian tribes that America sees as rivals and enemies: (1) Islam is in a holy war with the West from their perspective and a war on terrorism from an American perspective; (2) Russia has historically been a rival of America since WWII; (3) China who is America's current economic rival; and (4) African nations are, by proxy of Islam and being "have not" countries, are rivals as well. America has several enemies worldwide just as Rome had enemies at the fringes of its empire.

When we succumb to weakness and to nonsense, that is where decline starts. As the weakness grows and exposes bigger holes, that is where the tolerant group is enslaved or killed by the intolerant group.

Anything successful can be replicated. I'm not sure if people in a 63-gender tribe can replicate or reproduce fast enough to have a positive birth rate or enough cohesion to form a functioning unit over time. Or would the group just disband like a bad orchestra where none of the instruments ever really go together to form harmonious music?

If you win the lottery, that's great for you. You might have $10,000,000 cash in the bank the next day, but you aren't a success because you can't repeat winning the lottery by your own will.

Below is a list of the proposed 63 genders of the modern day:

#	Phys	Pers	Pref	Description
1	M	M	M	Masculine Homosexual Man
2	M	M	F	Masculine Heterosexual Man
3	M	M	A	Masculine Bisexual Man
4	M	F	M	Feminine Homosexual Man
5	M	F	F	Feminine Heterosexual Man
6	M	F	A	Feminine Bisexual Man
7	M	A	M	Androgine Homosexual Man
8	M	A	F	Androgine Heterosexual Man
9	M	A	A	Androgine Bisexual Man
10	F	M	M	Masculine Heterosexual Woman
11	F	M	F	Masculine Homosexual Woman
12	F	M	A	Masculine Bisexual Woman
13	F	F	M	Feminine Heterosexual Woman
14	F	F	F	Feminine Homosexual Woman
15	F	F	A	Feminine Bisexual Woman
16	F	A	M	Androgine Heterosexual Woman
17	F	A	F	Androgine Homosexual Woman
18	F	A	A	Androgine Bisexual Woman
19	AM	M	M	Masculine Homosexual Andromale
20	AF	M	M	Masculine Heterosexual Androfemale
21	HA	M	M	Masculine Male-Attracted Androdite
22	HM	M	M	Masculine Male-Attracted Hermaphromale
23	HF	M	M	Masculine Male-Attracted Hermaphrofemale

#	Phys	Pers	Pref	Description
24	AM	M	F	Masculine Heterosexual Andromale
25	AF	M	F	Masculine Homosexual Androfemale
26	HA	M	F	Masculine Female-Attracted Androdite
27	HM	M	F	Masculine Female-Attracted Hermaphromale
28	HF	M	F	Masculine Female-Attracted Hermaphrofemale
29	AM	M	A	Masculine Bisexual Andromale
30	AF	M	F	Masculine Bisexual Androfemale
31	HA	M	F	Masculine Bisexual Androdite
32	HM	M	F	Masculine Bisexual Hermaphromale
33	HF	M	F	Masculine Bisexual Hermaphrofemale
34	AM	F	M	Feminine Homosexual Andromale
35	AF	F	M	Feminine Heterosexual Androfemale
36	HA	F	M	Feminine Male-Attracted Androdite
37	HM	F	M	Feminine Male-Attracted Hermaphromale
38	HF	F	M	Feminine Male-Attracted Hermaphrofemale
39	AM	F	F	Feminine Heterosexual Andromale
40	AF	F	F	Feminine Homosexual Androfemale
41	HA	F	F	Feminine Female-Attracted Androdite
42	HM	F	F	Feminine Female-Attracted Hermaphromale
43	HF	F	F	Feminine Female-Attracted Hermaphrofemale
44	AM	F	A	Feminine Bisexual Andromale
45	AF	F	A	Feminine Bisexual Androfemale
46	HA	F	A	Feminine Bisexual Androdite

#	Phys	Pers	Pref	Description
47	HM	F	A	Feminine Bisexual Hermaphromale
48	HF	F	A	Feminine Bisexual Hermaphrofemale
49	AM	A	M	Androgine Homosexual Andromale
50	AF	A	M	Androgine Heterosexual Androfemale
51	HA	A	M	Androgine Male-Attracted Androdite
52	HM	A	M	Androgine Male-Attracted Hermaphromale
53	HF	A	M	Androgine Male-Attracted Hermaphrofemale
54	AM	A	F	Androgine Heterosexual Andromale
55	AF	A	F	Androgine Homosexual Androfemale
56	HA	A	F	Androgine Female-Attracted Androdite
57	HM	A	F	Androgine Female-Attracted Hermaphromale
58	HF	A	F	Androgine Female-Attracted Hermaphrofemale
59	AM	A	A	Androgine Bisexual Andromale
60	AF	A	A	Androgine Bisexual Androfemale
61	HA	A	A	Androgine Bisexual Androdite
62	HM	A	A	Androgine Bisexual Hermaphromale
63	HF	A	A	Androgine Bisexual Hermaphrofemale

I would argue that the same definition of success applies to groups of people, companies, armies, governments, and even tribes made up of people who are in the "middle genders" of 63 genders. Can these 63 genders reproduce and become their own tribe of people? I highly doubt it without the use of an artificial system to promote fertility; there is too much variation and too many compatibility issues and preferences.

How do you play matchmaker with 63 different genders and preferences? This is like a menu at a restaurant with 63 types of food, and you aren't sure what to order, so you walk out and go to a restaurant that is good at one or two dishes only. None of the best restaurants in the world are buffets. Do we need a buffet of genders? Are any of the dishes any good at a 63-dish buffet? Usually not. But you can have two really good dishes at a restaurant that focuses and defines its two really good dishes, instead of trying to make 63 dishes to please everyone and no one at the same time.

It's common sense that two well-defined concepts will be better than 63 ill-defined concepts. This is true for food, music, art, and business, and it's general common sense. Common sense is uncommon, though.

I don't think 63 genders could form its own coherent tribe. I have seen no historical evidence of a tribe that survived and grew to be mighty with 63 gender concepts to mix and match to reproduce. But groups of two genders only—men and women—form mighty nations: Germans are their own group, the French are their own group, the Chinese, the East Indians, the Americans are their own groups. Each group can self-propagate, grow, and prosper in great ideas and inventions. Sixty-three minority genders cannot self-propagate effectively over the long term. Are there any examples in history where a group of 63 genders have lasted 200 years? Or 1,000 years? Or do regular men and women take over and the 63 genders are just an artificial construct that are a temporary idea to be swept away by permanent truth over time?

If you dropped down an assortment of 63 gendered people into a group in the forest or on farmland, could you check on them in 50 years and find that their tribe had grown in number? Or would they be in decline? Could they maintain a positive birth rate of 2.1 or 2.2 to replace their dead every generation?

To answer that question, men and women in the Western world are only breeding at a rate of 1.2 children per couple, which is a negative birthrate and already in decline. That's regular straight men and women; they are currently failing at replacing themselves to keep our society alive.

Now imagine we added 63 genders into the mix. We would be wiped out so fast from our own preferences, "feelings" over reason, and the "need" to be different.

Chances are, the tribe made up of 63 unique genders would shrink in size and in a few generations then cease to exist. Furthermore, any children bred from a 63-gender tribe would likely be just regular heterosexual masculine men and regular heterosexual feminine women, eliminating the 63 minorities quickly. Sixty-three genders are created out of collecting all the minority outliers and giving each variation power to the point of meaninglessness. This is impractical and takes our minds off the real problems at hand, such as our survival of the tribe. That is why the government of Hungary realized this and abolished the subject of gender studies. Hard times are coming, so we will need strong men to bail us out.

We live in a strange world today, where every group and every minority has a megaphone, a channel, an outlet to scream at the top of their lungs for special treatment. We are living in the new Tower of Babel. It didn't work then, and it won't work now. In the case of 63 genders, the system makes very little practical sense, and I'm not sure why we would need 63, or 100, or 200 genders. Men and women are already not functioning on a basic level and are already into negative birth rates. Fifty percent of marriages are ending in divorce, and when divorce occurs, 70% of wealth is lost. Why complicate an already poorly functioning system of two genders with an even poorer functioning system of 63 genders? To even suggest further complication when the system is already failing is madness and an idea generated from the mind of an insane person. Why complicate something that already isn't working more? For feelings? To be unique and special? To be a unique and beautiful snowflake? It wasn't hard enough anyways? To feed our subjective preferences? All of the above? Or none of the above?

The big question comes down to, does this idea function in real life? I would say the answer is no. Sixty-three genders is a special luxury that comes from our tolerant, weak, yet advanced Western society where every minority has its own megaphone and is protected from the harsh realities of trying to survive each day in the wilderness or against other hostile tribes. The idea of 63 genders has grown out of the imagination of a human animal that has too much creative energy built up from not having to focus on survival, and the frontiers of survival are so far away that we create nonsense to pass the time.

In our current Tower of Babel, where minorities are ruling the roost, whoever screams the loudest gets attention from politicians to buy the votes of as many groups as possible for the lowest possible price.

In primitive warrior cultures and intolerant societies like the Muslim countries of today, I can almost guarantee that if you even think about saying you are one of 63 genders, you will be thrown into a pit and stoned to death. Intolerant societies are strong societies, and they usually increase in power over time until they become empires and then slip into decline like the Western world.

Our tolerance is our weakness. Their intolerance is their strength. Hard times create strong men. Welcome to the Islamic countries and African third-world countries where times are hard. You have to be tough to survive.

Our perpetual good times in the West have created multiple generations of weak men and tolerance. We are the weakened empire and the barbarians are at the gates; they are intolerant and they are violent.

So if we have 63 genders today, and if these genders have always existed but were not properly documented, where were all the nonheterosexual men and women existing throughout history? What did we do with the other 61 configurations of men and women in the world if they always existed? What was the previous procedure for handling these people?

They do not dominate the history books, which would suggest that throughout history they were not really recognized, marginalized, intimidated to be "normal," or simply killed. If these people are here now, they must have always existed, so where did previous versions of our Western society put the 63 transgender people if they always existed and were indeed naturally occurring in nature?

In today's world, we put the minorities on the big stage, with the big lights. We give them big microphones with very loud speakers, and we celebrate how different and special they are. They are snowflakes, beautiful and unique. We host parades for them, and our leaders, our prime ministers, and presidents wave and march in the parade smiling and happy to win the votes of these fringe groups and gain power.

Not long ago, these minority genders were locked up deep inside the dungeons of mental institutions and were called "crazy people" in the past. Men who thought they were women were likely thrown into the darkness of the mental institutions or called perverts and incarcerated into a prison system. Those men who used to be called "perverts" are now allowed to call themselves "women" and share a bathroom with a real 11-year-old girl, and this is just getting strange. How can you prove that the man is a transgender and not just a crazy pervert? Not long ago he would be in prison or a mental instruction for the same claims, and now we invite him into the girl's bathroom with young girls. This doesn't seem like a common sense good idea. Why must we bend over backwards for any group who screams the loudest?

> "*The object of life is not to be on the side of the majority,*
> *but to escape finding oneself in the ranks of the insane.*"
>
> MARCUS AURELIUS, *MEDITATIONS*

In less tolerant countries in the not-so-distant past, these "unique groups" of people were certainly killed because intolerant groups do not tolerate variations in men and women. The roles are defined when the group is concerned with its own survival. Desmond Morris in the *Human Zoo* iterated that as the densities and populations of humans grew over time, that is where abnormal behavior started to show. Put these same people in the wild, put them in a low-density environment, and would they change? The evidence is shown in animals, so why not humans?

Another place you would see these transgendered people would have been in the traveling circus. Have you ever heard of going to see the "bearded lady" at the freak show? That was likely where some of the transgender people were before we recently promoted them from the side show to the main stage in our society. Rome fell when it turned into "bread and circuses." The Western world is turning into a circus every day when you take the side show and promote it to the main act.

Another place you would find these unique creatures would have been the local eccentric dandies of the time who dressed in the energy of the opposite sex and likely held jobs as entertainers or something on the fringes.

The fringe has always been there in very small numbers. Somehow today, the fringe is the main attraction, and the previous main attraction—strong men who used to be the kings, fathers, community leaders, military leaders, and captains of industry—have lost the spotlight to people who subjectively redefine themselves depending on how they feel that day.

This is just plain weird. If you were to explain the idea of 63 genders to people in primitive countries where they focus on getting food for survival every day, countries in Asia, Africa, South America, or Eastern Europe, the ideas we have adopted would seem ridiculous and far-fetched because the primitive, intolerant countries, focus only on food-getting every day to live.

Such is life and survival.

These people living on the frontier of survival are explicitly not thinking about which gender they are or how much a sex change would cost. They are not trying to convince their 4-year-old boy to take hormone blockers and make him girl. Shame on us for considering that with a 4-year-old who is barely not an infant.

The 4-year-old can't make a decision on his gender yet, how could he? He's only 4! A 4-year-old can barely communicate and was in diapers not long ago. He doesn't even have his adult teeth yet. Letting him pick a gender is a ridiculous idea. What if he picks wrong and has some surgery or therapy too early and wants to switch back because he was confused? That is a disaster. It has lots of downside, with limited upside just to satisfy his unique and emotional need to be a snowflake.

If you are a man, you must choose to be a man, play your role in society and stick to it. To do anything else is unmanly, including switching genders to one of the other 63 options. There is one way to succeed in life and a million ways to fail. Choose success and ways that are self-sustaining and repeatable over snowflake-ideas based in emotion and feelings, which turn out to be false at some point anyways.

Stick to reason, stick to common sense, stick to simplicity; often the simpler the idea, the better. To complicate things just means you don't understand it enough.

To be a man is a simple idea; don't make it complicated.

"If you can't explain it to a six-year-old,
you don't understand it yourself."

ALBERT EINSTEIN

CHAPTER 20
THE DESTRUCTION OF MEN AND THE FAMILY

"Teach your son about god, be all powerful and absent."

STEPHEN COLBERT, COMEDIAN

Since the 1950s, men have been losing power in the Western world. Women have been increasing in power, which is not necessarily a bad thing. Maybe women were underrepresented before? But what has happened throughout this balancing of power process is that we now have reached a point of marginalization of the father, lack of strong men, and in several family cases no fathers at all.

Women are now wondering, where have all the men gone?

The father role has been marginalized mostly by the empowerment of women by (1) women taking on the masculine role of work; (2) the welfare state; (3) the divorce laws, family laws, child laws, and sex laws that favor women and give men almost no rights; (4) even TV sitcoms where the dads are bumbling idiots. This list could go on, but there are several attacks on strong men and fathers, and it's reached a point where (a) there are almost no strong men or fathers left, and (b) if you are a strong man or father, there is disrespect, name-calling, and even hate. Think of what has happened to Donald Trump since he got into the White House with violent public beheadings of Trump dolls by vindictive, social justice warrior women televised on TV. I thought this was America, not Islamic jihad where enemy prisoners are beheaded on TV for intimidation. The crusade to make women equal and more powerful has had a negative and backfiring effect where patriarchy has become the enemy, and there is now a public witch hunt to destroy patriarchy and eradicate strong men in general in favor of matriarchy and female empowerment.

Patriarchy is a word I heard in college when I dated a girl who took courses in gender studies. I also had a female friend in gender studies, and the university was a place where empowered women would walk around blaming their problems on the patriarchy.

Everything bad in the world apparently came from the patriarchy. The word *patriarchy* is of Greek origin, coming from *pater*, meaning father, and *archy*, meaning ruler.

This is like the 16-year-old teenage boy who blames all of his problems in life on his father. Our society is now the badly behaved teenager who is blaming all of life problems on "Dad" and the patriarchy. The popular public and media reaction to Donald Trump as the president is a perfect example of the popular narrative being so antipatriarchal that it is mind boggling. The media was actually playing up the "not my president" movement, which doesn't even make sense. He is the president; he won, that's it, there is no opinion after the election.

In Russia and China, rising countries and rising powers, Trump is respected and loved by the people. Those countries are on the upswing of history and are growing more powerful. America, on the other hand, is on the downswing, heading into decline, and Donald Trump was the strong man chosen to clean up the mess. However, the popular narrative and media in the USA are attacking the patriarchal ruler with all of their female empowerment might. When a society is rising, it rises from violence and patriarchy; when it falls it's from pacifism and matriarchy.

Patriarchy has been the structure where men have ruled the family and ruled society throughout history because men were the leaders and protectors of their tribes against danger and were in charge of the survival of the group against (1) the elements; (2) starvation and death by lack of food; (3) violence or attacks by other tribes; (4) violence or attacks within the tribe; (5) protection from predatory animals, lions, tigers and bears; (6) they were the best hunters and later farmers and later workers in the industrial age who made all the money and the women did all the house work; (7) they were decisive and aggressive in making choices about what to do next in the tribe; and (8) they did not have to leave their leadership posts for child-rearing or family responsibilities as women have to if they have to make the binary choice of family versus career. Both cannot be done well, and women are struggling with this idea today in the modern world by freezing their eggs until 40 so they can have a career and a late family.

"Men weren't really the enemy—they were fellow victims suffering from an outmoded masculine mystique that made them feel unnecessarily inadequate when there were no bears to kill."

BETTY FRIEDAN, *THE FEMININE MYSTIQUE*

Love it or hate it, patriarchy functioned for a long time in history, especially when the tribe had its survival threatened.

Even today in the USA and Russia, I would argue that Donald Trump and Vladimir Putin as rulers come from a population that is "feeling threatened" in its own survival, so the population has chosen strong men and rulers to be the patriarch of the tribe through hard times. When times are good we want Mom in charge; when times are bad we want Dad to fix our problems. Things are getting tough, so we have called out to our dads: Putin and Trump to come in to fix the hard problems.

In the medieval days, the serfs, the working class, would work the land, the forest, the mines, and the farms in exchange for protection from the king or the lord. If a band of hostile Vikings were to invade or raid the land, the serfs would flee into the keep or the castle for protection, and the strong man king would protect them. Survival in hard times has always come from strong men in power who could physically protect the tribe from violence or other threats.

In an attempt to equalize the sexes and bring more power to women, I would argue that we have completely marginalized the fathers of society. Doing so has brought about some destructive side effects:

Statistics on the Effects of Missing Fathers in Society:

- 63% of children who commit suicide are from fatherless homes (US Dept. Of Health/Census)—5 times the average.

- 90% of all homeless and runaway children are from fatherless homes—32 times the average.

- 85% of all children who show behavior disorders come from fatherless homes—20 times the average. (Center for Disease Control)

- 80% of rapists with anger problems come from fatherless home—14 times the average. (Justice & Behavior, Vol 14, pp. 403-26)

- 71% of all high school dropouts come from fatherless homes—9 times the average. (National Principals Association Report)

Father Factor in Education—Fatherless children are twice as likely to drop out of school.

- Children with involved fathers are 40% less likely to repeat a grade in school.

- Children with involved fathers are 70% less likely to drop out of school.

- Children with involved fathers are more likely to get As in school.

- Children with involved fathers are more likely to enjoy school and engage in extracurricular activities.

- 75% of all adolescent patients in chemical abuse centers come from fatherless homes—10 times the average.

Boys without fathers are more likely to end up in jail from lack of discipline; fathers often must take the role of administering discipline in the home. I have seen this firsthand in my own divorced family when my mother kicked my father out. No one was left to discipline my younger adult brother who would scream at my mother, not pay his rent, and fail to pay his loans to her. If Dad was around, someone would be around to fight back.

Boys learn sexuality and how to treat women from their father. Those boys who did not have a father at home did not have that sexual role model to learn their sexuality and thus can struggle to establish their own heterosexuality. Young men learn their sexuality from their father and learn to treat women in the same way that their father treated their mother.

Boys without fathers have a harder time finding their footing in life. They have no direct mentor who cares about them, and they don't learn about male tactical virtues such as strength, courage, mastery, or honor. These are things that their father needs to teach them. If there were more fathers in society left, I would not have to write this book, which is filling a gap for fatherless men—myself included. I have a father, but a marginalized, divorced father whom my mother banished from her home. I had to struggle from age 17 until today to find mentors and have flown around the world in the last 8 years hiring mentors, strong men around the world to teach me to become a leader in my business and several of the skills I should have learned from my father. This has cost me nearly $300,000 to learn from successful men, but I have made millions since my investment. The sad thing is, most men without good mentors will never make the kinds of investments to seek mentorship as I have—I am an extreme outlier.

Coming back to the reigning strong man in the United States right now, President Donald Trump, he started with a $1,000,000 loan from his father, Fred Trump, a $100,000,000 man in his life. And some people, weak people and dumb people, will claim that if they started with a million dollars they would be able to do what Donald did to reach multibillionaire status. I would argue strongly against that.

> **Fact:** Wealthy families, 2nd generation, has a 70% chance of losing wealth

> **Fact:** 3rd generation, has a 90% chance of losing wealth

A wealth transfer from first to second generation wealth, so from Fred to Donald, has a 70% chance of failing. Donald's kids, Ivanka, Don Jr, Eric, Tiffany, and Barron have a 90% chance of losing wealth, but I think Donald and his wives have done a good job of raising their children. I don't think there will be a loss of wealth in the third generation of the Trump family.

The point is this: the real value for Donald Trump was the mentorship he received from his father, and Donald had to step out of his father's shadow and eclipse the empire that his father built. I would argue Donald has eclipsed his father's business into the luxury arena, a global brand, into television and now as the president of the most powerful country in the world.

The popular media and the popular narrative in society hate this success. They are jealous, they hate the strength, they hate masculine power, they hate it when Trump tells the cold brutal truth like a man. This same hate is the hate that has been destroying fathers since the 1960s. It's a very dangerous force and a dangerous emotion to have in our society, and it destroys the basic fabric of society, which is the family.

"The truth will set you free, but first it will piss you off."

GLORIA STEINEM, *FEMINIST*

Girls without fathers are in an equally bad position or perhaps worse position without fathers:

Father Factor in Child Abuse—Compared to living with both parents, living in a single-parent home doubles the risk that a child will suffer physical, emotional, or educational neglect. The overall rate of child abuse and neglect in single-parent households is 27.3 children per 1,000, whereas the rate of overall maltreatment in two-parent households is 15.5 per 1,000.

Daughters of single parents without an involved father involved are 53% more likely to marry as teenagers, 711% more likely to have children as teenagers, 164% more likely to have a premarital birth, and 92% more likely to get divorced themselves.

Adolescent girls raised in a two-parent home with involved fathers are significantly less likely to be sexually active than girls raised without involved fathers.

- 43% of US children live without their father. [US Department of Census]

- 90% of homeless and runaway children are from fatherless homes. [US D.H.H.S., Bureau of the Census]

- 80% of rapists motivated with displaced anger come from fatherless homes. [*Criminal Justice & Behaviour*, Vol 14, pp. 403-26, 1978]

- 71% of pregnant teenagers lack a father. [U.S. Department of Health and Human Services press release, Friday, March 26, 1999]

- 63% of children who commit suicide are from fatherless homes. [US D.H.H.S., Bureau of the Census]

- 85% of children who exhibit behavioral disorders come from fatherless homes. [Center for Disease Control]

- 90% of adolescent repeat arsonists live with only their mother. [Wray Herbert, "Dousing the Kindlers," *Psychology Today*, January, 1985, p. 28]

- 71% of high school dropouts come from fatherless homes. [National Principals Association Report on the State of High Schools]

- 75% of adolescent patients in chemical abuse centers come from fatherless homes. [Rainbows for all God's Children]

- 70% of juveniles in state operated institutions have no father. [US Department of Justice, Special Report, Sept. 1988]

- 85% of youths in prisons grew up in a fatherless home. [Fulton County Georgia jail populations, Texas Department of Corrections, 1992]

- Fatherless boys and girls are twice as likely to drop out of high school, twice as likely to end up in jail, and four times more likely to need help for emotional or behavioral problems. [US D.H.H.S. news release, March 26, 1999]

Girls without fathers face a myriad of problems in life. They statistically are more likely to become strippers, prostitutes, sluts in school, or girls with Daddy issues who either stay with an abusive guy or psychologically seek a man to abuse them. Yes, that is a real thing. If women are abused when they are young, they seek abuse later in life from their lover because it's normal to them. We all want normal. Girls without fathers are more likely to be insecure women, women who are unable to keep a man, and women who are unable to stay married.

These young girls and women raised without fathers usually have a greater number of premarital sexual partners. When a woman reaches 15 premarital sexual partners, her chances of being able to have a stable marriage drop precipitously as per the chart below:

Having a father in the home has major positive side effects, especially when compared to the negative side effects that we have already explored on boys and girls who do not have fathers. Homes that have fathers who are at least present in the home have the following benefits:

- Responsible fatherhood research literature generally supports the claim that a loving and nurturing father improves outcomes for children, families, and communities.

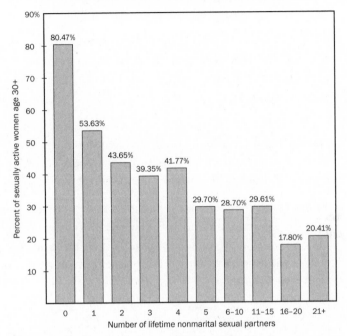

Women Who Have More Nonmarital Sexual Partners Are Less Likely to Have Stable Marriages

http://cdn.freedomainradio.com/FDR_2899_Marriage_
Partners_Study.pdf

- Children with involved, loving fathers are significantly more likely to do well in school, have healthy self-esteem, exhibit empathy and prosocial behavior, and avoid high-risk behaviors, such as drug use, truancy, and criminal activity compared to children who have uninvolved fathers.

- Studies on parent-child relationships and child well-being show that father love is an important factor in predicting the social, emotional, and cognitive development and functioning of children and young adults.

- 24 million children (34 percent) live absent from their biological father.

- Nearly 20 million children (27 percent) live in single-parent homes.

- 43 percent of first marriages dissolve within 15 years; about 60 percent of divorcing couples have children; and approximately one million children each year experience the divorce of their parents.

- Fathers who live with their children are more likely to have a close, enduring relationship with their children than those who do not.

- Compared to children born within marriage, children born to cohabiting parents are 3 times as likely to experience father absence, and children born to unmarried, noncohabiting parents are 4 times as likely to live in a father-absent home.

- About 40 percent of children in father-absent homes have not seen their father at all during the past year; 26 percent of absent fathers live in a different state than their children; and 50 percent of children living absent their father have never set foot in their father's home.

- Children who live absent from their biological fathers are, on average, at least 2–3 times more likely to be poor, to use drugs, to experience educational, health, emotional, and behavioral problems, to be victims of child abuse, and to engage in criminal behavior than their peers who live with their married, biological (or adoptive) parents.

- From 1995 to 2000, the proportion of children living in single-parent homes slightly declined, while the proportion of children living with two married parents remained stable.

https://thefatherlessgeneration.wordpress.com/statistics/

In America, the world's current empire and the Rome of today, there are two major groups of men that are under major attack that are needed to be present in their families and be the strong fathers that are required to build a free and good society.

The first endangered species of men is the white Christian male. The white Christian male is being systematically removed from the social discourse. He was once very important in the decision-making in society. When America was in its glory days, the white Christian male was very prominent in society indeed. He was a majority, and I would argue that America was made great and built on Christian and Judeo values.

The birth of the country and most of the good things that were produced in America—such as automobiles, freedom of religion, strong families, a strong military, strong religious morals, a well-defended functioning democracy, computers, and the internet—made America the richest nation on earth. Most of the innovation and initiatives came from white Christian males. Today, white Christian males are under attack and labeled as fascists, racists, sexists, homophobes, misogynist, Nazis, neo-Nazis, xenophobes, Islamophobes, and any other severe label to marginalize this group. This group used to be a powerful majority, and when it was a powerful majority, America was a very strong empire in the period of 1945-1970. This group is now becoming an endangered minority, and it's also a group that has been getting screwed on several things since the 1950s, including families, jobs, money, retirement, power, and influence. These people are frustrated, and many hail from the interior of the USA. They represent a major group that came out to vote for Donald Trump, a strong man, to save them from their problems. This is the group of "deplorables," as Hillary Clinton put it, but it's also the group that built America and is now being thrown into the trash bin.

The second group that American desperately needs right now is black men. This group has an even worse deal than the white Christian males and consists of the black men who are systematically being enslaved. Slavery never left America; they just repackaged it and resold it under a different name. Right now, the statistics on black male incarceration in the USA are appalling. I don't think that black males are bad men; the black population in the USA has always received the worst deals from the American government. America always tries to whitewash its very racist history, and it likes to forget that America was a major supporter of the Nazis pre-World War II. The Bush family has been linked to helping Adolf Hitler rise to power, just like the Bush family has been linked to helping the bin Ladens in the 2000s. In the 1930s and 1940s, Adolf Hitler was celebrated twice on the cover of *Time* magazine and once as man of the year (kind of like Barack Obama in 2012 was also man of the year). America is home of the Ku Klux Klan, which still operates today. Ironically, though, the KKK self-promotes on its website as a white male Christian protection group, which is the other major group of men under attack. It is ironic to talk about white Christian males, the KKK, and black males simultaneously under attack in the same breath, but such is the state of society. Men in general, white or black, are under attack in the USA.

Statistics of Incarcerated African-American Males

Researchers have been analyzing statistics on the *incarceration in the United States* of *African-American* males as to age, location, causes, and the impact on children. Approximately 12–13% of the American population is African-American, *but they make up 35% of jail inmates, and 37% of prison inmates of the 2.2 million male inmates as of 2014* (U.S. Department of Justice, 2014). Census data for 2000 of the number and race of all individuals incarcerated in the United States revealed a wide racial disproportion of the incarcerated population in each state: the proportion of blacks in prison populations exceeded the proportion among state residents in twenty states.

According to the National Association for the Advancement of Colored People (NAACP), African Americans constitute nearly 2.3 million of the total 6.8 million incarcerated population, and have nearly six times the incarceration rate of whites. A 2013 study confirmed that black men were much more likely to be arrested and incarcerated than white men, but also found that this disparity disappeared after accounting for self-reported violence and IQ.

https://en.wikipedia.org/wiki/
Statistics_of_incarcerated_African-American_males

The black population in the United States has very discouraging statistics when it comes to crime, incarceration, drug use, family statistics, and education. The deck is completely stacked against black people, as it has always been throughout history in the USA.

The saddest part about the current system for the black men and fathers in America is that when they enter the prison system, which is privately owned and a for-profit system in the USA (this seems corrupt), criminals in prison are stripped of their voting rights and are forced to work for almost no pay. This is exactly the same as pre-Civil War slavery in which black men could not vote and had to work for almost nothing, and ironically were still bound in chains.

To destroy a group of people, simply destroy the men. This has been the strategy throughout history in wars, kill the men, rape the women, enslave the children.

We can see the same pattern happening today in the Western world—kill the men (marginalize them), rape the women (women are giving themselves away sexually for free these days due to female sexual liberation), and enslave the children (children nowadays have a lesser chance of economically succeeding than their parents). Give the children worthless and meaningless "McJobs" for little purchasing power. Minimum wage does not allow you to afford a two-bedroom apartment in any state in the USA right now. Tell me this is not enslavement of the children and future generations.

This trend must be reversed, and it starts with fixing the men and bringing back the strong men.

A group of people, a tribe with strong men to protect them, can protect the women and protect the children. But if the men are marginalized, dead, imprisoned, or enslaved, the women and children are exposed. We are seeing the exposure of women and children to the elements of survival today, and it isn't good for women and children.

In divorce, sex, children, or family law, men have absolutely no power. Divorce today typically favors women over men when it comes to child custody, property, and money. The divorce laws are from a time when women could not work. The laws made sense back then to protect women from being cast alone into the streets with no money, no skills, and no way of surviving.

Today women are empowered, have careers, and many can make money and earn more than their husbands, but the laws still favor women over men when it comes to divorce. These prohibitive laws make young men question if they should even get married. I myself am 31, have money, own property, and severely question the legal and financial downsides and risks of getting married. It certainly is not an incentive to take the risk on something with a 50% failure rate and a potential loss of 70% of my wealth at the whim and emotions of a woman.

Why should my existence and success in this world be tied to the emotions of one irrational woman? This is a rational argument that many young men are making today and opting out of women and families all together. Porn and video games can fill most of the needs instead. To bring back families and marriages these laws need to be reexamined and brought into the reality of the modern world and the modern change in the balance of male/female power.

Another unspoken factor with marriage and divorce is the fact that the welfare system favors women over men as well. The welfare systems of the Western world will typically pay per child, and women usually have the custody of the children. In some ways, the welfare system has replaced the need for men as a provider, whereas in the past women with children were in dire need of a man to provide for them. Today there is no need for men at all. Single women with children can be figuratively "married" to the welfare system in lieu of marriage to man as a provider, and thus, if they emotionally don't like their husband or common-law boyfriend on a bad day, they can divorce him, attack all his property, money, wealth, way of life in perpetuity, take his kids, and then go to the welfare system for survival. Women used to need men for survival. Now they have welfare for that.

I take business coaching from a company called E-myth created by a man named Michael Gerber. Michael Gerber wrote the brilliant book on entrepreneurship called the *E-myth*, but I found out that he doesn't own his company anymore because his wife took his company in the divorce. This is madness! She can take the man's life's work just through the emotions and whim of a divorce?

This scares me as an entrepreneur and makes me not want to be married. Why would I risk my life's work and my intellectual property on the whim of a woman? How is it that divorce is allowed on merely the grounds of emotional dissatisfaction?

In the prewelfare days, women needed to stay with men and work out the marital problems because there was no welfare safety net to jump into if they wanted to leave their husband. This made women really think about divorce and splitting up the family because the downside and the risk to the woman were real.

The major problem with the destruction of the family is the current divorce rates that hover around 50%. As stated earlier, divorce destroys 70% of a family's wealth and creates a multitude of problems for both parents and children. We live in a divorce culture now where if we simply don't like our spouse anymore, we divorce them. If we find them unsexy because they are fatter, older, or balder now, we divorce them. If they have an affair we take no responsibility for lack of sexual connection and instead divorce them. If they aren't making enough money or make too much money, we divorce them.

The answer to most marital problems is now divorce.

There is a piece of wisdom that says, "never take advice from someone who doesn't have what you want," but a shockingly common practice today is for people in relationships to take relationship advice from single people. The single friend who can't hold a relationship together says: "Get a divorce." The therapist who is single and hasn't been on a date in 10 years says, "Get a divorce." The message across the board from single people to married people when times get hard is usually: "Break up, find another person."

The costs of acquiring a new marital partner are huge. Dating is expensive, takes a long time, the courtship process is a pain in the neck, and if you are older—30, 40, 50 ,60, 70, 80, 90—the older you get, the harder dating gets. Dating was fun in my 20s. I was young and dumb, and so was everyone else.

In my 30s, dating is a waste of time. The women left over who are my age at 31 are (1) ugly; (2) fat; (3) if they are pretty they have a child from a previous marriage or boyfriend that I do not want to look after;

(4) have a lot of mental problems from previous relationships; (5) are meaner to men because they are jaded; (6) in a big hurry to get married and tie up a guy, especially one with some money; (7) aggressive and want to know if you are "in or out" right away (rightfully so, they are running out of time); (8) aging horribly if they haven't taken care of themselves; or (9) adopting all sorts of masculine traits from having to survive on their own and make their own money (some of these masculine energy women seem more like men than women).

I imagine these problems compound over time the older you get. After her divorce my mother received an extremely rude awakening at the realities of dating as a woman at 50.

My mother used to be a "hot girl" when she was 18 and younger. She dated the alpha male athletes in high school and was pursued by the local NHL hockey players in town. She was engaged several times and must have been a prize back in the day. After she divorced my father, she was in her 50s, had extra weight, short hair, and was entering the dating pool of men.

Women in a study by Match.com always find a man their age to be most attractive until they reach 45. Beyond that, they always want a 45-year-old man who is at the peak of his sexual value.

My mother was courted by men who were 60, 70, or even 80 years old! This was a huge turnoff for her. She was also courted by men younger than I was, who were 23 and wanting some "sexual experience" from an older woman. The men her age (the peak sexual value of late forties) were (1) happily married, (2) dead, (3) gay, or (4) chasing young 20-year old-girls in a midlife crisis.

My mother didn't do the sexual math prior to divorcing my father. My father, on the other hand, is 6 foot 2, Swedish descent, handsome, in shape, charming, and fun to be with. He immediately got a woman just like my mother; in fact, his value in the dating market was very high in his late forties. I would go for lunch with my father, and the 22-year-old waitress would hit on him with his silver hair over me, a young man her age.

My father also "was a pilot" who would take his girlfriend flying in his plane, and he owned a sailboat. It all seemed very romantic.

Since his divorce my father has been with the same woman exclusively for more than a decade. This woman is almost identical to my mother, my father's long-term love. She is the same socioeconomic background, lives in the same part of town where my mother lived, is a resource teacher like my mother, has children like my mother, decorates her house in an eclectic way like my mother, shops at the same stores as my mother, and, ironically, bumps into my mother at teacher conferences.

My father was rejected from one reality for not providing enough money and support to the family. But at his peak sexual value, he was able to simply get another woman that he wanted and continued with his life living out the same patterns he had before.

My mother, on the other hand, divorced my father, lost a lot of her wealth and assets to him, has been single for 12 years, has tried dating but is experiencing the cruel reality that women peak in sexual value at around 20 years old. In her late 40s, 50s, and now 60s, her sexual value has dropped precipitously. A woman trying to date in her mid-40s and 50s experiences the same dating hardships that a young man in his 20s faces—she has little or no value in the sexual market. For a 20-something man, the women his age want older, more established men. Women in their 40s and 50s find that the men in their age pool want younger and more beautiful women. Men increase in value from age 20 towards 45; women decrease in value from age 20 towards 45.

Divorce is not good. No one really wins, except for lawyers and realtors, who profit off disaster. It's difficult to reverse a culture that has mechanisms in place to support divorce like welfare and the divorce laws that protect the economically weaker person to pillage the economically stronger person imperviously with no penalty.

As I type this, it has been 12 years since my parents' divorce, and part of me sees the reality for what it is and accepts it. The other part of me wishes they had just stuck it out and worked on their problems.

No one won, everyone lost, and this is how we live in this modern world of divorce. Fifty percent of our families lose in every way, and I don't think it has to be this way. All it takes is a change in mindset to go back to the values that we previously held in the '40s, '50s, and even the '60s.

Part of the issue with divorce today is that there is no support system for marriage. Previously, churches and religions provided maintenance systems for marriages, as well as access to a peer group of married couples who gave the message "figure it out" or "fix it if it's broken," instead of the current sea of single people saying, "Get a divorce." But with the decline of churches and religion and support systems for marriages, the future does not look good for marriage statistics because today's culture is openly hostile to marriages through pop culture, adultery websites like AshleyMadison.com that encourage cheating and even Facebook, or Instagram or Tinder and other social media, where it's easier than ever to start an affair or get attention from the opposite sex.

Child support is another major part of divorce that men lose on in a big bad way. Typically, men lose the children to the woman in a divorce or separation, but they are expected to pay fully through child support. This leaves a strange situation because the laws surrounding this practice were originally intended for a time when women could not work, and these laws were to protect an unworking woman stuck with the kids and to punish a man who would cast his wife and family out into the streets.

The reality today is that women work, and women can abuse this law to maliciously hurt their ex-man, take the kids, and force him to pay for years. These child-support policies also need to be reexamined and revised for the modern world if they are to persist with the current culture and attitudes around marriage and divorce today.

The current laws also work to destroy the fabric of society. The nuclear family with a mom, a dad, and a few kids is the basic atom of our society and the fabric that makes up what we are as a nation and group of people. Destroy the family, you destroy the nation. Destroy the father, you destroy the family because the children, the next generation, end up living much harder and baseless lives than necessary. The policies, laws, attitudes, and general popular idea that "we don't need Dad" or "Dad is unimportant" to a family are false—dangerously false—but we live in a world that thinks it doesn't need a dad. This destroys our current youth and future youth, which make up the future people of our country.

The weak men and weak ideas that we have prevalent in our societies today come from an elimination of fathers, masculinity, and discipline from the basic unit of society—the family. We now leave everything up to the state: state-run day care, state-run schools, state-run prisons. The state now serves as a figurative husband to single women with children living off the welfare system. The state is so powerful and almighty that it has become its own religion, its own god, eclipsing the religions that used to provide proven paths on how to live a successful life.

These guideposts are gone now, and we will be entering hard times to try to find the principles that have worked throughout history again at some point.

Source on Bush family and nazis: https://www.mondialisation. ca/the-bush-familys-links-to-nazi-germany-a-famous-american-family-made-its-fortune-from-the-nazis/5512243

Source on American Nazis pre-World War II; https://en.wikipe-dia.org/wiki/German_American_Bund

"The strongest drug that exists for a human being is another human being."

<small>UNKNOWN</small>

CHAPTER 21
PORNOGRAPHY
The Mass Castration of
Divine Masculine Power

In today's world pornography is the mass castration of divine masculine power. In Canadian prisons, the inmates are sometimes given "pizza and porn nights." Sometimes the public is outraged by this, but I can see why the prison system would want to sedate the violent, hyper-masculine, sexually frustrated, violent, and prison gay population in jails today.

I have heard that man produces upwards of 100,000,000 sperm a day. Other numbers on sperm counts as per Google are: a fertile male human ejaculates between 2 and 5 milliliters of semen (on average about a teaspoon). In each milliliter there are normally about 100 million sperm. If the concentration falls below 20 million sperm per milliliter, there is usually some trouble with fertility.

> Dr. Charles Lindemann's Lab: Sperm Facts - Oakland University
>
> www2.oakland.edu/biology/lindemann/spermfacts.htm

When a man ejaculates, he expends tremendous energy—actionable energy, sexual energy, and divine creative energy.

You can see the difference in the power of male masculinity and this divine creative force in the difference between an ox and a bull. A bull is a strong powerful male cow. He has huge horns, and you can see the viciousness of a bull in bullfights and at rodeos with how powerful and aggressive these animals are. A bull is usually the alpha male on the farm, and his job is to impregnate as many females as possible. In short, his job is to (1) fight other male cows for dominance and (2) fuck all the female cows in the population. Very masculine, very dominant, very alpha.

When you cut the bull's balls off—castrate him and take away his divine masculine power—he becomes an ox. A big, sedated, easy-to-control animal. A work animal, not aggressive and not much of a fighter, in fact, not much of an anything. If the ox could play videogames and order pizza, he would be living in his mother's basement playing video games and staying inside the house all day.

Such is the struggle of being a modern man. Bulls are dangerous and hard to control; oxen are docile and easy to control. It's no wonder that pornography has crept into the popular culture for what I believe to be a control mechanism over young men to keep them from rising in power.

Pornography, which is cheap, free, and abundant on any smart phone, tablet, laptop, or desktop computer, is instant. There are no waiting times, available in high-definition quality video, and there is literally an unlimited amount of porn out there for free or nearly free, and a man could literally die masturbating himself to death trying to watch it all or see every girl—much like a rat in a cage pushing a button that hits his dopamine receptors as much as possible until he drops dead from exhaustion. Rats have self-stimulated themselves to death in studies, and the modern man is just like the rat—masturbating into a hellish existence on earth through mediocrity and lack of results. To live a life of mediocrity is not much of a life at all. You might as well masturbate to death like the rat!

In human history, powerful kings have had harems of up to a few hundred women. Alexander the Great had over 450 concubines and several wives in his different conquered city-states, which he renamed Alexandria. Yes, Alexander named several cities "Alexandria" after himself; this was very confusing to look at on a map.

A tribal king in the ancient world would have his wife or wives, then several concubines. And as the ruler and the king, the alpha male, he would naturally need guards to keep his concubines and wives safe. So the king would castrate a few of his guards to make them eunuchs so they would have no sexual drive to tamper with the women. Just like the alpha male bulls and the oxen, the king would use castrated men to guard his women so his seed and his sexual dominance could be enforced upon the women of his harem and his guards could not be caught sampling "the merchandise."

Today, with men masturbating into oblivion at no financial cost, what we have is a mass daily minicastration or a minirape of these men, and the results are devastating over the long term.

In Napoleon Hill's legendary book *Think and Grow Rich*, there is a chapter on sexual transmutation. To paraphrase Hill as an interviewer of the 500 richest men in the world in the early 1900s, all of the richest men in the world at the time used a technique called sexual transmutation. Transmutation is when you deny yourself sexual release and transmute the desire for sex into money, results, and real power.

Sexual energy—specifically male sexual energy—is one of the most powerful forces on the planet. It is man's actionable energy, creative energy, which allows a man to create like a god, command like a king, and work like a slave to meet his goals and achieve his whims.

Turn Your Lust into Gifts

"When a man sees a beautiful woman it is natural for him to feel energy in his body, which he usually interprets as sexual desire. Rather than dispersing this energy in mental fantasy, a man should learn to circulate his heightened energy. He should breathe fully, circulating the energy fully throughout his body. He should treat his heightened energy as a gift which could heal and rejuvenate his body, and, through his service, heal the world. Through these means, his desire is converted into fullness of heart. His lust is converted into service. His desire is not

converted by denying sexual attraction, but by enjoying it fully, circulating it through his body (without allowing it to stagnate as mental fantasy), and returning it to the world, from his heart."

DEIDA, *WAY OF THE SUPERIOR MAN*

Usually, the motivation behind sexual transmutation for a man is a woman, usually the one woman he loves in his heart and mind—hopefully his wife—but it could also be the "other woman." A mistress.

Nonetheless, sexual transmutation is important, and I have personally used sexual transmutation in my most successful times in my life. The first time I practiced it, I made $42,000 in a week and wrote a book in 30 days.

This book and my previous book, *The Close*, have been written in the last month by practicing sexual transmutation and celibacy. In the last 30 days, I have produced over 200,000 words of text, in addition to running two multimillion dollar companies, planning and executing a national speaking tour, and managing several internet businesses, plus managing the buying of one investment property per week.

That may sound impressive to you, it may not, but my production, especially in the writing arena, is more output in one month than I have produced in the last 5 years combined. The creative results I have achieved in the writing arena are a result of saying "no" to random women and "no" to pornography and keeping my sexual energy to be used on my own creative and constructive endeavors.

As the famous saying goes:

> Create like a god,
> Command like a king,
> Work like a slave.

If you are masturbating into oblivion and blowing your load every day or twice a day, you, sir, are an ox and not a bull.

You will instead:

Create nothing,
Command nothing,|
Do nothing,
And be nothing.

You need to have your balls to do things that require balls, which is most things that are adventurous, dangerous, risky, or exciting in life. The work of a man is usually dangerous and filled with risk—it takes balls. Don't waste your own balls for pleasure; instead, save your balls for the danger, the risk, the battle, and the adventure.

Ejaculation Should Be Converted or Consciously Chosen

"There are many physical and spiritual reasons why ejaculation should be converted into non-ejaculatory whole body, brain, and heart orgasms. But there are also relational reasons. When a man has no control over his ejaculation, he cannot meet his woman sexually or emotionally. She knows she can deplete him, weaken him, empty him of life force. She has won. When a man ejaculates easily, he creates ongoing distrust in his woman. At a subtle level, she feels he cannot be trusted. She, and the world, can deplete and depolarize him easily. This subtle distrust will pervade the relationship. She will not only doubt him, but actually act to undermine his actions in the world. By undermining him she demonstrates and tests his weakness, but she also hopes that through such tests he can learn to remain full."

DEIDA, *WAY OF THE SUPERIOR MAN*

Men have accomplished tremendous feats, explored the earth, gone into space, created the atom bomb, the cure for polio, split the atom, created massive bodies of work and literature, built skyscrapers, sea vessels, submarines, invented cars, combustible engines, ion batteries, computers, the internet, and I would wager all of my money and wealth today to say that those men did it all for a woman (or gay boyfriend) whom they loved.

If You Don't Know Your Purpose, Discover It, Now

"Without a conscious life-purpose a man is totally lost,
drifting, adapting to events rather than creating events.
Without knowing his life-purpose a man lives a weakened,
impotent existence, perhaps eventually becoming even sexually
impotent, or prone to mechanical and disinterested sex."

DEIDA, *WAY OF THE SUPERIOR MAN*

All divine creation, all invention, all innovation—it was all to have an orgasm with a woman. The original burst of energy that creates life. The divine masculine energy that is the seed required to create life and other humans.

Women have tremendous power in the world because of their sacred life-giving energy and ability to create life. But the masculine side is powerful as well.

I have given great thought to this and some points on masculine sexual energy:

1) Women can have sex even when they are not necessarily aroused or "turned on." They have a vagina, which gets wet or not, but sex is still possible. Because of this, women can be violated, raped, or penetrated by a man even if they aren't interested.

2) A man must have an erection and choose a woman to have an orgasm. If he doesn't find a woman sexy, there is no sex; his impotence will render sex impossible. This is the reversal of a woman, where she can be chosen or raped violently by a man's erection.

3) If a man isn't into the woman, there will be no erection and thus no orgasm.

4) If a man isn't into the woman, he won't even get fully hard.

5) A man usually ejaculates if he likes the woman enough; if he doesn't like her, he won't ejaculate.

6) A woman may or may not have an orgasm; it's up to her mentally and emotionally to handle that, and the man must last long enough and be present enough for her to reach orgasm.

7) The male orgasm nearly always happens; the female orgasm is optional.

Everything I have written above is modern sexual protocol and especially from the world of casual "hookup" culture. But it's interesting to note that (1) the woman must choose the man to have sex, but (2) the man must choose the woman to get an erection.

> *"What is sexual is what gives a man an erection ...*
> *If there is no inequality, no violation, no dominance,*
> *no force, there is no sexual arousal."*
>
> CATHERINE MACKINNON,
> *TOWARD A FEMINIST THEORY OF THE STALE*

If the man has been masturbating all day, watching too much porn, and has a million young porn stars in his brain who are all hotter than the girl he is with, there is no chance of an erection. In fact, he probably isn't even going to call a woman, talk to a woman, or go out. He's going to order pizza, stay home in Mom's basement, and play his video games.

This is a violation of sexual transmutation and creative energy.

The man described above cannot invent anything, he has no creative energy stored, and he can't be effective in his work or serve his life purpose. He can't love his woman and has no energy to protect or love his family. The base energy that makes him a strong virile man is gone, robbed by himself.

As with all addictions and all sins, sins are a waste of energy. This is not a sacred book that relies on you to believe my arguments on blind "faith" simply because they are stated in the book. This is a secular book based on logic and reason and results. I present the logical arguments, and you can make your own decisions and come to your conclusions.

The sins of the world across all religions are simply a waste of energy that deplete your limited creative life force on stupid things such as lust, gluttony, greed, pride, wrath, sloth, and envy. They zap your life of its energy and will bring you closer to death. Sins bring you closer to death, but virtues bring you closer to life. In each choice we make each day, we must choose between life or death.

"It is better to waste your seed in the belly of a whore than to waste in thine own hand."

UNKNOWN

Start thinking of yourself like a battery with a limited amount of energy, a limited number of heartbeats. I have heard arguments for an unlimited amount of energy and unlimited amount of heartbeats, but that seems unlikely because we will all die one day. No human is immortal. We all have a lifespan, much like a battery.

"Do not act as if you were going to live ten thousand years. Death hangs over you. While you live, while it is in your power, be good."

MARCUS AURELIUS

Do you have a limited number of orgasms? Some would argue that you do. You will die at some point. Your time is limited by an unknown fixed point in the future. Between now and the point of death, you have a limited number of orgasms.

A limited number of breaths.

A limited number of heartbeats.

A limited number of shits.

And in the book *The Subtle Art of Not Giving a Fuck*, by Mark Manson, you also have only a limited number of "fucks" to give.

Don't waste your finite time and energy on this planet masturbating in your Mom's basement!

When I was 12, I used to stay up and watch the 18+ shows on late night TV. Of course, the Howard Stern TV show was on one of the channels on late at night, and in the 1990s Howard Stern was a challenging public figure who liked to stir things up and create controversy. Today, nearly 30 years later, he is tame by today's standards.

Howard Stern made a little side show called "porn jeopardy," or porn trivia, where two degenerate men would compete to answer the most porn trivia questions. These questions were very specific about which girl or guy was in which scene of which movie, etc.

Now this was the '90s, when porn was hard to get. If you wanted to watch porn in the '90s, you had to get in your car late at night, drive down to the porno store, walk in, risk your neighbor seeing you in the seedy store, pick out a movie, stare down the girl who works at the store, let her judge you on what you are renting, hand her $5 for the movie rental, drive home with your movie in a brown paper bag, and pop that VHS tape into your VCR, watch the video, then return it the next day in broad daylight hoping no one will see you. A great effort compared to the instant, free, easy access to porn today.

This was a major effort back then compared to the modern world of porn where you can have 482,000,000 results delivered in 0.27 seconds that Google offers you on your smartphone at any time of day. (I actually typed the word "porn" into Google while typing out this book to see how many results would come and how fast).

So these two men are playing porn trivia, and of course one of them works in a porno store. He answers every question and wins the game-show hands down. The other guy answered roughly a third of the questions correctly.

At the end of the game show, Howard Stern congratulated the winner of porn trivia, and then he paused for a moment and said, "No, actually, you're a major loser for knowing all the answers to porn trivia!"

Howard was right!

This guy in the 1990s was a major degenerate, and had his 15 minutes of fame on cable television.

In the '90s the porn aficionado would have been called a pervert, a weirdo, a degenerate, or any number of names.

My mother used to warn me against watching porn, claiming that it was for "weirdos and sickos who couldn't have real relationships with women." The porn epidemic has made it hard for men to have real relationships with women and has made men opt out. I'm 31, unmarried, and don't have a relationship with a woman at the time of writing. I probably fit into the "weirdo and sicko" category as my mother explained it, someone who "can't have a real relationship with women."

My mother was absolutely right.

Today, I would argue that a vast majority of men consume so much pornography that they could probably win porn jeopardy because porn is fast and free today. Anyone can get it in seconds with no cost. We are now a society of perverts, weirdos, and degenerates.

This has seeped into the female culture too with books like *Fifty Shades of Grey* being a #1 best seller. This is a real testament to the intelligence level of most women now (the book is written at a roughly grade 7 level when I tested an excerpt online for reading level). Here were the results:

Flesch-Kincaid Grade Level	6.3
Gunning Fog Index	8.8
Coleman-Liau Index	6.7
SMOG Index	9.1
Automated Readability Index	5.7
Average Grade Level	**7.3**

If the majority of men are porn-addicted perverts with porn in their pockets by virtue of a smartphone and books for women like *Fifty Shades of Grey* top the bestseller list when it is full of sadomasochism, bondage, butt plugs, vaginal sex, anal sex, oral sex, and a myriad of other pieces of kink delivered at an accessible grade 7 level at every library, airport, and bookstore in the world for young girls, what is going to happen next?

I fear to even peek into the future.

The Romans in their decline had legendary feasts in which the population would eat until they were full, force themselves to vomit, and then eat some more. In modern-eating contests, eating until you puke and then continuing to eat is aptly called "Roman rules." The ancient Romans would have a roman orgy, where men and women would just turn into a massive ball of bodies having sex in every which way.

This was the decline of the once intolerant empire that had become tolerant. The Romans had become amoral and weak in their decline. Then the violent barbarians came from the North, an intolerant warrior society, who stormed the gates of the once world powerful empire and slaughtered the Romans, and that was it for Rome. The orgy and expense of sexual energy ended in blood and a reign of massive destruction.

Tolerant societies are usually violently taken or enslaved by intolerant societies at some point; such are the cycles of history.

Just like the ox, men today are giving up their sacred sexual energy through porn, which satiates the hunger of a man, the hunger, the drive to succeed. Too many men nowadays are settling for less, saying, "It's good enough for me."

The minimalism movement is a derivative of the "good enough for me" mentality.

The tiny house movement (which are not tiny houses, but trailers) is a "good enough for me attitude."

This is an opt out of power, wealth, and success that men need to have to be men. I'm not saying you should be the most powerful man in the world or the richest man in the world, but I believe you should always be pushing for your potential in those areas and opting in to competition and avoiding giving up.

It's unmanly to opt out or give up.

A man has to try, try, and try again.

> *"Forward, forward and forward some more!"*
>
> GENERAL GEORGE S. PATTON

The waste of male sexual energy *en masse* today not only blocks the ability to "try" but also blocks the ability to "think and grow rich," as Napoleon Hill has titled his masterpiece on building wealth and success in a man's life.

> *"Thinking is the hardest work of all and*
> *that is why few people do it."*
>
> HENRY FORD

Thinking truly is hard work, and most men go through their entire lives without stopping to think about anything.

> *"All of humanity's problems stem from man's*
> *inability to sit quietly in a room alone."*
>
> BLAISE PASCAL, *PENSÉES*

The greatest innovations in my life have come from periods of my ability to sit still. Some men meditate, some pray, some slip into states of semiconsciousness. I practice fasting. Whatever you do to sit still in a room and do nothing allows you to think and access the "infinite intelligence" of the universe, as Napoleon Hill calls it, or God, as the religions of the world would call it. Porn and wasting your sexual energy disrupt the energy needed to connect your mind to the spiritual realm to think and create, and that can only come from sitting still in a room alone.

All great leaders and innovators have had their great inventions come from periods of sitting in a room alone.

Robert Kiyosaki wrote his hit book, the #1 personal finance book of all time, *Rich Dad Poor Dad,* alone in a cabin with nothing but a Macintosh computer, a tape recorder, and scraps of paper.

Bill Gates planned Microsoft alone in a hotel room with 6 yellow notepads on which to scribble his thoughts.

50 Cent turned his life around in prison, got his rap career together, made a decision to get out of drug dealing, and resolved to "get rich or die trying" by being alone in a jail cell.

Hitler wrote his manifesto in prison and became a great orator and visionary while sitting alone in prison.

Nelson Mandela achieved his great work in prison.

Jordan Belfort wrote *The Wolf of Wall Street* in prison, arguably his best work of his life. It relaunched his tarnished, broken, and failed career.

Newton discovered gravity alone on his mother's land after he fled the city due to a plague that was sweeping the land.

Moses came down from the mountain after 40 days of fasting with the Ten Commandments straight from mouth of God.

I wrote my previous book *The Close: 7 Level Selling* in 4 days in Costa Rica after an 18-day fast and solitude in the jungle.

The list can go on and on forever, but this divine creative energy cannot be accessed if you are blowing your load every day worshipping the goddesses of porn and mopping his seeds of creation off your belly every day.

The religions of the world agree that a man should live in one of two ways: (1) single and celibate or (2) married.

A single and celibate man can save his sexual energy and pour it into his craft, his purpose, his endeavors, become a success and attract the woman of his dreams.

A married man can practice sexual transmutation and the battery effect with his wife in which love and sex, when mixed, will energize a man, heal his physical, mental, emotional, and spiritual wounds and energize him to push further into his purpose.

The Three Purposes of Sex

Our sexual center has three potential purposes or functions:

1. Generation (Procreation)
2. Regeneration (Health Creation)
3. Spiritualization (Immortality)

Paschal Beverly Randolph MD was perhaps the most prolific writer on this subject and termed the spiritualized sex teachings "the Mysteries of Eulis," as outlined in his book, The Immortality of Love. *Freeman B. Dowd, a student of Dr. Randolph, summarized the esoteric nature of the sexual forces this way:*

"The creative power of man is due to the sexual nature, from whence his being is derived... The energy of the soul pours through the sex nature, and the volume of energy is in proportion to the capacity of the nature through which it flows, being drawn from the limitless ocean of energy with which the soul is connected." (Regeneration)

The Law of Exchange: Criteria for the One Flesh Union

To obtain the Regeneration and Spiritualization benefits described above, specific aspects of the sexual embrace must be met. *These criteria include* both a physical component and the emotional (love) intent.

The physical component of the One Flesh Union requires that intercourse be carried out as God designed: with the male organ in the vagina of his mate at the time of orgasm, with nothing to prevent or compromise the exchange of the physical fluids and resultant spiritual energy that occur during climax. Within the male and female sexual fluids exist hormones and natural chemicals beneficial to the physical and emotional stability of both individuals. It is as if the husband and wife were each poles of a battery and their fluids were the electrolytes that permit the transmission of energy produced between them.

Science is beginning to confirm the importance of the direct physical exchange of male and female fluids during sexual intercourse. A study in the Archives of Sexual Behavior (2002 June 31(3):289-93) *demonstrated that the women who were directly exposed to semen during intercourse (without interf erence from condoms) were less likely to be depressed. The researchers in this study concluded that such a response is due to the mood-altering hormones in semen that are absorbed through the vagina.*

It is essential that nothing in the sexual embrace prevent this mutual fluid exchange from taking place in the vagina because Regeneration and Spiritualization cannot take place without this exchange any more than a battery can function without its electrolytes. Any sexual practice that excludes this exchange diminishes our spiritual potential and loss of soul energy. Such common practices include, but are not limited to, condoms, masturbation, oral sex, anal sex and (the pull-out method).

Both the Old and New Testament biblical writers tried to instruct the people of their time period concerning the importance of the law of sexual exchange.

From http://www.soul.org/teachings/sex

If a man can obey the sexual laws of either (1) single and celibate, or (2) married and in love, he can unlock the vast spiritual power, creative power, and regenerative powers and become much stronger at an exponential multiplier than he is alone.

A metaphor used to describe the synergy of men and women who are married and working together as partners says that "two oxen equally yoked is equal to 12." The two become one flesh and synergistically powerful where 1 + 1 does not equal 2. Instead 1 + 1 = 12. That is the power of synergy and unlocking spiritual power through the proper use of sex.

As a business coach, I know from firsthand experience that married men with children always perform better than single men, single women, two male business partners, or any other configuration of people in setting up and growing a business. Married women with kids are also very powerful, but they usually play the feminine role of wife and mother and send their husbands in for business coaching or play a support role to him.

Divorced or single women forced into the masculine role will coach with me, but my clients with the most power to draw on are always married men with kids because of the reasons outlined above. Spiritual power and sexual power are what allow man to transcend his physical power and accomplish amazing feats that are unthinkable or impossible.

> *"Who you marry, which is the ultimate partnership,*
> *is enormously important in determining the*
> *happiness in your life and your success."*
>
> Warren Buffett, *Berkshire Hathaway CEO*

Buffett told Forbes that his first wife Susan Buffett was one of his "greatest teachers," along with his late father Howard and late mentor Benjamin Graham.

"The most important person by far in that respect is your spouse," said Buffett in a conversation with Bill Gates earlier this year. *"I can't overemphasize how important that is."Buffett and Susan were married until Susan passed away in 2004. Notably, she was the 17th richest woman* in the world, worked as a director for Berkshire Hathaway and served as the Buffett Foundation's *president.*

Buffett remarried in 2006 when he wed longtime friend Astrid Menks.

Berkshire Hathaway CEO Warren Buffett believes that making money means nothing without having another person, such as a spouse, to share the wealth with, according to a recent interview with Forbes.

"It's much more fun achieving things in life with a partner, there's no question about it," Buffett, 87, recently told the magazine. "It's really a huge advantage from a personal standpoint to have a wonderful partner.""That's true obviously in marriage, I mean that's the most important decision that you make," he added. *"Who you marry, which is the ultimate partnership, is enormously important in determining the happiness in your life and your success and I was lucky in that respect."And there is scientific research to back up Buffett's advice. A study published by Carnegie Mellon University* found that people with supportive spouses are *"more likely to give themselves the chance to succeed.""There were two turning points in my life," Buffett said in the HBO documentary "Becoming Warren Buffett." "One when I came out of the womb and one when I met Susie,"* as he called Susan.

The two met when Susan was going to be rooming with Buffett's youngest sister as a college student at Northwestern University, she says in an old video clip shared in the documentary.

"So I walk into their house, [Warren] was sitting in this chair and he made some sarcastic quip," she recalled. "So I made

one back. I thought, 'Who is this jerk?'"Buffett told Forbes that Susan taught him a lot about investing. He also credits Susan with teaching him to open himself up to the world emotionally.

"I just got very, very, very lucky. I was a lopsided person," Buffett said in the documentary. "And it took a while, but she just stood there with a little watering can and just nourished me along and changed me."Though you may not have a choice in determining how you were born and raised, Buffett said, "You have something to say about who you marry."

https://www.cnbc.com/2017/10/02/warren-buffett-says-this-partnership-will-determine-your-success.html

Bill Gates, one of the world's richest men, has been long married to his wife, Melinda Gates.

Jeff Bezos, also one of world's richest men, is married to Mackenzie Bezos.

On the flip side, divorce doesn't just take 50% of your wealth. Divorce usually destroys 70% of your wealth and also your mental, physical, emotional, and spiritual self.

A divorce can rob you of all your momentum in life, your purpose, your business, your company, your children, your family and drag out for 5, 10, or even 20 years after the marriage separates.

I know several men who had divorces last longer than their marriages. That is why Buffet, Gates, and Bezos, three of the world's richest men, would all say "marry the right person."

> *"Far too many people are looking for the right person, instead of trying to be the right person.""*
>
> GLORIA STEINEM

The two ways for a man to live sexually are (1) single and celibate, or (2) married and in love. This is so important to a man's success that in the early 1900s the government tried to outlaw bachelors. Bachelors—single men—were responsible for all the drinking, whoring, gambling, fighting, violence, rapes, stealing, and crimes. Thus, the government tried to outlaw bachelors.

Bachelors do not produce as much as married men and usually get into trouble because of their vices. Throughout history and across cultures, up until the 1950s when teenagers were invented (as they are an American post–World War II invention), both men and women went from living with their parents straight to marriage. There was no perilous middle period of bachelorhood in which men get perpetually stuck.

Where are all these sexual trends for young men going?

I recently read a collection of articles online that illustrated the utter destruction of love, virtue, and the proper use of sex. Pornography is now so rampant and so available that young teenagers, even tweens, like 12-year-olds and younger, are watching hardcore porn on their smartphones.

They aren't just watching softcore porn. They are watching hardcore gangbangs, anal, BDSM, and crazy things that no 12-year-old could, or should, ever imagine.

This exposure is nothing but pure evil, and this type of content was never intended for 12-year-old children. If an adult male was to expose a 12-year-old to that kind of content, he would be thrown in jail as a sex criminal. Why aren't the companies who expose such content online to children not treated as sex criminals then? This is wrong on every level, and nothing good can come from it.

When I was 12 in the 1990s, you would be lucky to get a peck on the cheek or a little kiss from a girl. According to the collection of articles that are coming out today on various blogs, young girls who are 12 are now bartering with young boys, and they are trading blowjobs for their first kiss.

This is not the Cinderella story, the Snow White story, or the Beauty and the Beast story that Walt Disney sold to the little girls. No one is singing "someday my prince will come" in this scene. Cinderella didn't blow the prince for a kiss! But this is where we are today—hardcore penetration of an orifice in exchange for your first kiss.

Pure evil.

When I read this, my heart broke. It seemed evil and twisted for a young 12-year-old boy to broker a blowjob done in advance, just so that an innocent little girl could get her first kiss. A kiss is innocent; little girls want their first kiss. It's fun, it's cute.

A blowjob is explicitly adult—it's sex, it's penetration, it's hardcore. Those are two incompatible ideas for a first exchange.

But such things are real today; the little girls and the little boys all have hardcore porn, and sex is no longer sacred. This is fatally damaging for the fabric of society from the most basic level, and my heart breaks to hear that this is the level we have degraded to.

"Someone has to be on top, why not you?"

GENERAL GEORGE S. PATTON

PART III

RELIGION, GOD, AND THE NEW GODS OF MEN: MONEY AND GOVERNMENT

Communist until you get rich

Feminist until you get married

Atheist until the plane starts to crash

THE HYPOCRITE DIARIES

CHAPTER 22
RELIGION FROM A
FUNCTIONAL PERSPECTIVE
To Keep Man from Returning
to Cannibalism

"The lucky ones died in the blasts. They were spared the fate of starvation, cannibalism, rape and slaughter. Where a man could be killed over half-eaten can of corn."

JOE REYES, AFTERMATH

"Until relatively recently, and with a very few exceptions, cannibalism would have been regarded as anything but normal. As a result, until the last two decades of the 20th century, few scientists spent time studying a topic thought to have little, if any, biological significance. Basically, the party line was that cannibalism, when it did occur, was

*either the result of starvation to the stresses related to captive
conditions. It was as simple as that. Or so we thought."*

BILL SCHUTT, *CANNIBALISM: A PERFECTLY NATURAL HISTORY*

Without an organized system or a way to live, man would degrade into an emotional mess of robbing, raping, killing bands of cannibals. Man needs religion to avoid degenerating backwards to a cannibal, which has happened several times throughout history, especially in hard times when men have eaten their dead for survival. Without religion, man cannot govern himself or delineate the boundaries in his daily life.

Religion has always played an important role in governing man, training his spirit, and bringing the tribes together. In fact, I would argue after studying humanity and the great inventions we have created—cars, spaceships, the internet, medicine, computers, irrigation systems, vitamins, vaccines, and any number of scientific inventions—the greatest invention to mankind is written religion. Without the base values of written religion, man is unable to form the base of society to allow for the other inventions to grow. If man cannot get past fighting in the mud and warring with his neighbors, he will never go to space. Religion is the fundamental base of civilization and holds man accountable for his actions. Religion was the base of the modern legal system and how we build our entire civilization around a set of values and a way to live.

As I mentioned earlier in this book, religion and governmental power systems go hand in hand. City-states Bc. in ancient Greece or the Viking tribes were pagans with several gods because the power of their city-states was decentralized with several chiefs and several leaders.

Next came the empire, which was seen in Rome, and paganism fell away to monotheism—specifically Christianity, one god to rule them all.

When the empires get so powerful and so large, totalitarianism sets in, and then we see movements like the Nazis, Communist Russia, and Imperial Japan, where the state is all powerful and the state becomes its own religion.

Men are now atheists in totalitarianism and are severed from practicing the spiritual realm as a new form of control over the population and keeping men from accessing their true power and growth through the spirit.

Atheism is a form of weakness: if the spiritual realm were a road and you needed to choose a religion to drive down the road, you have several options to move from point A to point B. You can choose to be a Christian, a Jew, a Hindu, a Muslim, a Buddhist, or any religion of the world to explore your spirit, the spiritual realm, how the universe works, and get down the road quickly and safely. The trouble with atheism as a religion is that it takes the energy of belief to be an atheist, but there are literally zero benefits to exploration of the spiritual realm. When you study the 100 richest people in the world, and yes, making money is a spiritual endeavor, 25% of them are Jewish, even though only 0.6% of the world's population is Jewish. Several wealthy and rich people are Christians or practice some other form of religion to explore the spiritual realm.

If you choose to opt out of the spiritual realm, you will receive little or no benefit or power from the spiritual realm. Man is four parts: mental, physical, emotional, and spiritual. The spiritual realm is the way for man to connect his finite self to the infinite. I chose to opt out of spirituality for many years at the popular suggestion of "science" and the junk philosophy served in the modern school system and universities. Through this popular ideology, I became an atheist because science could not prove that there was a God or even a spiritual realm. During this time when I followed the atheist belief system, I enjoyed the least power and success in my life.

Studying the spiritual realm through organized study and practice or religion has brought me greater power and success in my life, just as countless men have had success with an organized way to study God throughout history. The spiritual realm is infinite, and it is the most powerful of the four realms of a human being. The physical realm is flawed, temporary, and limited. The emotional realm is deceiving, finite, and often crippling. The mental realm relies on reason and logic and is also finite in its own limitations—Napoleon Hill calls this synthetic intelligence, which is limited in power. But the spiritual realm is unlimited in power, unlimited in reach, unlimited in access, and where man draws his infinite power from if he learns to access it.

Napoleon Hill calls this "infinite intelligence," and it is the divine ability to create.

Man is the only animal on this earth with the ability to create like a God; no other animal can do that. Infinite intelligence is another word for God; it is the collective intelligence that binds all thoughts and binds all things together. Some people call this the universe, a secular name for God. It is much harder to have a relationship with an abstract like "the universe" than to have a relationship with a personified entity like God.

"FAITH is the only agency through which the cosmic force of Infinite Intelligence can be harnessed and used by man."

NAPOLEON HILL

To be an atheist is to eviscerate and disconnect yourself from the most powerful realm—the spiritual realm—and you will be limited in every way. You will be ruled by fear because you will be limited in faith. Faith is the ability to leap logic and see the unseen. It is where all creative power comes from, and if you deny the spiritual realm, you will be only a fraction of the man you would have been by embracing the power of the infinite.

"Without leaps of imagination or dreaming, we lose the excitement of possibilities. Dreaming, after all is a form of planning."

GLORIA STEINEM

To understand the practical power of religion, after the fall of Rome, a monotheistic empire, to the barbarians, Rome fell backwards into a collection of city-states.

It was Charlemagne who began to reunite the tribal city-states, and he did it with religion. In the Dark Ages, religion became corrupt because of human nature, as all large human organizations eventually become corrupt with so much money and power. The continental European population was illiterate, and there were no books or copies of the Bible to read. The Roman Catholic Church became ultrapowerful, keepers of the written word, and modified the translations of the biblical text to serve their means. However, the Roman Catholic Church was masterful at uniting the tribes through religion and promises of heaven. Most importantly, the church showed the people how to live prosperous and productive lives.

In the 16th century, a man named Martin Luther proliferated the printing press and began to print his ideas and Bibles for the first time. The people had never been able to read the words of God or a Bible, as books were so scarce.

This lead to the Renaissance and the rebirth of Europe.

After the rebirth, Europe entered into a series of technological and social leaps, and it was because the average man could now read the written word of God for the first time.

The barbaric British tribes who had fought back the mighty Roman legions had become civilized. As civilized Britons, they were raided in the Dark Ages by the Northmen—the Vikings—fierce warriors who were unstoppable at the time with their high-tech ships and navigation abilities. However, it was the Christ-god and religion that sacked the Vikings, not muscles and war. The Viking kings decided to convert to Christianity for trade purposes and to unite their own warring pagan tribes into bigger empires.

The pattern being drawn here is that organized religion civilizes man, and civilization is the mass control of individual human emotions.

Civilization is good, we love civilization, without civilization we would be primitive apes fighting and digging in the mud to survive.

You may love or hate religion, but what you must not deny is the usefulness and ability to civilize man into a useful group of people and in giving man a portal into the infinite intelligence and the divine creative energy that he needs to survive and thrive in this world.

Infinite Intelligence vs. Synthetic Intelligence.

I quote Napoleon Hill's *Think and Grow Rich* in this part of the book frequently because he is able to bridge the gap between the sacred and secular.

To speak of the spiritual realm in a purely sacred way falls on deaf ears with a secular audience, and to speak of it in a secular way doesn't really capture the essence of the message. Such is the challenge of discussing religion and spirituality with anyone.

To make things simple, man has access to only two types of intelligence:

1) Synthetic intelligence, and
2) Infinite intelligence

Synthetic intelligence comes from already known facts, logic, other people's work, and the things that man can see and sense in his immediate periphery.

Infinite intelligence works in a completely different way. Infinite intelligence is where man can tap into the infinite minds and infinite intelligence that exist outside of his own mind. You might have experienced infinite intelligence when you are in the shower in the morning and have a brilliant thought, or maybe first thing out of bed in the morning you have a great idea. When you sleep and dream, you might be accessing infinite intelligence, or last thing before bed at night while you are falling asleep, your mind can access infinite intelligence. Infinite intelligence is responsible for the "eureka" moments when man becomes brilliant and makes game-changing discoveries.

Nearly every great man in history who has created something, invented something, or has become a great success inside and outside of the world of money has used infinite intelligence to his advantage.

Another word for infinite intelligence is God. People who have a relationship with God through prayer, organized religion, or church can access infinite intelligence much easier than people who fail to practice some form of religion. I make the argument that (1) religion is important for organizing large groups of people and instructing them on how to live productive harmonious lives, and (2) religion is important to man as an individual to access infinite intelligence and reach its full spiritual power, creativeness, and potential in his life purpose. A man is not a man without command and mastery over the spiritual realm.

To be an atheist and deny the acknowledgment of the spiritual laws and the spiritual realm is an expensive choice for yourself as a man and your potential.

I encourage you with every fiber of my being to explore the spiritual realm through a religion to connect to the divine intelligence that gave you and all things on this planet life.

Man claims that he knows how the world works through science, but science is primitive because we still cannot create life. Sure, we can clone animals and build GMO foods, but we cannot create life from scratch.

Life always has to come from a synthesis, something else that was divinely created, which we still don't know how to create. Although we are intelligent, we are not gods yet relying on our synesthetic intelligence and science to guide us. Only when man can create life from scratch without any synthesis of other cells or living things will we have reached the true level of the gods.

Science will always be a form of primitive synthetic intelligence in the face of the divine powers of infinite intelligence. To think that science has all the answers today is an ignorant thought.

Science is limited to a synthesis of published past knowledge and data. Infinite intelligence can shape the future, regardless of past data, and bend the future to man's will.

In the past thirty days I have written over 200,000 words, this book, and my previous publication *The Close: 7 Level Selling* by using the powers of infinite intelligence. The words in these books are pouring out of me with very little revision. To unlock your full power as a man and be a man who fully lives to his potential and lives his purpose, you must learn to communicate and work with infinite intelligence in your life to become the man you were born to be.

Power and the Invisible World

"Fetch me a fruit of the Banyan tree."
"Here is one, sir."
"Break it."
"I have broken it, sir."
"What do you see?"
"Very tiny seeds, sir.'"
"Break one."
"I have broken it, sir."
"What do you see now?"
"Nothing, sir."
"My son,' the father said,

"what you do not perceive is the essence, and in that essence
the mighty banyan tree exists. Believe me, my son, in that
essence is the self of all that is. That is the True ...."

Chandogya Upanishad, vi, 13

Inside the invisible essence of the seed is the power of infinite intelligence. How does the seed know to become a tree? Such is the power of the spiritual realm and the encoded plans for seeds to become trees, sperm to become babies, and eggs to become birds. We can synthetically replicate these life-creations in labs today, but we still cannot create life from scratch. We are limited in our powers and our knowledge, but the spiritual is truly infinite.

CHAPTER 23
NEW GOD
Money, the Economic Genocide
of the Middle Class

It's a great brainwashing process, which goes very slow[ly] and is divided [into] four basic stages. The first one [is] demoralization; it takes from 15–20 years to demoralize a nation. Why that many years? Because this is the minimum number of years which [is required] to educate one generation of students in the country of your enemy, exposed to the ideology of the enemy. In other words, Marxist-Leninist ideology is being pumped into the soft heads of at least three generations of American students, without being challenged, or counter-balanced by the basic values of Americanism (American patriotism).

The result? The result you can see. Most of the people who graduated in the sixties (drop-outs or half-baked intellectuals) are now occupying the positions of power in the government, civil service, business, mass media, [and the] educational system. You are stuck with them. You cannot get rid of them. They are contaminated; they are programmed to think and react to certain stimuli in a certain pattern. You cannot change their mind[s], even if you expose them to authentic information, even if you prove that white is white and black is black, you still cannot change the basic perception and the logic of behavior. In other words, these people ... the process of demoralization is complete and irreversible. To [rid] society of these people, you need another twenty or fifteen years to educate a new generation of patriotically-minded and common sense people, who would be acting in favor and in the interests of United States society.

Yuri Bezmenov, KGB Defector in an interview with
G. Edward Griffin

In our world today, we have a denial of God and a manufacturing of atheism in our school systems and universities in the Western world. The school systems and universities are systematic factories that pump the youth's brains full of communist propaganda and atheism as a religion. When America was the greatest country in the world, America's schools preached freedom, capitalist ideals, and Judeo-Christian values in the classroom that were the backbone of our great Western civilization.

We have since torn out the brains of our civilization—the capitalist philosophy—and ripped out the backbone—Judeo Christian values. Now we have a spineless, brainless body that runs on communist philosophy and atheism. This is one of the major sources of our weak men of today. Men with no fathers, raised by the state alone, who go to school in a communist factory and worship nothing and believe in nothing.

"A man who stands for nothing will fall for anything."

MALCOLM X

To replace God in the new Western philosophy, man now worships new gods in the Western world. The new gods in our weakened Western society are:

The New Gods of Man

1) Money: fiat currency, fake value, with no real value
2) The government: collectivist, communist philosophy, no real value to the individual man but rather the collective group
3) Science: Synthetic Intelligence modified by the universities for its own agendas, its benefit to an individual man very little, but rather to further larger agendas
4) Atheism: the belief in nothing

With the proliferation of these new gods, what we lose in return is:

1) Real value: families, loving marriages, children
2) A freedom-based government, where man is free to survive or fall on his own volition, ownership mentality disappears, and victim mentality takes over, where man relies on the government for survival instead of his own brain.
3) Infinite intelligence, God, and man's relationship with God, and his power to reach his full potential
4) Judeo-Christian philosophy, aka religion, which has built and created the greatness of a free America and much of the Western world

> *"That's L.A. (Los Angeles)—they worship everything and they value nothing."*

SEBASTIAN WILDER IN *LA LA LAND*

Like the Native Americans who traded real value—the island of Manhattan to the white man for a stipend of glass beads, baubles, and mostly worthless money—we today are trading our real value. We are trading our families, our marriages, our children, our freedom, our infinite intelligence, our relationship with God, and our proven successful philosophy for a pile of worthless nonsense: fake money backed by nothing, a collectivist communist government that is systematically taking the good things out of life, junk science that is manipulated by the universities for ulterior agendas, and atheism that believes in nothing.

"Only when the last fish has been fished from the river and the last tree has been cut down will you realize that you cannot eat money."

NATIVE AMERICAN PROVERB

A man who believes nothing will stand for nothing, and over time he will eventually become nothing.

This is the trade that destroys the empire. It's been slowly subverting Western society since the 1940s, and like a boiled frog, the temperature on the water has been slowly turned up one degree at a time, and before the frog can realize that the water is too hot and jump out, the frog is boiled.

We are very close to becoming boiled frogs in today's Western civilization.

If the frog was cast into a bubbling boiling pot of hot water, it would shock his senses, and he would have the sense to reject the boiling water and jump out to reject the changes. But these social changes are happening very slowly over 80 years, and we, the frogs, have lost all perspective on what made us into a strong society and why it worked.

We are entering hard times with a population of weak men. The weak men of today are not here because it is their fault. The changes that have occurred over the last 80 years have brought down the pillars of Western philosophy and beliefs that made us strong.

We have traded our strength for weakness, and this is our fatal error; it is philosophical battle, a spiritual battle, not a battle fought on the front lines with guns, bullets, and bayonets. This is a battle fought within the heart of each man, and the enemies are invisible, unkillable, and coming from all sides.

*"I see in the fight club the strongest and smartest men who've
ever lived. I see all this potential and I see squandering. God
damn it, an entire generation pumping gas, waiting tables,
slaves with white collars, advertising has us chasing cars and
clothes, working jobs we hate so we can buy shit we don't need.
We're the middle children of the history man, no purpose or
place, we have no Great war, no Great depression, our great
war is a spiritual war, our great depression is our lives, we've
been all raised by television to believe that one day we'd all be
millionaires and movie gods and rock stars, but we won't and
we're slowly learning that fact. and we're very, very pissed off."*

CHUCK PALAHNIUK, *FIGHT CLUB*

The empire of America became great when the middle class began to
appear and blossom in the early 1900s. One man, Henry Ford, was
responsible for designing the assembly line and essentially creating
the middle class. Henry Ford had the philosophy of paying his workers
more so he could sell more cars; this was a brilliant idea and an idea that
made America into the richest and most prosperous country for a time.

What we have had since 1960 is a systematic destruction of the middle class. A nation is a first-world nation when it has 3 classes—rich,
middle class, and poor. When the middle class disappears, the same
nation becomes a third-world nation with only rich and poor. As I
write this book, America's middle class is becoming endangered and
will shortly be extinct, while other countries like China, Brazil, Russia,
India, Mexico, and other emerging markets are gaining middle classes.

The middle class was based on slightly higher wages, higher skilled
labor, and value-added economies. The factories that used to make up
America's industrial strength were value-added businesses that created
real value in the economy, and America was a major exporter of added
value.

Today the factories are gone, and the rising countries mentioned above are gaining the factories that America lost. When the value-added jobs go, so does the middle class.

What we have instead now is a service economy where everyone performs a service, but very little of what we produce is "value added" or product production. President Trump is trying to reverse this trend, but I'm not sure he can reverse the decades of damage since the 1970s.

The middle-class dream made America great because an average man could work hard, make money, be the man of the house, raise a family, own a home, own a car, raise his kids, and be home from work in time for dinner. This middle-class dream is gone from America. No longer can an "average Joe," a working guy, "make it" in this country. As stated earlier in this book, a minimum wage worker can't even afford to rent a two-bedroom apartment. What kind of message does this send? If you work here, you can't afford to live here? This sounds like slavery and the third world instead of the beacon of hope and freedom that America used to be.

> *"That which is not good for the beehive*
> *cannot be good for the bees."*
>
> MARCUS AURELIUS

This trend is moving into a very dark place. We now see headlines from CNBC.com that read: "No full-time minimum-wage worker can afford a 2-bedroom apartment in any US state." This just became a reality at the end of 2017. What's next? The working people now must live as homeless?

The people cannot even afford to live, and we now have "tent cities" popping up in America. These are similar to the shantytowns that litter third-world countries in Africa. The third world is coming to America, delivered straight to our door, and it's coming fast.

Here is a list of "tent cities" that are named in the USA according to Wikipedia.

- Camp Hope, Las Cruces, New Mexico
- Camp Quixote, Olympia, Washington State
- Camp Take Notice, Ann Arbor, Michigan
- Dignity Village, Portland, Oregon
- Opportunity Village, Eugene, Oregon
- Maricopa County Sheriff's Tent City, Phoenix, Arizona
- New Jack City and Little Tijuana, Fresno, California
- Nickelsville, located in Seattle
- Right 2 Dream Too, Portland, Oregon
- River Haven,[6] Ventura County, California
- Safe Ground, Sacramento, California
- The Jungle, San Jose, California
- Temporary Homeless Service Area (THSA), Ontario, California
- Tent City (100+ residents) of Lakewood, New Jersey
- Tent City, Avenue A and 13th Street, Lubbock, Texas
- Tent City, Bernalillo County, New Mexico
- Tent City, banks of the American River, Sacramento, California
- Tent City, Chicago, Illinois
- Tent City 4, eastern King County outside of Seattle
- The Point, where the Gunnison River and Colorado River meet
- The Village of Hope and Community of Hope, Fresno, California
- Transition Park, Camden, New Jersey
- Tent City, Fayette County, Tennessee
- Camp Unity Eastside, Woodinville, WA

These are just the named tent cities that made it on to the list. Imagine how many unnamed or unlisted tent cities there are in the USA.

I cannot imagine how anyone would argue that these changes are good for Western civilization. I can see no benefits to the populace living in tent cities on the side of the highway. The real problem with the destruction of the middle class is not a political one, but rather a problem with the monetary system itself.

Henry Ford—the father of the middle class, the richest, most powerful man in the world in his time and the main study behind life-changing books such as *Think and Grow Rich*—has been attributed with saying:

"It is well enough that people of the nation do not understand our banking and monetary system, for if they did, I believe there would be a revolution before tomorrow morning."

HENRY FORD

What did Henry Ford understand about the monetary system that would make the nation revolt by tomorrow morning?

Let's examine money vs. currency to find the answers from history. What we must understand about money is that the only real money in the world is gold. Gold has had constant value throughout history and constant purchasing power in real goods. For instance, in ancient Rome, a gentleman could take a 1-ounce gold coin and trade it for a fine toga, a haircut, and a pair of sandals.

In the modern world, a gentleman can take the same 1 ounce of gold and trade it in for a finely tailored suit, a haircut, and fine pair of shoes.

And thus, in real purchasing power, gold has had a historical constant purchasing power. Gold is the only real money in the history of the world. All other forms of money are fake.

Until 1971, the US dollar was backed by gold. In August of that year, President Nixon announced that the US dollar would no longer follow

One gold coin (1oz) = a toga,
a pair of sandals and a haircut
in ancient Rome.

=

One gold coin (1oz) = a finely
tailored suit, a haircut, and a fine pair
of shoes in the modern world.

=

the gold standard. When America was great, the American dollar was the world reserve currency, and America had enough gold in its reserves so that anyone could take an American dollar and exchange it for real gold.

This was a powerful system, a brilliant system, and a real system for which to store and transfer value.

And then the Vietnam War happened, and countries around the world lost confidence in the United States, so they began trading in their US dollars for real gold. The treasury was starting to run out of gold, so President Nixon took the US off the gold standard and debased the currency.

Whenever a currency becomes debased, its value always reverts to its intrinsic value—zero at some point.

The Roman people were smart with their money. Roman men and women traded with real pieces of gold and silver, coins minted out of pure metal by the government. The Roman people handled gold and silver every day and knew the intrinsic weights of these metals. The Roman government did not dare to debase the currency because they knew they would be overthrown instantly by a militant population if they tampered with the real currency of the powerful empire.

Emperor Nero, one of the worst emperors in history, was the first Roman emperor to debase its currency. At a threat of killing the men working at the Roman mint and all their families, Nero had the middle sections of the silver coins hollowed out and replaced with an equal weight in lead. Nero then took the extra silver and built himself a luxurious new palace.

Does this story sound familiar?

In 2008 in the USA, the Wall Street bankers had screwed up their banking system by trading derivatives on value that did not exist—derivatives backed by values in homes that were overinflated. They had dug their own grave by violating the rules of value and sound business.

President Obama should have let the banks fail and let the economy crash to reset, but instead he robbed the people through quantitative easing, aka printing money. The government turned on the printing presses and began to print bailouts for the unethical bankers, the bad banks were saved, the Wall Street boys made huge bonuses (built themselves palaces), and the people started to trade a weaker currency, just like in Rome. It's important to note that when Emperor Nero debased the currency, that was the beginning of the major decline of the empire. Obama and his debasement of the currency in 2008 is a major marking for a decline of the American empire.

A real strong leader should have let the banks fail, charged the bankers with treason, and publicly shot or hanged them as criminals in Times Square in NYC. What really happened, however, is the criminal bankers got away—criminals who robbed the country, robbed the people, robbed the currency, and got even richer. In America, if you rob a 7/11 you go to jail, but if you rob the country you get rich!

Here are the effects of gold and currency since 1968. In 1968, the minimum wage was 31.31.

	1968	2014
Price of Gold in USD	$39.31	$1264.99
Minimum Wage USA	$1.25	$7.25
Hours to Earn Gold	31.45 Hours	174.48 Hours

If it took a young man working at McDonald's with no education, no skills, no experience 31.45 hours to earn a piece of gold in 1968; in 2014 that exact same man, still working at McDonald's with no education, no skills, no experience, would now have to put in 174.48 hours of labor to earn that same piece of gold. Assuming a 2,000-hour work year, here is the decline in real purchasing power for the average minimum-wage worker since 1968 when indexed USD to gold.

1968 Minimum-Wage Purchasing Power vs. 2018 minimum wage-purchasing power in the USA

40 hours a week of work for 50 weeks of the year, 2 weeks off is 2000 hours per year			
	1968	2014	2018
Minimum Wage USA	$1.25	$7.25	$7.25

Continued on next page

Continued from previous page

	1968	2014	2018
Gold Price 1oz USD	$31.34	$1,264.99	$1,349.30
40-hour work week in Money $	$50	$290	$290
40-hour work week in Gold oz	1.5954	0.2293	0.2149
40-hour work week in USD indexed to 2018 Gold Price	$2,152.68	$309.33	$290.00
Monthly pay in 2018 purchasing power USD	$8,610.72	$1,237.31	$1,160.00
Annual pay in 2018 purchasing power USD	**$103,328.65**	**$14,847.75**	**$13,920.00**

So according to the math above, if the workers had continued to be paid in gold as they were in 1968, right before going off the gold standard, annual minimum wage should be around $103,328.65 to keep up with the same purchasing power that a minimum-wage burger flipper at McDonald's would have had with zero training, zero education, zero skills. Yes, America was indeed a great country when the lowest-skilled person was making $103,328.65 per year and getting two weeks off for vacation.

A $103,328.65 annual minimum wage did make America great indeed. Perhaps Donald Trump's presidential slogan "make America great again" is relevant?

Here are the 2018 purchasing power numbers. A worker today on minimum wage is only making $13,920.00 and thus can't even afford to rent a 2-bedroom apartment. Do you see the problem with this? This is not a political power problem. It's not a Democrat or Republican problem. It's a money system problem just as Henry Ford warned us. Hard times do create strong men; this relationship with purchasing power, gold, and money is rigged against anyone who works for money.

Let's examine what kind of job and education you would need today to keep up with a burger flipper from 1968:

Top 25 best-paying jobs in America in 2018 according to CNBC.com	
1. Anesthesiologist	*14. Marketing Manager*
Mean salary: $269,600	Mean salary: $144,140
2. Surgeon	*15. Podiatrist*
Mean salary: $252,910	Mean salary: $144,110
3. Obstetrician and Gynecologist	*16. Lawyer*
Mean salary: $234,310	Mean salary: $139,880
4. Oral and Maxillofacial Surgeon	*17. Financial Manager*
Mean salary: $232,870	Mean salary: $139,720
5. Orthodontist	*18. Sales Manager*
Mean salary: $228,780	Mean salary: $135,090
6. Physician	*19. Financial Advisor*
Mean salary: $201,840	Mean salary: $123,100

Continued on next page

Continued from previous page

7. Psychiatrist	**20. Business Operations Manager**
Mean salary: $200,220	Mean salary: $122,090
8. Pediatrician	**21. Pharmacist**
Mean salary: $184,240	Mean salary: $120,270
9. Dentist	**22. Optometrist**
Mean salary: $173,860	Mean salary: $117,580
10. Prosthodontist	**23. Actuary**
Mean salary: $168,140	Mean salary: $114,120
11. Nurse Anesthetist	**24. Political Scientist**
Mean salary: $164,030	Mean salary: $112,250
12. Petroleum Engineer	**25. Medical and Health Services Manager**
Mean salary: $147,030	Mean salary: $109,370
13. IT Manager	
Mean salary: $145,740	

Source:https://www.cnbc.com/2018/01/09/these-are-the-25-best-paying-jobs-in-america-in-2018.html

So the burger flipper guy would have been the 26th best job on this list at $103,328.65 in 2018's purchasing power. Keep in mind, the burger flipper guy has no education, no student debt, no skills; he just shows up to work and runs the grill. Note that to run the grill at McDonald's today is much harder. The menu has over 100 items now. Back then the menu was much easier to make as well.

So what does it cost to make the incomes above in education?

Below are the average costs of tuition fees at US universities in 2017 and 2018. This is grim.

Average Fees at US Universities, 2017–18

	Public two-year colleges	Public four-year colleges (in-state fees)	Public four-year colleges (out-of-state fees)	Private non-profit four-year colleges
Tuition and other fees	$3,570	$9,970	$25,620	$34,740
Room and board	$8,400	$10,800	$10,800	$12,210
Total (per year)	$11,970	$20,770	$35,420	$46,950

Source: College Board

Source: https://www.topuniversities.com/student-info/student-finance/how-much-does-it-cost-study-us

A student in the US who goes for a four-year degree, which is now worthless, is going to end up nearly $100,000 in debt after graduation. He can never bankrupt his way out of—it follows him for life—and because the money is inflated, he gets taxed at a higher tax bracket than people in 1968. He has to be highly skilled, a smart worker, and perform complex jobs just to have the same purchasing power as a 1968 McDonald's burger flipper. Student debt is a modern bond into slavery; many students can never get out from under that monetary bondage, not even through bankruptcy, because of the laws regarding student loans.

This is part of what is crippling the young men in this country and forcing young women to work alongside men just to live. In 1968 the women could stay home and look after the family, and their men could pay the bills. Today it takes a man, a woman, and credit cards just to stay afloat. Such is the current state of our corrupt fiat monetary system—an evil system that must be abolished!

So does this trend of purchasing power decreasing over time get better or worse over time?

The answer is, it will get worse until the average man can't buy bread.

This story has already happened throughout history in countries around the world. When the average man is so poor that he can no longer buy bread—a revolution happens.

In Russia in 1917, the average man couldn't buy bread, and he was protesting in the streets. The Russian czar, the emperor, sent his military to shoot the protestors. The military was demoralized from losing World War I and shared the sentiment of hardship with the civilian protesters. The military turned on the czar, and 11 assassins were sent to kill the czar and his family of 11 people, including women, children, and babies. The czar and his family were brutally murdered without mercy by those 11 assassins.

Following the assassination of the czar, the military took over the government in Russia, and they plunged the country into 79 years of communism until 1991, when the Soviet Union dissolved. Those 79 years were a brutal regime, and the death toll in Soviet Russia is estimated at around 20–100 million, but it's almost impossible to determine how many people actually died.

If an estimated 20 to 100 million people were murdered by the brutal regime in communist Russia, then how many others died under other communist regimes?

The Black Book of Communism, Estimated number of victims

In the introduction, editor Stéphane Courtois states that "Communist regimes ... turned mass crime into a full-blown system of government."According to Courtois, the death toll amounts to 94 million. The breakdown of the number of deaths given by Courtois is as follows:

- *65 million in the People's Republic of China*

- *20 million in the Soviet Union*

- *2 million in Cambodia*

- *2 million in North Korea*

- *1.7 million in Ethiopia*

- *1.5 million in Afghanistan*

- *1 million in the Eastern Bloc*

- *1 million in Vietnam*

- *150,000 in Latin America*

- *10,000 deaths "resulting from actions of the international Communist movement and Communist parties not in power."*

Courtois writes that Communist regimes are responsible for a greater number of deaths than any other political ideal or movement, including Nazism. The statistics of victims include deaths through executions, man-made hunger, deportations, and forced labor.

https://en.wikipedia.org/wiki/The_Black_Book_of_Communism

A plunge into communism happens when the people are sold that communism is better than their current form of government, usually a monarchy or tyranny. You can see from the stats above that communist regimes are brutal, major killers of people, and the countries listed above are not real producers of value on the world stage. Would you want to move to any of those countries to live for a long period of time? The answer is usually "no."

Communism enriches the people who are in government and impoverishes the people by stealing from them. Sadly, we are moving towards a communist regime in our philosophy and current attitudes. This weakening of philosophy is a cause of the weak men in our society, and if these philosophies persist in our universities and schools, we will one day have full-blown brutal communism in the Western world.

> *Former Soviet-era deception expert Yuri Bezmenov laid out a* blueprint for communist subversion of any targeted nation back in the 1980s. That blueprint looks remarkably like what Obama and the radical left just pulled off over the last eight year ... *with the help of the lying mainstream media and cultural subversion via movies, TV, Jon Stewart, fake news, false flags, and an overthrow of the public education system (Common Core, an anti-education indoctrination / obedience scheme).*

> *Bezmenov is well known for saying:*

> *The highest art of warfare is not to fight at all ... but to sub-vert anything of value in the country of your enemy until such time that the perception of reality of your enemy is screwed up to such an extent that he does not perceive you as an enemy, and that your system, your civilization and your ambitions look to your enemy as an alternative, if not desirable then at least feasible. That's the ultimate purpose, the final stage of subversion, after which you can simply take your enemy without a single shot being fired.*

> ...

> ***The four stages of subversion—from Yuri Bezmenov, Soviet KGB subversion expert***

> 1. ***Demoralization.*** *It takes 15–20 years to demoralize a society. It includes influencing (infiltration, propaganda, etc.) of various areas where public opinion is shaped: Religion, educational system, social life, administration, law enforcement systems, military and labor-employer relations.*

> *Exploit the people within the society who are ideologically opposed to the system. Use small groups of agents from foreign*

nations. Distract people from real faith and replace it with artificial faiths in other systems.

In education, distract them from learning something constructive, pragmatic and efficient. Instead of mathematics, chemistry, history, teach them sexuality, home economy, anything to distract.

In social life, replace traditionally established institutions with fake organizations. Take away the initiative from people, take away the natural links between individuals and replace them with bureaucratically controlled systems. Establish social workers' institutions ruled by bureaucracy. Eliminate the family and replace the main concern with the paycheck from the government.

In government, replace elected officials with un-elected bureaucrats who control the people.

In the major media like the New York Times, you don't have to be an excellent journalist. You have to be exactly a mediocre journalist.

For the power structure: It is slowly eroded by those who do not have qualifications nor the will of the people.

Law enforcement: Put into place a slow substitution of basic moral principles, where someone who used to be a criminal is now considered a victim.

Labor relations: Destroy the traditionally established links of bargaining between employer and employee. Obedient workers follow their leaders.

Democracy is not a system of equality. It is a system where diverse people of different backgrounds have the chance to compete and thrive.

2. **Destabilization.** *Destabilize all the accepted institutions and organizations of your enemy.*

There is no crime if a professor introduces a course of communism or Marxism into a California college.

The radicalization of negotiations between labor and employers. "Normalizing" violent protests.

The media places itself in opposition to society, to alienate the people.

Subversive "sleepers" now become leaders in society and actively include themselves in the political process. Now, homosexuals make it a political issue to "demand human rights" and instigate violent clashes. Black against white. It doesn't matter, it's about creating antagonistic clashes. This is destabilization.

The sleepers are KGB agents. They become leaders to destabilize the targeted nation. Thus, the agent is already a respected citizen of the United States. He even gets money from the government for his struggle labeled "human rights."

3. **Crisis.** *The process starts when the legitimate bodies of power cannot function anymore. Instead, artificial bodies are injected into society, such as non-elected committees. They claim power on how to run your life. If power is denied to them, they take it by force. They are often half-baked intellectuals from Harvard or somewhere, they think they know the answers to social problems.*

The population at large is looking for a savior to solve the crisis that has been artificially created. They call for socialist government, centralized power. A savior is needed. The savior is then provided as the foreign nation, or the sleeper agents, they call it a revolution. They say, "I will lead you."

The two alternatives here are: 1) Civil war. 2) Invasion.

4. **Normalization.** *This stage is to make the subversion results seem "normal" to the people. "Your country is normalized."*

At this point, the workers don't demand a revolution anymore. This is stabilizing the country by force. Activists, liberals, social workers, homosexuals, professors and Marxists are being eliminated because they are not needed anymore.

The new owners need stability to exploit the nation and take advantage of the victory. The Marxists shoot their own revolutionaries.

Once the subverted culture is "normalized," the only way to reverse the course of the country is through military intervention.

The most difficult and simplest answer against subversion is to start it before the "demoralization" stage. Bring back religion to restore stability to society. (Halt "cultural Marxism" from marching forward.)

As part of normalization, allow the criminals to have "civil rights" and bring crisis to the country. To defend against this, do not allow them to take political power... do not elect them into power. It must be driven into the heads of the American voters that a person like that is an enemy of the state.

Restriction of certain freedoms would prevent sliding into crisis. To curb unlimited power of the trade unions would save the economy from collapse. To introduce a law to stop private companies of raping public opinions in the direction of consumerism. No company must have a right to force you into buying more unless you want.

Demoralization is the easiest thing to reverse. Restrict the import of propaganda. The unrestrained import of Soviet journalists... it has to be stopped. They won't be offended, they will respect America more. My colleague appears on Nightline and Ted Koppel asks him, "What do you think?" What can he think? He is a propaganda mouthpiece for the Soviet empire.

The process of demoralization will not start at all if the country prevents the importation of foreign ideology. You don't have to shoot every foreigner... but when he offers you junk in the disguise of shiny something, you have to tell him, "No. We have our own junk."

If the country is strong enough to stop the importation of ideas which are foreign, then the whole chain of subversion can be prevented.

Many societies throughout history collapsed the moment they lost religion. The idea of human beings as intelligent, moral agents of God can prevent collapse. But all the technology and computers will not prevent collapse. No one will fight to defend "2+2=4" but millions will fight to protect God and religious faith.

The answer to ideological subversion is very simple. You don't have to shoot people. You simply have to have faith and prevent subversion ... not to be a victim of subversion. Strike not with force but with the superiority of your intellect.

https://www.naturalnews.com/2017-01-09-communist-subversion-of-america-is-nearly-complete-left-wing-media-soviet-style-overthrow-yuri-bezmenov.html

So there you have it. We are in stage 3 subversion in the Western world as outlined by Yuri Bezmenov, Soviet KGB subversion expert. The Western men have been made weak, the family has been destroyed, women have been made into lesser men and taken away from their sacred purpose and jobs, money has been debased, religion has been marginalized and moved to the fringes, and politics has become a virtual circus. The next steps are (1) civil war or (2) invasion.

Rome was invaded by barbarians after a civil war and split into east and west.

History is just the same story over and over again with different costumes. What is happening in America already happened in Russia nearly 100 years ago. What is happening in America already happened in Rome. The fall of Russia and the fall of Rome are just echoes of the same story happening over and over again to empires throughout history. It starts with making the men weak and then hard times set in. Good times create weak men, weak men create hard times, and hard times create strong men.

You might think that subversion is conspiracy theory, you might still deny the fact that our society is being subverted by outside philosophies and undermined in values, you might think "that can never happen here," but subversion has already been used in North America to wipe out the ruling group of people and take their land and everything valuable to them.

CHAPTER 24

NATIVE AMERICAN GENOCIDE

British Style versus American Style

"Any man who thinks he can be happy and prosperous by letting the government take care of him, better take a closer look at the American Indian."

HENRY FORD

I am Canadian born and bred and live in Winnipeg, Manitoba, Canada, the murder capital of Canada. Winnipeg gets a bad reputation from other Canadian cities because if you go to the downtown core, what you may see will sadden you and potentially horrify you. On some days, there are literally bodies of passed out, drug-induced, drunk, hurt, bleeding, incapacitated aboriginal men and women lying on the streets. Sometimes you don't know if they are dead or alive; their bodies have been twisted by hard lives, alcohol, fighting, diabetes, and many have lost limbs, toes, or fingers to disease. Right in the heart of downtown there are several missions, low income housings, government housings, pawn shops, hotels and bars where these people live.

It is hardcore.

I have stood on the streets of the south side of Chicago, a notoriously dangerous "black" part of Chicago with gun violence that is always advertised in the American national media. It is not as scary, and the black population in the south side of Chicago is not nearly as messed up as in downtown Winnipeg, the reigning murder capital of Canada.

I have traveled to all the major cities in Canada, and Winnipeg has the worst downtown of any major Canadian city because it is scary and sad to see the remnants of a British genocide floating around in the downtown core, the Canadian aboriginals.

Canada, like America, is a huge landmass colonized by Europeans, namely the French and the British, starting in roughly the 1600s. How the Americans and the British (who later became the Canadians) dealt with the native populations was cruel, destructive, and genocidal, but each empire carried out the genocide in different ways.

American Indian genocide stats:

- **10 million+**—Estimated number of Native Americans living in land that is now the United States when European explorers first arrived in the fifteenth century

- **Less than 300,000**—Estimated number of Native Americans living in the United States around 1900

- **5.2 million** identified as American Indian or Alaska Native in the 2010 census

  http://endgenocide.org/learn/past-genocides/native-americans/

The Americans wiped out the natives with open war—guns, germs, and steel—and the old cowboy movies that characterize Americans as cowboy culture show the same cowboys over and over again slaughtering Indians or getting slaughtered by Indians. What the Americans did to their Native American Indians was similar to what Hitler did with the Jews in WWII, open frontline genocide of a people.

"To establish the American Republic, our forefathers exterminated Indian tribes. The Indians were no better. James Mooney, a pioneering ethnologist whom the native Americans of the late 19th century regarded as a friend, said, 'The career of every Indian has been the warpath. His proudest title has been that of warrior. His conversation by day and his dreams by night have been of bloody deeds upon the enemies of his tribe. His highest boast was in the number of his scalp trophies, and his chief delight at home was in the war dance and the scalp dance. The thirst for blood and massacre seemed inborn in every man, woman, and child of every tribe.'"

HOWARD BLOOM, *THE LUCIFER PRINCIPLE*

North of the US–Canadian border, the British had a far more sinister way of doing away with the aboriginal populations of Canada. Rather than open war—guns, germs, and steel—the British used subversion to destroy the aboriginals in Canada. This is much more dark and sinister.

They destroyed the Native American religions, raped the women, and stole the children into British schools to replace their religion with the religion of the British empire. Families were destroyed, the men were destroyed, children were ripped away from mothers, sons were taken from fathers, and today we have the remnants of a British genocide, carried out through subversion rather than open warfare as the Americans used on their Indians.

The British subversion of the Canadian aboriginals followed the exact same four steps that are happening right now in our own Western culture. When a group of people or a nation is subverted, there is no need for open warfare. The people can destroy themselves, marginalize themselves, and all you do is roll in at the end and rule the broken people.

The four stages of subversion—from Yuri Bezmenov, Soviet KGB subversion expert

1. **Demoralization.** It takes 15–20 years to demoralize a society. It includes influencing (infiltration, propaganda, etc.) of various areas where public opinion is shaped: Religion, educational system, social life, administration, law enforcement systems, military and labor-employer relations.

The aboriginals had their religion destroyed first, and the children were thrown into British schools. The children were sexually abused and taken from their parents. Intergenerational knowledge from fathers to sons and from mothers to daughters was lost. This fatally damaged the aboriginal people as a group. I would argue that this break, this loss of knowledge, is part of what has made them so broken for centuries. The aboriginal way of life was lost and poorly replaced with the British way of life.

2. **Destabilization.** Destabilize all the accepted institutions and organizations of your enemy.

Demoralization leads to destabilization. The organization of the leadership and the aboriginal tribes was destabilized, and I would argue it has never really been put back together again. A once strong and proud people—strong warriors and strong men who had their own culture and way of life—was completely destabilized to the point of not being able to revert back to what they had before. Once weakened through destabilization, it's almost impossible to get those traditions of strength back for the aboriginals or any other group, for that matter.

3. **Crisis.** The process starts when the legitimate bodies of power cannot function anymore. Instead, artificial bodies are injected into society, such as nonelected committees. They claim power on how to run your life. If power is denied to them, they take it by force. They are often half-baked intellectuals from Harvard or somewhere. They think they know the answers to social problems.

The legitimate bodies of power in the aboriginal community do not function. The modern native reserves and aboriginal chiefs on several native reserves have been proven to be corrupt over and over again, and they steal the money intended for the people. Life on the reserves is hell on earth, as I have seen the people come off the reserves firsthand, with rotten teeth, addicted to drugs, gas huffers, several addictions, and missing limbs, toes, and fingers because of diabetes. Some reserves don't even have running water or any fresh food. Coca Cola is cheaper than milk, and there is no healthy nutrition in the processed food that is only available on some reserves.

The aboriginal bodies of power are gone and have been replaced with government institutions to "help them," but these are artificial bodies of intellectuals do nothing to actually help the people. Government bodies are only concerned with their own power and how to increase their own power.

4. **Normalization.** *This stage is to make the subversion results seem "normal" to the people. "Your country is normalized." Normalization is usually where the weakened people are taken by force and there is no resistance left in the broken and weakened people. They welcome their enemy as a savior with open arms and as a real solution to their problems.*

After stage 3, crisis, the subverted people become normalized, and the new way of life becomes the new normal.

This leads to invasion or civil war. I would argue that the Canadian aboriginals in Winnipeg are in more of a state of civil war with the murders in the city being in the same part of town and the same groups of people killing each other over and over again. It's a very hard and sad life for the Canadian aboriginals.

In other ways, the aboriginals have been invaded and sent into remote pieces of shitty land called "reserves" while the British took over the best land for themselves and became rich in the process.

The Canadian aboriginals were invaded by the British and subverted, and to this day they still live in a state of civil war, where they fight each other for scarce resources on far away remote lands called reserves and in the ghettos of Winnipeg.

Rather than fight, the strong, powerful, proud aboriginal warriors from a strong warrior culture in open warfare, the British subverted the Canadian aboriginals instead. They let the native populations succumb to weakness, took their religion, their education, their strong men, their fathers, broke up their families, and let them get addicted to amoral activities such as drinking, drugs, and sex. Once a people like that is weakened, you won't have to fight them anymore. They will fight and kill each other, and then they simply need to be ruled until they wipe themselves out through civil war.

This is the power of subversion.

Is this right? Absolutely not, but life isn't fair.

Is this happening to the strong men of the Western world right now? Are we being subverted? Is this a growing trend since the 1960s?

You decide.

Human tribes with better technology, guns, germs, and steel are always invading, destroying, and subverting less advanced tribes.

What is startlingly apparent when comparing the Native American genocides to Canadian aboriginal genocide is that the Americans used force—guns, germs, and steel—to take the land from the American Indians. This was something that the Nazis studied and admired about America—the mass genocide of the Native Americans by force. In Canada, the British, with less military man power, used the invisible forces of subversion, which is much subtler and much darker and brings about more horrifying results. This is like the Russian KGB subversion tactics that have been used on America and the West since the Cold War to break down their enemy. Instead of force in the form of bombs, nukes, tanks, and soldiers, they have started to subvert the culture and philosophy and weaken the men so they can never fight back.

The aboriginals you see walking around downtown or passed out on the pavement in Winnipeg are but a shadow of a once proud and strong people. They were strong men who took care of their women and their tribes. I think the Canadian aboriginals were so strong that the British didn't wish to fight with them at all. The Apache warriors in the United States were one of the most savage and feared warriors in history. To fight Apaches in open combat was risky, costly, and dangerous. The British chose subversion instead of open warfare with the Canadian aboriginals out of pure practicality.

Instead of fighting these mighty warriors in one-to-one combat, the British subverted their culture much like we are being subverted in the Western world into leftist, collectivist, Marxist, and feminist ideals. This weakens and eliminates the strong men of society by opening the doors to civil war or invasion.

Why face your enemy in open combat when you can destroy him from within?

As the great warrior Sun Tzu wrote about subversion and subduing the enemy without ever fighting a war or a siege because of the high costs of open warfare. In *The Art Of War*, Sun Tzu writes:

III. Attack by Stratagem

1. Sun Tzu said: In the practical art of war, the best thing of all is to take the enemy's country whole and intact; to shatter and destroy it is not so good. So, too, it is better to recapture an army entire than to destroy it, to capture a regiment, a detachment or a company entire than to destroy them.

2. Hence to fight and conquer in all your battles is not supreme excellence; supreme excellence consists in breaking the enemy's resistance without fighting.

3. Thus the highest form of generalship is to balk the enemy's plans; the next best is to prevent the junction of the enemy's forces; the next in order is to attack the enemy's army in the field; and the worst policy of all is to besiege walled cities.

4. The rule is, not to besiege walled cities if it can possibly be avoided. The preparation of mantlets, movable shelters, and various implements of war, will take up three whole months; and the piling up of mounds over against the walls will take three months more.

5. The general, unable to control his irritation, will launch his men to the assault like swarming ants, with the result that one-third of his men are slain, while the town still remains untaken. Such are the disastrous effects of a siege.

6. Therefore the skillful leader subdues the enemy's troops without any fighting; he captures their cities without laying siege to them; he overthrows their kingdom without lengthy operations in the field.

7. With his forces intact he will dispute the mastery of the Empire, and thus, without losing a man, his triumph will be complete. This is the method of attacking by stratagem.

http://classics.mit.edu/Tzu/artwar.html

The Art of War was written in the sixth century BC, over 2,000 years ago, but the principles of warfare and destroying your enemies still ring true today. Technology may change, but human nature does not. Subversion was an ancient tactic back then and is still being used today. To deny the subversion of Western culture today is foolish and ignorant. It is much better to put the issues in the open and solve them like men, strong men who can identify and solve problems before we become the conquered aboriginals of tomorrow.

One more thought about subversion: since World War II America has been a major force in the world exporting its culture, food, music, entertainment, and way of life into countries all around the world. These countries have their own cultures subverted when American culture takes over. Subversion is happening every day all around the world, but it is an invisible force, not something you can see. Man has trouble fighting an invisible enemy. A real enemy, a flesh-and-blood enemy, a

Hitler to fight and kill is easy to band men together against a common foe, but an invisible force that comes in slowly like a poisonous gas is impossible to stop.

Do not take subversion lightly. It is just as destructive, or potentially more destructive, than an atom bomb. If a city is bombed, you can gather the people together and rebuild it much like Japan rebuilt after being nuked in World War II. But a tribe that has been subverted cannot even philosophically rebuild their philosophy, attitudes, and activities that they became successful on before. That is why subversion is so destructive. A strong man can stop a man like Hitler with guns, bombs, tanks, and planes, but not even a strong man can stop a slow subversive force that erodes the culture from within. Just look at Trump in America right now. He is attempting to reverse the subversive forces in his own backyard while the subverted groups of the popular media and popular narrative fight him harder, more unfairly, and more openly and viciously through character assassinations and the media. No amount of overt power can stop a subversive force. It has to be stopped on the basic level: man to man.

Subversion is a war of ideas and a war of ideals instead of a war of muscle, blood, and steel.

Subversion is a war for the hearts and minds of the people instead of a war for their land. Win their hearts and minds and they will welcome their enemies in and give their land away freely without a fight.

Such is the subtle and corrosive power of subversion.

CHAPTER 25
NEW GOD
"Science" and Worthless Academia

"Man, whose tool of survival is the mind, does not merely fail to teach a child to think, but devotes the child's education to the purpose of destroying his brain, of convincing him that thought is futile and evil, before he has started to think."

AYN RAND, *ATLAS SHRUGGED*

Academia, the universities, the philosophies taught, and the entire educational system in America and the Western world has become a subversive force to manufacture the weak. These educational systems are worshiped as the new gods in our Western world with the old wisdom "go to school, get good grades, get a good job, and you shall live happily ever after."

That old wisdom is from 1929 when the Great Depression hit and people flocked from the farms into the cities to get jobs. In 1940, 5.5% of American men and 3.8% of American women had degrees.

A degree used to be special and something elite that roughly 1/20 people would have. It truly was special in 1930 or 1940.

As of 2016, 33.2% of men and 33.7% of women had four-year degrees.

> *"Distract people from real faith and replace it with artificial faiths in other systems.*
>
> *In education, distract them from learning something constructive, pragmatic and efficient. Instead of mathematics, chemistry, history, teach them sexuality, home economy, anything to distract."*
>
> **The four stages of subversion—from Yuri Bezmenov, Soviet KGB subversion expert**

The degrees of today are more worthless than ever for several reasons:

1) The subjects that are offered are worthless to a young man getting a vocation in the world. Here are some worthless degrees: gender studies, aboriginal studies, art history, art therapy, music, sexuality, home economics, and anything else that doesn't directly equate to higher earnings or income, such as engineering, physics, math, chemistry etc. I know this all too well with a major in English and a minor in music. Sure, it was fun to read poetry and old stories in books, but it sure didn't help me secure meaningful work in the marketplace.

2) Too many people have degrees today, making the supply of degrees in the job marketplace devalued. You are better off to get a practical trade such as plumbing, electrical, carpentry, metalworking, pipe fitting, etc.

3) The cost of post-secondary education, especially in the USA, is ridiculous. It makes no sense to spend $120,000 on a degree to make $30,000 in an office. You cannot pay off

Percentage of the US Population Who Have Completed Four Years of College or More from 1940 to 2016, by Gender

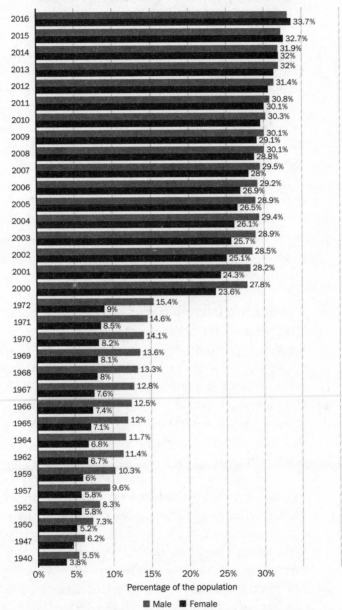

Year	Male	Female
2016	33.7%	
2015	32.7%	
2014	31.9% / 32%	
2013	32%	
2012	31.4%	
2011	30.8% / 30.1%	
2010	30.3%	
2009	30.1% / 29.1%	
2008	30.1% / 28.8%	
2007	29.5% / 28%	
2006	29.2% / 26.9%	
2005	28.9% / 26.5%	
2004	29.4% / 26.1%	
2003	28.9% / 25.7%	
2002	28.5% / 25.1%	
2001	28.2% / 24.3%	
2000	27.8% / 23.6%	
1972	15.4% / 9%	
1971	14.6% / 8.5%	
1970	14.1% / 8.2%	
1969	13.6% / 8.1%	
1968	13.3% / 8%	
1967	12.8% / 7.6%	
1966	12.5% / 7.4%	
1965	12% / 7.1%	
1964	11.7% / 6.8%	
1962	11.4% / 6.7%	
1959	10.3% / 6%	
1957	9.6% / 5.8%	
1952	8.3% / 5.8%	
1950	7.3% / 5.2%	
1947	6.2%	
1940	5.5% / 3.8%	

Percentage of the population

■ Male ■ Female

https://www.statista.com/statistics/184272/educational-attainment-of-college-diploma-or-higher-by-gender/

the student debt, and you cannot go bankrupt to get out from under it. If you can't go bankrupt on student debt, is this not a new form of bondage and slavery? The system is broken.

4) To spend four years on a degree is too slow. I would argue that with modern learning systems, the internet, video, online video conferencing, coaching, and mentoring, it shouldn't take someone four years to earn an undergraduate degree. My degree took me four years in time, but there was only six months of content. Considering you can go into business and become a self-made millionaire in five years, I don't see a need to waste 4–12 years in a university to become a PhD (Poor Helpless and Desperate) or a BA (Barely Able) to suddenly not find meaningful work. Why not go into sales and make a career for yourself instead? Sure, that requires some personal development, but who doesn't need to develop new skills to win in this ever-changing world?

5) The workplace and job markets are changing so fast you are obsolete by the time you graduate.

6) Employers generally don't care about degrees (I am an employer, but I never look at anyone's education). Instead, employers care about results: what can you do for me? How can you make me money? There are some jobs that require degrees, but those are government-regulated jobs such as medicine, law, and education.

7) Universities often eviscerate the creativity and thinking ability of men and women, and the people who graduate are no longer creative and are worth less than people who think creatively. People who think creatively are ironically the "uneducated" people who didn't have their minds destroyed in a four-year institution to learn to think like everyone else on the assembly line.

8) Many of the skills learned in university must be unlearned or relearned in the workplace. I had to relearn how to write because academic writing is different from writing that

influences and sells. Why get an English degree then? I'm not sure; to me it was a poor use of time and money.

9) You spend four years without earning money while you go to university. This is stupid; earn money. It's a manly thing to do. So many students don't bother working in university for favor of studying. I would argue that working and getting real experience is more important than studying the obsolete nonsense taught in modern universities these days.

10) The professors don't practice what they preach; they are virgin sex therapists. The people who teach business school have never run a business. They say that those who can't do, teach.

11) The cutting-edge material available in a university is likely at least five years old by the time it becomes available to students. This is because of the publishing and academic sourcing system. To publish academic papers and make something a "fact" takes too long. Rather than base your facts on common sense and "cause and effect," you must research, source, get published in an academic journal, then be taken as fact. This takes several years. This is too slow for the real world, where every six months, the world has changed dramatically due to the compounding effect of faster and better technology.

"Man is the only animal that cripples his children's ability to survive."

Ayn Rand

Students treat the university as if it is God; the university is supposed to be a storehouse of knowledge and a place for higher learning. Instead, most universities are a place where creativity goes to die. They are impractical versions of trade schools and sell things that are outdated and deliver them in antiquated ways.

In 2005, I signed up for the innovative new program at the University of Manitoba—jazz. Jazz has not been a relevant music since 1960, yet the university, being 45 years behind reality, was offering a brand-new subject of study. How out of touch can you be with reality? I asked my professors at the time if we could learn sampling or digital music; they had nothing to teach. DJs were just starting to proliferate in popular music, and live music was becoming antiquated in the real world of the music business.

Even the business schools are out of touch because the universities rely on published books and published academic papers to be "truth and good sources." This is bullshit in the new world; information moves too fast. Publishing physical academic papers is too slow. They are reactive and behind the cutting edge nowadays because of the velocity of technology.

This publishing system is antiquated and manipulated for ulterior motives when it comes to medicine, drugs, and other studies such as "global warming." Science, or what the popular masses deem to be science, is created in universities to serve an agenda, and not for the real knowledge of truth of a subject.

"Today's science is tomorrow's laughingstock."

STEFAN AARNIO

Our broken education system comes from Prussia, and Prussia no longer exists. Kindergarten is a German word that means "garden of children," and Prussian schools were designed to create obedient workers, soldiers, and employees. They were not designed to create free thinkers who challenge the system and the crap that is served to them every day.

Prior to formal schools, the way to transfer knowledge from man to man was through masters and apprentices. If you wanted to be a blacksmith, you lived and worked with the blacksmith and you were his apprentice. I believe that the relationship between masters and apprentices, and mentors and mentees is the true way to learn. In my own education company, we coach and mentor students all over north America to learn complex subjects such as real estate investing with none of their own money, sales, negotiation, and other hard-to-learn subjects through coaching, mentoring, and master/apprentice relationships.

People have been learning successfully throughout all of human history in master–apprentice relationships. Only in the last century have we decided to violate these important ways to learn with classrooms and industrial style learning—which doesn't work well.

I come from an education family—a family of teachers. Last summer while driving out to the lake, my mother lamented that the kids are no longer showing up to the classroom in her high school.

I said, "The classroom is obsolete, Mom."

The kids are smart, they can Google the information, they can use a calculator, they can watch a video online for free on YouTube. They don't have to sit there and listen to a shitty teacher who sucks at teaching go through some 20-year-old textbooks that have no weight in reality anymore.

Kids are smart, the system is dumb, and the system needs to die like the dinosaur it is and be reworked. Masters and apprentices need to be brought back, and technology needs to be leveraged to speed up the education process. The 12-year school curriculum between kindergarten and grade 12 is only 12 years to socially condition the students into obedient workers and has nothing to do with actually teaching. The purpose of the school system is to dumb the students down and make them slow and unable to think on their own.

I explained to my mother that in my education company, the students don't show up to my classes anymore. They get their learning over the phone, one-on-one coaching, online in a video bank, webinars, group coaching, direct text and email access to their coach and through media consumed at home with CDs, DVDs, boxed manuals etc. (Yes, I'm writing this in 2018 and we still use hard media like CDs.)

My last classroom session I held should have had 80 students show up, but only 23 showed up to class. The rest had learned on their own time, got the results they wanted in real life, and saw no need to come to class.

My education company also doesn't do tests or mark students; instead, they do a real live project where they flip a house and make real profit. Real profit in their pocket is their report card, not some stupid card that says, "Billy didn't show up to class or is unengaged." No one cares about that.

To create strong men once again, I think we need to see a return to the historical education system of masters and apprentices, coaches and mentors. That is the best and fastest way to transfer real knowledge, not some textbook garbage.

Donald Trump is the reigning strong man in the USA at the time of writing this book. He went to Wharton School of Business, one of the best business schools in the USA, but he gives very little credit to his success for his degree from Wharton. Instead, he attributes his success to his mentor, his father, Fred Trump, a $100,000,000 man who mentored Donald to be strong.

Masters and apprentices, fathers and sons, mothers and daughters, mentors and mentees, and coaches—that is how knowledge is practically transferred throughout generations. Today, our classrooms and universities are mostly obsolete and broken.

Statistics on Wealth Transfer and Knowledge Transfer from One Generation to the Next:

"Wealthy families, 2nd generation has a 70% chance of losing wealth 3rd generation has a 90% chance of losing wealth"

http://time.com/money/3925308/rich-families-lose-wealth/

To transfer knowledge from one generation to the next is a perilous task, and that is why wealth is lost from one generation to the next. The same applies to "how to be a man." With no father to teach a man how to be a man, the boy will stay a boy forever. Without proper mentoring programs, young men will continue to be weak men until they are mentored by a strong man to learn the skills they need to survive.

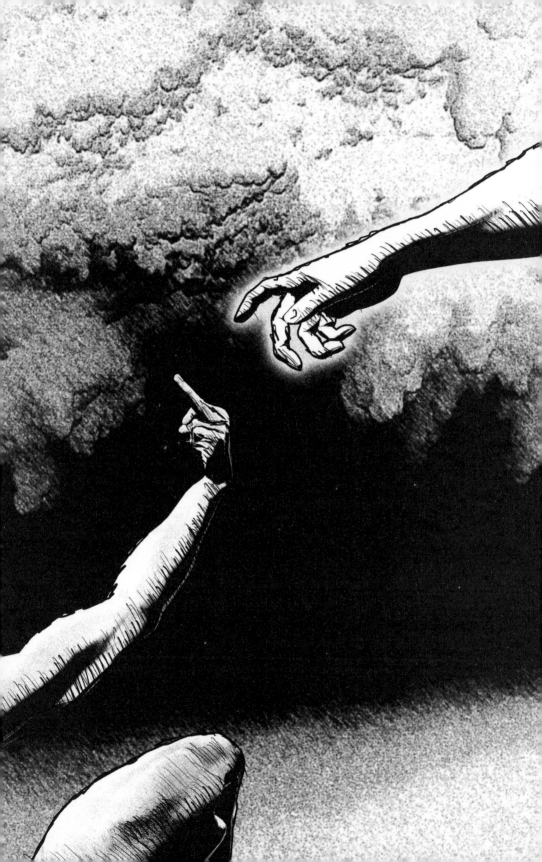

CHAPTER 26
NEW GOD
Atheism: Killing the Sacred Cows

*"All diseases of Christians are
to be ascribed to demons."*

St. Augustine

The man in the bar and the man in the church are looking for the same thing. They are both trying to find God.

I have often stayed up late staring into my computer screen at 3:00 a.m. trying to find God.

I have swiped my way through dating apps looking at women in the middle of the night, again hoping to find God.

I have often said that online dating is "staring into the mouth of hell hoping to find God," and as dark as it sounds, men in today's world, weak men, try to find God in all the wrong places, and this futile seeking in the wrong places keeps men lost and weak.

s throughout history collapsed the moment they
The idea of human beings as intelligent, moral
:an prevent collapse. But all the technology and
not prevent collapse. No one will fight to defend
"2+2=4" but millions will fight to protect God and religious faith.

The answer to ideological subversion is very simple. You don't have to shoot people. You simply have to have faith and prevent subversion ... not to be a victim of subversion. Strike not with force but with the superiority of your intellect."

Mike Adams

America became the greatest nation in the world in the mid 1900s and was born a great nation in 1776 because it was founded on Judeo-Christian values. Religion is a philosophy, a system of organized living, a fundamental technology of civilization, an ancient way to pass knowledge from one generation to another, and a way to build on strong values that allowed empires to be built. Without such technology of religion, man would be living today digging in the mud, scavenging to live, and roaming the countryside as bands of cannibals. Religion is the technology and the system that keeps man from his darkest self and from the darkness of his own human nature.

We have Saturdays off for the Jewish Shabbat and Sundays off for the Christian Sabbath. Thus, we have a five-day workweek, with Saturday and Sunday free to rest and pursue our passions in life.

So many great things in America come from Judeo-Christian philosophy, and this has led to the abundance of creativity in America. It has allowed business people the opportunity to try and fail. With bankruptcy, men can have a second chance to "try again" and avoid debtor's prison. This was a new idea in the new world of America versus the old world of Europe, Asia, or the Middle East.

America (as a nation born of great philosophy and religious ideals) had the most abundance, religious freedom, economic freedom, the ability to rise or fall based on your own virtues, and freedom from a caste system like in India or other countries. The laws are merciful; they will not cut off your hands if you steal, they will not pour acid on your face if you are a woman, and they will not mutilate your clitoris as they do in Africa. America is a great place because of a merging of the Judeo and Christian philosophies.

The Jewish faith is one of the smartest and oldest faiths in the world. The Jewish faith is a very old technology and has had more time than other religions to prove its success over time. Places that adopt the Jewish faith are advanced in technology and are highly prosperous. Israel is one of the most technologically advanced, prosperous countries on the planet because of its strong philosophy and Jewish faith.

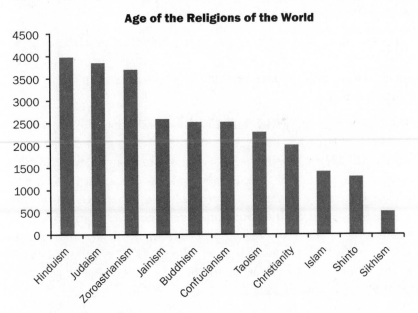

http://www.beliefnet.com/columnists/religion101/2012/10/how-old-are-the-religions.html

In his book *Thou Shall Prosper,* Rabbi Daniel Lapin lays down the 10 commandments for making money. The Jewish faith as a technology has built-in mechanisms for living a prosperous life and becoming wealthy. These include simple things such as get an education and a high-paying profession; these are staples in the Jewish culture and philosophy. Many Jewish people become lawyers, doctors, and accountants because that is encouraged in the culture. Other simple ideas include never retiring; this leads to life-long earning and wealth.

There is no magic in the Jewish philosophy, just a set of great ideas that work and bring success and prosperity. Are the Jewish people really God's chosen people? Who knows, but what is known for sure is that their philosophy certainly makes them achieve great results in business and in life. What came first? Being great then being chosen by God? Or being chosen by God and then being great? This is like the chicken and the egg paradox. What is undeniable is that the Jewish faith and philosophy makes for very successful people.

The Christian faith is another prosperous faith that practices forgiveness, freedom, celebrates creativity, resourcefulness, a conservation of man's sexual energy, marriage, families, children, and an entire list of other benefits.

The blending of the Jewish and Christian philosophies has been the backbone of what has made America great. If you do not believe my words, simply look at countries that are not Christian or Jewish in faith and ask yourself, do you want to move to those countries? If you live in a Western country, the answer is probably "no." There is a reason why people from non-Christian and non-Jewish countries from around the world want to come to Canada, America, Sweden, Germany, France, Britain, and other developed first-world nations. They are great places to live and are constantly at the top of the charts for being generally great places to work and play.

The reverse is not true, however. People from great countries that have Judeo-Christian values *do not* want to move to countries devoid of those philosophies. You likely do not want to move to Turkey, Syria, Libya, Afghanistan, Iraq, or Iran. Those people want to come here because of our values, but we don't want to go there because of their values.

This is not racism or hate. It simply is that the Judeo-Christian values are an advanced technology and are progressive compared to the backwardness of some countries around the world. These countries embrace philosophies that are 500 years behind, and the Jewish and Christian people have already grown past those philosophies. Would you want software from 500 years ago on your computer? Probably not. The newer, more relevant, updated software is usually what you want, not 500-year-old medieval software. For example, Islam as a religion is roughly 500 years younger than the Christian religion. The Christian religion is much younger than the Jewish religion. The older and more established the religion, the more advanced and tested its philosophy. In effect, since Islam is 500 years behind Christianity, they are effectively living with the brutal and violent ways of life that was seen in the Christian medieval times. If you are 500 years behind in philosophy, then why would anyone in the modern age or the Western world want to return to a thinking process from 500 years ago? The Middle Ages were a hard and violent time, and that is why people from the Islamic countries want to move to the West. But the people from the West don't want to move into Islamic countries.

In our schools and universities, the Judeo-Christian values that built great countries like America are being subverted in favor of atheism. Atheism literally means "without god."

a·the·ism
'āTHē͟ˌizəm/
noun

    disbelief or lack of belief in the existence of God or gods.

    synonyms: nonbelief, disbelief, unbelief, irreligion, skepticism, doubt, agnosticism; nihilism

    "atheism was not freely discussed in his community"

To fill the minds of the youth and young people, especially "educated" young people with post-secondary educations with "atheism," destroys the base values and philosophy of the country. When you destroy the philosophy first, the design of fundamental information, everything else in a culture is destroyed over time as well. This is true for individual people, companies, countries, or any group of people. Philosophy, attitude, and activity determine everything in your life. To replace a successful philosophy with a totalitarian philosophy of atheism where the state becomes the new god is the ultimate subversive move towards destroying an empire and weakening the men.

Rome as an empire grew with a stoic philosophy based on cause and effect, denial of pleasures, and reason. In the height of Rome, stoicism was a religion based on personal ethics and was against making decisions based on emotions rather than reason. *Stoicism* is a school of Hellenistic philosophy that flourished throughout the Roman and Greek worlds until the third century AD. Stoicism is predominantly a philosophy of personal ethics that is informed by its system of logic and its views on the natural world. According to its teachings, as social beings, the path to happiness for humans is found in accepting this moment as it presents itself, by not allowing ourselves to be controlled by our desire for pleasure or our fear of pain, by using our minds to understand the world around us and to do our part in nature's plan, and by working together and treating others in a fair and just manner.

It was founded in Athens by Zeno of Citium in the early third century BC. The stoics taught that emotions resulted in errors of judgment, which were destructive, due to the active relationship between cosmic determinism and human freedom, and the belief that it is virtuous to maintain a will (called *prohairesis*) that is in accord with nature. Because of this, the stoics presented their philosophy as a religion (*lex divina*), and they thought that the best indication of an individual's philosophy was not what a person said but how a person behaved. To live a good life, one had to understand the rules of the natural order, since they taught that everything was rooted in nature. Later stoics—such as Seneca and Epictetus—emphasized that, because "virtue is sufficient for happiness," a sage was immune to misfortune. This belief is similar to the meaning of the phrase "stoic calm," though the phrase does not include the "radical ethical" stoic views that only a sage can be considered truly free, and that all moral corruptions are equally vicious. From its founding, stoic doctrine was popular during the Roman Empire—and its adherents included the Emperor Marcus Aurelius. It later experienced a decline after Christianity became the state religion in the fourth century AD. Over the centuries, it has seen revivals, notably in the Renaissance (Neostoicism) and in the modern era (modern stoicism).

https://en.wikipedia.org/wiki/Stoicism

Rome died when it began to take on epicurean philosophy and the relative weakness of Christian values versus stoic values. Epicureanism and Christianity were incredibly soft in Roman times compared to the warrior culture and warrior philosophy of the stoics. Rome was born out of war and combat, which led to a hardness that the Christians at the time did not have as a young religion. Good times had created weak men once more.

Also important in the history of atheism was Epicurus (c. 300 BC). Drawing on the ideas of Democritus and the atomists, he espoused a materialistic philosophy wherein the universe was governed by the laws of chance without the need for divine intervention. Although he stated that deities existed, he believed that they were uninterested in human existence. The aim of the epicureans was to attain peace of mind by exposing fear of divine wrath as irrational.

One of the most eloquent expressions of epicurean thought is Lucretius' *On the Nature of Things* (1st century BC) in which he held that gods exist but argued that religious fear was one the chief cause of human unhappiness and that the gods did not involve themselves in the world.

The epicureans also denied the existence of an afterlife and hence dismissed the fear of death. Epicureans were not persecuted, but their teachings were controversial and were harshly attacked by the mainstream schools of stoicism and Neoplatonism. The movement remained marginal and gradually died out by the end of the Roman Empire.

https://en.wikipedia.org/wiki/History_of_atheism

Atheism is of little or no value to the average man as a belief system because out of the four parts of a human being (the physical realm, the mental realm, the spiritual realm, and the emotional realm), atheism denies the spiritual realm all together and by collateral damage denies the emotional realm as well. This leaves man with half of his capacities: only mental and physical.

You are much more than a mind and a body. The modern atheistic view proclaimed by institutions and universities claims that you only have a mind and a body. However, that view denies man of the true spiritual and emotional power deep within his soul. This power is the power that great men have drawn on to build the great creations of history or lead the world-changing movements.

If you deny man of his greatest power, it will keep those who have power in power and will prevent those who do not have power from rising. This is a gambit to keep the bureaucrats, the rich, aristocrats, the wealthy established people in power and to keep younger groups of men from rising.

Are We Created or Are We Evolved?

This has been a hot topic in American schools: should we teach evolution or creation? I have been full circle on the topic of creation and evolution in my life, and my beliefs have changed as I have learned more about the world and how it works.

When I was a child, I was taught that God created man; this made sense to me as a child. Then I grew up, entered the high schools and the universities with the best-known science at the time, and we were taught about Darwinism and evolution—which is a religion unto itself. No one really knows if we were created or evolved. Both theories rely on faith and have limited evidence, where faith must make up the gaps in the logic. In the evolutionary theories, somehow single-celled organisms and primordial ooze evolved into fish, then the fish walked up on land and became lizards, then the lizards lost out to mammals, etc. The story made sense in school, and so I subscribed to the religion of science and evolution.

Now I am 31 years old. I have lived life, seen people die, seen people be born, watched things come and go from the world. I have written several books, destroyed my first novel (that I wrote at age twelve), created art, destroyed art, loved women, lost women, led men to success, and led men to failure. In my limited life experience with all the things I've created, won and lost, I believe in intelligent design.

*"Failure is simply the opportunity to begin
again, this time more intelligently."*

HENRY FORD

The world does not operate in a chaotic thrashing of randomness. That is a nihilistic view of the world in which there is nothing, no intelligent design, just randomness thrashing against itself. Nihilism and postmodernism is Marxist, and what has been pumped into our universities since the Cold War to subvert the Western philosophies and way of life. Nature is not random, nor is life random. There is an incredible amount of design in our world, and we have not been able to find any other intelligent lifeforms yet in our solar system in our brief history. The earth is very special, and humanity is unique. We are one of a kind, but who created us? What created us? What intelligence designed us? The universe is infinitely intelligent, and the evidence of this intelligence is everywhere and nowhere all at once. This infinite intelligence is invisible, so some may claim that it does not exist, but look at the following things we use that are invisible, yet we know they exist:

1) Radio waves
2) Microwaves
3) Electricity
4) Wireless phones
5) Wi-Fi
6) Sounds that are above 20,000hz that we cannot hear with our ears
7) Cloud computing
8) Software stored on computers
9) Data stored in hard drives Hard drives
10) Data stored in Microchips
11) Thought
12) Ideas

All of these invisible forces exist; we use them daily, and yet some claim that infinite intelligence, which is also an invisible force to be used every day, does not exist. Here are some questions for those who do not believe in intelligent design and may feel that we are evolved rather than created from an infinite intelligence:

Some Questions for Evolution that I Believe DO NOT Have Good Definitive Answers from the Scientific Community.

1) If we evolved from "apes," then why didn't all the "apes" evolve? Wouldn't we all evolve the same? Are we going to claim that some apes just weren't lucky enough to get a ticket in the evolution race? The scientific answer would blame the apes that didn't evolve on "they just didn't"? Or perhaps we wiped out our competitors; why not wipe out all the primitive apes then?

2) Humans are the only animal on the planet with an ultra-advanced brain that we cannot replicate through science, and we will find out in the coming decades if we can recreate a human brain or superior synthetic creation through artificial intelligence. Will we become gods? Who knows. Our human brain has a neocortex, a thinking brain. We can communicate in complex language, think into the future, recall the past, create art, create poetry, write, read, build machines, and build empires. No other animal on the planet has anything near the capacity to do what we can do with our thinking brain. Why didn't the other animals evolve these capacities? Wouldn't every animal be evolving an advanced thinking brain to survive? Why is humanity the only animal that again won the evolutionary lottery and received such a gift? Some science people have argued that we wiped out the competitors ... really? Why aren't there lizards or fish with advanced thinking brains who can create tools? Was the thinking brain genetically added to primitive protohuman

and a gift from our creator, who also had a neocortex and the ability to create? Several other planets we have discovered are barren and cannot support life. Why is our planet the only one we can find that can support life? When we find other planets with life, will we become the gods and designers of new life? Or will the new life we find be our god and designers?

3)   In studying the skeletal remains of protohumans and evolution, there is a massive leap between the humans of today with a thinking brain and the subhumans. What caused such a massive leap? Wouldn't evolution be slow and gradual? What outside force acted on that primitive animal to make him into man?

4)   Structures such as the pyramids in Egypt were built with more advanced forms of measurement, alignment, stone cutting, stone moving, and stone laying, and they line up precisely with the constellation Orion's belt. Our speculative history tells us that slaves created such structures; this is improbable, because slaves do relatively imprecise work and could not have built such structures. We cannot recreate the pyramids today with the modern tools we have in construction, so who built them? Who is smarter than man on this planet to be able to build such structures? Why do these structures exist all around the globe in different cultures and different times of history, and yet we have no real explanation about these structures? What intelligence did we have custody of as a race at the time that we lost? Was it human intelligence at all? Was it higher intelligence of the creators or the gods?

5)   Man's brain is able to connect to the spiritual realm through the pineal gland. No other animal has such capabilities to wield the spiritual universe and create. Why didn't the other animals evolve such creative capacity? Why is there only one animal on earth with this capacity? Would there not be evolved competitors around the globe? Lizards, fish, birds, wouldn't they evolve a thinking brain

too? If evolution is random or the universe is random, wouldn't we have randomly evolving animals who also have thinking brains like us?

6) Specific fruits and vegetables are shaped to resemble and heal specific organs in the body. Were these created by the people, gods, or entities that designed man? It would appear so; no other food can be digested fully other than fruits and vegetables.

Digestion Times for Different Foods

Foods	Digestion time	Foods	Digestion time
Watermelon	20 minutes	Potatoes	1 hour
Oranges, grapes	30 minutes	Brown rice, oats, millet	1.5 hours
Apples, pears, cherries	40 minutes	Soya beans, peas, kidney beans	1.5–2 hours
Fresh tomatoes, cucumbers, celery	40 minutes	White cheese	1.5–2 hours
Boiled spinach, cauliflower, maize	45 minutes	Chicken without skin	1–2 hours
Boiled egg	45 minutes	Beef	3–4 hours
Boiled root vegetables: carrot, beetroots, turnip	50 minutes	Cheese	3–4.5 hours
Fish: cod, salmon, herring	30–60 minutes	Pork	4–5 hours

We can survive on meat, dairy, bread, and man-made foods, but eventually we will have diseases and become sick unless we only eat fruits and vegetables. Is this intelligent design? Man's jaw is designed to be an herbivore as indicated by the ability to move side-to-side and molars for grinding vegetables and fruits. A carnivore has sharp teeth and a jaw that cannot move side to side to rip flesh. Our colon is much too long to digest cooked meat, whereas a carnivore like a tiger has a short colon. If you feed cooked meat to a tiger, he dies. If you feed flour to a rat, he dies. Feeding foods to animals that they aren't meant to eat kills them. Is this intelligent design? We are designed to only eat fruits and vegetables that are shaped like our organs and specifically heal them. If we eat foods that are outside of our design, we get sick. This is like putting diesel in a Formula One race car. The car would not run well, or the engine would break. Who designed such a system? Did they design fruits and vegetables at the same time they designed us?

7) The human body can clean itself, regenerate itself, and sort out nearly all health issues through fasting. Is this intelligent design or is it just random luck? You can reset a computer by turning it off and restarting it, as the designers of computers put into plan. You clean a plumbing system by shutting the water off and cleaning the pipes, as the designers of the plumbing system planned. Those are man-made systems designed to be cleaned and "rebooted" if they become clogged. We have a built-in reboot system to clean and fix our bodies when they become sick and clogged like a computer or a plumbing system. Who designed that? Was that random? All animals on the earth stop eating and fast if they are sick, and we are designed to do the same. Who designed the highly intelligent fasting reboot system?

"Everyone has a physician inside him or her; we just have to help it in its work. The natural healing force within each one of us is the greatest force in getting well. Our food should be our medicine. Our medicine should be our food. But to eat when you are sick is to feed your sickness."

HIPPOCRATES

"Instead of using medicine, rather, fast a day."

PLUTARCH

When an animal, such as a dog or cat, is sick, its natural instinct is to refuse food. When the crisis is over, and the internal healing work has been accomplished, the appetite will return naturally, of its own accord.

The human organism also has a fasting instinct, just like that of other animals. Evolutionary adaptation has made our bodies very efficient at storing energy reserves and drawing upon them when food supplies are scarce. Fasting is as old as mankind, perhaps even older. As far back as historians can see, men have been fasting for one reason or another. It seems to be a universal practice.

The ancient Greeks were great believers in fasting. Hippocrates advocated in favor of it, as is shown in the above quotation. Plato said that he fasted for greater physical and mental efficiency. Aristotle, his pupil, also fasted. Both Galen and Avicenna also prescribed fasts for their patients.

> http://www.greekmedicine.net/hygiene/Fasting_and_
> Purification.html

1) This primitive book you are reading had a primitive creator, and it is a primitive creation. You are a complex creation, so what complex creator created you? Someone authored this book; who authored you and the information in your DNA? Surely there was an author to write your code. Books don't write themselves. Nothing is created without a creator. We can likely agree that a book cannot exist unless someone created it, so who created the only life-supporting planet we can find, the animals, the fruit, the vegetables, the trees, and the humans? Was there not an author to that book as well?

2) As advanced as we are in science, we cannot create life from scratch. Why not? We can synthetically create life by splicing genes and grafting things together, but we cannot create new life from scratch. Is this divine power that we do not possess? Inside the seed exists a tree. There is intelligent design in the seed. Inside a sperm and egg exists a human when mixed. Is there not design there as well? Who authored such creation? Our science cannot author

this creation from scratch. There must be a higher intelligence who could create such a thing.

3) How can we explain a soul? Or a spirit? When we die, the soul leaves the body. We cannot get it back, we cannot create a soul, we cannot recreate a soul, we are not immortal and perhaps can never be. Who created the soul? Who authored such a thing that we cannot make?

4) How could something as delicate and advanced as a human eyeball or human brain, which we cannot currently replicate or synthesize with our current technology, be an act of randomness and random evolution? Is there not intelligent design in such an advanced creation? This book had an author. Who authored the human brain? Who was the architect of the human eyeball? Those are advanced creations. Were these very complex, more complex than anything we have created so far as a species. Are such delicate creations as the human eye and brain not designed by someone or something?

5) Do things change over time? Do animals breed and selectively choose traits that are more favorable to the environment as Darwin said in his work? The evidence seems to be there for evolution and adaptation as animals and humans change with their environment. Even still, who created the environment and the animals? There is no such thing as something from nothing. What caused all the life on this planet to be?

I ask these questions because I am a creator and designer, and I know the energy it takes to create primitive objects like books. In fact, a book is a glorified notepad of paper and usually takes two years and a huge team of people to produce. It is only a pad of paper, not a self-sustaining ecosystem of life, not a life-sustaining planet, not an autonomous human being with a soul. This book was authored by an author, but who authored the world? Nothing is random in the universe; we claim randomness because we cannot see the greater patterns that are invisible to us.

Humans are wired to see patterns. If we can't see a pattern we claim randomness, but nothing is random. The patterns are just too large, too broad, too invisible, and too complex for us to see. Much like the message in this book is that hard times create strong men, strong men create good times, good times create weak men, and weak men create hard times. That is an invisible 80-year cycle; it exists, and our problems come from not understanding the invisible cycle, which is the purpose of this book.

When you attempt to discover the answers to the questions about intelligent design as I listed above, you may start to study the spiritual realm and the force that binds all things—the infinite intelligence of the universe or the God, as some religions personify this intelligence. I am not telling you to believe what I believe. I am only asking you to think and find the answers to these major questions for yourself. Think deeper on the mysteries of this world that we do not have satisfactory scientific answers for but our primitive and ever-changing university-based religion of "science" claims to understand.

To teach children in school evolution is like claiming we know how the pyramids were built. We don't know, and we don't even have good evidence to pretend to know. Some would argue that shoving one religion down everyone's throat in school is wrong, but we do it anyway via the worst possible religion called atheism. It is of no benefit to our people. To have a 2000-year-old technology (Judeo-Christian values) on how to live a good and productive life and then delete the software in favor of a 70-year-old nontechnology, aka atheism, is not progressive but regressive. Atheism eviscerates the spiritual realm from man and by doing so the emotional realm as well. This weakens the men and denies them of their true spiritual power, which is infinite power and creative power.

At least when Christianity was taught in American schools the children learned the values that their country was built on and how to live a virtuous, moral, productive, and successful life. That is powerful unto itself. To fail to know the values that your tribe is built on is what will destroy your tribe in the long run. The Roman Empire had Roman values, a common religion of stoicism in the beginning, "for the senate and the people," and they were a mighty group of strong men and women in history until they compromised their values and violated their success principles for pleasure, weakness, and emotions.

I am convinced that written religion is the greatest invention of the human race. Without written religion, we could have no supertribe. We would be too busy violating one another to invent computers, the internet, artificial intelligence, spaceships, food systems, transportation, or any other invention. Written religion is the base of civilization, and without it the human race would degrade backwards into cannibalism. If a plane crashes in the mountains, the survivors turn into cannibals in three days, eating the dead to stay alive. How long can you live without eating? As a man who practices fasting, I know that a human being can survive on water without food until you are 2% body fat. A healthy male is 15% body fat, and a healthy woman is roughly 24% body fat. If you are obese you might be 65% body fat and can probably survive for a year without food. The truth is people can live for quite a long time without food, but not long without water. What remains true is we have time to survive on our own fat and food-matter stored in our organs before things get dangerous and we starve. Yet people get emotional and scared and succumb to cannibalism after three days, why?

Man is weak, ruled by his emotions, if he does not use his mind and use reason to survive. We are cannibals on an animalistic and physical level. The only thing keeping us from cannibalism today is the thin veil of civilization we have dangling in front of our faces and our value systems that are still loosely based on successful religions of the past. Religion is the technology to keep man from degrading into an animal, a cannibal, by harnessing the power of his mind and spirit for greater things in life.

"Man's mind is his basic tool of survival. Life is given to him, survival is not. His body is given to him, its sustenance is not. His mind is given to him, its content is not. To remain alive, he must act, and before he can act he must know the nature and purpose of his action. He cannot obtain his food

without a knowledge of food and of the way to obtain it. He
cannot dig a ditch...without a knowledge of his aim and of
the means to achieve it. To remain alive, he must think.

"But to think is an act of choice. The key to what you so recklessly
call 'human nature,' the open secret you live with, yet dread to
name, is the fact that man is a being of volitional consciousness.
Reason does not work automatically; thinking is not a mechanical
process; the connections of logic are not made by instinct. The
function of your stomach, lungs, or heart is automatic; the
function of your mind is not. In any hour and issue of your life,
you are free to think or to evade that effort. But you are not free to
escape from your nature, from the fact that reason is your means
of survival—so that for you, who are a human being, the question
'to be or not to be' is the question 'to think or not to think.' ...

"Man has no automatic code of survival. His particular
distinction from all other living species is the necessity to act
in the face of alternatives by means of volitional choice...
Man must obtain his knowledge and choose his actions by
a process of thinking, which nature will not force him to
perform. Man has the power to act as his own destroyer—and
that is the way he has acted through most of his history."

AYN RAND

Ironically, Ayn Rand, the author of that passage above, was an atheist, but she created powerfully and harnessed the faith of the spiritual
realm through her work. Whether man denies or confirms the spiritual
realm, it does exist. A woman like Rand could have never created such
work if she did not have faith and understanding of the spiritual world
as a creator who can turn the unseen into the seen.

The human brain is three brains in one: the reptile brain, the mamma-
lian brain, and the neocortex, his upper brain. The neocortex is man's
only tool against the elements and other animals. There is a darkness in

man when he succumbs to fear, hunger, envy, hate, and anger. Man can either become a god who creates, looks after his family and his tribe, and raises his children to become self-propagating creators and gods themselves, or man can become a feral animal, cannibalizing his fellow men to live and feasting on the flesh of the dead.

The Ten Commandments in the Bible outline man's violent and feral tendencies to kill, steal, rape, fornicate, and worship false gods (like we do today—money and government). This old technology has helped man advance throughout the ages to the next level of civilization:

1) *"I am the Lord thy God, thou shalt not have any strange gods before Me."*
2) *"Thou shalt not take the name of the Lord thy God in vain."*
3) *"Remember to keep holy the Sabbath day."*
4) *"Honor thy father and mother."*
5) *"Thou shalt not kill."*
6) *"Thou shalt not commit adultery."*
7) *"Thou shalt not steal."*
8) *"Thou shalt not bear false witness against thy neighbor."*
9) *"Thou shalt not covet thy neighbor's wife."*
10) *"Thou shalt not covet thy neighbor's goods."*

http://www.dummies.com/religion/christianity/catholicism/
catholicism-and-the-ten-commandments/

The fact that man has needed 10 commandments to avoid the darkness of human nature is indeed revealing about the ten dark things that man will do first if he becomes a feral, unthinking, emotional animal acting upon his urges and whims. Man becomes a violent barbarian, killing, raping, stealing, pillaging, and violently taking that which his unpredictable emotions dictate.

At some point in history, man was ill-behaved, and the original laws of man had to be written in the form of 10 commandments to rule man and civilize the beast into a coherent group. Those commandments grew from a hard time and created strong men to enforce the commandments from keeping men from degrading into criminals, adulterers, and, worst of all, cannibals.

With the removal of the technology of religion and the framework from which to live, there is a risk than man will slip back into his dark feral ways and become more like an animal than a god.

So what is man's relationship with God?

Man's relationship with God has become challenging, especially with the proliferation of atheism as the reigning religion in our schools and universities. The "educated" people in the universities have become the new gods of man with their theories, papers, publications, and science on what they believe to know based on data, studies, and facts from yesterday.

I would say that the modern man, the weak man, would deny that God or a creator, an infinite intelligence, a universe governed by design and spiritual laws, or a central binding force in the universe even exists. To deny that there is a creator to this world is like denying that you have a mother and father of your own. You were created—by your own mom and dad. Something created you. There is design to you as a human being!

If man's relationship with God is mostly denial now, then how can we reverse the trend?

The way to connect to the infinite intelligence and the divine is to clear your mind of all the noise that is civilization and just listen to the nothingness.

Some people call this meditation, some call it prayer.

Some people mediate to be with God, while others pray, which is scientifically proven to trigger the same brain mechanics. Prayer and meditation stimulate the brain in the same way.

"FAITH is the head chemist of the mind. When FAITH is blended with the vibration of thought, the subconscious mind instantly picks up the vibration, translates it into its spiritual equivalent, and transmits it to Infinite Intelligence, as in the case of prayer."

NAPOLEON HILL

Some people pray, some people meditate. I fast; I practice fasting, which indeed connects me with infinite intelligence, removes my weaknesses, and sorts out my mind, body, soul, and emotions.

To connect with divine power, you need to enter into a dreamlike state. As mentioned above, your dreamlike state may be through prayer, meditation, fasting, or several different methods, but the commonality of you connecting to the ultimate creative force in the universe is through a dreamlike state.

> *"Be still and quiet, tune in with the Infinite Intelligence,*
> *and continue in right thought, right feeling, and*
> *right action, and you will arrive at your goal."*
>
> JOSEPH MURPHY

To get the mind into a dreamlike state, you must remove all distraction from the mind. The mind is most creative and powerful under one or more of the following mind stimuli as outlined by Napoleon Hill in his work *Think and Grow Rich*:

THE TEN MIND STIMULI

The human mind responds to stimuli, through which it may be "keyed up" to high rates of vibration, known as enthusiasm, creative imagination, intense desire, etc. The stimuli to which the mind responds most freely are:

1) The desire for sex expression
2) Love
3) A burning desire for fame, power, or financial gain, MONEY
4) Music
5) Friendship between either those of the same sex, or those of the opposite sex.

6) A Master Mind alliance based upon the harmony of two or more people who ally themselves for spiritual or temporal advancement.
7) Mutual suffering, such as that experienced by people who are persecuted.
8) Autosuggestion
9) Fear
10) Narcotics and alcohol

This book, *Hard Times Create Strong Men*, was written in 11 days by connecting with infinite intelligence and by communicating through a dreamlike state.

Your weaknesses, your sins, and your addictions will take you away from your purpose on this earth and the work that you are here to do. To find your divine purpose and what you were put on this earth to do, you must connect to God, to the infinite intelligence, to the force that binds all things and listen for the answers.

The infinite intelligence has everything you need, but you can never connect to it if you deny its existence, and you can never connect to it if your life is full of addiction, fear and distractions. Cut the fat and cut the extra distractions; less is more.

Men throughout history have had their biggest breakthroughs by stripping it all away and going into nature, perhaps into a cabin or perhaps into a jail cell to be alone and one with God. There they find their purpose, their character and their work much like Jack the Giant-Slayer found his golden goose, his woman, and his singing by climbing up into the dreamlike state of the beanstalk.

"Remember, meditation will bring you more and more intelligence, infinite intelligence, a radiant intelligence. Meditation will make you more alive and sensitive; your life will become richer."

RAJNEESH

"I don't need a priest between me and God."

UNKNOWN

I agree with the statement above. You can connect to God, the infinite intelligence, at any time. You don't need a priest, but I still encourage using the technology of organized religion to help you navigate the spiritual realm to learn faster and become stronger spiritually in a faster way.

You can walk down the road of the spiritual realm without any help, and it might take you your whole life to find your purpose, your calling, and the divine information waiting for you in the collective infinite intelligence. You may have that information instantly, or you can wait and struggle for your whole life. Which would you choose? You can use proven technology to take a vehicle and move faster down the road. I encourage the faster way.

Only you can choose the vehicle to explore the spiritual realm. I don't recommend any one religion. I have no opinion about which religion man chooses; it doesn't matter. But man certainly needs a religion because a religion will keep him from his darkness, his cannibalistic side. The technology of religion, any religion, is better than no religion. Are some religions better than others? Probably, but still in math, 1 is infinitely greater than 0.

The technology of religion is for you to explore. Throughout history men have seen success and have connected to the same infinitely intelligent force the Christians call God in different ways.

"I know this world is ruled by Infinite Intelligence. It required Infinite Intelligence to create it and it requires Infinite Intelligence to keep it on its course ... It is mathematical in its precision."

THOMAS A. EDISON

It's kind of like connecting to the internet through a Mac computer or a PC. At the end everyone is connected and on the same internet.

I use the Judeo-Christian words of God and the values here because they have built the Western world that we live in. The Western world and the Judeo-Christian technology have been proven to be successful here. In other places and in other times in history, men have used different names but the same methods to connect to the same unifying force.

How does man serve the binding force that connects all things?

Man can serve God, the force that binds all things by living his purpose and reaching his potential. That is your #1 job in this lifetime on this planet. It might take you time to find out what that purpose is and what your potential is, or maybe you will never know, but to find your purpose and your potential, you will find it by cutting away the distractions and reaching deep inside of your essence when all else has been taken away.

> *"The things you own end up owning you. It's only after you lose everything that you're free to do anything."*
>
> Chuck Palahniuk, *Fight Club*

How Can Man Find God?

You will find God by taking away the distractions in your life. By stripping away your addictions, getting rid of the porn, getting rid of the video games, and focusing on what your purpose is. Focusing on service and giving and becoming a man of production and value rather than a man of consumption.

> *"From Christ on down to Edison, the men who have achieved most have been those who met with the most stubborn forms of temporary defeat. This would seem to*

*justify the conclusion that Infinite Intelligence has a plan, or
a law, by which it hurdles men over many obstacles before
giving them the privilege of leadership or the opportunity
to render useful service in a noteworthy fashion."*

NAPOLEON HILL

You can only communicate with God when your mind is clear, through prayer, mediations, a dreamlike state from waking up or going to bed. There is infinite intelligence in the spiritual realm for you to make you whole and make you complete as a man. You just simply need to access it. The first step is to cut the distractions, the parasites, the time wasters, and the wastes of your vital life energy—your sins. This will leave you free to connect and see what you truly need to see.

*"Live a good life. If there are gods and they are just, then they
will not care how devout you have been, but will welcome you
based on the virtues you have lived by. If there are gods, but
unjust, then you should not want to worship them. If there
are no gods, then you will be gone, but will have lived a noble
life that will live on in the memories of your loved ones."*

MARCUS AURELIUS

PART IV
POLITICS,
A SYSTEM OF
ORGANIZED HATE
AND THE SYSTEMATIC
EXTINCTION
OF THE WEST

"**Politics** *as a practice, whatever its professions, has always been the systematic organization of hatreds.*"

HENRY ADAMS

CHAPTER 27

IN THE LAND OF THE BLIND

Men Can No Longer See
Their Enemies

"In the land of the blind, the one-eyed man is king. In the darkness, the man with the candle is an easy target."

MICHAEL GRANT

The current political climate has destroyed man's ability to identify problems and threats in the Western world. We are disabled from our tools of discernment and judgment.

To question the popular narrative of the media and government today is a political suicide mission and damning to a man and his social standing.

If a man questions why two men should want to get married, or why that is part of the popular narrative, he's a homophobe.

If man questions why a 4-year-old boy is taking hormone blockers to become a girl, he's an ignorant, backward hick.

If a man questions why there is a cross-dressing man in the girl's bathroom at the same time as his 8-year-old daughter, he's hateful and ignorant.

If a man questions why militant and extreme radical Muslims whom his country is in an official "holy war" and an official "war on terrorism" with are allowed to enter his country, he's a racist, xenophobe, and Islamophobe.

If a man questions why the Mexican government is dumping prisoners from jail on his borders and wishes to build a wall to let the official, chosen, legal Mexican immigrants into his country and keep the unofficial and illegal people out, he's a hater of Mexicans.

If a man questions anything to do with women and women's roles in society, he is a sexist or misogynist.

If a man goes on a date with a woman and is too aggressive, he's a rapist.

If a man goes on a date with a woman and he is not aggressive enough, she feels unsexy and thinks he's gay.

The art of thinking, logic, reason, and debate has been violently cut out of our society, and anyone, specifically men, who questions any part in the popular narrative are condemned, labeled, and banished to the fringes of social relevance.

It happened to Donald Trump in his race to become president. The popular media story was that Trump was a joke. I have studied Donald Trump since 2007 (before his run for presidency in 2016) when he was famous as a real estate celebrity. He's a self-made billionaire; nothing about him is a joke. But the media painted him as a joke because he started to call out the problems in America that were destroying and dismantling the country. When he spoke out against objective problems identified by reason, the people subjectively lashed out at him emotionally because their feelings were hurt.

These same people refused to accept him as their president, saying, "He's not my president." Again, this is not based in reality or reason; it's just a feeling of him "not being my president." I'm sorry, but he did indeed become the official president.

This is like a little child saying, "Dad, I don't want to go to bed," when Dad says, "Go to bed." That's the level of argument happening here. The child has a feeling of not wanting to go to bed, because he thinks it's best for him. Dad knows that for his child to live a happy, healthy, and productive life, he needs to go to bed now.

Sometimes the medicine of what we need is bitter, and there is no "spoonful of sugar" to make the medicine go down as Mary Poppins used to sing about in the wonderful imaginary world of Disney.

In less tolerant countries like China and Russia, those people who oppose their leader openly in such a way would be rounded up and shot. China and Russia don't mess around; they have policies against attacking the leaders. They are concerned with their own self-preservation and growth as a tribe, and people who speak out against the leaders are punished and quickly made public examples of.

We have become so weak in America that even the tribal leader when attacked can't fight back with anything more than a Twitter account. Men cannot question some of the political agendas unfolding in front of their eyes for fear of harsh character assassinations. Even I fear for my own well-being by exposing such problems by writing this book. Books that challenge the popular narrative are threatening and are banned like George Orwell's *1984* or Aldous Huxley's *Brave New World*. Those men told the truth, and their work was attacked for that truth.

Politics has traditionally been about property, who gets to keep what property, and what property is redistributed to the poor. Now, politics has become a subversive force silencing the men who can defend the tribe from external attackers or invaders. As I mentioned, politics has been traditionally about property and money. Thus, if you don't have property, you vote for the left because you wish to take someone else's property and give it to yourself. If you own property you vote for the right because you wish to defend your property and keep it for yourself. If you don't really own much property, you might be somewhere in the middle and take some of someone else's property and give away some of your own. It's all about power, money, property, and procurement of resources for oneself. We all vote for whatever benefits us the most.

Political leanings change when you have resources or do not have resources.

> *"If a person is not a liberal when he is twenty, he has no heart;*
> *if he is not a conservative when he is forty, he has no head."*

JOHN ADAMS

People on the right typically live on the frontiers of survival: they run businesses, own farms, own real estate, own land; they could lose everything at any time to disaster, their own ignorance or negligence, the elements, the markets, or another hostile and invisible force. For the people who live on the right side of the political spectrum, daily survival is real and practiced, so they can keep their enterprises and lives running.

People on the left are protected by the state and wish for more protection. The frontiers of survival are so far away that they use their energy for pleasure, family, relaxing, or anything other than survival because the state sends them a check every month to keep the challenges of survival away.

Such is the disparity in philosophy of the left and right, the rich and the poor. America's founders rightfully predicted that if they ran a democracy, eventually the democracy would lead to a race to the bottom, a pandering for cheap votes from the poor to win public favor and get elected into power. Politicians have been brokering weakness for power throughout history. It's a sad trade and should be stopped, but such is human nature, and such is the nature of bribes for votes.

The brokering of weakness for power happened in Rome during its demise, and the same happened in the election of Donald Trump versus Hillary Clinton.

Clinton, on the left, won the popular vote. But the electoral college—the second tier of political power—voted for Trump. Trump became president.

The founders of America were smart enough to know that the people are too stupid to govern themselves. In Rome, the general populace voted for breads and circuses and free grain for all until the barbarians sacked the gates and wiped out their civilization.

Can the popular vote be wrong? Yes, and it often is. Whatever the masses are doing or thinking, stay away and do the opposite.

"Only two things are infinite, the universe and human stupidity, and I'm not sure about the former."

ALBERT EINSTEIN

The American founders learned from ancient history from Greece and Rome and thus created America as a republic with an electoral college in place to prevent the bottom, the poor, from voting themselves free benefits out of weakness.

When it comes to voting, I have the extremely old-fashioned view that only landowners should be able to vote. At least you have a stake in the country and you own a share. If you own a share, you care about the good of the country and the group. If you don't own anything, how can you really care about the health of the group? There is a vast amount of land to buy in the country, and cheap land in remote places. Anyone can work hard, save up, buy some land cheaply somewhere, and get a vote, but I know this old system that preserved the health of the country is never coming back in this lifetime.

America is currently practicing the race to the bottom with food stamps, free abortions, free healthcare, free or subsidized housing, and other benefits that were meant to be safety nets and temporarily used but now have now become permanent ways of life for people on the bottom to live. The only reason why we allow the bottom to live on those programs in perpetuity is because the politicians need to buy votes with weakness. This is why democracy cannot last as a permanent form of government.

CHAPTER 28
MASCULINE VS. FEMININE
POLITICAL POWER
Bonobos vs. Chimps

Excerpt from Jack Donovan's ***book*** The Way of Men

What would happen if men got spoiled, gave up and gave in to women completely? How would that society operate?

The evolutionary theory of parental investment suggests that because reproduction is costly, members of the sex which makes the lesser parental investment will compete for sexual access to whichever sex makes the greater parental investment. In humans and most mammals, females are forced to make the greatest investment in reproduction ...

Human males evolved to compete for access to females because female reproductive investment is a valuable prize. Males can exist in the all-male world of the gang, but females quite literally represent the future. Men create a perimeter and establish security. They create a rudimentary hierarchy, order and seminal culture of us vs. them. To perpetuate the us, they need women. So they try to figure out how to get women, and how to get "access to their reproductive investment ..."

The Way of Men is the Way of the Gang, but a gang of men, alone, has no future. The all-male gang ends with the death of the last man. Men want to be remembered, they want their tradition to survive, and they want sex. Ultimately, these psychological mechanisms and desires will allow them to pass on their genes. When there is competition for resources—including women—it is good strategy for a gang of men to create a patriarchal hierarchy, eliminate neighboring rival gangs, take their women, and protect the women from rival gangs. This is exactly what many primitive tribes do. This is the basic strategy of the gang.

What happens when competition for resources is radically reduced?

What happens when women get their way?

Two of our closest primate relatives, chimpanzees and bonobos, illustrate some of the differences between the way of males and the way of females.

Wrangham and Peterson argued that in spite of cultural determinist theories and a lot of wishful thinking about peaceful pre-historic matriarchies—the evolutionary, archaeological, historical, anthropological, physiological and genetic evidence overwhelmingly suggests that humans have always been a patriarchal, male-bonded party-gang species that engaged in regular coalitionary violence. This was a brave conclusion, because both authors seemed to be whole-heartedly against violence. As self-described evolutionary feminists, they offered suggestions as to how we might end male violence now that men have the means to wreak havoc well beyond what their primitive ancestors could do with powerful arms and simple tools. Aside from selective breeding to reduce violent alpha tendencies in males—a program that seems to be underway, albeit accidentally—and the establishment of one world government, Wrangham and Peterson suggested that we look to the gentle bonobo apes for guidance.

Chimpanzees and bonobos are both close relatives of humans. Both have much in common with people, but when it comes to social structures, the chimps are more apt to live in small groups led by a hierarchical gang of males, whereas the bonobos tend to live in larger, more stable parties with a greater number of females and the females maintain coalitions that check male violence. Chimpanzees organize to the benefit of male reproductive interests, and bonobos organize to the benefit of female reproductive interests. Chimps follow The Way of Men. Bonobos follow The Way of Women.

Zoologists for years have studied different ape societies to see how they function and to draw parallels between how apes behave and how man behaves.

In the ape world, there are the patriarchal, male-ruled chimpanzees who live in areas with scarce food resources; they hunt and live on the meat of the smaller monkeys whom they kill and eat. Their society is a male-dominated gang culture where the males will be violent towards other males and females for dominance in the tribe. If resources are plenty, the male gangs will unite and form alliances into larger groups. When resources are scarce, they will break into smaller hunter groups to efficiently hunt the land for survival. Mating is done as the males see fit, and the male chimps will take the females of their group or of another group where they have fought and killed the males for mating purposes and to assimilate into their tribe. The female chimps are not socially dominant, and the social structure runs around the alpha male, the king. Females are grouped together, but the males dominate.

The Chimpanzee Way:

Chimpanzees can mingle in larger parties if they are able to make alliances, and if food is plentiful. Chimps and humans prefer high-quality foods, and male chimps actively hunt for meat, especially red colobus monkeys. Chimpanzees compete for resources when they are scarce, so they break up into smaller gangs. This is a "partygang" social structure because of this flexibility in party size. Under stress, they revert to patri-archal gangs run by male relatives and bonded male allies. Females move (and are moved) from gang to gang. Males compete for sexual access to females, but males also some-times court the females and escort them away from the stress of male competition. Females who do not have children some-times join males in hunting and raiding activities. Females are subordinate to males in the chimpanzee social hierarchy, and they are expected to demonstrate submission. When a young male comes of age, he will usually make a big show of it, and start pushing females around until they acknowledge him as an adult male. After he achieves that, he'll stop making such a big to do. However, chimpanzee males do batter females sporadically to maintain their status and show the gals what's what. Males who come of age spend a lot of time together, but also spend a lot of time competing for status with each other. Their contests are often violent, and on rare occasions two males have been known to form an alliance and murder the alpha male. Humans might recognize this as patricide or tyrannicide. For chimps, in-group competition is less import-ant than competition with other groups. Chimpanzees and humans are the only two members of the great apes where males form coalitions to go out and raid or eliminate mem-bers of a neighboring gang. Alpha chimps will occasionally gather up other males, go out to the edge of their range, try to catch a member of another gang unaware, and murder him. This is similar to the "skulking way of war" common among primitive humans, who also engage in guerilla raiding. Over time, males will pick off all of the other males of the neigh-bor gang, absorb the remaining females into their own group, and mate with them. Because chimpanzees hunt, defend and aggress as a coordinated gang, they have to be willing to put aside internecine competition and maintain close bonds with each other. Primatologist Frans de Waal wrote:

"... the chimpanzee male psyche, shaped by millions of years of intergroup warfare in the natural habitat, is one of both

competition and compromise. Whatever the level of competition among them, males count on each other against the outside. No male ever knows when he will need his greatest foe. It is, of course, this mixture of camaraderie and rivalry among males that makes chimpanzee society so much more recognizable to us than the social structure of the other great apes.

Donovan, *The Way of Men*

Humans have lived like chimps throughout history in violent patriarchal societies, with violent gang culture. When resources become scarce, humans have split off into smaller groups to efficiently hunt.

On the opposite end of the spectrum are the bonobos. Bonobos are a matriarchal ape society where the females rule and the males, with less responsibilities, become weak. The bonobos live in different territory than the chimpanzees or gorillas, and their food source is plentiful and replenishable. They are mostly vegetarians but will sometimes eat meat if they can get it. The bonobo tribes are much larger and need a replenishable food source as a base to support the tribe, as they avoid hunting.

The female bonobos run the tribe, male violence is discouraged, and if a male gets violent at all, the other females will gang up on him to stop the violence. Food is so plentiful, and there are no major threats, so the females practice getting the food and the males laze about in the sun all day. They participate in masturbation and homosexuality with their excess of energy and time that is no longer needed for hunting, whereas the chimps live in a hostile environment, cannot afford to waste their sexual energy, and must hunt to survive.

The Bonobo Way:

Bonobos eat many of the same foods that chimpanzees like, and they will eat meat when they find it. However, bonobos don't share their territory with gorillas, so they are able to eat the kinds of portable herbs that gorillas eat. Wrangham and Peterson believe that this is one of the key differences between chimps and bonobos. Bonobos have a staple food source that is easy to find. They don't have to compete for resources even when many foods are out of season, so they can more or less relax all year long in a peace of plenty. The males compete for status, but they seem less concerned about it because status for bonobo males doesn't mean much. Bonobos don't compete for mates. Each male just waits his turn, and the females are happy to oblige anyone who comes knocking. For the bonobos sex is social, and bonobos have both homosexual and heterosexual sex. Bonobo males don't know who their kids are, because any of the kids could be their kids. The mother makes all of the parental investment. Bonobo males do know who their mothers are, and they remain bonded to them for life— they often follow their mothers around throughout adulthood, and mothers intervene in conflicts on a behalf of their sons. Males don't spend a lot of time together in bonobo groups, but females build strong friendships with one another. When males start trouble, the females band together to put a stop to it quickly. Bonobo females are in charge. When one group of bonobos comes in contact with another group, the female bonobos will be the ones who make the peace, and generally they will start engaging in hoka-hoka with each other—that's what natives call bonobo girl-on-girl action. Then the females will start mating with the males from the opposite group. The males just sit around and watch, shrug their shoulders and eventually join in.

Jack Donovan, *The Way of Men*

So here we have two very different ways of living, and humanity has, for the majority of human history, lived in a patriarchal, chimpanzee way where the food was scarce and the tribes had to rely on hunting, resource gathering, and male dominance for survival. Now, with a much larger supertribe, the females have taken over, and we live in a bonobo-style tribe that is almost the opposite of the ways that man used to live throughout his history. What is the cost of this? Weak men and strong women.

You can still find strong men today in our society on the frontier of survival. If you go into the countryside on a farm, the men are still strong and the women are women. But the larger the city, the larger the center, the larger the tribe, the more bonobo we become, and the weaker the men become. And thus, it seems as though just like with female and male sexual power, there never really is a balance when it comes to sex. If a man has multiple women, he has the power; if a woman has exclusivity, she has the power. The same is true with matriarchal societies and patriarchal societies—each have a cost and a benefit and a directly inverse conflict of interest. The more you have of one, the less you have of the other. Like freedom and security, the more freedom you have, the less security you have, and the more security you have, the less freedom you have. Maximum security is maximum security prison; maximum freedom is living in the forest alone.

A Conflict of Interests:

Bonobos and chimpanzees are adapted to different environments, and their social structures follow from what those environments have to offer. Bonobo society favors female interests. Female coalitions hold sway over politics, and female bonding is more important than male bonding. Males are bonded to their mothers and don't know who their fathers are. Females stay together for life. In chimpanzee society, females are somewhat isolated and stay with their young when they are children, while males enjoy both rivalry and camaraderie, and stay with their fathers, brothers and male friends for life. Chimpanzee society favors male interests. Wrangham and Peterson believe that bonobos offer a "three-fold path to peace" because they have managed to reduce violence between the sexes, reduce violence between males, and reduce violence between communities. In response to the mass destruction inherent to modern warfare, many men have searched for ways to abandon the "warfare system" that attends patriarchy, and they have looked to women for guidance on coalition building and finding a more peaceful way to live. Those who believe human warfare is somehow unnatural will find little objective support for this theory in history or the sciences. Human societies are complex, and aspects of both bonobo and chimpanzee patterns are familiar enough. But male aggression, male coalitional violence, and male political dominance have all been identified as "human universals"—meaning that evidence of these behaviors have been found in some form in almost every human society that has ever been studied. Scientists only began to study bonobos as a separate and distinct species in the 1950s, because bonobos evolved in a small, sheltered range. Chimpanzees have a much larger range, and have adapted to more diverse environments. Humans and chimps clearly have more in common in terms of social organization. It is likely that while humans are smarter and have far more complex social arrangements than chimpanzees, male bonding and male coalitional violence have been constant features of human and pre-human societies. The following table shows the differences between various aspects of chimpanzee societies and bonobo societies—it shows two ways, two extremes.

Jack Donovan, *The Way of Men*

The major question I have when looking at chimpanzee vs. bonobo society is, is the constant of human war the only determining factor between a patriarchal and matriarchal society?

Does a society shift from a birth out of "hard times create strong men" and male domination into patriarchy and establishment to create "good times and weak men" where the women take over and matriarchy becomes the new system of power? Is brutal and violent war the catalyst that changes the society in a decline from female driven back to male driven? Must we be on the edge of survival and oblivion to bring the strong men back?

"As long as man exists, there will be war."

GENERAL GEORGE S. PATTON

Male Interests vs. Female Interests

	Male interests (Chimpanzees)	Female interests (Bonobos)
Resources	Variable, sometimes difficult to obtain	Readily available
Hunting priority	High	Low
Male alliances	Yes	No
Female alliances	No	Yes
Sexuality	For mating	For pleasure and socialization
Homosexuality	Minimal, uncommon	Frequent, common
Political dominance	Males	Shared, but female coalitions have most influence
Males - Parent bonding	Father, brothers, patrilineal Males spend time with mothers during youth, with males for the rest of their lives, with females for mating	Mothers
Females - Parent bonding	Mothers, females may leave gang	Mothers, matrilineal, females generally stay in party
Males batter females	Yes	No
Males rape females	Yes, but rare	Why bother?
Females acknowledge male dominance	Yes	No
Range defended	Yes	Sometimes
Intergroup raiding	Yes	No
Border patrols	Yes	No

Source: Jack Donovan, The Way of Men

Wars seem to be constant throughout human history. especially when resources get scarce. When that happens, humans become violent. In earlier chapters we talked about subversion of our American society by communism and that the final stages of subversion of our society and values end up in

1) invasion (war against the external enemies), or
2) civil war (war against the internal enemies).

Will this time of weak men that we live in eventually come to a grinding halt when we hit hard times that will be sorted out by war? We might believe that war will not come onto our own American soil, or that the violence can't happen here. We tend to think that violence happens in other places, but just because the violence isn't happening here on Western soil doesn't mean that it can't come home.

> *Wars against men are known to fewer and fewer of us. Mandatory conscription for the Vietnam War ended the year before I was born. Since then, the United States has effectively created a class of professional contract soldiers who do the government's fighting in faraway lands. Average men know more about collegiate basketball than they know about a given overseas conflict.*

> *Like the bonobos, we don't have to worry about hunger. We barely have a reason to get up off the couch. Until the recent extended recession, jobs were fairly easy to come by, and almost all of the men who wanted to work were able to get a job. Welfare and social assistance programs provide safety nets for many others, and few American men living today grew up in a home without a television. True hunger and poverty and desperation, the way people know it in Africa, is rare even for those who are officially considered poor. Diseases that wiped out populations in the past are treatable, and people recover fully from injuries that would have been fatal one hundred years ago. If anything illustrates the surreal plenty we live in today, it is the fact that we have problems like epidemic obesity. People are able to sit in their homes and eat until they are so fat they can't move.*

Jack Donovan

So with the poem that is the premise of this book:

> Hard Times Create Strong Men
> Strong Men Create Good Times
> Good Times Create Weak Men
> Weak Men Create Hard Times

Through the hard times of civil war or invasion, the hard times create strong men again, and the cycle is set to repeat just as history seems to repeat itself exactly every 80 years or so. Forty years on an upswing, 40 years on a downswing, and 80 years is the magical number because it is 40 times two.

Forty is an important magic number in human history because there is a saying, "By the age of forty, man has seen all that he can see." Traditionally throughout history, men have lived to be roughly 40.

The number 40 is also important in the Bible. Jesus, Moses, and many others fasted or meditated for 40 days.

Forty years is how long it takes for the pendulum of society to swing entirely in one direction. To go all the way into good times takes 40 years—20 years on the way to good times and 20 years swinging back to the middle, back toward hard times. Then the pendulum swings back into hard times—20 years getting worse, and then 20 years getting better. The entire cycle of history looks like this:

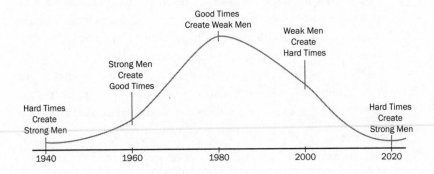

Hard Times Create Strong Men (20 years of hard times 1940 to 1960)

Strong Men Create Good Times (20 years of good times 1960 to 1980, the start of feminism and the decline of Western strong men)

Good Times Create Weak Men (1980 to 2000 the proliferation of weak men and degradation of the original values that made men strong)

Weak Men Create Hard Times (2000 to 2020 back into hard times, which will force men to become strong again)

Every 80 years, if we want to see the future, all we must do is look literally 80 years back in the past when the swinging pendulum of history was in the exact same spot as today. As I write this, we are in 2018, and 80 years ago was 1938, right before America got officially involved in World War II.

We are ready for a major war and a major hard time as dictated by the cycles of history. Just as sure as the tide moves in and out a cycle, history repeats on a cycle. Such is the human condition.

In 1940, World War II was just starting to ignite on a global level. That was when the WWII generation was galvanized by fire, blood, sweat, and tears into becoming the "greatest generation" through the destruction of what was sold as the "war to end all wars." We always think the current war is the last war, but humanity has a short memory and bad amnesia. Alas, the cycle of history repeats.

Why is 80 years the magic number for history? And why do we look 80 years in the past to see today? Eighty years is a vitally important number because it takes 40 years to grow a human generation. One generation grows up swinging in one direction, and their children will look at their parents and swing in the opposite direction. To swing one way or the other takes a human lifetime—40 years for a generation to grow up and swing society in one direction and then 40 years for their children to grow up and swing in the opposite direction.

This is illustrated in fashion; whatever is cool today in fashion is usually old trends from 20 years ago. Literally, 20 years ago is "retro" and "cool" because the kids of today who are 18 were not even born to see what was cool 20 years ago. They can't see the greater invisible force of the pendulum.

Forty years is relevant because that is where the young people commit to "doing it differently than my father or mother did." The children compensate by going in the opposite direction of the parents, and then their children compensate by going their 40 years in the opposite direction of their parents. This brutal tug of war—one direction for 40 years, then the opposite for 40 more years—is a major part of man and his innate flaws. To repeat what he already knows to be bad for him simply because he forgot his hard, bloody, violent past is silly and shortsighted.

We live in a good time today that has created weak men, so I am writing this book to swing the pendulum back to strong men, because we have been weak for far too long. I am a student of history and know that the pendulum is ready to swing back into violent hard times with full force shortly.

Eighty years is a magic number because it is two cycles of 40. Everyone who was alive 80 years ago, at this exact same part in the cycle, is now dead. My grandmother, born in 1920, was alive and contributing to the WWII war effort as a nurse 80 years ago. As I write this, Grandma is turning 98 years old. She will not live much longer, and of course when we plunge back into the darkness and hard times of the repetition of history, Grandma will no longer be alive. The men and women of 80 years ago are now gone. They lived through the horrors of hard times and had firsthand experience, stories, and knowledge to warn us against the horrors they lived through. Instead of being alive to warn us against our own ignorance and weakness, these people born 80 years ago are (1) dead, (2) disabled and unable to communicate with us anymore, or (3) marginalized by society and rotting in isolated old-folks homes.

We no longer listen to our elders and think that our valuable elders have nothing to contribute, when in fact they are the keepers of the most important knowledge in society, which is firsthand experience. That is why history is, as Stefan Molyneux pointed out, the "same damn story over and over again just with different costumes."

We can't see or recall what happened 80 years ago, and we think "it won't happen to us." This is a fallacy of human nature; we always think we're different, we always think that our situation is different, but it never is!

The violence of history has and always will swing in 20-, 40-, and 80-year cycles because a lifecycle of a human being is only 40 years. I believe we are designed to live only 40 years. We have managed to live longer—to 80 or 100 years—with recent medicine and nutrition. That is great, but from looking at history with all of the problems, wars, famines, and plagues, it seems that man has only been able to get to 40 consistently throughout history, and then he is an "old man" at 40 when he dies.

We can see that history moves in cycles. A nation, a society, a tribe is born out of patriarchy and male dominance because the environment is hostile, and the hard times create strong men. As the strong men build the prosperity of the tribe or the nation, strong men bring prosperity and good times through their sacrifices. Good times create weak men as the new generations of man enjoy the spoils that their forefathers left behind for them. Just like a rich kid who becomes useless, unable to fend for himself, degenerate, addicted to drugs, sex, and gambling, he cannot survive in the gangster-tribal way that his tough entrepreneurial father or grandfather did.

The first generation makes the wealth, the second generation spends the wealth, and the third generation talks about the wealth.

The good times become a poison of comfort and excess, a breeding ground of weakness, and we slip into matriarchy as the women take over. The physical threats are gone, and the strong men aren't needed and can relax or become marginalized. The threats are no longer present, we are not worried about the frontiers of survival, and through our ignorance of our violent past and complacency, the tribe allows its enemies to grow within and begin to circle on the edges of the tribe.

"Anything in excess is poison."

THEODORE LEVITT

This leads our society to one of two options, as we have always had in the past:

1) Civil war from weakness, resources getting scarce and the tribe goes to war with itself, like a body fighting itself with

an autoimmune disease, weakening itself for an invasion OR

2) Invasion from an enemy strong man tribe hungrier for resources, the weak men of our tribe, the weak tribe are violently killed by a strong man tribe, and the women are sexually assimilated and children are enslaved.

The real question is, do female-ruled societies survive and persist throughout history? Or are they just temporary before a fall? Are female dominated societies a sign of the times that will be violently taken by an external patriarchal, strong man tribe at some point?

> *"Masculine republics give away to feminine democracies, and feminine democracies give way to tyranny."*
>
> ARISTOTLE

I would make the counterargument, "do male ruled societies survive either?" The answer is no. Male-ruled societies give away to female-ruled societies through too much comfort and weakness as the poem of "Hard Times Suggests":

Hard Times Create Strong Men (1940, World War II)

Strong Men Create Good Times (1960, Height of American prosperity)

Good Times Create Weak Men (1980, Decline after 20 years of feminism and comfort creating weak men)

Weak Men Create Hard Times (2000, September 11th terrorist attack and major decline of America through the crash of 2008 and beyond)

Hard Times Create Strong Men (Present day, 2020)

2020 is where we will begin to get the next generation of strong men through forced hard times as the cycles of history indicate. I write this book in 2018 as the pendulum is about to swing into "hard times create strong men."

Are female-driven human tribes able to persist and survive over time? The answer is "no." A group of strong men coming from hard times will eventually invade, and the institution of war wipes the dominant women and weak men out.

Is war an institution? Yes, it is always happening. Somewhere on the globe resources are scarce, and humans are killing each other violently to survive. You can see this in the poorest ghettos of America. Even in my hometown of Winnipeg, Canada, the murder capital of Canada, the poor are violent and fighting each other for survival, in Winnipeg the historically highest murder rate in my country.

As long as resources are scarce, as long as there are men, as long as men desire women and a better life, there will be war.

History is full of movements of have-nots rising up against the haves— young men fighting old men for resources and women. So war will never leave us as long as we have men. But the strong men, the violence, and the wars eventually turn to times of peace and stability when the women can take charge and rule the tribe.

Unfortunately, as illustrated, these are times of decline, and other violent tribes of men, who are the have-nots of the world, see our abundance, see our plenty, hate us, and despise us for what we have. They want what we have, and they will violently take it. Violence took Rome with the barbarians storming the gates to take what they wanted, women, land, money, slaves, and power.

Will it happen again to us?

I would argue that the barbarian invasion has already started.

CHAPTER 29
THE WORLD BELONGS TO WARRIOR CULTURES

"Know thy self, know thy enemy. A thousand battles, a thousand victories."

SUN TZU, *THE ART OF WAR*

The world belongs to warrior culture.

As the poem says:

> Hard times create strong men,
> Strong men create good times,
> Good times create weak men,
> Weak men create hard times.

Such is the cycle of history.

The cycle fluctuates between war and peace, war and peace over and over again. At some point, there is always mass violence, killing, and murder, and this is just the nature of men.

Peace is unsustainable unto itself, because we live in a world of haves and have-nots. Inevitably, there is a gang, a group of have-not men out beyond the frontier. The Romans called them barbarians, and these barbarians eventually show up at the gates and kill everyone for women, land, and treasure.

The barbarians are strong men christened by hard times. They are violent, masculine, and live in a warrior culture. They want the luxuries of civilization, they want women to reproduce with, and they are willing to use violence to get it.

Thus, because war is always inevitable with the clash of the haves and the have-nots, the world belongs to the warrior cultures.

The men of the West were once warriors and farmers. The dawn of Western culture was born out of intolerance. Societies are born out of intolerance, and they die when they become too tolerant to function. We are reaching that point of tolerance in America right now, where we are getting overtolerant, and every crazy thing brought by any fringe group to the popular narrative or media is tolerable.

After gay marriage was legalized, the new agenda on the political docket is to legalize pedophilia with groups like NAMBLA (The North American Boy Lovers Association) attempting to join in the LGBTQ group. Islamic immigrants want to marry children as young as 9, as is customary through their religion in some parts of the world, and now the precedence of gay marriage has opened up the next frontier: "why not marry kids?" Tolerance is a problem because it sets a precedent for weakness. The new argument is: if I can marry a man and I am a man, can I not be free to love whoever I want? What if I love this child? Can I not marry the child? This is an actual argument on the fringes of the popular narrative right now, and I hope that we don't legalize pedophilia because that is a real step backwards into the Middle Ages for civilization.

Tolerance leads to weakness and weakness leads to hard times. Hard times leads to war and violence. War and violence christen men through blood and flame making them strong men, galvanized against hardship.

America was born as an intolerant nation. The war for independence from the British empire was born out of an intolerance for the crippling taxes that the empire was placing on the ragtag group of farmers living in the Colonies across the ocean. These farmers, the men, became warriors, got pissed off, and started killing Redcoat British soldiers until the British had to go home to lick their wounds.

The Americans started as the barbarians, and the British were the empire. The Americans were intolerant; the British were so big and fat that they grew to be tolerant. After the Victorian British empire fell, the American empire rose to power, and simultaneously the Russian empire rose as well. Two backwater countries of farmers and country boys had become the empires. These country boys who were too primitive to be a threat rose up as the world leaders and world's superpowers post–World War II.

Rome was birthed on intolerance and died after it became too tolerant to function.

Greece was birthed on intolerance and died after it became too tolerant to function.

Right now, the rising star in the world of warrior culture and intolerance is the religion of Islam, which is much more powerful than a nation of barbarians. It's a multinational religion spanning over the entire third-world with over 1 billion members. Imagine 1 billion have-nots pissed off and angry at infidel Western values in Europe and America. Imagine 1 billion angry men with pulsing testosterone and testicles with over 100 million sperm each ready to spread their seed and take the women of their slain enemies.

Islam is growing more rapidly than any other religion in the world, according to a new report by the Pew Research Center that says the religion will nearly equal Christianity by 2050 before eclipsing it around 2070, if current trends continue. The Pew is a nonpartisan fact tank that informs about issues, attitudes, and trends shaping the world.

"The main reason Muslims are growing not only in number but in share worldwide is because of where they live," says Alan Cooperman, Pew's director of religion research, said in an interview with NPR. "Muslim populations are concentrated in some of the fastest-growing parts of the world." The Pew report on the matter states that "as of 2010, Christianity was by far the world's largest religion, with an estimated

2.2 billion adherents, nearly a third (31 percent) of all 6.9 billion people on Earth. Islam was second, with 1.6 billion adherents, or 23 percent of the global population."Those numbers are predicted to shift in the coming decades, as the world's population rises to 9.3 billion by the middle of this century. The Pew projects that, in that time, Islam will grow by 73 percent, while Christianity will grow by 35 percent—resulting in 2.8 billion Muslims and 2.9 billion Christians worldwide.

Islam is spreading like wildfire, and many of the countries that Islam takes as members of their tribe are from poor third-world nations.

Empires fall when they become too tolerant and too complacent and comfortable to be able to identify the hostile barbarians at the gates. History is littered with the carcasses of slain empires that were violently destroyed and trampled on by a barbarian horde.

China has become a strong nation through intolerance. They used to be very strict with their policies, but as the Western culture seeps into the Chinese culture and the incomes go up, China will gain a middle class, and grow comfortable and tolerant as well.

Why Nazism Failed versus the Success of Communism and Islam

In the 1930s and 1940s, Nazism became a powerful and popular movement in Germany, and there were Nazis around the world who had belief systems shared with Adolf Hitler and his religion based on blood. They believed that Nordic Aryans (a very loose undefinable term but were thought to be Nordic blonde hair, blue-eyed people) were the master race and were superior to all other groups of people.

Hitler had a very simple racial ideology (that also branched into other philosophies):

1) Nordic Aryans were the master race.
2) Slavics were a slave race.
3) All other races were below that.

The idea at the time was embraced by people in Europe and abroad even in America. Nazism was popular, but it has been whitewashed from American history after the Nazi death camps and genocides were exposed after the war.

Whoever wins the war gets to write the history books.

The trouble with the Nazi philosophy based on blood and race is that it is not exportable to other groups of people. Only northern Europeans with blonde hair and blue eyes could fit into the blood-based ideology.

Officers in the Waffen-SS lamented turning down great soldiers because they didn't fit the strict racial criteria to be in the elite Waffen-SS. Soldiers had to be 6 feet tall (at least 5 feet 11 inches) with no dental cavities and a traceable pure Aryan blood lineage back to the 1700s. Sure they could select a certain type of person, but they could not export this ideology, or replicate it in other groups of people, and so Nazism was limited to Germany, America, and a small minority of northern European countries.

Even non-Aryan countries like Italy, Greece, and Spain had to dubiously claim that they were Aryan, and a questionable system of "Mediterranean Aryans" was established, where Mussolini, who was not a northern European and did not have blonde hair or blue eyes, somehow became an "Aryan." Hitler himself did not fit the Aryan description either.

So dubious was the racial blood philosophy that for Nazi Germany to somehow ally with Japan, the Germans had to claim that the Japanese were "honorary Aryans," which completely violates their blood philosophy and Aryan master race philosophy and shows just how inexportable the Nazi ideology was. They could not take over the world quickly because they couldn't manufacture enough Aryans to do the job.

When the Nazis were taking over Poland and Eastern Europe, they had to decide out of the mostly Slavic populations which men and women could be "Aryans" and which ones couldn't. They didn't really have a real system for this, so it came down to "does this person look Aryan or not."

There was no real science behind it. In the end, Nazism failed.

On the other hand, the exportability of an ideology is what made communism so powerful.

The Vietnamese could be communists, the Russians, the Cubans, the Cambodians, the North Koreans, and on and on. Communism was exported like a wildfire across the world because it was an easy movement for anyone to join. It was a convenient way for the have-nots to band together into a gang and rise up and fight against the haves.

The exportability, the easiness, the stickiness, the adaptability of an idea is key to the success of it over time, and the easier something is to adopt, the bigger and faster it can grow.

Islam today is the fastest-growing religion in the world:

Muslims Projected to be Fastest-growing Major Religious Group

Estimated percent change in population size, 2015–2060

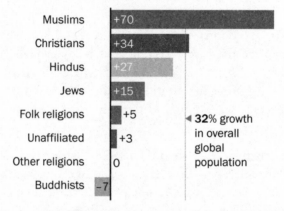

Islam is an ideology that lends itself perfectly to third-world countries of have-nots and promises the young, hungry, military-aged men enormous gains and an upside with a dream of world domination.

This is the same promise that Hitler gave the young men of Germany, but he couldn't export his ideas fast enough to other groups of people outside of his own group. He couldn't recruit black men from Africa, the Arabs from the Middle East, or anyone who wasn't pure Aryan. This was one of Hitler's fatal strategic flaws.

The Islamic ideology, like communist ideology, is proven to be widely exportable, violent, and intolerant.

That is an explosive mix of factors that is mortally threatening to the good of the Western world.

People who are poor, the have-nots, the frustrated youth of history who want to seize power, have always attempted to rise up through violence to take what they have always wanted: a better life, the luxuries they do not have, and the women of their enemy to reproduce and create offspring.

This haves versus the have-nots has been proven over and over again throughout history.

The youth versus the establishment has been proven over and over again.

The intolerant taking over the tolerant has been seen over and over again.

The primitive barbarians sacking empires has been seen over and over again.

This is why the world and the future belong to warrior societies. Good times create weak men, which always follows with strong men from other tribes coming to invade.

The barbarians are at the gates. Should we let them in?

"It is better to die on your feet than to live on your knees."

EMILIANO ZAPPATA, MEXICAN REVOLUTIONARY

CHAPTER 30
EXTINCTION: THE OBSOLESCENCE OF MEN

"Everything not saved will be lost."

NINTENDO

M other nature has a wonderful law, the law of use. The law of use is: things that get used get stronger; things that do not get used get weaker.

*"Anything given to you in life will be violently
taken back if you fail to earn it."*

STEFAN AARNIO

If you do not use your body, it becomes weak.

If you do not use your mind, it becomes weak.

If you do not use your spirit, it becomes weak.

If you do not use your emotions, they become weak.

Strength and being a strong man come from use.

If you use your gifts that are given to you, your gifts shall become stronger.

However, anything given to you that you fail to earn over time shall become lost and will be taken back by the ebb and flow of life.

Part of the problem with men in today's world is that they are no longer needed. There is virtually nothing that a man can do that a woman cannot do and thus, this is part of the problem with men becoming weak.

Women have become men, and men have become women. We don't need men anymore, so they wither and become weak like an unused muscle or a mind left unchallenged.

Women can fight wars with guns and bombs and soldiers.

Woman can be police officers and drag you off to jail.

Women can be prison guards and bash your head with a nightstick and put you in solitary confinement.

Women can be firefighters and drag you out of a burning building on their back.

Are any of the jobs above ideal for women and the natural strengths and divine gifts that women have? No, I don't believe that it's a woman's job to do any of the jobs listed above; in fact, I would wager that women would do a worse job than men for these reasons:

When it comes to danger and life-threatening decisions, that is where men and women become defined in their work and their jobs. When survival is on the line, I want the best man for the job. I don't want to take a gender studies class and learn about the theory of how men and women are equal. Men and women aren't equal; they are recip-rocal complementary opposites. Equal is homogenous and useless. Complementary and opposite is a powerful combination where men and women fiercely need each other.

If men and women are truly equal and the same, why not just have *sports* instead of men's and women's sports? If there was just *sports* instead of gender separated sports, there would probably be an extreme minority of women participating in the mixed gender sports. Generally, women's bodies are built differently, and they are unable to compete physically with the bigger, stronger, testosterone-filled men on the field.

There is no girls basketball in real life. In girls basketball there is a lower hoop, and a smaller ball, and the girls are shorter and less aggressive than the 7-foot tall black men in the NBA who will dunk over your head. In real life, there is only one type of basketball—the NBA. The men come out, and the little boys and girls go home and take their toys with them. Real life is reserved for the strongest, the smartest, the fittest for the job. In fact, as a 6'4" white male, I would be small and never make it in the NBA. Bigger black males dominate the sport, and rightfully so, because they are better at the job than smaller white males.

Success in real life is about having the best man for the job, and sometimes that doesn't include women.

Why not put the men and women together at the Olympics? If that were the case, women would complain: "This isn't fair. We can't compete with the bigger stronger men. Please give us a separate Olympics so we can compete against ourselves out of weakness."

Why the case for equality, then? What happened to complementary or reciprocal? What happened to two halves needing each other? What happened to having an offensive squad and a defensive squad on a team, instead of having everyone just chase the soccer ball around hoping to score?

Men have become obsolete to women.

Women have become obsolete to men.

They are equal and homogenous, and there is no reason to be together anymore.

This has come from the equalization of genders, homogenization of genders, feminism, destruction of men, and the creation of a bonobo-style weak man society.

Men are no longer needed to serve a purpose, which is to work and provide. Welfare can take care of them instead. They are no longer needed in the home or on the farm or in the military. Men are no longer needed—period. Welcome to the homogeneous mix of a gender-neutralized mankind.

Perhaps in the future, a theoretical sci-fi future, we will just have women, sperm banks, and turkey basters of semen to propagate the human race. Think it sounds crazy? Aldous Huxley predicted in his book *Brave New World* that humans would no longer be born in the near future, but instead would grow in test tubes. We are getting close to that point right now, and we are indeed entering a brave new world.

In the book *Brave New World*, a banned book during the author's time because it had offensive but truthful ideas, John—called the Savage because he lived on the Savage Reservation, but also because he was the only naturally born character in the novel—is brought from savage humanity, the frontier of survival, into the brave new world of the high-tech future. At the end of the book he goes insane and flogs himself just to feel human again and then hangs himself to end his life. Does John the savage in *Brave New World* represent the repressed man and what modern man has become? Now that man is obsolete, and unneeded, is the answer to the problem self-destruction and suicide as *Brave New World* subtly suggests?

Instead of men being the backbone of the family or important in the workplace, they are an inconvenient afterthought.

Not needed.

Not required.

Strictly optional.

The way we treat men is the same way we treat dogs today: when you get a dog as pet to love and cherish, the first thing you do is cut off his balls immediately and emasculate him. We do the same with men. As soon as they start acting like young men with aggression and defiance in schools, we metaphorically castrate the young men, cut off their balls, and treat them like badly behaved girls. It's proven that girls and young women do better in school because they can sit there and be obedient and listen. The young men, with 100 million sperm pulsing inside of them and raging testosterone flowing through their veins, can act like delinquents, convicts, and challenge authority. The young men are acting out, trying to form a party-gang to ensure their own survival, and we break them up and put them in detention; we shame them until they give up their masculine tendencies and turn into girls instead. There is no room for male-dominated gang culture inside of the school system today, which is an official mandate, but it is part of what being a man is about.

Men, strong men, once were the center of attention on the stage of society in the 1940s and even in the 1950s. They were real-life heroes that younger men wanted to be like. Nowadays, instead of the starring role on the stage of the play, men have nothing but a cameo appearance. They show up for a few minutes, say a few lines, they "check in" to pay child support, or see their parole officer, then they are ushered out the back door of the theatre.

Employment equity has flushed men right out of certain parts of the workforce. Whenever I fly in an airport and get patted down by the TSA, I rarely find a strong white male working in the TSA. Every minority is represented, every gay man, lesbian woman, black, Hispanic, Asian, crippled, American Indian, but no white males. The mandate for equality and for empowering minorities has made the previous majority, white males, an endangered species.

Gone are the warrior cultures that needed men to survive. They exist elsewhere in the world, namely in Islamic nations, Africa, South America, and hard places where men must violently fight to survive. But instead we have the neutered beta males in the Western world waiting for the gates to open and barbarians to violently finish them off.

Man is one part banished and one part imprisoned in the Western world nowadays. He is banished from the home, not needed, especially if he has a divorce, unless his exwife wants child support. He is banished from several workplaces through employment equity. He is banished from the gang-tribe of other men who used to survive and go out and hunt together and do manly things. Such groups are discouraged today, and he is imprisoned by the laws, family law, anything to do with sex law, and even laws around seeing his own children.

To illustrate the cage and imprisonment of the last remaining strong men in our society, I'll finish with a story: When I was in university I had a jazz professor who was 6'5", black, and he must have been a large and muscular 250 pounds. He was a huge man, bigger than a refrigerator, had a booming voice, and had made it as a jazz musician. This man, my professor and mentor, was a strong man, and I admired him. He mentored me one-on-one in my music career, and I am very grateful for the lessons he taught me. He was indeed a strong man.

This man was a dominant alpha male. He had made it on the streets of New York, had served in the American military, fired guns, blown up grenades, lived to tell about it, lived off his jazz music, and now had earned a position of power in the faculty of music. He had fought his way through the lines of survival into the comfort of the institution. He had it made, almost like earning an early pension.

He was totally different from any of the other effeminate, intellectual, nerdy men with beards and glasses in the faculty. He was raw, real, authentic, and had survived in the real world. He was the kind of guy you wanted to defend you on the front lines, in the trenches of the war, fighting your enemies for survival. He was tough, but he had your back. He had been to the frontier and made it back alive. This gave him charisma.

He was strong, and I was young—about 17 at the time—and he was tough. He didn't take any bullshit; he walked like the alpha male, strutted like a gangster, talked like the alpha male, flirted with the young women like the alpha male, and rightfully so, he was the king of his domain.

Things didn't work out, and I quit the school of music after a year. I remember crying out of weakness and having a chat with him backstage in a service hallway at the last gig I played at. I remember he respected my decision to quit. He sat and listened, and I cried. I was frustrated. He was stoic in the moment and respected my quitting, but he warned me to refrain from talking trash about him or his program, or I would "end up on the wrong side of history." It was a very manly thing to say; he was a little bit gangster, it was intimidating, but he was the tribal gang leader, so it was fine to me.

I was honorable, so I left quietly and moved on to the next chapter of my life.

Fast forward 14 years later, and this professor of mine is now caught in a witch hunt with the media. Students came forward claiming that "he took my drum sticks away from me," "he mocked me," "he was mean," I "felt uncomfortable about him," and of course the media lynched him. Ironically, he was a big black man, and in the Deep South they actually lynched black men until not that long ago. The mob would hunt down the big black men and hang them by their necks from trees if they did something wrong. Today in the university, the modern institution of power, they metaphorically hunted my mentor down and lynched him, the big black strong man, for his crime of being a dominant alpha male in his environment.

Sadly, things don't really change much in history.

He was a good man—had a wife, kids, seemed faithful enough. His wife supported him by responding to his press inquiries during the attacks students were making on him. He was out of the country of Canada and in his home country of the USA, and he would not respond to comments, but the lynch mob was out there looking to lynch the strong man.

The same lynch mob has come out looking for Donald Trump for being the alpha male and the dominant strong man and tribal leader.

My mother sent me articles about the lynching of my mentor. I believed he was acting normally as he always did, but the times had changed, and you can't be an alpha male anymore, especially in a big institution like a university. I read the articles my mother sent me and the accounts from students who claimed that he was off-side. Nothing seemed out of the ordinary for his normal behavior, but he was an alpha male, from the real world of survival, dominant, intimidating, and all the good things that men are on the frontiers of survival. I appreciated those qualities about him and learned from him.

What had changed though was the narrative in society. Female empowerment had grown in leaps and bounds in the last 14 years, and Trump was getting smashed in the media every day as a "racist," "sexist," "homophobe," "Islamophobe," "Mexican hater," and worst of all say-ing "mean things." The Harvey Weinstein scandal was just coming out, and the "me too" movement by women was becoming vastly popular with every single woman coming out with a rape story or abuse story. My professor was eliminated because he was no longer needed. He was now ironically "on the wrong side of history" and a victim to an invis-ible change and a sign of the times.

If we were in a survival situation, he's the first guy you would want to handle an emergency or a life-threatening situation. He was a strong man that you wanted on your team if your life depended on it. But your life wasn't in danger, so instead you had him eliminated because he threatened you. Welcome to the darkness of human nature. Eliminate the threats to you before they become threats.

As the lion who takes over a new territory, kill the cubs of your compet-itors before they grow up to challenge you.

But in our safe zone, our world of comfort, our world of women, our world of weak men without any threats from the frontier, my alpha male professor was obsolete and thrown into the trash bin of society.

I believe he lost his professorship at the university and had his charac-ter assassinated in the media.

Where is he now?

I'm not sure, probably lying low until things cool down.

Men are obsolete now, especially strong men, who have "fallen on the wrong side of history."

CHAPTER 31
A HISTORY OF VIOLENCE
The Rise of Rome

"Remove justice, and what are kingdoms but gangs of criminals on a large scale? What are criminal gangs but petty kingdoms? A gang is a group of men under command of a leader, bound by a compact of association, in which the plunder is divided according to an agreed convention. If this villainy wins so many recruits from the ranks of the demoralized that it acquires territory, establishes a base, captures cities and subdues people, it then openly arrogates itself the title of kingdom, which is conferred on it in the eyes of the world, not by the renouncing of aggression but by the attainment of impunity"

St. Augustine, City of God. 4-4

Thug life: an excerpt from *The Ways of Men* by Jack Donovan

AS THE STORY GOES, Rome was founded by a gang:

The Romans believed that Romulus and Remus were the distant descendants of Aeneas, who wandered the Mediterranean with a small band of survivors after the ruin of Troy. These exiled Trojans—the few remaining ambassadors of a proud but defeated tradition—were guided by the gods to Latium, where they intermingled with the Latin people of Italy. The former Trojans thrived there and founded the settlement of Alba Longa—just southeast of modern Rome.

Many generations passed, and the eldest son of each king took the throne until Amulius ousted his older brother Numitor. Amulius murdered Numitor's sons and forced his daughter Rhea Silvia to become a Vestal Virgin, assuring that the exiled Numitor would have no heirs to challenge his own. However, Rhea gave birth to twin boys, and rather than admit an indiscretion, she claimed that they were fathered by Mars, the god of war. King Amulius didn't buy her story. He had her chained and ordered her sons to be drowned in the Tiber river. The men charged with this task left the boys exposed in the swampy shallows of the flooded river and assumed the current would carry them to their deaths. According to legend, it was there that they were rescued by a thirsty she-wolf and suckled on her hairy dugs. The grandsons of Numitor were then discovered by shepherds who took the boys in and raised them as their own.

Thanks in part to a vigorous country life, Romulus and Remus grew into strong young men known for hunting and for fearlessly confronting "wild beasts." They also gained a reputation for attacking robbers, taking their loot, and sharing it with all of their shepherd pals. The generous twins were also fun to be around, and their merry band grew. During a festival, they were ambushed by the bitter robbers, and Remus was brought before the King Amulius on poaching charges. While Remus was in custody, Numitor suspected who the twins really were.

Meanwhile, Romulus organized his band of shepherds to kill Amulius and free his brother. The shepherds entered the city separately and gathered together at the last moment to overwhelm Amulius' guard. Romulus succeeded in killing the tyrant king, and after learning his true heritage, he restored the kingship to his grandfather Numitor.

The reunited twins then decided to found a city together on the land where they were raised. However, the two men quarreled over its naming and the dispute became heated. The brothers challenged each other, and in the end Romulus triumphed, killing his beloved twin brother Romulus and his friends then set to work organizing the government of the new city that bore his name.

According to the historian Livy, one of the first things that Romulus did after making some rudimentary fortifications was to establish the religious rites that would be celebrated by the people of Rome. In addition to the rites honoring the local gods, Romulus chose to observe the Greek rites of the heroic god-man Hercules, known for his great strength and for his "virtuous deeds."

After identifying a constellation of gods and setting a rough spiritual course for his tribe, Romulus advertised the city of Rome an asylum where all men, freeborn or slave, could start a new life. A motley collection of immigrants from neighboring tribes traveled to Rome, and he selected the best men to help him rule. These men were made senators and designated "fathers" (patres) of the Roman tribe. Their heirs would be known as patricians. With the city fathers, he created order through law.

Lacking women, the men of Rome knew their city would die with them. Romulus sent out envoys to surrounding communities to secure wives for his men. Their offers of marriage were refused, however, because the young men of Rome had no prospects, no reputations, and were generally regarded as a dangerous band of low-born men. Insulted, Romulus and his men hatched a scheme, and invited the people of neighboring communities to a festival. During the festival they seized the unmarried girls. Their parents were furious, and the other tribes affected made war with Rome, but Rome prevailed over all militarily except the Sabines, with whom the women themselves helped to make peace to save both their fathers and their new husbands. The Sabines decided to join the Romans, and it was through this successful "rape" of the Sabine women that Romulus ensured the future of his new tribe.

Romulus continued to strengthen and defend his tribe through calculated military action, and he was loved by the rank and file of his men-at-arms. These rough men— Romulus's big gang—secured the city and made its growth possible. They were Rome's guardian class, and their unbeatable fighting spirit would characterize the Roman people for centuries.

One day, as he prepared to review his troops, Romulus disappeared with a violent clap of thunder. Livy suspected that he was torn apart at the hands of his senators, who were contentious and tended to conspire, as men close to power often do. The Roman people preferred to remember Romulus as a great man of divine lineage who lived among the people as one of them, who was known for his meritorious works and courage in battle, and who finally took his rightful place among the gods.

There are many founding myths of cities, and countless myths that establish a totemic lineage of a particular people. In the absence of certain recorded history, this is the myth that Romans chose to believe about themselves. It is the spirit of the tale that endures, and it can tell us something about The Way of Men.

Romulus and Remus were betrayed and abandoned. They were left to die and saved by a wolf. Livy admits that the wolf might have easily been a country whore, but it doesn't really matter—they were raised wild. Romulus and Remus were raised "country." They had practical know-how and they knew the value of a hard day's work. They were given a simple upbringing, uncomplicated by court politics or the soft moral equivocation that attends urban commerce. They were virile and upright youth.

The early life of Romulus and Remus is a Robin Hood story. They roughed up other men, seized their stolen loot, and shared it with their poor friends. They were alpha males, natural leaders of men. They were tough, but they weren't bullies. They were the kind of men who other men look up to and want to be around. They were the kind of guys who men choose to lead of their own free will. They had heroic qualities, but they were as flawed as any men—and when the brothers fought for status, as brothers often do, one of them had to lose.

Romulus' "merry men" were basically a gang. They were a rowdy bunch of country boys who came out of nowhere to attack a king and upset the status quo. When Romulus staked out his territory and announced that it would be an asylum, he attracted hooligans with little money or status of their own. Some were former slaves. Some could have been wanted men. They had little to lose, everything to gain, and no real investment in the communities they came from. Rome was Deadwood; it was The Wild West. Romulus organized these unruly men and established a hierarchy. He founded a culture, a religion, a group identity.

Like any bunch of young men, Romulus' thugs had reproductive interests. Romulus tried the nice route, sending ambassadors out to inquire about getting his men some wives, but his men were laughed out of town. No father of means was going to send his daughter out to some camp to marry a man with no prospects. So Romulus took the women. The Romans were able to keep the women and start families because they were strong and effective fighters. They didn't give in. They fought for a new future, and they won.

The Roman tribe used violence and cunning to expand its borders, and men from many tribes became Romans. The expansion of Rome served the interests of the descendants of the tribal fathers: the patrician class. However, Roman economic and military power also benefitted many other citizens and noncitizens living within Roman territory. Protected by

Roman might, men were able to specialize and live their lives as laborers, craftsmen, farmer, and traders. Many men were able to live relatively nonviolent lives. The Roman definition of manliness expanded to include ethical virtues that were less specifically male, but more harmonious with a more complex civilization

However, the Romans who rested in the lap of protection still hungered for the drama of violence. They became spectators of violence and bloodsport. Gladiators fought each other to the death to entertain the Roman tribe, and the people crowded into massive stadiums like the Circus Maximus to watch chariot races highlighted by gory wrecks. There were chariot racing "color" gangs who brawled after the events like today's soccer hooligans. Political figures, landowners, and merchants employed gangs of armed young men to intimidate their opponents, tenants, and business rivals.

Rome was founded by a gang, and it behaved like a gang. To paraphrase St. Augustine, it acquired territory, established a base, captured cities, and subdued people. Then it openly arrogated itself the title of Empire, which was conferred on it in the eyes of the world, not by the renouncing of aggression but by the attainment of (temporary) impunity. Rome slowly collapsed from the inside as it became a giant, pointless, corrupt economic machine. The Roman machine, like the American economic machine, could no longer embody the virile ethos of the small bands of rebellious men responsible for its creation. Gangs of armed young men existed throughout its rise and fall, and there were gangs long after the glory of Rome was left in ruin.

The story of Rome is the story of men and civilization. It shows men who have no better prospects gathering together, establishing hierarchies, staking out land and using strength to assert their collective will over nature, women, and other men.

Empires rise out of violence, killing, slavery, and the hard times that create strong men. For example, the Egyptian empire rose out of violence, killing, and slavery.

> *"Militarily, Egypt towered over its neighbors. Its public buildings were carved with solemn scenes of Egyptian warriors leading huge masses of conquered peoples off to slavery and beheading the unruly types who refused to go along with captivity. No one could challenge the mighty empire. Not if he wanted to live to talk about it. Like ants in the colony with the biggest territory, Egyptians lived the good life."*

HOWARD BLOOM, *THE LUCIFER PRINCIPLE*

The Persian Empire rose out of violence, killing, and slavery.

The Persians were unlettered and uncouth. But they loved a good fight. It wasn't long before this mob no one had ever heard of overwhelmed the Assyrians and the Medes—Babylon's two rival superpowers. Then the Persians turned on the isolated Babylonians. You can imagine who won. The irony came a few decades later. By now, the victorious Persian rulers had turned from barbarians to urbane city dwellers. True, they still traveled up into the hills to eat and drink with the old folks for a few weeks. But then they went back to their estates, their servants, their armies of bureaucrats, and their imported luxuries. One by one they took over the superpowers of the day, finally subduing Egypt in 525 BC. The Persian superorganism was now the master of the international pecking order. Of course there were still dangers. But the Persians knew exactly where to look for them. Or so they thought. Like the Babylonians before them, the Persians were blind to the barbarians, and expected trouble only from nations celebrated for military might. They forgot that the real threat often comes from a people everyone has totally dismissed. So the great Persian leader Darius didn't even bother with the scarcely civilized yokels who squabbled interminably on a bunch of islands and rocky coasts to the west. It was a big mistake. The western upstarts provoked a fight. When some of the cities under Persian rule revolted, the insignificant foreigners sent a fleet to help them out. Then these outlanders proceeded to burn down Sardis, capital of the western segment of the Persian Empire. The Persians, determined to teach the impertinent nobodies a lesson, ordered a naval detachment to administer punishment. Like the group of helicopters once dispatched to rescue American hostages in Iran, the invincible Persian fleet ran into technical problems. It was wrecked in a storm. In 490 B.C., the Persians tried again. This time, they sailed off to the homeland of the upstarts and clobbered one of their pitifully backward towns into the turf. But the nobodies turned the tables. They sent the invading Persian troops running and destroyed seven of the Empire's momentarily victorious ships.

Howard Bloom, *The Lucifer Principle*

The Greek empire rose from backwater barbarians fighting the civilized Persians to a sophisticated empire after defeating the Persians. The Greeks rose out of violence, killing and slavery:

The Persians had had it. They were determined to make these half-baked rednecks from a land scarcely marked on the map rue the day they tangled with Persia. Emperor Xerxes gathered an armada of mind-boggling size. Its ships numbered well over a thousand. What's more, according to Herodotus, the Persians put together an army of 1,700,000 men, including troops from every territory of the Empire— Arabia, Bactria, Media, Assyria, Ethiopia and Libya. Even the distant Indians contributed their heaviest transport vehicle—the war elephant. The resulting military force was so vast that it stretched farther than the eye could see. Provisioning it with food and equipment took four years and the resources of an entire continent. Whenever the Persian host marched to a fresh campsite, it literally ate every available bit of food and drank every potable drop of water in expanses dozens of square miles in size. Says Herodotus, "There was not a nation in Asia" the Persians didn't take with them. And "save for the great rivers there was not a stream... [their army] drank from that was not drunk dry." The folks they were marching to conquer couldn't come anywhere near this logistic sophistication.

But the barbarians the Persians considered beneath contempt won the war. They were called the Greeks. In the 490's B.C., years before the first major Persian-Greek war, when he was informed that the burning of Sardis had been pulled off by a landing party of Athenians, the exasperated Persian emperor Darius had been forced to ask, "Who are the Athenians?" Now, presumably, he knew. One hundred and fifty years later a Greek who even his fellow Greeks called a barbarian would conquer the entire Persian Empire. His name was Alexander the Great.

Howard Bloom, *The Lucifer Principle*

The Roman Empire began as a rabble of barbarians and ended up as a sophisticated empire. At the beginning Rome was built on violence, killing, and slavery.

The rise of America came from unsophisticated barbarians in the eyes of the British empire after World War I and America's ultimate rise to superpower status after World War II.

America was born out of violence, killing, and slavery in 1776 and rose to superpower out of the same violence, killing, and slavery through taking the world currency as the US dollar.

(Alexander the Great rising up as a barbarian to take Persia from Darius) ... was as unlikely as the Vietnamese turning around and conquering the U.S. But it happened. In fact, in history it happens over and over again. It happened in 1870 when the French were forced to fight a country which just a few years earlier had been a disorganized clutter of rag-tag mini-states ruled by comic opera princes. The land of Napoleon was rated by every armchair general as the mightiest military force on the Continent. But France lost. Its army was chopped up like ground round. Its glorious capital, Paris, faced the humiliation of a foreign army marching down its streets. The upstart nation that had brought France to its knees was ... Germany. An equally surprising fate occurred to England when it trained its guns on the superpowers of its day in two world wars. When the smoke had cleared, two backward nations of Johnny-come-latelies ended up dominating the world. These countries, whose inhabitants had usually been regarded as just one small step above the primitive, were The United States and Russia. The moral is simple. Never forget the pecking order's surprises. Today's superpower is tomorrow's conquered state. Yesterday's overlooked mob is often the ruler of tomorrow. Never underestimate the third world. Never be complacent about barbarians.

Howard Bloom, *The Lucifer Principle*

Although the current American Empire has a "strong moral code," whatever that means, and claims to have abolished slavery, I would argue that slavery was never abolished America; it just put on a different costume. Look at the prison system for the black population who are stripped of their voting powers and forced to work in privately owned prisons for privately owned corporations. Is that not slavery? Look at the minimum wage slaves who cannot afford a 2-bedroom apartment in any state, or the middle-class debt-slaves who have to work two jobs just to pay for their homes. Or how about the mom and dad slaves at two jobs in the middle class just to pay interest on loans on money that never existed in the first place. Or what about the "tipping wage" for mostly women and minorities at $2.13 an hour in some states where these people have to live on tips to survive. Rome had slave girls and boys. America has slave girls working for $2.13 an hour to live on tips, which is one level above begging for money on the street. Slavery is persisting in the United States, but it's just packaged in a "happier" and "nicer" way that looks different from what we tell ourselves slavery is.

The old slaves in America were not allowed to read; the new slaves in America won't read no matter what.

The old slaves in America lived on plantations and owned nothing. The new slaves in America "own stuff" like cars, TVs, houses, fast food, video games, beer, and porn. They feel better about their situation, so they don't bother rising up. George Orwell said in *1984*, "The people will not revolt. They will not look up from their screens long enough to notice what's happening."

> *"The best way to keep a prisoner from escaping is to make sure he never knows he's in prison."*
>
> FYODOR DOSTOEVSKY

Slavery in the most basic sense is where a person works the entire year and at the end has nothing to show for it; most Americans fit into this category in the poor and middle class. Sure, they own some worthless consumer goods at the end of the year, such as a big screen TV, but those items are not of real value.

All empires are built on the backs of slaves.

With the demonstrated rise and fall of several empires dating back to the Egyptians and all the way up to the modern day, with the American empire losing a war to the barbarians in Vietnam, will the rise of the Islamic empire be next? Will a new religious empire from Islam be the next wave of barbarians that swarms the shores of America and Europe to cause violence, enslave the population, and rape the women?

Will they bring violence, killing, and slavery to our gates?

It could happen.

With the "refugee crises" going on in Germany, Sweden, France, and several civilized countries, I have seen firsthand footage of hordes and hordes of young military-aged men. They look like an army coming in to take what they want. The refugee migrations appear to have a disproportionate number of men in them when compared to women and children. Sweden and Germany have had major problems with their women being raped and their men being beaten by roving gangs of Muslim refugee men.

To counter this, white-power German biker gangs are also roaming the streets to unleash vigilante justice on these invaders and beat up any Muslims they see. I previously stated that the history from 80 years ago is ready to repeat itself. Roughly 80 years ago, gangs of German thugs roamed the streets as the Brownshirts bringing a man named Adolf Hitler to power, who was leading a group of pissed off and impoverished Germans who had been sacked by brutal war reparation payments that they could no longer pay. The German men were have-nots and rose up to take back what they had lost.

Does the street-level violence and "justice" in Germany not resemble the street-level violence of 80 years ago with the Brownshirts and Adolf Hitler? History always repeats itself, especially in 80-year cycles.

The major shifts in a society always start on a street level, with small gangs and units of men, and then they increase into larger and larger groups and finally into large tribes and supertribes. This is the beginning. If history continues the trends outlined above, we could have a rude awakening from the backwater barbarians who do not even have an established military but instead show up on our soil in primitive boats claiming to be refugees with nothing but their bare fists, testosterone, and muscles looking to fight.

Greek mythology tells us the story of Troy and how it was sacked by using the Trojan horse tactic. After a 10-year long war and eventually a siege, Greece had surrounded Troy. The walls were impenetrable, so the Greeks devised a plan. They built a Trojan horse, a beautiful wooden statue as a gift to give to the Trojans as a sign of peace. The

Trojans happily welcomed the horse as a gift from their departed Greek enemies into their mighty walls. But when night fell, the elite Greek soldiers led by King Odysseus snuck out of the horse and brutally massacred the sleeping Trojans.

Could this same story, with a modern spin, be happening right now? Except instead of with a Trojan horse it is happening with dingy little boats and marches of refugees who "come in peace"?

I will let you decide from the examples in history above.

The popular view in the political narrative and in the media is that "we are helping the Muslim refugees," "Islam is peaceful," "we have to have to be compassionate and let them in." These are the words of our female leaders, our bonobo women leaders who would be the first to go if violence were unleashed from inside of our country or if Sharia law took over. A record number of Swedish women have been raped by Muslim refugees as Sweden has grown very relaxed, liberal, and "progressive" over the years. Sweden is a neutral country in war and used to have a decent military to defend its borders from neighboring superpowers like Russia, Britain, and Germany, but they have recently downsized their military. Good times create weak men, weak men create hard times. Now the women are getting raped from invading refugees from within. What's next?

As a Swedish dual citizen myself, I'm afraid to know.

The media does not play tapes or history records the times when an unsophisticated, violent, desperate group of have-nots with nothing to lose and everything to gain are unleashed on a "free, peaceful and tolerant society led by women and weak men?" Those historical records usually end in slaughter, mass murder, butchery, killing, and rape.

> "Kill one man you're a murderer,
> Kill millions of men, you're a conqueror,
> Kill them all, you are God."

> **Jean Rostand**

> "Veni Vidi Vici.
> I came, I saw, I conquered."

> **Julius Caesar on conquering
> the once indomitable British tribes.**

Please refrain from thinking that I am hating on one particular group or singling out Islam.

The Vikings were barbarians who sacked the Empire—English city-states at the hands of Ivar the Boneless, who was a ruthless killer.

We love, celebrate, and worship "our" killers like Julius Caesar and hate "their" killers like Saddam Hussein, who is portrayed as a barbaric butcher of innocent lives. In the end, a killer is a killer, killing is neutral, it's a means to an end. There are no real morals or ethics in war. There are rules of engagement such as "don't shoot hostages," but the winners of wars shoot hostages just like the losers of wars. However, the winners are never war criminals. Only the losers are documented as unethical, amoral, and war criminals. The winners paint over their crimes with white paint and whitewash their dark war crimes. The winners paint over their crimes with white paint in the same way that the Americans white-washed the charred Whitehouse after the British infiltrated the country and set fire to it. White paint can cover up a lot when it comes to history.

The hypocrisy on killing is the "us and them" tribal high school foot-ball dynamic taken all the way—this is part of being human. No matter how hard we try to remove it and have world peace, it's never going away; it's a part of our biology and what makes us human. When it comes to our enemies, there are two sets of morals and ethics. When we kill it's justified and our enemies are subhuman. When they kill us, it's a crime.

Unsophisticated groups of have-nots have always toppled technologi-cally and socially advanced haves in the bloody pages of history over and over again.

Instead of the Ivar the Boneless facing off against Alfred the Great, we have George Bush sending his crusaders in to fight Osama bin Laden.

Instead of Julius Caesar and the Gallic tribes lead by Vercingetorix, we instead have Donald Trump and Vladimir Putin blowing up Islamic fighters together in Syria. It's the same damn story over and over again, just with different names and different costumes.

A man's duty is to do his work. Today we contract out all our society's killing to professional killers in the military, but we might have a time when men are called upon to make killing their work once again. If that time comes, the men who are strong men will have to step up to their temporary work as has happened in history over and over again.

Men would be farmers or factory workers in peacetime, and when the war sirens rang, they grabbed their swords or rifles and marched into battle to defend their land, women, children, and way of life.

If your tribe, your society, your group required you to kill, would you do it?

Could you do it?

Do you have the killer instinct that the barbarian on the other end of the gun barrel has?

He wants to kill you and take everything you have ever loved, cherished, and valued?

Who pulls the trigger first?

> *"In a man-to-man fight, the winner is he who has one more round in his magazine."*
>
> ERWIN ROMMEL, GERMAN FIELDMARSHAL IN WWII, THE LEADER OF THE AFRIKA CORPS AND THE DESERT FOX. FROM HIS BOOK *INFANTRY ATTACKS*.

History is full of examples of sophisticated empires that were born out of violence, killing, and slavery. Men were made strong in the hard times of birthing a nation, and as they grew rich, fat, complacent, and tolerant, they became weak and docile on the way down.

These empires never considered that the unsophisticated barbarians on the fringes would ever break through the gates and bring back the violence, killing, and slavery that their prosperity was built upon.

Primitive barbarians could never hurt us...right? Say the weak men safely behind the city walls.

"Pride comes before a fall "

PROVERB

Apartheid was legal.

The Holocaust was legal.

Slavery was legal.

Colonialism was legal.

Legality is a matter of power, not justice.

Anonymous

CHAPTER 32
BARBARIANS AT THE GATES
The Fall of America

The Barbarian Principle: *"A thousand men who fear not for their lives are more to be dreaded than ten thousand who fear for their fortunes."*

DENIS DIDEROT

A position at the top of the pecking order is not permanent. Far from it. Animals who make it to the peak know that simple fact. They see that yesterday's adolescents have become today's restless adults, and watch warily as these youthful challengers size up the odds of knocking their elders off the top of the heap. Dominant beasts remain vigilant. But a strange thing happens to nations at the pecking order's apogee. The dominant superorganism sometimes goes to sleep. It falls complacently into a fatal trap, assuming that its high position is God-given, that its fortunate lot in life will last forever, that its lofty status is carved in stone. It forgets that any pecking order is a temporary thing and no longer remembers just how miserable life can be on the bottom. The results are often an unpleasant surprise. We all know that Rome was picked apart by peoples any respectable Roman could see were beneath his contempt. The barbarians didn't shave. They wore dirty clothes. They were almost always drunk. Their living standard was one step above that of a mule. Their technology was laughable. They usually couldn't read and write. And they certainly had no "culture." What could these smelly primitives do? They could fight.

Howard Bloom, *The Lucifer Principle*

When Americans go to the theatre to watch *Star Wars* or the *Hunger Games,* they cheer for the rebels, the have-nots, the young teenagers, the women. The youth like Luke Skywalker and Princess Leia from *Star Wars* and Katniss Everdeen, the 16-year-old female protagonist in the *Hunger Games,* capture that rebellious essence, the youth, the vigor, the purity, and innocence of the rebellion. Katniss takes on the evil empire oppressing her family, and the villain in the movie—an old white man named President Snow.

I recently watched *Star Wars: The Last Jedi,* and I literally fell asleep in the middle of the movie because it was neutered by Disney, who now owns *Star Wars*. The narrative was: women, blacks, the youth, Asians, the poor, and a whole bunch of minorities (and some incompetent weak men) against the rich and old white men in the empire.

It was cliché and such a display of the popular narrative that I fell asleep in the middle.

They say that clichés are so common they are meaningless. The entire movie was one big cliché, a story so common in our narrative it failed to become a distinct or meaningful piece of art.

So I fell asleep in the middle of the movie.

No amount of lasers, robots, or spaceships could keep my interest in something so blatant and bland to the social conditioning that is happening today. At least in the 1970s, *Star Wars* had competent young men fighting the old-man empire as rebels.

The Last Jedi has almost no competent men left. In fact, the men in that movie really suck: good times create weak men.

In the *Hunger Games*, the story is set in an alternate universe based on Rome in which the story takes place. The alternate post-American futuristic Roman universe is fully equipped with bloody gladiator games, an oppressive Roman-style American government, and tribes of poor have-not barbarian teenagers who wish to overthrow the empire. The story is full of Roman names like Cato and Panem, which is the name of the nation. Panem, which is supposed to be a post-apocalyptic America, means "bread," which is an allusion to "breads and circuses."

The gladiator games of Rome were the "breads and circuses" that the bloodthirsty Romans loved to watch. Fittingly, the oppressive empire in the *Hunger Games* loves to watch blood sport as well.

The irony is, we, the Western world, are the evil empire and not the rebellion.

We are Darth Vader and the endless waves of Stormtroopers invading primitive backwater societies and utterly crushing their way of life.

We are the sinister and menacing faceless-foot soldiers in the *Hunger Games* from District 2 who are cold-blooded killers and who carpet bomb women, children, and innocent civilians.

We are the Empire, and we kill and exterminate the disorganized bands of teenagers running around in the desert who are "freedom fighter" rebels in both *Star Wars* and the *Hunger Games*.

But somehow, we cheer for the rebels. We cheer for the barbarians even though we are the Empire.

Sometimes reality is stranger than fiction. It seems ironic, but ironic is an understatement.

We want the rebels to win, but we are the Empire stomping people down daily across the world and bombing families with robotic predator drones that are controlled by our young men with Xbox controllers.

The young American recruits had played so much Xbox and had done so much killing through video games, they didn't need much actual training to fly predator drones across the world and bomb the primitive barbarians and teenage rebels across the world. How clean, how convenient—real killing done through a TV with an Xbox controller! It might be a good thing that the men of today are doing so much simulated killing through video games, because that literally might be how the wars of the future are fought. With a keyboard and mouse or with an Xbox controller in Mom's basement with a real live predator drone blowing up real people across the world.

Why send a man if you can send a machine? Stay in the comfort of your basement and be home in time for dinner after the killing is done for the day.

But we go home and watch *Star Wars* and cheer for Luke Skywalker; yet we are governed by Darth Vader himself. We think we are the Jedi, but we are indeed the Sith. We are the bad guys, the evil Empire, the human butchers on the world stage. No wonder the barbarians of Islam hate us and what we represent. When you see the evil Empire on the big screen in the movies, you know they are evil right away, so why is it so hard for us to see our own evil and our own darkness? It's because tribally, our killers are good, moral, and justified.

Their killers are bad, amoral, unethical, and subhuman.

Our killers are defenders of freedom; their killers are terrorists.

They call themselves freedom fighters; we call them terrorists.

One man's freedom fighter is another man's terrorist.

One man's God is another man's devil.

This is like the primitive, tribal, high school football rivalry, but with real bullets.

This is real life, where the winner plays for keeps. This is live ammo, you might get shot, and if you get shot, you might die. The Empire doesn't strike back. The Empire strikes first!

In the blockbuster movie *American Sniper*, we patriotically follow Texas hero Chris Kyle, one of the top 10 most deadly snipers in history, in his story from being a country boy and learning to hunt deer with his dad all the way up to his days as a modern crusader in Iraq hunting terrorists and Islamic barbarians. His rival in the movie is an Olympic Syrian sniper. The movie depicts the humanity of both sides and the reality that is tribalism and war. Chris Kyle has his beautiful wife and baby at home, and he's going to war to defend his country, his people, his wife, and his baby—all in the name of freedom!

The Syrian sniper is a mercenary, an athlete, and a top caliber sniper just like Chris Kyle.

If they weren't in a war and were just hanging out at the gun club, having beer, and talking about guns, they would probably be best friends. Their kids might play together, or their wives might have lunch together once in a while. The Syrian sniper has a beautiful wife and a baby as well and is just trying to make a living shooting American soldiers on video camera for $20,000 apiece and trying to earn the bounty for his family by killing Chris Kyle, who has a $180,000 bounty for the "Crusader."

He wants to win for his freedom and to protect his family and his baby. Who am I referring to in that last line? The answer is both Chris Kyle and the nameless Syrian want to "win for his freedom and to protect his family and his baby." It's the same story on both sides. Both men want freedom, but only one man gets freedom in the competition—the one who shoots the other man in the head and spills his brains all over the walls.

There is only one trophy given out in this contest, and second place is buried among the dead and wiped nameless from the history books.

I respect both Chris Kyle and the Syrian sniper as men. They are doing their jobs and protecting their tribes. They are good, trustworthy men who are doing their best to ensure their survival. But in history, one wins and one loses. This is not a soccer game where everyone gets a participation trophy and ice cream on the way home even if they lose.

In the real life of tribal competition, the losers are brutally eliminated from the gene pool.

"For you to be free, someone else must be enslaved."

UNKNOWN

My mother went to Mexico on vacation some years ago, and she wanted to experience "authentic Mexico." So she left the resort that has military soldiers with machine guns, gates, guards, and barbed wire around the resort to protect the rich, fat, white gringos from the locals.

In her naiveté, my mother stepped out into the hostile frontier of survival into her idealistic idea of "authentic Mexico" away from the guards (the men who were hired to fire their guns to protect her) and gets on a bus as an old, white, heavyset Canadian woman.

The Mexicans spotted the intruder and they robbed her.

Why would they do that? She couldn't understand why someone would rob her.

As a government teacher, my mom has lived her life inside the frontier, inside the safe perimeter, protected and sheltered. She couldn't understand what it would be like to be hungry, desperate, and a have-not.

My mother has had a great life; she has never been without.

The Mexicans on the streets in "authentic Mexico" had never had anything, so they took what they wanted.

"They hate what you represent, Mom," I explained. "You represent everything they don't have. They are the have-nots, and you are the have."

It's not personal. It's just the business and gang culture of human nature.

She was the Empire, and they were the rebels.

She was the bank, and they were the robbers.

Everyone is just looking to survive.

The Western world is great, though; there are marvelous things in the West.

We are not all bad, and we would like to think that we are not so evil. The West creates, innovates, can build fantastic products and feats of engineering that even the pharaohs of Egypt couldn't imagine: a car, a computer, a cellphone; we build homes, have credit, credit cards, finance, cheap trips, cheap food, cheap clothes, access to medicine if you get sick, and we have all the luxuries in the first world. We are sitting at the dinner table in the first world eating a big plate of sizzling juicy prime-cut steak while the third world, a hungry dog, is watching us eat our dinner. The dog is well behaved today and just watching; he's drooling, and smiling, and panting as a dog normally does. We think he's cute, we think he's harmless, but if we turn our back for a second, or take our eyes off that juicy steak, the dog will jump up on the table and snatch our dinner from us.

It's not racism, and it's not Islamophobia or Mexican hate; it's just that you are the kid eating a cookie on the playground, and another kid is looking at you, and his mom didn't pack him a cookie for lunch. He doesn't have a cookie, and he wants yours. He's hungry and imagining how good it's going to taste when he puts your cookie, that sweet, chocolatey morsel in his mouth.

If the teacher at school goes away or out of sight for a moment, the other kid might punch you in the face and take your cookie away from you.

Would it be right for him to do that?

No, but we are talking about human nature and not idealistic morals, ethics, or "the way that things ought to be."

This is not gym class, where everyone gets a trophy because they ran in the race, or where everyone gets an "A" no matter how fat he is or how slowly he runs. We don't get the ability to opt out of the race altogether and get your mommy to write you a note to exempt you from gym class. Gym class is mandatory, and everyone has to run.

In the race of real life, only first place gets a trophy. Everyone else gets nothing or gets buried for competing. And if you are a loser in the race game of real life, no one is there to buy you an ice cream at the end. In fact, if you come in second place in history, as we have seen earlier in this chapter, second place gets violently murdered, the women get raped, and the children get enslaved. You don't want to be second place when it comes to the frontier of survival.

"The kid on the playground who is always afraid of getting punched in the face always gets punched in the face."

50 CENT, RAP SUPERSTAR WHO GREW UP IN THE
HARD TIMES GHETTO DEALING DRUGS.

"Everybody has a plan until he gets punched in the face."

MIKE TYSON, HEAVYWEIGHT CHAMPION OF THE WORLD

When you compare the greatness of the Western world, which has stemmed from a Judeo-Christian philosophy and values system, and look at the third world, it's easy to see why they would want to come here and live in the luxury that has been built here. It's truly amazing, and even the poorest people in Canada or America live better than the kings of ancient Egypt. Food is more plentiful and cheaper, the shelter is heated or cooled, transportation is easier, infant mortality is far less, and the entertainment—TV, porn, and videogames—provides luxuries that the ancient kings of Egypt would probably have given it all just to experience.

They want to come here, but the reverse is not true.

We don't want to go there and live in the world that they have built. The same woman who emasculates men and claims equality as her highest virtue, while also claiming that Donald Trump is racist, will also want to let more Muslim refugees into the country because it's compassionate, fair, and equal. Diversity and multiculturalism are her values, and she's not considering what happens when a tolerant woman like herself becomes the unprotected minority to the majority of militant Muslim men.

Will those men from intolerant and violent societies be tolerant and peaceful with her and honor her untraditional feminist ideals that she learned in gender studies class at the university? Will they let her bare her breasts in public? Will they let her dress provocatively in the way she wants? Will they give her equal opportunity in life? Likely not!

Will things be good for her then? Probably not.

Sharia law isn't very fun for women. She will be forced to cover her body with a burka. If she acts out, she might get some acid on her face to disfigure her. She will have her clitoris mutilated to sexually numb her pleasure so only her dominant Muslim husband can have pleasure from sex. She may also have her hand cut off if she tries to steal something. If she cheats on her husband, she will be thrown in a pit and stoned. She might find this to be a shock, because Sharia law and Islamic countries operate in a very different way from the ways that the empowered women of the West are used to. In many Islamic countries women can't even drive or leave the house without her husband, father, or brother as protection.

When a tolerant society is met with an intolerant society, the intolerant society will usually murder the tolerant society. Such is human history.

Just like my mother on the Mexican bus who was robbed and had her wallet and cellphone taken, I wonder what a majority of intolerant, radical, violent Muslim men will do to our tolerant, empowered, bonobo women who get up on stage and talk about "pussy" and "vagina monologues" and decapitate dolls of their male strong man leader Donald Trump for a laugh.

Perhaps the intolerant Islamic men will become tolerant in a moment of idealistic compassion? Probably not.

I would venture to say that the intolerant Islamic men will instead decapitate those Western women as infidels and a disgusting aberration of what a woman should never be in the world. A disgusting aberration is the sentiment that they feel towards the Western empowered woman.

The strong men of Islam do not tolerate the nonsense that women have been pulling off in the Western world since the 1960s.

Is this good or bad? It doesn't matter.

It's just how things are; don't get emotional or idealistic about it.

The irony of the empowered Western women showing up at the train station in Sweden with signs welcoming hordes of masculine, soldier-aged men who are 100% intolerant of the liberal Swedish way of life is mind-blowing. We have become so weak that we cannot even see the barbaric invasion and war of ideology that are happening right in front of our faces.

We are blind.

The Judeo-Christian values and philosophy have made us, the West, into creators and leaders in the world.

What does the third world or the barbaric hordes create? Very little.

I'm sure that the Roman government asked themselves the same questions of the Germanic tribes they were oppressing with crippling taxes. "What do they make? Nothing! They don't even shave!" This, of course, would have been followed by the famous last words, "They are of no threat to us."

But then those barbaric hordes came over. ...

They came a little closer. ...

Then we let them inside the gates. ...

They butchered us, the Romans, in an epic blood-letting to take Roman land, seize our possessions, rape our women, and enslave or murder our children:

> *"Man's greatest good fortune is to chase and defeat his enemy, seize his total possessions, leave his married women weeping and wailing, ride his gelding (and) use the bodies of his women as a nightshirt and support."*
>
> GENGHIS KHAN

"In Shakespeare's The Life of Henry the Fifth, the King promised his enemies that unless they surrendered, his men would rape their shrieking daughters, dash the heads of their old men, and impale their naked babies on pikes. Today, if a military leader made a promise so indelicate, he would be fired and publicly denounced as an evil, broken psychopath. I can't call Henry an unmanly character with a straight face."

JACK DONOVAN, THE WAYS OF MEN

"He butchered three of them with an ax and decapitated them. In other words, instead of using a gun to kill them he took a hatchet to chop their heads off. He struggled face to face with one of them, and throwing down his ax managed to break his neck and devour his flesh in front of his comrades. ... I ... award him the Medal of the Republic."

GENERAL MUSTAFA T'LAS, SYRIA'S MINISTER OF
DEFENSE PRAISING A HERO OF THE 1973 WAR WITH
ISRAEL BEFORE THE SYRIAN NATIONAL ASSEMBLY

The damage of letting the Germanic barbarians infiltrate the perimeters of Rome was so great that Europe went into nearly 1,000 years of darkness—the Dark Ages. This was one of the worst times in all of human history. The once mighty Roman Empire decomposed into warring city-states, Europe's population fell by almost 50%, libraries were burned, knowledge was lost, people were killed and enslaved, women were raped, and people were cooped up in city strongholds with high walls to keep out the bands of roving gangs.

Trump wants to build a wall to keep out the Mexican criminals and drug dealers who are supposedly illegally crossing the border into the USA. Rome had several walls to protect the people from the danger of the frontier. When Rome fell, they needed major walls on their smallest cities just to survive against the barbaric, raping, killing hordes.

Rome had problems with its borders and with the barbarians on the frontier. Things do not change throughout history. When Donald Trump announced his presidential bid, there was talk of walls and protecting the border, much like ancient Rome that had problems with its borders:

> When do we beat Mexico at the border? They're laughing at us, at our stupidity. And now they are beating us economically. They are not our friend, believe me. But they're killing us economically.
>
> The U.S. has become a dumping ground for everybody else's problems.
>
> (APPLAUSE)
>
> Thank you. It's true, and these are the best and the finest. When Mexico sends its people, they're not sending their best. They're not sending you. They're not sending you. They're sending people that have lots of problems, and they're bringing those problems with us. They're bringing drugs. They're bringing crime. They're rapists. And some, I assume, are good people ...
>
> It's coming from more than Mexico. It's coming from all over South and Latin America, and it's coming probably—probably—from the Middle East. But we don't know. Because we have no protection and we have no competence, we don't know what's happening. And it's got to stop and it's got to stop fast.
>
> (APPLAUSE)
>
> TRUMP: Islamic terrorism is eating up large portions of the Middle East. They've become rich. I'm in competition with them ...
>
> I would build a great wall, and nobody builds walls better than me, believe me, and I'll build them very inexpensively,

> I will build a great, great wall on our southern border. And
> I will have Mexico pay for that wall.
>
> https://www.washingtonpost.com/news/post-politics/
> wp/2015/06/16/full-text-donald-trump-announces-a-
> presidential-bid/?utm_term=.b620f418aa35

In that speech, Trump's presidential announcement speech, Trump identified several of the problems that Rome faced before and after the fall: the have-nots coming in and causing problems for the have's. The solution back then was to build a wall. The solution today is to build a wall.

History does not change, just the costumes; it's the same story over and over again.

The amazing part is, if people break into your house and you want to lock your door or put up a wall to keep them out, that's common sense. But in today's popular narrative, when Trump mentions basic protection measures for the perimeter of the tribe, weakness cries out: "You're racist," "You're an Islamophobe," "You're sexist," and "You're a homophobe!" Dissenters call Trump names and assassinate his character, but they offer no real logical arguments against the basic idea of building a wall to keep out the barbarians.

The most fundamental logical argument lies in the wording of who can enter the country and who cannot. My father is an immigrant who came legally to Canada; he has kept his landed immigrant status, and that's fine with the government. The fact that America even has to have a debate about keeping "illegal" immigrants out is ridiculous. There are legal immigrants who should stay and "illegal" immigrants who should go. I am a 6'4" white male from Canada, and they treat me with major scrutiny at the border, especially if I bring my Swedish passport instead of my Canadian one. As a non-Canadian European trying to cross into the American border, I have had to (1) sign a green card visa, (2) declare I am not a Nazi refugee from 1945, (3) declare I am not a Nazi refugee from 1933, (4) declare that I don't have AIDS, and (5) be searched with a drug dog sniffing down my body. I was also thrown in a jail cell temporarily while they ripped my entire car apart at the land border.

Getting into America is a pretty tough process, and I can see why some people would want to skip the line and come in illegally. Getting in legally is a major hassle.

Even though they treat me badly at the border in America if I go in on a Swedish passport instead of a Canadian one, I understand their policies. People illegally entering the country is bad; people entering the country legally is good.

There is no emotional argument here, just who is approved and who isn't. Sneaking in or breaking in doesn't make it right for a person to come into a country, any country. Here's what the more publicly popular presidents Bill Clinton and Barack Obama said about the same issue and garnered major support:

In President Bill Clinton's 1995 State of the Union Address, Clinton Received a Bipartisan Standing Ovation for His Tough Rhetoric on Illegal Immigration

PRESIDENT BILL CLINTON: "All Americans, not only in the States most heavily affected but in every place in this country, are rightly disturbed by the large numbers of illegal aliens entering our country.

The jobs they hold might otherwise be held by citizens or legal immigrants. The public service they use impose burdens on our taxpayers.

That's why our administration has moved aggressively to secure our borders more by hiring a record number of new border guards, by deporting twice as many criminal aliens as ever before, by cracking down on illegal hiring, by barring welfare benefits to illegal aliens.

In the budget I will present to you, we will try to do more to speed the deportation of illegal aliens who are arrested for crimes, to better identify illegal aliens in the workplace...

We are a nation of immigrants. But we are also a nation of laws. It is wrong and ultimately self-defeating for a nation of immigrants to permit the kind of abuse of our immigration laws we have seen in recent years, and we must do more to stop it." (Bill Clinton, Remarks at State of the Union, Washington, D.C., 1/24/95)

https://gop.com/flashback-democrats-talked-tough-on-immigration-rsr/

In President Barack Obama's 2013 State of the Union Address, Obama Called for Putting Illegals "Behind The Folks Trying to Come Here Legally"

Transcript:

PRESIDENT BARACK OBAMA: "Real reform means strong border security, and we can build on the progress my administration has already made—putting more boots on the Southern border than at any time in our history and reducing illegal crossings to their lowest levels in 40 years.

Real reform means establishing a responsible pathway to earned citizenship—a path that includes passing a background check, paying taxes and a meaningful penalty, learning English, and going to the back of the line behind the folks trying to come here legally.

And real reform means fixing the legal immigration system to cut waiting periods and attract the highly-skilled entrepreneurs and engineers that will help create jobs and grow our economy." (President Barack Obama, Remarks at State of the Union, Washington, D.C., 2/12/13)

All three presidents, Trump a Republican, Clinton a Democrat, and Obama a Democrat, all are giving the same message. Secure our borders. This is the job of men, securing the perimeter to protect the women and children.

What changes from speech to speech is:

- Trump's language is the strongest, most direct, most matter of fact, and he is explicitly telling you who is coming into the country, identifying his tribal enemies, men of other tribes who are coming here to cause harm to his tribe—drugs, crime, rapists, criminals—and he is telling you where the enemies of the tribe are coming from: Mexico, Latin America, and potentially the Middle East. The have-nots coming for the haves and the barbarians to America's Rome.

- Clinton makes a similar speech to stop illegal aliens who are coming here to take our jobs away, use the public services, welfare, and be a burden to the taxpayer. The enemies are unidentified. Why they may harm the tribe is simply a money drain on the system. The word "illegals" protects the tribe from the reality of where the illegals are coming from. The threat is not really identified.

- Obama makes the weakest speech of all in his weak man rhetoric about "folks," "illegal crossings," and background checks, learning English and bringing in high value entrepreneurs and engineers. His speech is the most happy-go-lucky, and he cannot identify his tribal enemies or why they are a threat. This is the way of the weak man society we live in today. The tribal leader can't even identify his tribal enemies or threats to the tribe, and this makes him a bad man and a bad tribal leader.

The same message is delivered in three ways. Clinton and Obama received standing ovations from both Democrats and Republicans. Trump gets called a racist. Why is the same issue getting different results from the same group of people?

We have the weak man message of Obama who cannot even identify his problems, but this makes the weak popular narrative of the media and the people happy because there is nothing offensive in his words. His words are threatening to his own tribe because as a man, he is failing to identify the nature of the threat on the perimeter and what might happen if the tribe is infiltrated by outsiders (rape, murder, crime, drugs, other barbaric acts).

Clinton's speech is focused more on the financial picture and money, which everyone understands. The people could understand that there is a cost to illegal aliens, and he's getting a little more visceral to talk about money. Money is a visceral subject. Clinton is somewhat identifying a threat in a way that other people can understand, but he is not showing the cruel reality of a barbaric invasion.

Trump gives the strong man speech; he tells the people exactly what is happening and who is threatening the tribe. He doesn't overtly make any racist claims. There are no value judgments or prejudices or inherent emotional "hate" inside of his words, but they are interpreted as "racist" by the hypersensitive media and the popular narrative of the population. Trump successfully outlines the problems and even offers a solution—build a wall.

This strong man message appealed to the people in America who have been on hard times for a while and are considering the survival of themselves and their tribe. The strong man message was also threatening to the female, bonobo narrative of political correctness, and they smeared him as "racist," "xenophobic," and "Islamophobic" merely for doing the job of being a man who is a leader: identifying threats and protecting the tribe.

This begs the question: if in our modern world, the strong man cannot even identify the problems and threats that could potentially harm him and his tribe, how is he able to do his job as a man? How is he able to survive in the real world when his opponents and tribal enemies don't care about political correctness, but the female bonobo preferences of the population bind him to it? If his enemies are violent, and he cannot meet them with the same violence because of female preferences and feelings about violence in general, then how can he protect the tribe?

This is a major philosophical problem, for if you cannot identify a problem you can never solve it.

If you cannot own a problem, you can never solve it.

Love Trump or hate Trump, he owns his problems and he gets them solved. That's why he is a good man and a good, strong leader for his tribe. That's why roughly half the country voted for him. It was not popular to vote for Trump. He lost in the popular vote, but the electoral college, the brains of the country (as the founding fathers put in place to protect against a Roman-style "grain for votes" race to the bottom by the populace) vetoed the popular vote, which is usually wrong anyway, and put a strong leader in charge.

The Human Race to the Bottom and the Lowest Common Denominator in Civilization

On June 26, 1931, comparative psychologist Winthrop Niles Kellogg and his wife welcomed a new arrival home: not a human infant, but a baby chimpanzee. The couple planned to raise the chimp alongside their little baby boy.

The experiment worked well in the beginning, and at first the chimp was ahead of the little baby boy in his development. But after a while something strange happened; rather than the chimp acting more like a human, the human baby started acting more like a chimp. Thus, after roughly 9 months of trying to get the chimp to act like a human, the entire experiment backfired, and the human started to act like a chimp.

"In short, the language retardation in (the human baby) may have brought an end to the study."

> https://www.smithsonianmag.com/smart-news/guy-simultaneously-raised-chimp-and-baby-exactly-same-way-see-what-would-happen-180952171/

This experiment illustrates humanity's race to the bottom. When people of high and low value are mixed, the top doesn't pull up the bottom, but rather the bottom pulls down the top to the lowest common denominator.

This is how gravity works in real life; it works for people as well.

"Show me your friends, and I'll show you your future," the old adage says.

When you have five loser, beer-drinking, pot-smoking friends who can't get a job, you will be the sixth loser, beer-drinking, pot-smoking friend who can't get a job.

Even if you want to get your life together, environment always wins over time.

It is idealistic to say that we can and want to bring up these other societies and groups into our own and raise them up to the levels of civilization we have set for ourselves. What is more realistic is that we will come down to the third-world level instead of pulling them up to first-world levels. It simply takes too much effort to pull up. Pulling down is much easier, as has been demonstrated with barbarian invasions throughout history.

Instead, what we see by letting in the third world, the have-nots and the "primitive barbarians," is a degradation and a loss of our own culture that is relatively advanced and took hundreds of years to build since the Renaissance and the Dark Ages ended. The Dark Ages were a horrible time when the barbarians sacked Rome. What followed were 1,000 years of misery and half the population died. Could the same be happening now?

We see a dumbing down of our own people, our own schools, where we keep catering to the dumbest person, the slowest person. Trump understands this, and although he has a self-professed genius IQ, he publicly speaks at a grade 4 level.

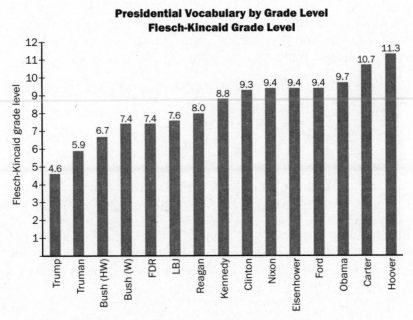

http://s.newsweek.com/sites/www.newsweek.com/files/styles/
embed-lg/public/2018/01/08/flesch-scale-trump-use.PNG

I know for a fact that this is a skill learned over time to dumb your speech down so even the most mentally handicapped person can understand what you are saying. As a public speaker myself, I am likely speaking at a grade 9 level, and yet I need to bring it down to grade 4.

Sometimes when Trump slips up and uses his true vocabulary, he lets out highly sophisticated and obscure words that the public doesn't know.

brag·ga·do·cious
ˌbragə'dō(t)SHəs/
adjective
US *informal*
adjective: **braggadocious**
> boastful or arrogant.

> "It sounds braggadocious, but I don't think I ever dropped a pass in a game."

This makes the public feel that he is "dumb" for making up a word, but in fact he is ultrasmart for (1) speaking at a grade 4 level so all can understand and (2) accidentally letting his grade 4 routine slip and saying a sophisticated or obscure word that the public does not know.

Words that they do not know, words above their level, threaten the mob.

Do not threaten the mob.

Will the People Kill their Liberator? The Man Who Sets Them Free?

In ancient Greek times, the philosopher Plato wrote a short allegory of "the cave." The cave has been used throughout history to compare the ignorant with the enlightened and describe how man treats those who try to free him from his own ignorance.

Plato: THE ALLEGORY OF THE CAVE

In the famous work by Plato, *The Allegory of the Cave*, Socrates is explaining to his friend Glaucon that there is a group of prisoners chained in a cave staring at a wall with their back to a fire.

Beginning

The fire illuminates shadows on the wall, and the prisoners are all staring at the wall as the light of the fire flickers.

Shifting around on the wall are shadows of stone or wood artifacts that man has made, some of the shadows are talking to each other, and some aren't as the shadows flicker across the wall.

And if the prisoners have their heads fixed, they will see nothing but shadows, and if they are given time to talk it over, they would regard the fake shadows as real beings.

When they hear sounds of people walking behind them, moving around the objects of wood and stone that project onto the wall, they would suppose that the shadows were talking to them or making the sounds themselves.

These people have nothing to consider in life but just the shadows on the wall and the noises that the shadows make.

Let's suppose one man was freed from his chains and could stand up, look around, and see the mouth of the cave. If he looked at the brightness of the fire or the mouth of the cave, he would be blind to the wood and stone artifacts that projected the shadows on the wall.

SOCRATES: What if this prisoner was told that the things he saw in the blindness were the real beings and that he is seeing more correctly compared to the men staring at the shadows on the wall. Would he believe that the shadows on the wall were more real to him than the stone and wood in front of him?

GLAUCON: The answer is of course.

SOCRATES: And if he were forced to look into the flame of the fire itself, would it not blind him, hurt his eyes, and he would want to go back to looking at what was easy and comfortable for him before—the shadows on the wall?

GLAUCON: Of course.

SOCRATES: And what if a liberator, or someone were to drag him into the light, up the steep and rocky ascent into the daylight at the mouth of the cave and into the sun, would he not want to go back and look at what he was comfortable looking at before?

GLAUCON: Of course.

SOCRATES: And the prisoner being dragged into the sun, would he not feel pain and rage and extreme blindness from the glare of the sun? And would he not be blind and fail to see the things that have are revealed to him in plain sight?

Would it not take some time to get his eyes to adjust to the light outside the cave?

GLAUCON: Of course it would.

SOCRATES: And as his eyes adjust, would it not be easiest for him to look at shadows and reflections of people and objects in water?

GLAUCON: Yes, of course.

SOCRATES: And as his eyes further adjust, then wouldn't he be able to look at the objects themselves instead of just the shadows and reflections of water?

GLAUCON: Yes, of course.

SOCRATES: And wouldn't he be tempted to look up into the heavenly dome called the sky? But it would be too bright for him, so he would have to start by looking at it at night when it is easier on his eyes.

And when he was ready, would he not be able to look directly into the sun and wonder about what the sun was and what sort of thing it was? Of course.

And after studying the sun, (1) wouldn't it be apparent to him that the sun causes both the seasons and the years?; (2) wouldn't it be obvious that the sun governs all light of what he sees now?; (3) wouldn't it be obvious that the sun is the origin of all the things that the people in the cave see in one way or another?

And when he considers his journey and transformation that he has undergone to leave the cave and get to the sun, don't you think that this prisoner would think of his fellow prisoners and feel sorry for them?

GLAUCON: Yes, of course!

SOCRATES: However, what if the people in the cave had honors and awards for knowing which shadow would appear on the wall at what time? And in which combinations and in which sequence the shadows would appear next?

And now that this prisoner had escaped the cave, do you think he would want to return to the cave and compete for the esteemed honors of memorizing the shadows? Or do you think he would rather be living above ground "off the land with nothing but his bare hands" or performing menial peasant work in the sun? I would think that he would prefer anything but going back to darkness of the cave.

And if that prisoner were to return to his position as before in the cave, would he not find that his eyes were once again filled with darkness?

GLAUCON: Yes, very much so.

SOCRATES: And while the prisoner's eyes are readjusting to the darkness and he is trying to describe the shadows in the dark again, would he not be exposed to ridicule and criticism by the other prisoners?

GLAUCON: He certainly would.

SOCRATES: And certainly, they would tell him that by going up to the surface, he has ruined his eyes and thus it does not pay to leave the cave.

And if the prisoners in the darkness can get a hold of the liberator who comes down into the cave and break them free of their chains and bring them up into the light, would they not kill him if they could?

GLAUCON: They certainly will...

https://web.stanford.edu/class/ihum40/cave.pdf

So will the people kill their liberator? When stuck in the darkness and watching false shadows glide across the wall in the dark, will they kill the man who brings them to the light?

They most certainly will.

The modern-day cave is the living room, and the fire and shadows are the television and the media.

We have this exact allegory happening right now in our society. The masses are watching the shadows of the media glide across the cave wall every day, and they believe what they see to be true. But the shadows are manipulated and are man-made messages for a purpose.

When someone comes to take them to the light, to the truth, to reality, to what is actually happening, they violently fight this liberator as if he is their mortal enemy.

It is so dark in the cave, it is so comfortable, it is so easy, they have esteemed awards and honors for knowing the false truths and half-truths of the media, and they dare not compromise all that they have to risk going to the surface and learning the real truth.

Weak people don't want the truth; they want to feel comfortable.

There are four types of people:

1) Those who want to be comfortable
2) Those who want to be right
3) Those who want to be liked
4) Those who want to win

A strong man knows he must face ugly truths to win. It's part of the job of being a man, carry out the mission, do your job, whatever is required. But the people who live for comfort will resist the discomfort of reality. They will stay in the cave and cling to the false shadows and media messages.

If these ignorant people will try to kill their liberator and try to kill the truth, then what does that say about being a bringer of truth?

Donald Trump comes to the American people as a strong man and a liberator, a protector, a father figure with practical solutions, and what do the people do to their liberator? They would kill him if they could. This literally has happened on television with female comedian Kathy Griffin literally beheading a doll of Donald Trump on TV. She is trying to kill her liberator if she could, and that is power of darkness, the power of ignorance, and the power of the manipulated shadows on the wall.

The Romans brutally murdered and crucified a preacher named Jesus as he came with lessons from God on how to live a better life. The Romans murdered their liberator, the man who was there to show them the way, and later Rome fell to the violence of the Germanic barbarians.

The messages we see on the wall, the shadows, the media, always have an agenda, and as we established earlier in this book, the media messages are subversive, the messages in the school are subversive, the destruction of religion is subversive, the destruction of the family is subversive, feminism as a movement is subversive, and all of this is to weaken the protectors of the tribe and weaken our society to a point so that we can be taken without war or even without force. We will beg to be taken because the images of the shadows will have become so strong in our minds. We will see them for pure truth in our minds, even though they are manipulated and false.

Only when you believe in false truths would you seek to kill your liberator.

To bring truth to the masses is an extremely dangerous business. But as a strong man, it's a necessary part of the dangerous job of being a leader. The survival of the tribe counts on you.

"Everything we hear is an opinion, not a fact.
Everything we see is a perspective, not the truth."

MARCUS AURELIUS, *MEDITATIONS*

CHAPTER 33
THE EMPIRE STRIKES FIRST

"Who controls the past now, controls the future now, who controls the present now, controls the past."

GEORGE ORWELL, *1984*

History has constantly been manipulated and whitewashed by the victors and winners of wars. The losers have always been condemned and made out to be demonic.

All empires are violent, and empires know that it's better to "strike first" than to "strike back" as in the George Lucas *Star Wars* movies.

Although America was supportive of the German Nazis prior to WWII, the war was won by America. Thus, America's Nazi support has officially disappeared from history, along with many eugenics organizations that sterilized poor people, black people, and mentally challenged people and were on the same thought pattern as the German Nazis who proposed the "final solution" of killing all the undesirables in their tribe.

Cleaning up the history books is a way to strike first as a victorious empire and avoid having to strike back later.

America committed genocide with the American Indians, and it's romanticized by Hollywood as cowboys and Indians instead of the reality that it was mass murder and robbery of the people who lived here before us. Nazi Germany attempted genocide with several groups in Europe, namely the Jews. But Germany lost the war, so they are immortalized as demons in the history books. America got to repaint over its demons with a whitewashed paint brush as they whitewashed the charred White House after the British invaded America and set fire to the presidential house in the brief War of 1812.

Why strike back when you can strike first?

America has a history steeped in racism. Americans enslaved several groups of people, including the blacks and the Irish. The US has a violent and brutal history of conquest, world domination through financing puppet dictators of the third world, eugenics movements (much like the Nazis), concentration camps like Guantanamo Bay in Cuba, and atrocities by association like an alliance with Joseph Stalin, the butcher who killed more than 20 million of his own people during his brutal communist regime. Stalin killed more people than the demonized Nazis ever did with their calculated mass killings, but we whitewash communism and Stalin in the universities. After all, Stalin was our ally, and communism is the reigning philosophy of the schools and universities in America. This is part of the problem with the subversion of what made America great in the first place—a commitment to freedom, free markets, capitalism, freedom of religion, protestant work ethic, and Judeo-Christian values.

America has a racist and militant history. But today, with the zeitgeist of Donald Trump, the past actions and policies of America become invisible to the popular public, and Trump is thrown into the fray as a scapegoat for current policies that are congruent with past policies.

Trump doesn't want to let Muslim refugees into the country. The US is unofficially at war with Islam, and Islam is officially in a holy war with the West. In World War II, America accepted no German refugees and no Jewish refugees, even though people were being rounded up and taken to ghettos or gas chambers.

Trump recently barred refugees and people from 7 Islamic nations that the USA is illegally bombing according to war laws. Instead of supporting this policy, the people decried this very normal American policy as "racist." America is a historically racist and intolerant country, but with the weakness prevalent in today's society, Americans call one man, Donald Trump—a martyr, the one and only racist. I do not believe Trump as a man is fundamentally racist, sexist, homophobic, or Islamophobic as the popular media claims him to be. I think he is a good man—not a nice man—but a strong man looking after his family and his tribe and trying to do what he believes to be the right thing.

This is just the same as Darth Vader in *Star Wars: Episode III* trying to do the right thing by saving his wife Padme from death. The road to hell is paved with good intentions. When Darth Vader tries to save his fated-to-die wife from death itself, he converts to the dark side. He kills the young Jedi, dismantles the Jedi order, and loses his legs and one of his arms as well as his skin, his appearance, and the man he used to be in order to "do the right thing" and save his wife.

Darth Vader is the villain—just a strong man who tried to "do the right thing"—but he brought hell upon himself by trying to be good and just.

Donald Trump is our Darth Vader; he runs the Empire and bombs those teenagers in the deserts of Iraq and Syria instead of Tattooine and Alderaan. He is a villain to the rebels, the women, the youth, the have-nots, and the weak. But in his heart, he is trying to do what is right for his tribe, his family, and his people. Ironically, the word *Vader* is Dutch for "father." We live in a society where Dad is bad; fathers are mean and are pushed to the fringes of society in favor of Mom and empowered women.

Trump is the elected official leader of a violent empire that is traditionally racist, sexist, homophobe, intolerant, and Islamophobic. Thus, he has to carry the weight of America's past sins. In the same way that Jesus had to bear the weight of the cross and the sins of all his people before being brutally crucified at the hands of the bloodthirsty and barbaric

Romans, perhaps Trump is being figuratively—or perhaps literally at some point—nailed to a cross to "die for the sins of his people?"

I don't think it is right, but it doesn't matter what is right or fair. It simply is. The people are a mob, and they have a vicious and violent mind of their own.

What will the future of the mob and the Empire who strikes first look like if the current trends continue?

In the 20th century, two famous futurist writers gave us two versions of what they believed the future of the West would look like.

George Orwell and his mentor, Aldous Huxley, wrote two very different versions of what the future would look like, although they were both dystopias.

George Orwell predicted that we would enter a Stalinist future in 1984, where men are isolated, there is no family or love, and the government has thrown the people into perpetual war. The government spies on the people through technology, fearmongering, media control, revisionist history, the dumbing down of language and change of language, doublespeak, doublethink, and never-ending war with three world superpowers to keep the current government in power through martial law. In this dystopia, man is left alone to survive in the abyss of the technocracy. In some ways, the protagonist faces the question "what does it mean to be a man?" as he is alone in the abyss and darkness of the world that Orwell created in *1984*. All things that made a man a man—women, family, children, his work, his duty, money, privacy, and freedom—have been stripped from him. He is alone, he is isolated, and he is weak.

In *1984*, through manipulation of words, media, and beliefs into twisted lies upon lies and versions of reality that serve the government agenda for control, "we ... believe the lie until it becomes the truth."

This book and narrative was extrapolated by Stalinist policies in which the government would become totalitarian and all powerful and oppress the people. *1984* was written in 1949, and some would argue that we are living in the world of *1984* in modern America. I could see why. The famous words of George Orwell predicted the future we live in today:

"The people will not revolt. They will not look up from their screens long enough to notice what's happening."

ORWELL, *1984*

"Orwell didn't have a crystal ball, what he did have was an understanding of the human condition and its weakness. Apathy."

RASHELL HABIB

Orwell's mentor, Aldous Huxley, painted a different picture, a more American, less Stalinist picture in his book. *Brave New World* is Huxley's 1932 dystopian novel. In this American-style future, man has no pain, and he is not even born by female vaginal birth anymore. There are five castes of humans, from the tall, blonde, beautiful Alphas all the way down to the mentally retarded, short, ugly, and barely functioning Epsilons who can hardly function in the most meaningless tasks. Everything in society is planned, childbirth is obsolete, and babies are preselected to be Alphas, Betas, Gammas, etc. The lower classes are mentally retarded with alcohol to dumb them down to the lower levels and jobs of society. The society in *Brave New World* was admittedly a bonobo society with sex orgies rampantly taking place. Women have contraception, so there are no accidental vaginally born babies. Every need, every single thing is taken care of. There is no pain, just drugs called Soma, which is the favorite way to entertain yourself or friends. Getting high on Soma, participating in orgies—a painless life of all pleasure and no pain—again brings man to the question, "what does it mean to be a man?" When John the Savage is brought into the sleek dystopian world of all pleasure and no pain, he goes mad and flogs himself just to feel pain and be alive again. John the Savage has no place in his brave new world, so he hangs himself once he realizes he no longer belongs.

On some predictions, Orwell was right. In 2018, *1984* has climbed back up the charts of bestselling books and has become shockingly relevant to the world in which we live today.

In other predictions, Huxley was right about our drug-induced sex culture, bonobo-like masturbation, and the meaninglessness of sex. Childbirth may become obsolete soon when we look at the way families and women no longer need men for their basic functions.

Where do men fit in with the future of the Empire? It's hard to say.

In Orwell's future, men are oppressed, isolated, monitored, and put into Stalinist "cages," alone and obsolete. In Huxley's future, men are high, sex addicted, and not need for work in the way that they traditionally have been.

Surely, in both futures, there are men required to be on the frontlines of the endless war to do the killing and the bombing and to be the storm troopers for Darth Vader. But in either future, the average man of the Empire at home—the solo man—is like a rat trapped in a cage. He is denied what makes him a man. In our current form of reality, we see both traits of *1984* and *Brave New World* manifesting as reality.

Man is neutered, like a house pet, caged and sedated into a role he has never known before. He was once the base unit of the Empire, the nucleus of the family and the building block of a strong society. The Empire has grown so big and so efficient that it no longer needs him to be strong or to do what he once did.

How long can this Empire last?

CHAPTER 34
WHY "SHITHOLE" COUNTRIES ARE INDEED "SHITHOLES"

"A = A"

ARISTOTLE

"You can paint a turd gold, but it is still a turd."

WESTERN COLLOQUIALISM

In 2018, Donald Trump was alleged to have asked the following question behind closed doors in the White House in a meeting with lawmakers: "Why do we want all these people from 'shithole countries' coming here? Why do we need more Haitians? Take them out." Trump had been meeting with Illinois Democratic Senator Dick Durbin and South Carolina Republican Senator Lindsey Graham to discuss the visa lottery. One person briefed on the meeting said when Durbin got to Haiti, Trump began to ask why we want people from Haiti and more

Africans in the US and added that the US should get more people from countries like Norway.

https://www.cnn.com/2018/01/11/politics/immigrants-shithole-countries-trump/index.html

Haiti and Africa vs. Norway

I went to Haiti myself in 2016. I saw a country ravaged by natural disaster and debilitating poverty. I had donated to a friend of mine's charity and had donated enough to build a house for a family of eight people, a mom, a dad, and six children. When we got out of the airport and loaded onto the bus, I got to see the disaster Haiti had become.

Literally seas of trash filled the ditches along the sides of the road and sprawled on for miles and miles. The cities were left in ruins after the Haitian earthquake in 2010 that devastated the country. You couldn't tell the difference between a live-in house and ruins. The people were living in ruins.

It was all ruins.

At that time, it was six years since the disaster, and the entire country was still a wake of destruction—seas of trash and impoverished, very skinny people wandering the wasteland with nothing productive to do.

Haiti had become hell on earth.

"The road to hell is paved with good intentions."

Proverb

The American Red Cross raised more than half a billion dollars to bring relief to Haiti after the devastating 2010 earthquake, but it grossly overstated what the money bought. Although the organization claimed to have provided housing to more than 130,000 people, it actually only built six permanent homes, according to a report by ProPublica and NPR.

http://time.com/3908457/red-cross-six-homes-haiti/

To give you some perspective on what it costs to build a home in Haiti, as donator to my friend Frank McKinney's Caring House project, my $5,000 donation was enough to build a permanent concrete dwelling for a family of eight. So what did the Red Cross do with half a billion dollars to build six homes if you can build a home for $5,000 in Haiti? Who knows? They are an NGO—a nongovernmental organization—that lights money on fire and uses the money for their own corruption and internal expenses. Such waste should be criminal, and the people running the Red Cross should be put in jail for fraud.

When I saw the home that my $5,000 built, my heart broke: myself and the group I was traveling with had collectively donated $250,000 to build a village. But each home in the village was tiny and was about the size of an American shed. The people literally slept on the bare concrete floor, with not even straw to soften the floor, no pillows, and no blankets. They had no crops, no animals, no businesses, no intellectual property, no marketable language. The Haitians speak Creole French, which is not really a language; it's a bastard dialect of French. With that language, you can't even open a call center and employ the Haitians to answer the phone. No one wants Creole French in the marketplace. The global marketplace wants American English as a marketable language. Creole French is an obscure and low value language on the world stage.

The homes we built were in the middle of nowhere. We had to ride the bus for quite some time to reach the site, but still the homes were an improvement from what the people were living in before—shacks of scrap metal, wire, wood, and garbage. Like a bird building a nest, the Haitians built shelters out of whatever they could find. A concrete bunker house was a major improvement.

Still, my heart broke, because I saw these people who had nothing to do and no way to make money.

When Haiti was crippled in the earthquake in 2010, NGOs rushed in to provide aid. This was incredibly destructive for the Haitians because it wiped out all local entrepreneurs from restarting the local economy. Tom's shoes came in and gave everyone free shoes. They destroyed the local shoemakers in Haiti because no one can compete with free shoes. Then the American corn came in, the rice came in, and all these other free handouts came in to Haitians. This systematically destroyed the farms. Rice prior to 2010 was a luxury in Haiti, and now with all the free rice from the handouts, everyone eats rice frequently.

At the zoo there is a sign that says, "Don't feed the bears or they will get weak and dependent." In Haiti, they need a sign that says, "No more handouts for the Haitians, please. Your gifts are crippling them and destroying their entire economy and society."

As I write this, it's 2018 and Haiti is not in a better position than they were 8 years ago; in fact, the generosity of the West has further crippled Haiti.

As the famous proverb says, "Gifts make slaves." The Haitians became broken in spirit, broken in language, broken in commerce, and had become a broken people wandering around in seas of garbage even in the middle of the night with no lights as I witnessed from the bus as we drove through the broken cities at night.

What businesses could you bring to Haiti?

Haiti was traditionally a French slave colony from the times of Napoleon. The people there are black, Africans, and speak a strange Creole French that I imagine derived from a slave-spoken version of French. The island is shared with the Dominican Republic. On the Haitian half of the island, there is the most extreme poverty in the Western hemisphere. But on the other half of the island—the Dominican Republic—is opulence and luxury resorts. It's ironic that such luxury takes half the island, and the other half is made of broken slaves with an unmarketable language, no industries, and no hope. Like the Canadian aboriginal Indians, the "generosity" of the white man has subverted the Haitian culture and turned the men weak. The weakened men in Haiti no longer need to perform the tasks of survival, and thus, the culture and the people are destroyed.

Is Haiti a shithole? Yes, it is, absolutely. I have been there and stood in the dirt and experienced it with my own eyes. Why deny that fact? If you cannot own the problem or identify the problem, how can you ever fix it?

I am not making a value judgment of the people in the country, but it is a burning tire fire of a mess that is not going to change unless major moves are made. One move is to pull out the "generous" NGOs from the West that have subverted the Haitian men into weakness and destroyed the culture and man's ability to provide for himself and survive.

How can these broken men provide value? The answer is they cannot provide very much.

Trump is right to ask; do we need more Haitians? Do we need more people from broken and screwed-up countries in Africa? America is the sophisticated empire like Rome. Africa and Haiti are the backwater tribes of barbarians.

Ironically, Trump asks, "Why don't we get more Norwegians?", which is a country that is consistently considered to be more advanced than America in many ways, including social programs for the people. It has been seen in the headlines of the news that "every Norwegian is a millionaire" due to the government taxing the oil companies in the oil-rich nation at 78% and then investing the siphoned off royalties to create investment funds that provide social programs, high wages, and tuition-free university.

In America right now, an empire in decline, the story is much different from that of Norway. America does not tax its oil to invest and create social programs for a better life for the people; instead, America has some of the worst social programs in the world often compared to third-world nations like Brazil as the USA slips into decline. The wages in America are going down in real purchasing power indexed to gold, which was illustrated in an earlier chapter, and universities cripple the youth with enormous debt and useless liberal arts degrees. These reasons alone make America look barbaric compared to the socially sophisticated Norwegians.

And thus, is the question, if Haiti is a shithole compared to America, then is America a shithole compared to Norway? Immigration statistics would show that not many Norwegians want to move to America relative to Americans who want to move to Norway. One man's shithole is another man's paradise. What remains true is that the world is divided into haves and have-nots. The have-nots always want a better life and to join the haves. The haves do not want to move into have-not "shitholes," which is human nature. It's cold, it's brutal, it's honest, and what has destroyed countless empires in history has been the invasion of people from "shithole" countries into civilized nations. When the "shithole" barbarians get close to the Empire, they either storm the gates through invasion or bring the country down from within.

Is America going to be the world's next shithole? That could depend on who America lets within its borders. The barbarians are currently standing at the gates. There are billions of people in the world with nothing. These are the have-nots who are looking for a better life and to enter the gates of America to seize all the wonderful things of the American dream.

The have-nots want the world of the haves.

But the haves avoid the world of the have-nots.

The Norwegians avoid moving to America, and many Americans avoid moving into the third world. Why trade down if you are doing well?

Ironically, it's okay to avoid moving your place of residence from the first world to the third world, but if America keeps importing enough third-world people, eventually America will turn into an official third-world nation with broken welfare systems and social services that will burst from the sheer weight of people riding the system for free.

As in Rome, "free grain for votes" was the exchange of weakness for power. Today it's "food stamps and free abortions" for votes. These third-world immigrants and refugees are built-in free votes for the politicians who want to stay in power. There is an agenda to expand the voter base by bringing these people in because they are dependent on the system and need the government to survive.

When a human baby and a human chimp are raised side by side, the chimp doesn't get smarter and rise to the human baby's level. Instead, the human baby starts to act like the much less sophisticated and dumber chimp. The human's language becomes retarded as our

Western language is down to a grade 4 level now, and it continues to decline into meaningless abbreviations on the Internet, such as "Lol," "brb," "hbu," "lolz," "rofl," "bb." The language that took thousands of words to develop is literally degrading into meaningless nonsense in front of our eyes.

When it comes to society, we will always stoop to the most basic, dumbest, and lowest common denominator. If we do not wish to move to the third-world shithole countries like Haiti, then why import more people and bring the third world to your doorstep and into your home?

If you don't want to visit and eat in a pizza in a restaurant, then why order home pizza delivery? If you bring pizza into your home, you will end up eating pizza, and you are going to eventually get fat and sick if you do it enough times.

If you don't want to be fat and sick, (1) don't order home delivery pizza, (2) don't go to pizza restaurants, and (3) if pizza finds its way into your home, throw it out. This is common sense, and we all understand it when it comes to pizza.

Like getting fat on home delivery pizza, America, when delivering the third world to its doorstep, will become the next third world because like the baby and the chimp, the people at the bottom do not elevate themselves to the higher levels of civilization. How could they with the broken, trash, American education systems that cannot compete on the world stage? The American high schools are not competitive for a first-world country, and the postsecondary education is inaccessible for these third-world immigrants.

The higher levels of civilization take hundreds or thousands of years to push through developmentally—traditions, religion, institutions, training, and education. Instead, the bottom drags down those at the top down quickly in one or two generations until humanity has reverted back into the bloody, violent reality of the haves versus have-nots, which is a constant theme throughout history.

For most of human history, humans survived by digging in the mud. We will go right back to digging in the mud if we bring in enough people from other countries who actually dig in the mud all day for survival.

Perhaps it is time to stop ordering pizza and go on a "no pizza" diet? Maybe it's time to order some food that is good for the body?

What happens over time to empires that allow enough barbarians from "shithole" countries inside the gates of the Empire?

The Fallen Empires of History and Where They Are Today

Greece was once a mighty empire. Under Macedonian control, by virtue of Alexander the Great, Greek ideas spread all over the known world at the time. Greece was once a mighty superpower, and then they grew complacent and were taken by barbarians. Today, Greece is one of the least relevant countries in the European union. It is riddled with debt and was invaded repeatedly in the past by Muslim countries. The Greeks were once blonde like the Germans or the Swedes. Through loss of wars and rapes of blonde Greeks by dark Turks and other invaders, the Greeks now have dark hair, and very few blondes are left. Greece has degraded from an advanced civilization to a marginalized, indebted state with no real military inside of the EU, begging for handouts as a have-not country in the European Union. The men don't work much, and they have early retirement, which is creating a massive burden for productive countries like Germany and Sweden, where the age of retirement just got pushed into the 70s to pay for Greeks who retire in their 50s.

Rome was another empire that spanned the entire known world. They had great technology, libraries, philosophy, leisure time, low taxes, and life was great for a Roman in the Roman empire. Today all that is left of the Roman Empire is Italy. Like Greece, Italy is not a significant player in Europe economically, technologically, or in any other way. In fact, after Rome was sacked and the libraries were burned, Rome itself was never really significant again in history. Italian merchants and traders during the Renaissance and the rebirth of art, science, and music did take place with commerce and banking in Italy in the 1600s, but as a fallen people, they have never really recovered to a world power as they were before the fall. From barbarian invasions and countries like Turkey coming in through historic invasions, these people have adopted darker hair, skin, and other traits from their darker invaders who have violently attacked them and raped the population over history.

The sun never set on the mighty **British** empire in the Victorian age, which controlled 25% of the world's landmass. Through complacency, comfort, falling behind in technology, and generally underestimating the unsophisticated barbarians—the Germans, Americans, and Russians—Britain lost two world wars in battles with the "primitive" Germans. The Germans were ultimately defeated, but Britain lost all of its influence to two backwater societies of mostly farmers and country boys: America and Russia.

Britain today still has some influence in the world of finance, but she is a backwards state compared to the technological and economically superior empires in Asia or even America. Britain still holds a hand in finance, which gives them limited power on the world stage, but they have recently "Brexited" from the European Union and are isolating themselves into weakness once more. They have lost most of their colonies, and are not relevant on the world stage economically, militarily, philosophically, or in any other way other than finance, though the great British pound took a major hit with Brexit and severance from the European Union. The same spirit and movement that brought Donald Trump into power—the average man being pissed off because he is marginalized and weakened by the government and instructions—voted to go back to the basics and separate from the policies that have been screwing him for so long. Trump in America and Brexit in Britain are born of the same spirit, the spirit of the average man getting screwed and frustrated with the policies that have marginalized him over the last 40 years.

In the great **American** Empire, America gained power as a primitive and "backwards" tribe in World War I. This gang of country boys, farm boys, and devoutly religious men took the world by surprise with military superiority in two world wars. By the end of World War II, America had seized world domination from Britain and Germany, and it kept

Russia's spreading communism at bay through proxy wars in smaller countries. America has had a prosperous democracy for more than 200 years, but they are making the same mistakes that Rome made back in the day. "Free grain for votes" in Rome has become "Free food stamps and abortions for votes." American culture has turned from manly strength to a gender-neutral apathy that is turning into male weakness and destruction of the once great society. Strong men are no longer relevant in the American culture, and an air of piousness has entered the American populace in which the American people believe that they are invincible on the world stage and can never be taken down.

Across the oceans in an ideological world war, the **Islamic** barbarians of third-world have-nots from the Middle East and **Africa** are the fastest-growing religion in the world, growing by 70% last year and reaching membership in the billions. They are the have-nots, the barbarians of history, and they are looking for ways to penetrate the American Empire, destroy it, and take the resources, land, and women for themselves.

Every band of barbarians in history has looked at the empire and wanted to topple it. They have started with small attacks like terrorist bombings and 9/11. They lure American forces into the historical killing floor of the Middle East to butcher American soldiers and drain the American treasury with endless wars that are unwinnable against an invisible enemy—ideology and "terrorism." I put "terrorism" in quotes because it is an invisible enemy that can never be defeated. Hitler could be killed, but "terrorism" is an idea and can never be stopped. "Terrorism" is manufactured through our own fear and own ideas. Sure there are barbarians at the gates and have-nots across the world who wish to see America burn, but the idea of "terrorism" will persist forever because it exists in our minds.

Invisible enemies—ideas—can never be killed. They can only be fought with equal or greater ideas and truth, not bullets, missiles, and aircraft carriers.

Now the barbarians are sending boatloads of refugees to Europe, marching large groups of men into continental Europe and attempting to send these same soldier-age men into America to bring down the empire from the inside, just like the plots of *Star Wars* or the *Hunger Games*. The empire must be brought down from within. The Greeks, the barbarians at the time, defeated the Trojans by infiltrating their impenetrable walls with a Trojan horse filled with young and strong soldiers who mercilessly slaughtered the sleeping Trojans and made history.

President Trump has been trying to stop his tribal enemies from breaching his perimeter to get inside and harm the women and children inside his protection, but the popular media narrative and the popular cultural narrative are at ideological war with his strong man ideologies.

The war of ideologies and the subversion of American ideology and the destruction of the invisible ideas that made America great are underway, and as we saw earlier, the four stages of subversion will end in (1) civil war or (2) invasion.

America is more divided than ever, and groups that previously weren't violent are becoming violent. Women, through groups like ANTIFA (anti-fascism), and even the social justice warrior women are getting more aggressive and violent. Democrats and Republicans throw a lot of "hate talk" around. There are small political riots in the streets. Civil war could happen, especially if the currency collapsed or there were a severe oil crisis and the people could not get food.

America is an armed population with over 300 million guns. America has had a civil war before that split the country in two. Supposedly, this war was over the moral and ethical argument of slavery, as history officially claims, but the other story is that the North wanted to unite the states into one superpower for conquest. A violent uniting of the tribes? That has happened before several times as well in history.

So which will it be? Death by invasion or death by civil war? Only time will tell. If America decays enough philosophically, it may be without slaughter. Instead, the barbarians may simply waltz in and take what they want from the haves in history as the weak men sit there and watch like a group of sexually sedated bonobos watch the apes from other tribes fuck their women and sire offspring that the cuck, male bonobos, will have to raise.

Who cares?

Why bother?

Think of the male bonobos as they watch from afar, like the young men of today watching pornography and other men fuck women that they can't have at home in the safety of their mother's basement. Pornography is the ultimate cuck move. Watch another man fuck a woman you want to have. How is that manly?

In small tribes of 150 people or so, genes were the way to dominate. The king had sexual access to 50% of the women, and he built his own internal tribe of many children to protect himself and his DNA. As the tribes grew into supertribes, tribes that were so large that one man could not maintain such sexual access, a new way to rule was with ideas also known as memes.

Memes are the keys to world domination, and the battles of the future will be won and lost with ideas and ideology. The Nazis lost out to the communists because their memes and ideology could not spread fast enough. Islam right now as a meme and ideology is spreading through the third world like wildfire, bringing great promises to large groups of have-not barbarian men who wish to sack and plunder the Western world. Christianity was a meme that superseded the warring tribes of Europe after the fall of Rome and united the tribes again under the Holy Roman Empire.

One question that needs to be examined when looking at the memes of the world is, are two ideas compatible or not? Especially in the world of immigration and especially in the world of immigration of the third world into the first world or the West. Some people from third-world countries have compatible memes and ideologies with the West.

I live in Winnipeg, Manitoba, the third largest Filipino population outside the Philippines. Each year we receive thousands of Filipino immigrants sponsored by their families into the new and great country of Canada—a big upgrade from the streets of Manila. The Filipino people share the Christian meme with Canadians, and they work hard in mostly hospitals as nurses or healthcare orderlies. They have families, sponsor in two or three families, and have communities, barbeques, and church events. I love working with the Filipino population because they work hard, and their memes are compatible with the memes that made Canada into a great country in the first place—Judeo-Christian values.

Other groups that fit in nicely with Western values are Chinese, Japanese, East Indians, South Koreans, Hindus, Mexicans, Eastern Europeans, Polish, Ukrainians, Europeans, South Africans, and South Americans. These people from these places have similar memes and similar values that work and can fit together with the West. These countries have proto-Indo-European influences or ties to Christianity that make them compatible with the West. The northeast Asian countries are compatible because they are in many ways more civilized and have a higher IQ than the West.

In Canada we have a "multiculturalism" policy that creates a mosaic of cultures, and we embrace this idealistic idea as a good thing. It is a good thing and works when the memes and ideas of the groups are compatible. It works when the groups agree to "be Canadian" at some point, whatever that means and work together. It does not work when the memes are incompatible or violent with one another.

CHAPTER 35
SHOULD OUR CIVILIZATION GO 500 YEARS BACKWARDS?

It has been said that a preacher named Jesus died in the year 30 A.D., and Christianity took over Europe as the Roman Empire weakened into tolerance and later fell. The Roman Empire was shattered by Barbarian hordes, Rome didn't survive, but Christianity did. Ideas and memes are hard to kill because they are spiritual and of the mind. They do not exist except in the minds of men.

Mohammad was a warlord and lived at around 570 A.D. and began spreading his philosophy and religion—his meme—across the Middle East, Turkey, and Africa. The Muslims were so hungry for territory and power that at one point the Ottoman empire was a vast, sprawling, Muslim empire that controlled much of the Middle East until the end of World War I. Herein lies the rub. Christianity is nearly 500 years ahead of Islam in ideology, and this is simply because Christianity is 500 years older than Islam and has had more time to grow, explore, and move from intolerant warrior culture to a tolerant, pacifist, female-ruled culture.

This 500-year gap explains why the Islamic people are so different from the Christian people. The Jews, the Christians, and the Muslims in their religious narratives are all somewhat describing the same spiritual laws and same stories form three different perspectives on one God. They have different names for the same God and fight to the death about the small difference in ideology and for small pieces of land in the Middle Eastern desert. Such is the power of memes.

While Islam covers its women in burkas to hide and protect them from raiding, militant bandits and rapists, in the early nineteenth century, Christian women wore bonnets covering most of their heads, much like a burka, dresses down to their ankles, and were covered up to the neck and the hands. Not a single piece of flesh was seen on a woman's body, much like the Islamic dress of women today.

In Islamic Sharia law, they practice barbarism and medieval things that we cannot comprehend in the modern West. They behead people ceremoniously, pour acid on women's faces to teach them a lesson, practice female clitoral mutilation to rob women of pleasure, and cut off hands, ears, noses, and limbs to teach people lessons in the violent and bloody Sharia law.

This seems like butchery and barbarism to the West today, but we forget our own butchery and barbarism of 500 years ago when medieval Europe was doing the exact same things in the exact same point of their development. Female mutilation, covering of women for protection and property, cutting of hands of thieves, public beheadings, and cutting off ears, noses, and limbs to teach people a lesson.

Julius Caesar was famous for cutting off the arms of his conquered enemies and sending his enemies running into the countryside with no arms, bleeding, to run to their doom. He then slaughtered women and children in sacked states or would sell scores of conquered women and children into slavery for his own profit and plunder. Caesar got rich off selling slaves and winning wars.

We celebrate Julius Caesar and love him and study him because he was our killer and not their killer.

Hitler was their killer. Caesar was our killer.

Saddam Hussein was their killer. George W. Bush was our killer.

Osama bin Laden was their killer. Barack Obama was our killer.

It's the same idea over and over again.

So does it make sense to mix a people with a modern ideology of compassion, tolerance, and weakness with a group that is 500 years behind and in a militant, violent, and intolerant state? I would say no; this is a bad idea for the same reason that you don't leave a steak with a dog. If given the chance, the dog will eat the meat. Can you really blame the dog? It's in his nature.

The Scorpion and the Frog

A scorpion and a frog meet on the bank of a stream and the scorpion asks the frog to carry him across on its back. The frog asks, "How do I know you won't sting me?" The scorpion says, "Because if I do, I will die too."
The frog is satisfied, and they set out, but in midstream, the scorpion stings the frog. The frog feels the onset of paralysis and starts to sink, knowing they both will drown, but has just enough time to gasp "Why?"

Replies the scorpion: "It's my nature ..."

http://www.aesopfables.com/cgi/aesop1.cgi?4&
TheScorpionandtheFrog

Should we let the violent, intolerant, militant people from Islam into our pacifist, tolerant, and weak society from the West? What do you think will happen? Likely a large slaughter of us or them. In America, the philosophy is different than in Canada. In Canada, we preach an ideology of multiculturalism, where other cultures can come in and "have it your way" like the philosophy of Burger King.

In America, instead of a mosaic, where every group can have it "your way," America has traditionally been an intolerant, violent, warrior society of its own and has had a melting pot ideology where you become American when you emigrate to America.

The trouble lies in America's tandem philosophy of religious freedom. America was born out of oppressed people looking for religious freedom. There are more than 35,000 sects of Christianity in the world, and to run a Judeo-Christian nation, you need to have religious freedom to accommodate all those types of Christianity. However, the new problem with Islam moving in is that because of their religious freedom, they do not have to assimilate into the melting pot. The melting pot conflicts with the religious freedom, and thus the system for dealing with this new kind of problem is not established.

The founding fathers were worried about the King of England coming back over the ocean to reclaim his backwater American outpost, so they put several mechanisms in place, including religious freedom and a right to bear arms in the Constitution.

They probably did not think of the time 200 years in the future when America would be fat, lazy, weak and ready to die, bloated on its own richness, and surrounded by hostile barbarian hordes that were willing to take it at any moment and that these barbarians would infiltrate the perimeter through "religious freedom" and "refugee status."

The founding fathers couldn't see it coming, like the Trojans couldn't see the Trojan horse coming full of young, virile, Greek warriors ready to kill every last Trojan man and rape every single woman into submission to take as war plunder for his own tribe and children. The founding fathers probably didn't consider that American birthrates in the civilized empire would reach low levels of around 1.2 children per family, whereas these religious freedom refugee barbarians would come in and have up to 8 children per family.They probably didn't consider the welfare system that would keep those 8 Muslim children alive because infant mortality in 1776 was high.

The balance of society used to be rich people had 2 children, poor people had 8 children. Infant mortalities and hard lives would kill 6 poor children, so rich and poor both had 2 surviving children. Such was the balance of capitalism and the free economy. It also had built-in population control for the rich and the poor.

Today, what we see is rich Western families having 1.2 children and poor families on the welfare system having 8 children. Instead of 6 children dying, modern medicine keeps them alive, welfare keeps them alive, and in fact gives bonuses to single moms for having more kids.

The 8 children grow up to vote more welfare programs and "free grain" for themselves, while the 1.2 rich children are surrounded and bred out of existence.

What happens in 50 or 100 years when this trend has gone on for several generations and the poor Muslim refugees have outbred the Westerners to a point of majority for them, and a minority for us? What happens when they can vote in Sharia law and subjugate Western people and Western ideology to memes and ideas that we grew out of 500 years ago in the Middle Ages? This would be a very rude awakening in history, but as the four stages of subversion go, in the end, the cycle ends with (1) civil war or (2) invasion.

In the case of birth rates, there is no need to invade. Just have enough kids funded by the welfare system, and in 50 years, you will have enough voting power to skip the invasion and go straight into enslavement of the weakened and subverted American people.

> *"Appeasing of governments which revel in slaughter is an invitation to worldwide catastrophe."*
>
> FANG LIZHI

Our own divisiveness on every single political policy is polarizing the people of America and truly portraying politics as what it is: "a system of organized hate."

Politics today is mostly junk debates that resemble the rhetoric and intelligence levels of professional wrestling like WWF or the UFC on TV.

A list of junk debates to entertain and distract the people and media from real issues that need to be solved:

1) Gay marriage vs. straight marriage
2) Abortion vs. abstinence
3) Free healthcare vs. no free healthcare
4) Free university or not free university
5) Free birth control or no free birth control

6) Guns or no guns
7) Legalize pot or not
8) Legalize prostitution or not
9) Transgender bathrooms vs. no transgender bathrooms

Most of these arguments are pointless and do not really matter in the big picture. The real problems—the real debates that must be had to ensure the survival of the group—are lost to the stage time of the "Pro Wrestling" entertainment politics and junk debates, dumbed-down entertainment debates that mostly have nothing to do with how to run a country successfully. These are the subversive arguments that the former KGB agent Yuri Beznemov warned us against. This is part of Stage 3 in the subversion of a people. The only stage left in social subversion is Stage 4, "normalization," which ends in violence, lots and lots of violence until the society has been "normalized"—a KGB euphemism for saying "shoot anyone who objects to the new regime." Instead of talking about how to create strong men, defend the tribe, defend the American philosophy and ideology as Trump has been trying to do, the popular media and popular feminist driven narrative keep bringing us back to the most unimportant arguments of all and galvanizing people into viscously polarized groups that hate each other over the most meaningless arguments. Instead of coming together as a tribe against a common enemy we can see, the enemies of today are invisible, and thus we stay at home, eating our cheap and free food stamp food, and forgetting about the real problems that are going on:

1) The loss of fathers
2) The loss of the family
3) The loss of effective religions
4) The loss of strong men
5) The loss of real jobs in the country
6) The loss of borders and protection
7) The loss of respect on the world stage
8) The loss of strength in our military and integration with the average man
9) The loss of what it means to be American
10) The loss of what it means to be a man

The divisiveness and the hate that permeates through modern-day America make me afraid for the future as groups like ANTIFA (the antifascists, hard-left and communist ideology) go out in the public picking fights with nonviolent neo-Nazi protestors at the removal of an old relic confederate statue.

The new groups like ANTIFA are made of women, weak men, the subversive rejects of society who are viscous, hateful, and will attack other groups sometimes without even thinking.

In the big picture, who really cares about the taking down of an old confederate statue? The statue is a symbol, a small symbol of an old and forgotten time, and people are volatile, rioting and losing their minds over it. What would happen if the country ran out of fuel or food for a few days? What would the violence look like with 300 million guns on the street?

The question is, will it be civil war first? Followed by invasion as groups like ANTIFA and what I believe will be a rise of a new "white power" group akin to the Nazis to protect the loss of white interests? It happened in Germany when the Germans were getting screwed by the French in the post WWI war reparations, and it can happen again.

Just remember that the Nazis were the national socialists. America has become socialist, and I can see a rise of Nazis once more. These Nazis will be opposed by equally violent communist groups like ANTIFA, but at the end of the day, history has already demonstrated the mortal hate between the NAZI group and the communists in Germany in the 1930s, and to see this again would be just a repetition in the bloody pages of history.

CHAPTER 36
WOMEN AND THE
FALL OF MAN

*"I would rather die a meaningful death
than to live a meaningless life."*

CORAZON AQUINO

Are women our weakness as men?

Man alone is nothing. A group of men is nothing. They need women to have a future—to procreate, to have families, and to have children. The sexual value of women is high because a woman produces one egg a month, while a man can produce 100 to 300 million sperm in each ejaculation.

Men must compete for women, the scarcer and more discerning gender of the species. But there is a point where men become weak around women.

When a man has multiple women, he has all the power. The women must compete for the one alpha male, share him, and maybe even have group sex or threesomes with him. This is the masculine, gangster, fantasy that men try to access through violent movies, internet porn, and video games. Man has the power and the women are subjugated.

But what happens when the woman has the power? In a monogamous relationship, the woman has complete control of the sexual access. The man has hundreds of millions of sperm each day that he has every violent urge to unload into her womb, and he socially, by the law, by the customs of our modern world, must have permission and access to her body to get his release.

> *"My dear Friend,*
>
> *I know of no Medicine fit to diminish the violent natural Inclinations you mention; and if I did, I think I should not communicate it to you. Marriage is the proper Remedy. It is the most natural State of Man, and therefore the State in which you are most likely to find solid Happiness."*

BEN FRANKLIN, ON CHOOSING A MISTRESS

The woman must consent; he cannot rape her, or he is a criminal and goes to jail. So in a monogamous relationship, where the woman has all the control over sexual supply, the woman has the power, and this is where the exchange of power begins.

They say that when a woman loves a man, he becomes her strength. When a man loves a woman, she becomes his weakness. This is the exchange of sexual power.

She becomes strong, and he becomes weak.

She becomes more masculine in the sexual exchange and he more feminine.

Without women, there is nothing—no men, no future, no tribe. Men need women, men desire women, men want sex, and a man is incomplete without a woman. Men will do stupid and self-destructive things just to have a chance with a woman.

I have stood in front of a gun prepared to die before for a woman I loved.

I have flown across the country on a whim and urge for a woman several times on no notice and just put the plane ticket on a credit card without a promise of anything but to see a woman I loved.

I have spent sums of money equal to the annual salaries of my employees on a woman I loved in a single year, just to impress her and keep her happy.

I have pursued a woman I loved in spite of multiple death threats left in my voicemail from her father. We still snuck out to be together anyways.

Love is maddening, and love is madness. Love makes men and women insane. Men will do insane things for love.

If there were no women there would be no use for money, sex, violence, conquest, land, or anything at all. Men would just stay at home playing video games all day, fixing small problems that don't really exist. Men are useless without women to win and women to protect.

Paradoxically, are women the destructive force in our society?

Do they make man stupid and weak to a point of his own demise?

Think of cuck culture, where man loves a woman so much he'll let her have sex with another man.

I'm ashamed to say I have experienced giving away a woman I loved into the sexual free market to have her sleep with other men of her choice. It broke my heart, but she was my weakness, and I loved her to the point of compromising my own life and identity for her. This was the wrong move, but it's an emotional place that men get to where they lose all perspective on what being a man really is and what is allowed and not allowed in love.

Do women bring men to a point of feminine weakness, tolerance, and compassion when we need masculine strength, intolerance, and stoicism?

Let's explore three stories famous stories from history that all illustrate a similar point.

THE STORY OF THE SNAKE
As performed by Donald Trump

On her way to work one morning
Down the path alongside the lake
A tenderhearted woman saw a poor half-frozen snake
His pretty colored skin had been all frosted with the dew
"Oh well," she cried, "I'll take you in and I'll take care of you"
"Take me in, oh tender woman
Take me in, for heaven's sake.
Take me in, oh tender woman," sighed the vicious snake

She wrapped him all cozy in a curvature of silk
And then laid him by the fireside with some honey and some milk
Now she hurried home from work that night as soon as she arrived,
She found that pretty snake she'd taken in had been revived
"Take me in, oh tender woman
Take me in, for heaven's sake
Take me in, oh tender woman," sighed the vicious snake

Now she clutched him to her bosom, "You're so beautiful," she cried
"But if I hadn't brought you in by now you might have died"
She stroked his pretty skin and then she kissed and held him tight
Instead of saying thanks, the snake gave her a vicious bite
"Take me in, oh tender woman
Take me in, for heaven's sake
Take me in, oh tender woman," sighed the vicious snake

"I saved you," cried the woman
"And you've bit me heavens why
"You know your bite is poisonous and now I'm going to die"
"Oh shut up silly woman," said the reptile with a grin
"You know damn well I was a snake before you took me in!"

The woman opens up her world to the poisonous and viscous snake whom she compassionately looks after with milk and honey. The viscous creature turns on her, poisoning and killing her as she is blinded by feminine virtues like compassion, nurturing, and tolerance.

What Trump recited are lyrics from Al Wilson's 1963 song, "The Snake." The lyrics were inspired by *The Farmer and the Viper* from Aesop's fables.

THE STORY OF ADAM AND EVE
Biblical

The story of Adam and Eve in the Bible is another story with a woman and a serpent, who turns out to be Satan himself. Adam and Eve live in paradise, they know no pain, no childbirth, have unlimited food to eat, the best fruit, and they are allowed to eat from any tree as instructed by God their Creator except from the tree of knowledge.

One day, Eve sees the serpent, and he corrupts Eve's mind into tasting the fruit of the tree of knowledge. She is seduced by the serpent, tastes the fruit, and the wrath of God is unleashed upon man.

Eve makes Adam taste the fruit as well, and Adam and Eve are cast out of the Garden of Eden, paradise lost, and onto the barren soil of the earth, where they will have to till the barren soil to grow crops and live. They will have to go through the pain and suffering of childbirth. They will age and become mortal, human, and flawed in the process.

Again, we have a snake seducing a woman into doing something that is mortal to her and her man, self-destructive, and generally stupid. But the woman's innocence and curiosity, the feminine energy to play and explore and make friends and be playful and adventurous, lead humanity from paradise into a painful existence of aging, childbirth, and work on the barren soil versus a life of pleasure and perfection in the Garden of Eden.

THE STORY OF PANDORA'S BOX
Greek

The Greeks had an older version of Adam and Eve's story. As history has demonstrated over and over again, "same damn story, different costumes."

When Zeus was so angry at Prometheus for giving people fire, he was also mad at the people who had tricked him into taking the wrong bag of meat. Zeus got back at the people by getting Hephaistos to make a beautiful woman, whom he named Pandora (which means all-gifts).

Epithemeus and Pandora's Box

Zeus sent Pandora down to earth and gave her as a present to Prometheus' brother, Epimetheus. Zeus told Epimetheus that he should marry Pandora. Also, Zeus sent Pandora with a little box, with a big lock on it. (Actually in the earliest versions of this story it is a sealed pottery vase.) He said not to ever open the box, and he gave the key to Epimetheus.

But Pandora was very curious about what was in the box. She begged Epimetheus to let her open it, but he always said no. Finally one day he fell asleep, and she stole the key (or broke the seal) and opened the box (or vase).

What Was in Pandora's Box?

Oh! Out of the box flew every kind of trouble that people had never known about before: sicknesses, worries, crimes, hate, envy, and all sorts of bad things. The bad things all began to fly away like little bugs, all over the place. Pandora was very sorry now that she had opened the box! She tried to catch the bad things and put them back in the box, but it was too late. They all flew away.

What Does the Pandora's Box Story Mean?

But the very last thing to fly out of the box, as Pandora sat there crying, was not as ugly as the others. In fact, it was beautiful. It was Hope, which Zeus sent to keep people going when all the nasty things got them down.

The story of Pandora explains why bad things happen to good people, by telling us that it's because our ancestors were bad, long, long ago. We owe a permanent debt because they tricked Zeus with a bad sacrifice. The Jewish Bible has a similar idea with Adam and Eve eating the apple.

https://quatr.us/greeks/pandoras-box-greek-mythology.htm

Women, relative to men, are a double-edged sword. On the one hand, they provide men hope with childbirth and a future and an ability expand the tribe. Women are a source of power for men, inspiration, energy, sex, and healing. They are a prize to win in battle and conquest and a prize to defend from other men and other tribes.

But women are also the weakness of men, for they can singlehandedly destroy a man as is outlined in the three ancient stories above that contain ancient wisdom.

Women are creators and women are destroyers. Women represent the beginning of man's expansion from a gang into an empire. Is the reversal true as well? Do women also represent the fall of man from an empire into death or bondage?

In violent patriarchal societies, females move from one group of strong men to another, as with the chimpanzee culture.

In violent male-driven, patriarchal gangs, women move from group of dominant men to dominant men. If the men become weak, stronger men come in and kill the weak men. A variation is also true; if the men are proven to become weak, the women will join the tribes of the stronger enemies and abandon or have the former weak men who were formerly their mates marginalized or killed off.

Cuck culture is an example of this. The woman is more powerful than her weak man and thus subjugates the weaker man into a slave role to a much more dominant man who is better for the woman's survival in the long run. The cuck man plays a feminine role; the woman plays herself as the great creator and destroyer, and the new stronger alpha male plays the masculine role.

If men become weak, their women will throw them to the wolves.

I saw this happen with my own mother and father firsthand. It was a painful experience to watch.

Is this a function of women who create life and become the ultimate destroyer of life?

If a man is too weak for his woman, she will betray him by leaving him for another gang, another stronger man, cheating on him and opening up her reproductive organs to a stronger man who can give her a stronger chance of survival for herself and her offspring.

In other words, she will join a stronger gang, and her payment to enter the gang will be sex.

Do women betray their men when the men can no longer prove to be the tribal leaders or provide the protection they biologically and subconsciously think they need?

Is this betrayal of women destroying weak men a twisted survival mechanism of women? If this is performed on a large scale, is it the ultimate mega-cuck? The ultimate hypergamy?

Betray the man who has become too weak, have him killed, then go find a strong man? Reproduce and the strongest genes live on?

The strategy seems brutal, but it seems to offer women better survival options that make sense on a biological level.

No woman appreciates a weak man. Women are always looking for strength, whatever that concept means to them. They want a leader and they want to be lead. In a world of weak men, women will do what it takes to find a strong man, even if it means marginalizing, further weakening, and even destroying her own weak men to find stronger men to mate with.

"Women encourage killers. They do it by falling in love with warriors and heroes. Men know it and respond with enthusiasm ... What have human females gone for in nearly every society and time? "Courage" and "Bravery." In short, violence.

HOWARD BLOOM, *LUCIFER ON WOMEN—*
NOT THE PEACEFUL CREATURES YOU THINK

*"Family means no one left behind
and no one is forgotten."*

DAVID OGDEN STIERS

AFTERWORD

STORY OF MY FATHER: IT'S NEVER TOO LATE FOR REDEMPTION

My dad never had a father.

My dad was born in Helsinki, Finland, in 1958 .

His father, my grandfather, was a young boy in 1942 when the Russians invaded Finland.

Finland is a raw strip of land between two historically mighty empires: Russia and Sweden. The Swedes dominated in the Dark Ages and up to the Renaissance with fierce Viking raids and warriors pillaging all the nearby lands, including Finland, to kill, plunder, and rape. They were fierce European barbarians who became rich through the spoils of war.

In the other direction were the Russians, another fierce group of warriors who are always looking to add another piece of land to their border on the frontier.

Stalin and Hitler made a deal in World War II. Hitler would get Poland, and Stalin would get Finland. And so, the fight was on.The Russians invaded the Fins. The Fins had to defend their homeland from this seemingly unstoppable Russian steamroller.

They called it a steamroller because Russia had so many people that they would send two men into battle with only one rifle. When the first man with the rifle got shot and died, the second man would grab the bullets he was given, load up his dead comrade's gun, and keep fighting. Such was the Russian steamroller.

The Russians practiced quantity, and the Fins practiced quality. The Fins fought back with highly skilled Finnish ski troops. White ghosts draped in white sheets, gas masks, skis, and sniper rifles that would pick off scores of Russian human fodder with bullets and grenades until they ran out of ammo or got shot.

Finnish War hero Simo Hayha was celebrated around the world for being the deadliest sniper in history—over 500 confirmed kills. Simo Hayha was a farmer from the Finnish countryside, and he butchered Russian troops with a steel sight, no scope, and snow in his mouth to hide his breath.

His nickname was the "white death," and he brought the afterlife to any Russian soldier who was unlucky enough to enter the steel sight of his rifle.

My dad's father was a young boy at the time, 15 years old. His job was to radio coordinates in the trenches, hop on a little rickety bicycle, and move to the next position with a new message before the Russian artillery would find his position and the bombs would start dropping.

As a young man, my grandfather saw a lot of horror—dead people, scores of them—he saw misery, he saw atrocity, and he saw things that a 15-year-old boy should never see.

He developed post-traumatic stress disorder. At the time, the medicine for that undiagnosed problem was alcohol. My dad's father couldn't sleep at night, so he would drink until the demons went away.

He also ran a successful business after the war when he was older, and he had a son—my father. The business my grandfather ran was a Finnish foundry with 17 employees that made complex bronze statues and works of art. The employees practiced metallurgy, chemistry, and other advanced industrial technologies at the time. My grandfather was a brilliant man when he was sober.

When he was drunk, he would come home and pick fights with my father, who was only 12 at the time. My adolescent father would barricade his door in the middle of the night to keep his drunk dad from breaking into his room and beating him. My grandfather, as an alcoholic, had a slew of broken promises made to my father. "I'll take you to the soccer game," but he never did. This was how my dad lived when he was 12. The drinking started to get out of control.

One day, my grandfather had been drinking and driving and crashed his car in the ditch by his home. The police came and my young 12-year-old dad with his mom let my grandfather escape the cops before they arrived. The cops looked at my 12-year-old dad for an explanation.

To defend his father, my dad said, "I was the one who crashed the car."

The cops looked at my dad skeptically and said, "You drive better than that." They had nothing, no evidence, so my grandfather got off scot-free for drinking and driving.

Eventually my father's family dissolved. His father reached a point where he would drink into oblivion. My father moved with his mother to Stockholm, Sweden, in his teens and later to Yellowknife in Canada. They followed my dad's sister, a young 21-year-old, hot, Finnish trophy wife who was married to a guy so old he could have married either my dad's sister or her mother, and no one would have blinked.

My dad later moved to Winnipeg, fell in love with my mother, and in 1986, I was born.

I had a great childhood, and my teen years were pretty good. In high school things started to unravel, and when I was 17 my mother divorced my father because he wasn't doing his job as a man. He wasn't providing for himself, for the family, and I watched her humiliate him in the kitchen of our marital home.

He was on his knees begging for a second chance. She towered over him, a little 5'4" woman to his 6'2" frame bent on his knees like a prisoner waiting to be executed, and she laughed at him.

In that moment of laughter, two hearts were broken, his heart and my heart.

I got to watch the destruction and betrayal of my father by his woman, his wife; mother of his children; his bride.

He wasn't producing, and like so many women in history, she marginalized him, emasculated him. I think she had ideas that she could get a better deal, a better guy. Maybe she thought she was still 18 and smoking hot.

But those ideas never materialized. She was alone after she broke his heart. Today she has a dog instead of a man. As Tony Robbins says, if you want to fill your needs for love and connection but can't communicate well enough for a human—get a dog!

My heart also broke in that moment. I watched my ideal man, my father, become smashed like a porcelain doll tossed onto cement. She smashed him for me, right in front of my eyes, and there was nothing I could do to stop it.

I was helpless in this moment. I didn't want to see my father beg like a slave. I didn't want to see my mother stab my father in the back by laughing at him in front of my face. But there was nothing I could do. It was their struggle, it was between them, and it had nothing to do with me.

I remember acting tough about the divorce. I was 17, a man now, I told myself. I had a hot blonde girlfriend. We had sex; men have sex. I drove a car. I had little part-time jobs. I had work. I had money. I was a man.

I thought the divorce wouldn't hurt me, but it hurt me more than I could ever know. I thought divorce would be easier at 17 than if I had been 3 or 4. My conclusion about divorce from my firsthand experience is that there is no good age. Whether you are 5 or 50, no matter what age you are, the pain and the hurt are the same.

The reason why the hurt is the same is because you get to see your idols, your perfect man and perfect woman, the base of your knowledge, become destroyed and turn into demons right before your face. If one parent dies, the survivor immortalizes the dead parent as a saint. My mother lost her father fairly early in her life from an aneurism. He was an entrepreneur, a salesman, who worked himself to an early death. He smoked, he drank, he ate red meat, and he even cheated on his wife with her best friend.

His wife, my grandmother, forgave him, but never forgot.

He died before I was born. I never met him, but everything we heard about my mother's father was saint-like. We might as well have named him a saint, because he was dead, and he was perfect, a spiritual ideal that was never to be corrupted by the flaws of the physical realm. They say that the spiritual realm is perfect, but the physical realm is flawed. When you die, and become immortalized, you become perfect forever, immortalized in the minds of your loved ones.

My father didn't die. My mother executed him in front of my face, but she didn't kill him. Instead, she shattered the definition and idea of what it means to be a man. I didn't recover from this broken hole inside of me—this gaping wound, this spiritual and emotional abyss—until cathartically writing this book for you.

I wrote it for you, but in the process it helped heal some deep and mortal wounds that were driving me to become addicted to sex with too many women and rich foods that were killing me.

For 14 years those wounds stayed open, until the therapy of writing this book.

For 14 years my dad wandered this mortal plane wondering what to do with himself next? Should he commit suicide? That was a real option he shared with me in one dark moment. He lost his business in the divorce and took a shitty job driving limos. He started to take pilot lessons and told me once in a moment of misery that he frequently thought of crashing the plane and killing himself.

He lost it all, everything that it meant to be a man. He lost his work, his woman, his family, his ideals, his identity, his social position in a good upper middle-class neighborhood with good friends. All smashed in an instant.

My father wandered sideways for 14 years, spending more and more money on pilot lessons until he was nearly $100,000 in credit card debt.

He had a new woman now, a good woman, and this woman had experienced a divorce of her own at nearly the same time. It was a miracle that he met his new woman because she was nearly the exact same person as my mother. She was a similar body type, similar age, also a teacher and specifically a resource teacher. She had the same taste in home décor, an offbeat eclectic taste that was chic yet rustic, and she had four grown children of her own.

My father lost his first marriage because he could not fulfill his purpose of work and produce for the family. My mother punished him for his inability to be a man, and she was forced into the masculine role of becoming the breadwinner, and it pissed her off because she wanted to be a feminine stay-at-home mom like her mother.

Fourteen years later, my dad called me and told me that he might get kicked out of his new woman's house because he couldn't pay his bills. The pilot debt had caught up to him, at nearly $100,000, and under a crippling 25% interest, my dad found himself in a bankruptcy position.

"Go bankrupt" I commanded him, an order. I was now 30, had my economic life together, had become a success financially, and it hurt me to watch my dad repeat the same mistake again 14 years later.

He never grappled with his purpose of being a man.

The demons of his father's PTSD and the horrors of war that drove his father to drink had transferred into my father.

My father, a child of an alcoholic, had so much emotional damage from his youth, specifically when he was 12, that when the pressure was on, rather than fight or flight, my dad became paralyzed and turned into a 12-year-old boy who froze like a mannequin.

He learned to freeze when his dad was drunk and might hit him. If you freeze, you might not get hit. If you move, the hit would come.

These demons had transferred from my grandfather, to my father, and now to me. More than 50 years of pain and suffering from unresolved wounds from war. When would the demons die?

"Live as if Your Father Were Dead

A man must love his father and yet be free of his father's expectations and criticisms in order to be a free man."

DEIDA, THE WAY OF THE SUPERIOR MAN

My father showed up at my condo shortly after I told him to go bankrupt, and he had a pathetic resumé with him. He was like a dog with his tail between his legs, and it was extremely painful to watch. I suddenly became the father to my father and had to show him what employers wanted.

He wanted to work for me in real estate. At that time I had a company with nearly 10 employees, and I felt bad for him, so I invited him to a negotiation seminar I was putting on and later hired him in my real estate acquisition team buying real estate at 40–60 cents on the dollar.

My dad was the 44th best negotiator at the class out of 46 negotiators; the two who scored lower than my dad in the tournament left early and didn't complete the seminar. My dad was the absolute omega male in the room, the lowest chicken in the pecking order.

I reluctantly hired my father and placed him under my senior managing partner, instructing my partner to "fire him if he sucks."

I looked my dad in the eye and said, "I will fire you if you suck, so you have to do your job."

My dad learned how to call real estate people and pick the bones of the market for little morsels of meat.

I treated him like any entry level acquisitions salesperson, paid him a $0 salary and put him on straight commission, barked at him like a dog, and swore at him when he wasted my time or brought junk deals to my desk. I was initiating him into the all-male masculinity of the gang, my gang that had carved out survival and existence on the frontier for years. My gang had no place for weak men on the frontlines. You hunted, you killed, you ate what you killed. If you didn't kill, you didn't eat. Such is the law of the jungle.

Finally, after 6 weeks of calling and nose-down-ass-up work ethic, my father landed 3 real estate deals in one week.

He was earning his keep, he was doing his work, and he was earning the trust of the tribe and the trust of his woman again.

My father was on the road to recovery and becoming a man and taking responsibility for his life.

My father never had a father. He never had someone to teach him the hard lessons and the ways of men. My father was never initiated into the gang and brutally abused during the initiation as men are.

The holes that sunk my father in his marriage came from the holes that his father had stabbed into his heart and spirit at age 12. The holes never healed, and my dad was wounded, as if he had a physical disability. But it wasn't physical; it was an emotional, mental, and spiritual disability, much more fatal to a man's survival.

The holes in my father transferred to me when I watched him beg like a slave in front of my mother. My idea of what it meant to be a man was completely obliterated and until writing this book 14 years later, I had wounds, holes, and demons that haunted me every day.

By writing this book and fixing my broken definition of what it means to be a man, I am slowly closing the holes, and the bleeding is starting to stop.

I have ironically become the father to my father, his mentor, his strong man to show him how to succeed and make his way in the world against the hostile forces of the frontier.

It's backwards, but I'm okay with it.

You can teach an old dog new tricks, and redemption is always available as long as you are alive.

I get to work with my father every day and study him and study what it takes to be a man. I have to be the leader of the tribe—lead with masculine energy and sometimes be violent in my actions and decisions.

I am a good man but not a nice man.

My father was a nice man, but not good at being a man.

I am roughing him up on the front lines of the frontier. He will get some cuts, scrapes, and bruises, but he will live. It's part of his masculine gang initiation.

I will shape him through my gang culture to show him how to be good at his work, to earn the trust of the tribe, earn the trust of himself, and earn the trust of his woman again. He was broken, and I am doing the work of fathering him, loving him as his father should have, and teaching him the lessons his father never taught him before the demons and darkness consumed him and dragged him into the abyss.

Some people ask if I am ashamed to be fathering my father.

I am not ashamed at all; it's a privilege and an honor to serve him as he served me when I was young. The things he couldn't teach me, I can teach him, and I love him no matter how good or bad of a man he chooses to become.

He will become strong in my gang, in my culture. On the frontiers of survival there is no room for weakness. He will either live or die by virtue of his skills, his work, his effort, and his commitment to his purpose. He will have to fight back the elements, the land, and gain ground in the jungle to survive.

"If he sucks, just fire him," is the policy on the front lines.

In the trenches, it's, "If he runs from battle, just shoot him in the back."

The tribe cannot afford a man who cannot do his job; this is the way of gang, this is the way of the tribe, this is the way of men.

When my father showed up on my doorstep looking for a job, he was a rough lump of coal.

I took that coal and have applied heat and pressure ...

One day, if he sticks to the honorable path of his work and his purpose, learns what it takes to become a man and own his problems, he will transform into a diamond.

It's never too late for redemption.

"*Nowhere can man find a quieter or more untroubled retreat than in his own soul.*"

MARCUS AURELIUS, *MEDITATIONS*

REVELATIONS

Dear Reader:

I write this book without ego.

This book was explicitly not written for me, or my pleasure. It was written out of pure necessity, the mother of all invention, to save the weak young men around me.

Upon some introspection, writing this book "hard times create strong men" has, in a way, replaced what an ancient boy-to-man ritual would have done for me if I had grown up in a culture of men and lived on the frontiers of survival.

In several cultures around the world, the young boy is taken from his mother by the men of the tribe when he is 12 or so, and taught how to be a man. At some point, they might put him in the wilderness alone with no food, no water, very little tools, and he must survive.

The question: What does it mean to be a man came into my mind at age 17 through experiencing my parents' divorce. To see my father begging on his knees, crying, and asking my mother for a second chance and her laughing at him, shattered my father as an ideal man in my mind forever. The truth became apparent. My father was mortal, not perfect, and not a godlike being I thought him to be. He didn't have the answers. He just did his best, and sometimes he failed—his best wasn't enough.

He was flawed, he was imperfect—such is the life of being a man.

A lot of my ongoing emotional pain, spiritual pain, mental pain, and physical pain from that moment lasted for 14 years and has been traced back to my shattered definitions of what a man truly is.

My perfect father was no longer perfect; my mother destroyed him in front of my eyes, and I was unable to redefine what it means to be a man against the confusing backdrop and noise of society's ideas of "what a man ought to be." There is a huge difference between what ideals will say "he ought to be" and "what a man truly is and what it means to be a man."

In real life, there is no "should" or "ought to be." There only is what exists in front of our faces, staring back at us as we examine it.

My pain was coming from my avoidance to examine my definition of what it means to be a man and examine myself against that definition and judge my actions and choices according to that code.

At age 23, I was lost and reading *The Game* by Neil Strauss, trying to fill a hole inside of myself and trying to weakly answer, "what does it mean to be a man?" But really, I was a horny young man and just "wanted to get women into bed" without looking at my own interior problems of the mind, spirit, and emotions. My definition of a man was shattered at the time and ill-defined. I bedded many women, I got what *The Game* promised me, but I also was left with too many girlfriends, too much sex, which also led to the women hating me when I didn't move on to a relationship with them. Eventually, I found myself facing a spiritual bankruptcy and a darkness inside of me that I avoided for years.

The hole inside my heart turned out to be a gaping spiritual abyss. I became engulfed by a blackness and a nothingness. I would spend hours staring into a computer screens late at night, at 3 a.m. on video games, dating or pornography websites, struggling to find God like the man in the bar, staring into his beer; or the man in the casino who stares into the slot machine hoping to catch a glimpse of God the divine creator.

What I found and what all men find in their addictions and false hopes to find God in all the wrong places is that there is nothing. Man can only find the blackness of the abyss in his addictions.

"Man looks in the abyss, there's nothing staring back
at him. At that moment, man finds his character.
And that is what keeps him out of the abyss."

LOU MANNHEIM IN THE MOVIE *WALL STREET*

As I write this letter to you on January 29, 2018, only 19 short days ago, I was fasting on just water, no food, no supplements, in the middle of the jungle in Costa Rica, literally in the middle of nowhere with no cell reception, practically no internet, and surrounded by jungle, farms, and wild beasts. Just myself in my robe, as Marcus Aurelius the great Roman Emperor must have sat. Like Aurelius in his book *Meditations*, I too was alone with my thoughts, my demons, my fears, my weaknesses, and my addictions.

Eighteen days of water, no food, and self-inflicted stoic hardship that most men would never subjugate themselves to was, in retrospect, extremely important for my life and character development.

I had chosen to fast for health reasons. I gave up seeing doctors years ago, and instead I prefer to go on a long fast in the winter to clean my body, and, as I have discovered along the way, my mind, emotions, and soul became clean as well.

When you starve your weakness in the jungle, you starve your demons and addictions too. Through sin we become pure, and if you starve the demons long enough, the demons will die and you shall live. You will become a pure man with a clean mind, body, soul, and spirit to see the world cleanly in the way that it truly is; and not warped by your demons, your pain, your suffering, your fears, your addictions, or your mind-altering substances.

While fasting in the jungle this second time (last year I had fasted for 30 days on water in the jungle), I had a spiritual awakening. One of the messages that came to me from the divine power of infinite intelligence, aka God, was "do less," so this year I am committed to "doing less." I have canceled complex plans that were not important to me as I found upon true examination, I stopped calling my eight girlfriends I had in December prior to my fast, and they stopped calling me.

In the space I created for my mind that I have created from "doing less," I have written two books in the last 30 days, produced just over 200,000 words of writing (the average novel is 50,000 words), and I am doing my work as though it were my divine duty and my words are channeling directly from God himself as my demons have been starved and my mind is clean to be a conduit for true thought.

This Book Was Created out of Necessity, the Mother of Invention

Writing this book has replaced the boy-to-man rituals that other cultures used in the past, such as forcing the boy in the wilderness to survive or fast alone in the elements. I was fasting 18 days in the jungle this year, and I started writing this book on January 18, 2018, only 11 days ago; it is a massive work, my magnum opus and over 150,000 words, and approximately the size of 3 books that would normally be 50,000 words. But my spiritual awakening and commitment to "doing less" have brought me the ability to see the truth more clearly and do more of the work required of me.

When my young male employees said, "You're mean," and began to whine like boys in the bodies of men, something triggered in me, and this book was written in almost the same way Mozart wrote his music, blazingly fast and with almost no revisions.

The question "What does it take to be a man?" has been eating my soul for the last 14 years. At times it seemed as if I was possessed by an evil demon, and in the last 11 days, I have woken up every morning and fought that demon and stayed up some nights well past midnight until dawn at 6 a.m. fighting, grappling, and slaying the demon.

Like the boy in the wilderness who is fasting might encounter a wolf and be forced to fight and kill it until the boy dies or the wolf dies, I have been fighting the demons within every day until the demons die and I live as a stronger man than I was before.

If the boy kills the wolf in the woods and survives to find himself, he gets to come home and be a man and be a part of his tribe.

Slaying the demons in this book have brought a clarity and peace to my mind that were not there before, and knowing that my clarity can help other men see the things they could not before closes the spiritual hole that I have had in my heart for quite some time. Service and duty are man's higher purpose. I am happy to have served you in the pages of this book and wish to continue to be of service to you if I can.

"The happiness of your life depends upon the quality of your thoughts."

MARCUS AURELIUS

Writing this book has indeed been a spiritual process. There are hard questions in this book that I have attempted to answer as best I can. I know that some of my answers will be strong, and some will be weak. But I am like any man; I am imperfect, and I am flawed.

Like any man, I do what I can with the tools I have at the time.

I do my work—whatever work is required of me—and I earn the trust of my tribe by getting them what they need to survive.

It has been an honor to lead you through this book, and I hope you have been challenged and have benefitted from watching me slay my demons on the pages of this book, and perhaps you have slain some of your own by reading my work.

If this is the case, you have become a stronger man in the process.

The boy in the forest would become a man in a matter of days or weeks. This process of catharsis and spiritual demon slaying has taken me 14 years, from age 17 until 31, going on 32, for me. The revelations in this book have come quickly over a matter of 11 days, like the boy in the forest with the wolf might experience, but it might have taken the boy 14 years to enter the forest.

It took me 14 years to enter my spiritual battleground to fix the wounds inside of myself and begin to wage war on the spiritual demons that were lurking inside of me.

I hope this book can help you slay your demons and fill any holes you might have carried inside of yourself, especially around the question: "What does it take to be a man?"

So, the questions have been answered, and the demons have been slain. What can you do now to apply this book to your life?

Be the man who lives his purpose, does his work, and is always striving for his potential.

Reach out to me any time you need me. You may email me at my office at support@stefanaarnio.com, or you may phone the office at 204-285-9882. My assistant will connect you with me.

This is my fifth book I have written, and by the end of this year, 2018, I will have eight total official publications in print. Each one of my publications has been to enhance my business of consulting others in real estate or business coaching. They are simple tools made for other men so they may do their work better. If I can help you do your work better, that would be good for both of us.

But this book as of today has no "backend." I have nothing to sell you. I have no course on "how to be a man," although that may come if I get enough requests from men and women wanting firsthand training on the ideas in this book. It happened before in history. I wrote a book and ended up with an accidental training business that turned into a surprise success.

When I started writing books, I wrote a little book called *Money People Deal: The Fastest Way to Real Estate Wealth* and self-published it. It raised roughly $5,000,000 of working capital for my real estate investment company in one year and also accidentally spawned a real estate coaching and consulting company that has since done millions of dollars of business.

Mostly men have followed my work as they wish to fulfill their divine purpose as men and do their work; 88% of my audience as of today is men, 12% are women who are typically forced into the masculine role of moneymaking through hardship: divorce, loss of spouse, or forced to be the breadwinner. I have had thousands of people reach out to me over the years for mentorship in real estate and business. I could envision a similar thing happening in the "how to be a man" space if this book resonates with enough hearts and minds as "money people deal" did for men wanting to make money and do the work.

But as I said in the beginning:

I write this book with no ego.

This book is not about me, it's about you:

What comes of it, comes of it.

My benefit in writing this book has been the catharsis and slaying of demons that should have instructed by my father, my original mentor, 14 years ago, but he was ill equipped to bring me from boyhood into manhood.

Other men in my supertribe, other books, and my own spiritual awakening while fasting in the jungle have brought me the answers I have needed to bring myself spiritual maturity and inner peace.

You may contact me at any time, and I will see if I can help you.

No guarantees.

I'm not sure if I can help you directly or not, but I will try if you reach out.

I understand what it's like to struggle in life as a self-made man and to struggle with the questions in this book, as I have struggled in the hardest ways with the main question and the source of my pain for a long time: "What does it mean to be a man?"

If you want to see the future, just look at the past.

This book might have begun on my hard drive as an emotional rant about bitchy little man-boys who weren't doing their work, but as I began to inject it with sources and examples of history, it began to thicken into a nourishing rational soup—a solid argument backed up on rational thought, not emotions.

The past holds all the clues of what will happen next in the cycles of history.

I fear for the future because I have seen the violence—the atrocities that man has committed in the past—by studying the pages of history. Through my studies, I can see that inevitably hard times are coming for us in the Western world.

We are Rome, and the barbarians are literally at the gates. We are weak, cannot even identify these barbarians as a threat, and like every other empire in history, we will likely fall to the barbarians because of our own blindness from too many years of Good Times Creating Weak Men.

I believe the hard times will officially start in 2020, perhaps with a war or major currency or oil crisis. We may not have a bloody war, but we are living in an economic war today. The 20 years that follow 2020-2040 could indeed be the hardest of times seen in the Western world, and the men of my generation may be forced to man up and become strong men like in the past, or perhaps we may, as men, become killed, wiped out, or thrown to the side and completely marginalized.

We might have a violent war, and conscription could come back. It has been roughly 80 years since World War II, and as the pages of history have taught us over and over again, by the times an event is 80 years in the past, we are bound to repeat it because as a species, the human race, has amnesia and can't remember the horrors we lived through only a short 80 years ago.

Such is the premise of this book, Hard Times Create Strong Men.

What's Next for You?

What you must do now is focus on being the best man you can be. Do your work, whatever kind of work that is required of you, to earn the trust and respect of your tribe and your women. You must then pursue your potential as it pertains to your mental, physical, emotional, and spiritual realms.

The Western world needs strong men right now to be leaders in preparation for the hard times coming.

Do your duty—that is what it means to be a man:

> *"Everything, a horse, a vine, is created for some duty.*
> *For what task, then, were you yourself created? A man's*
> *true delight is to do the things he was made for."*

MARCUS AURELIUS

As a man, you have a duty to yourself, a duty to your tribe, a duty to your woman, a duty to your children. The word *duty* is purposely kept vague because men serve a variety of jobs, and depending on what your tribe needs of you, you must serve.

Marcus Aurelius was the man who ruled Rome at its height of power and spent his last days on the frontier, leading his troops and fighting the Germanic barbarians, as was his duty at the time. His book *Meditations* has been a powerful book on leadership throughout history, since he died in his 50s at the peak of the Roman Empire. Such was the wisdom he left behind on how to be a man that his thoughts are still wildly popular today through his books, and leaders from around the world seek to emulate him in business, the military, and in life.

Look to Marcus Aurelius to understand the world, the demons, and the barbarians around you.

Marcus Aurelius was just a man, no different than you and I, but he was the leader and emperor of the world's superpower at the time. Her studied Aristotle and tested and trained his mind and philosophies to be a sound and just ruler. You must do the same: train your mind, body, soul, and emotions to reach your potential and be a good and just ruler of your domain. Use your power for good, no matter how large or small your power is.

Choose wisely because the things you do today compound upon themselves and vastly affect the results you get tomorrow in bigger and stronger ways you can ever imagine.

Choose to become a Strong Man, like Marcus Aurelius in his time, a stoic, a leader of his people, a master of his domain, and a man that other men would die for and who men throughout history have wished to be.

Choose wisely what you do with your time and your actions, choose strength over weakness, because your choices today determine your future in bigger ways than you could ever imagine, for;

"What we do now echoes in eternity."

MARCUS AURELIUS, *MEDITATIONS*

You are self-made and you are on a journey. I salute you in the pursuit of your highest and greatest self.

Respect the Grind,

Stefan Aarnio

HARD TIMES PERMISSIONS

"Americano," Brian Setzer Orchestra, Hal Leonard Permission, pending

Fight Club, Chuck Palahniuk, Penguin Random House, pending

Way of Men, Jack Donovan, pending

Atlas Shrugged, Ayn Rand Institute

Way of the Superior Man, David Deida

Sexual Market Value video, Stephen Molyneux, pending

The Human Zoo, Desmond Morris, pending

"Emerging Adults: The In-between Age," Christopher Munsey: Monitor (June 2006) 37(6): 68, pending

11 Rules for Life, Charles J. Sykes

Wolf of Wall Street, Red Granite Pictures, pending

Young Man Blues, The Who, pending

Hot-Crazy Matrix video, Dana McLendon

"The communist subversion …," Natural News Network

"Hard times create strong men …" quote, G. Michael Hopf, Those Who Remain

The Lucifer Principle, Howard Bloom

"The Snake," Oscar Brown Jr. estate, pending

MORE BOOKS BY
THE AUTHOR

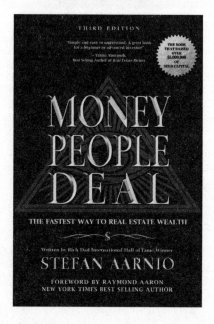

To Order, go to MoneyPeopleDeal.com

Stefan Aarnio is one of Canada's leading up and coming Real Estate Entrepreneurs and the winner of Canadian Real Estate Wealth Magazine's "Joint Venture Partner of the Year." Starting with only $1,200, Stefan has built a multi million dollar portfolio for his partners and has earned himself a spot on The Self Made List. Stefan has accumulated properties at an alarming pace through his understanding of Real Estate Joint Ventures—The Fastest Way to Real Estate Wealth. Stefan's philosophy is simple, find great deals, build a fantastic team, pay everybody and create partnerships for life.

MORE BOOKS BY THE AUTHOR

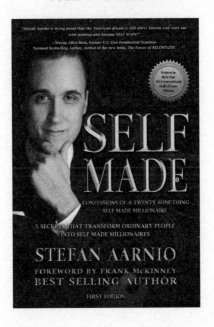

What does it take to become a self-made millionaire? Many have wondered, few have succeeded. *Self Made: Confessions of a Twenty-Something Self-Made Millionaire* follows the real life story of Stefan Aarnio, award winning real estate investor and award winning entrepreneur through the struggle of starting out with zero cash, zero credit and zero experience in his pursuit of financial freedom. Inside *Self Made*, you will discover the 5 Secret Skills That Transform Ordinary People into Self-Made Millionaires. These skills are mastered by the rich, purposely not taught in school, and are hidden from the poor and the middle class. Join Stefan on his journey as he faces financial ruin, meets his life-changing mentor, and transforms his mind, body, and soul to become Self Made.

Visit **SelfMadeConfessions.com** to order and receive your bonuses!

MORE BOOKS BY THE AUTHOR

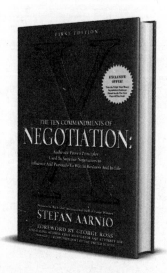

To Order visit Xnegotiation.com

What are The Ten Commandments of Negotiation, and why do we need them? Years ago in a study, 150 CEOs were contacted and were asked for the top three personality traits desired for the company's best negotiators. The top three desired traits were:

1. Personality

2. Knowledge of human nature

3. Ability to organize information

The Ten Commandments of Negotiation are time-tested fundamentals based on these top three desired traits. If you can obey the Ten Commandments, you will be successful more times than not in any negotiation.

To Order visit Xnegotiation.com

MORE BOOKS BY
THE AUTHOR

Stop selling start closing

The fastest way to increase your income is by learning to sell!

Close more deals, close bigger deals, get your copy at
7levelSelling.com

MORE BOOKS BY
THE AUTHOR

The *High Performance Journal* is the perfect complement to the Blackbook.

High performers who journal daily, write down their goals and measure their success incrementally will always outperform those who do not test and measure their success.

This journal has been designed with you in mind and is a tool for you to achieve your dreams. Big dreams are made up of small successes that slowly add up into big successes.

TheHighPerformanceJournal.com

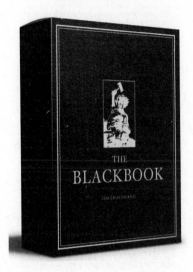

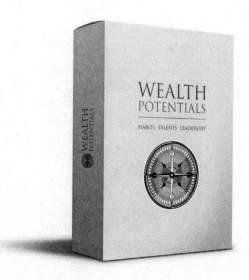

Bill Gates, Henry Ford, Oprah Winfrey, Steve Jobs, and Warren Buffet all made their money in different ways. How will you make your wealth?

Find out with the *Wealth Potentials* personality test that measures 1) Your habits, 2) Your talents, and 3) Your leadership to show you how you will build your fortune and also the next steps you need to take to remove the roadblocks and reach your full potential.

How will you reach your potential for wealth?

To Find Out, visit WealthPotentials.com and take the test!

STEFAN AARNIO'S

BLUEPRINT
TO CA$H

Stefan Aarnio's Blueprint to cash is the
perfect "next step" for anyone curious
in learning the fundamentals of buying,
fixing and selling homes for profit!

BlueprintToCash.com

For more information on Stefan Aarnio's award-winning system for finding, funding, and fixing homes, please visit **TheSystemToCash.com**

Other Books
by Stefan Aarnio

The Oracle, the Queen, the Princess, and the Whore,
Hard Times Vol IV

Letters to a Scorpion, Hard Times Vol III

Dead Man Walking, Hard Times Vol II

Hard Times Create Strong Men

Money People Deal:
The Fastest Way To Real Estate Wealth

Self Made

The Ten Commandments of Negotiation

The Close:
7 Level Selling

Visit StefanAarnio.com for 1on1
coaching or to order books

For a full list of products, please visit
stefanaarnio.com/store

For 1 on 1 coaching, visit
StefanAarnio.com

To book speaking engagements with Stefan
please email **support@stefanaarnio.com**
or call 204-285-9882